CELTIC PLACES AND PLACENAMES

To my sons Adam and Simeon

'A people without the knowledge of their past history
is like a tree without roots.'
Marcus Garvey

Bronze depiction of Taranis, Celtic god of thunder.

CELTIC PLACES AND PLACENAMES

HERITAGE SITES AND THE HISTORICAL ROOTS OF SIX NATIONS

JOHN MOSS

First published in Great Britain in 2022 by
PEN AND SWORD HISTORY
An imprint of
Pen & Sword Books Ltd
Yorkshire – Philadelphia

Copyright © John Moss, 2022

ISBN 978 1 39908 747 6

The right of John Moss to be identified as Author of this work has been asserted by him in accordance with the Copyright, Designs and Patents Act 1988.

A CIP catalogue record for this book is available from the British Library.

All rights reserved. No part of this book may be reproduced or transmitted in any form or by any means, electronic or mechanical including photocopying, recording or by any information storage and retrieval system, without permission from the Publisher in writing.

All illustrations and maps have been drawn and supplied by the author.

Typeset in Times New Roman 10/12.5 by SJmagic DESIGN SERVICES, India.
Printed and bound in the UK by CPI Group (UK) Ltd.

Pen & Sword Books Limited incorporates the imprints of Atlas, Archaeology, Aviation, Discovery, Family History, Fiction, History, Maritime, Military, Military Classics, Politics, Select, Transport, True Crime, Air World, Frontline Publishing, Leo Cooper, Remember When, Seaforth Publishing, The Praetorian Press, Wharncliffe Local History, Wharncliffe Transport, Wharncliffe True Crime and White Owl.

For a complete list of Pen & Sword titles please contact
PEN & SWORD BOOKS LIMITED
47 Church Street, Barnsley, South Yorkshire, S70 2AS, England
E-mail: enquiries@pen-and-sword.co.uk
Website: www.pen-and-sword.co.uk

Or

PEN AND SWORD BOOKS
1950 Lawrence Rd, Havertown, PA 19083, USA
E-mail: Uspen-and-sword@casematepublishers.com
Website: www.penandswordbooks.com

Contents

Introduction	vii
Part One: Common Celtic Place Name Elements	1
Part Two: Cornwall, the South East & the Isles of Scilly	7
Part Three: Ireland Northern Ireland (Ulster) & the Republic of Ireland (Eire)	32
Part Four: The Isle of Man	74
Part Five: Scotland & the English Borders	82
Part Six: Wales & the Marches	154
Part Seven: Celtic River Names	193
Part Eight: Celtic Mountain Names	206
Part Nine: Bronze & Iron Age Hillforts	216
Part Ten: Cairns, Barrows, Henges, Monoliths & Stone Circles	237
Part Eleven: Celtic Crosses	257
Part Twelve: Brittany	265
Bibliography	269
Useful Online Resources	271
Index	272

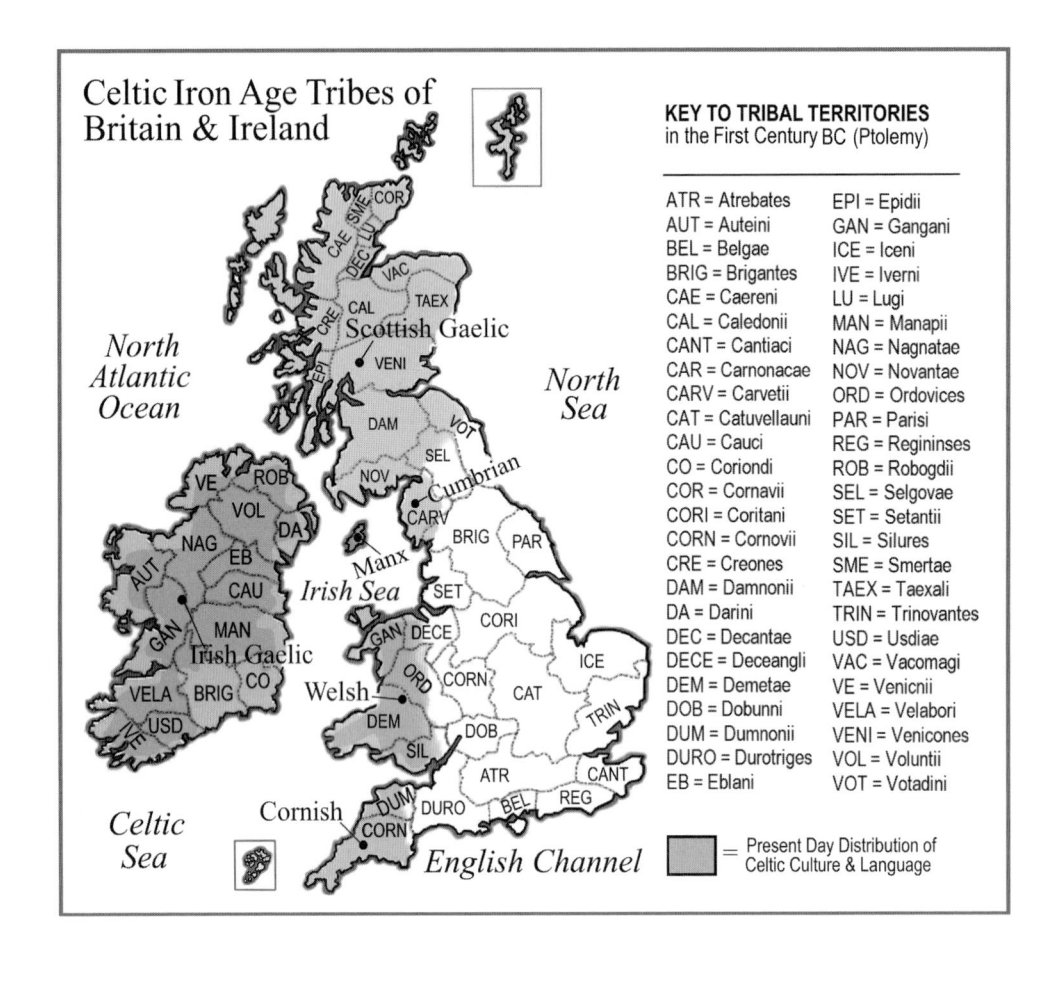

Celtic Places and Placenames

Celtic Iron Age Tribes of Britain & Ireland

KEY TO TRIBAL TERRITORIES
in the First Century BC (Ptolemy)

ATR = Atrebates	EPI = Epidii
AUT = Auteini	GAN = Gangani
BEL = Belgae	ICE = Iceni
BRIG = Brigantes	IVE = Iverni
CAE = Caereni	LU = Lugi
CAL = Caledonii	MAN = Manapii
CANT = Cantiaci	NAG = Nagnatae
CAR = Carnonacae	NOV = Novantae
CARV = Carvetii	ORD = Ordovices
CAT = Catuvellauni	PAR = Parisi
CAU = Cauci	REG = Regininses
CO = Coriondi	ROB = Robogdii
COR = Cornavii	SEL = Selgovae
CORI = Coritani	SET = Setantii
CORN = Cornovii	SIL = Silures
CRE = Creones	SME = Smertae
DAM = Damnonii	TAEX = Taexali
DA = Darini	TRIN = Trinovantes
DEC = Decantae	USD = Usdiae
DECE = Deceangli	VAC = Vacomagi
DEM = Demetae	VE = Venicnii
DOB = Dobunni	VELA = Velabori
DUM = Dumnonii	VENI = Venicones
DURO = Durotriges	VOL = Voluntii
EB = Eblani	VOT = Votadini

= Present Day Distribution of Celtic Culture & Language

Introduction

In a sense, there were no such people as the Celts. Certainly the people to whom it has been ascribed would not have called themselves by the name. They remained essentially separate tribal groups with their own particular names and identities, and were never a unified people as the term 'Celt' might imply. The peoples who occupied the land which the Romans called 'Britannia' were known to them simply as 'Britons'.

However, there is a broad consensus of opinion that a race of people of Indo-European descent, who shared a common gene pool element, did migrate westward from central Europe to the Atlantic coast around seven thousand years ago, during the Mesolithic period, (sometimes called the Middle Stone Age). Some of the earliest sources describe these ancient tribes as the 'Keltoi', of whom the most influential commentator was the Greco-Roman astronomer and mathematician, Ptolemy. Many later sources are based upon his work.

The descendants of this early cultural group are limited nowadays to the British Isles and islands, to Ireland and Brittany on the north-west coast of France. These forebears dominated Western Europe from the eighth until the first century BC.

The people we call Celts were actually a construct dating back to the ancient Greeks, who saw the Keltoi as a unified barbarian race. In fact, apart from loosely sharing varying dialects of a common Gallic language and certain cultural traits, they were distinctly separate entities, and would not be formally called Celts until the eighteenth century. They were often at war with each other and their territories were fiercely fought over and defended.

One of the recognised culturally cohesive factors in the Celtic world was the Druids, and a great deal of speculation surrounds their status and function in Iron Age society. The Romans knew them as 'druidae', and similar names persisted in Old Irish where they were known as 'drui', meaning 'sorcerer', in Old Cornish as 'druw', and in Middle Welsh as 'dryw', meaning 'seer'. It is widely believed that they were a learned class who served as priests, teachers, physicians and authority figures, but as they left no written accounts, it is possible that they were no more than village or tribal elders or wise men. The name 'druid' may be derived from a Celtic word meaning 'knower of the oak tree'. The earliest known records of the Druids come from the third century BC, but over the following centuries they became the stuff of folklore and legend, attributed with mystical powers.

Later Roman writers accused the Druids of presiding over human sacrifices, and there is some anecdotal evidence for this, as recorded by Julius Caesar in his *Commentarii de Bello Gallico* (*Commentaries of the Gallic War*). These accusations led to their persecution, especially from early Roman converts to Christianity, forcing the practice of Druidic veneration underground. Suppression of the Druid orders continued to be actively pursued by the Roman government under first century emperors like Tiberius and Claudius, so that virtually all references to them had disappeared from written history by the second century.

As to the development of the Celtic languages, the debate continues as to whether they arrived directly from Continental Europe, or whether they gradually evolved over many millennia in the British Isles and islands from the original Indo-European languages. It is also not clear whether the development of the Irish Gaelic came directly from Europe or whether it arrived later via mainland Britain.

Some have argued that when the incoming migrant Celts interbred with the existing pre-Celtic population, a mixed language inevitably resulted, much in the same way that Norman French and Anglo-Saxon combined to create the form of Middle English which Chaucer used to write his *Canterbury Tales*. Whatever that hybrid language sounded like, it was basically Celtic.

The commonality of these Celtic-derived dialects is amply illustrated by the words they used for 'rock' or 'stone'. They are remarkably similar in all of the Celtic nations' vocabulary: in Welsh the word is 'carreg', in Irish it is 'carraig', in Scots Gaelic it is 'craeg', in Breton 'karreg', and in Manx, 'carrick'. Clearly, these are all derivations of a similar or identical source.

Julius Caesar considered there to be three distinct languages in Britain, spoken by tribal peoples he identified as the Aquitani, Celtae and Belgae. According to his account, they were three quite separate peoples. However, nowadays we consider them to have spoken dialects of the same or related Celtic languages. These dialectic variations, according to contemporary analyses, divide them into two basic types: first, Irish, Scottish and Manx, which are called Goidelic Celtic; second, Welsh, Cornish and Breton, which are known as Brittonic (sometimes written as Brythonic) Celtic.

In his writings concerning these 'barbarians', even Caesar made little distinction between the Aquitani, the Belgae and the Celtic tribes. 'We call them Gauls', he wrote. His first two forays into Britain in 54 BC and 55 BC were short lived and the legions failed to advance much beyond the River Medway in Kent, so fierce was the opposition from native tribes. However, when four Roman legions under the new Emperor Claudius returned in 43 AD, they made a secure landing on the south-eastern shores of Kent and Sussex, and quickly overran Colchester, the capital of the Catuvellauni tribe.

Native Britons were quick to recognise the common threat which the Roman advance posed, and hitherto belligerent tribes were forced into uneasy alliances. The Romans were met with fierce and equally savage opposition from the reorganised

Introduction

Cantiaci, Iceni and Brigantes tribes. However, in the face of the superior power and might of Rome, the native peoples of southern England were either beaten into submission, assimilated, or gradually pushed back into the western and northern regions of Britain. Those that lived in the remote regions of Scotland, Cornwall and Wales were less severely affected by the inexorable advancing Romanisation that ensued. Many Cornish tribes from the extreme south-west of Britain took refuge across the English Channel and settled in Brittany in Northern France.

Wales was seen as something of a frontier and to a large extent the Romans stopped short of venturing much beyond its borderlands. Its troops were stationed in places like Caerleon and Chester, around the border country, what later became known as the Welsh Marches.

Neither were Scotland and Ireland fully conquered, so that they were able to avoid the kind of integration into the Roman Empire to which the rest of Britain was subjected. Julius Agricola, the Roman Governor of Britain, who led the legions in the second campaign, had made some headway into Lowland Scotland, fighting battles with its natives. Even he eventually determined that permanent occupation was unsustainable and moved his troops back to the English borderlands. This was partly prompted by other conflicts in Eastern Europe, and the withdrawal of substantial numbers of troops in the defence of Rome.

The Emperor Hadrian later commissioned the building of an eighty-mile-long wall across the north of Britain, stretching from Wallsend in the east to Carlisle in the west, thereby isolating Scotland and its Pictish tribes. The wall effectively marked the northern limits of the Roman Empire as he saw it. Later, another defensive earthwork was built further north by Antoninus, seeking to make his mark by extending the empire even further. In the event, his weak earthen rampart and ditch system soon proved ineffective and was abandoned as forces withdrew back to the security of Hadrian's Wall.

Thus, the Scots, Welsh and Irish tribes retained their unique customs, religion and culture. Similarly, Cornwall's distance from the south-east and Europe beyond, separated as it was by the River Tamar, enabled its people to retain a degree of autonomy as well as a continuance of the Cornish language.

Despite the Roman occupation of much of mainland Britain, its islands remained relatively protected by their isolation, and after the Roman legions withdrew in the fifth century, many of Britain's indigenous people retained an identifiable vestige of the old Celtic language in the several dialects that we recognise today. Over time, despite inevitable adaptations and modifications, traces of the original can still be read and heard, where Erse, Gaelic, Cumbric, Cornish, Manx and Brittonic Welsh still survive. These dialects are still commonly found, not only in spoken language, but in the names given to the places where their speakers live.

In considering this subject I set out to explore the sources of ancient British places and place names, in the full realisation that many Irish, especially those living in Eire, would balk at any suggestion that they are British. But, for the

Celtic Places and Placenames

purposes of this book, and as a convenient portmanteau term, I have included places and settlements of the British Isles and islands as well as Ireland, very much as the Romans might have regarded them. I also accept that many Scots, especially those of the Orkney and Shetland Islands, might feel they owe more to Scandinavian languages than to European Gallic, as might the Manx speakers of the Isle of Man.

That said, for want of a better explanation, they are what I have called 'Celtic Places'. They are typified by what follows, some several hundred townships, villages and ancient ritual sites of Cornwall, Ireland, the Isle of Man, Scotland, Wales and Brittany in north-western France.

Part One

Common Celtic Place Name Elements

Though by no means exhaustive, the following lists of word elements are provided so that readers may begin to understand the meaning and interpretation of some of the place names which have been included in this book.

Ancient/Old Irish (Gaelic/Erse)

AGH/AUGH	field, land
ANNA	marsh, bog
ATH	ford, river crossing
BAILLE	district, township
BALLY/BALLINA	place of
BARR	top, head
BEN	peak
BILE	sacred tree
BLAR	bare, exposed
BRAEN	rain, moisture
BRAN	raven
BRUGH	mansion, palace
BUN	root, bottom
CAEL	slender
CARN	heap, pile of stones
CATH	battle
CENN	head
CILL	church
CLOCH	stone
CLUAIN	pasture, meadow
CNOC	hill
CONGA	isthmus
CUILEN	whelp, pup
DAIR/DARACH	oak, oaken
DONN	brown
DORN	fist, pebble-shaped
DUB	black
DUN	fort, stronghold
EISCIR	ridge

EO	yew tree
FAILL	cliff
FAL	rule
FER	man
FINN	white, fair
FLAITH	lord
GAL/GAEL	foreigner, stranger
GLAIS	water, stream
GLAS	green
GLENN	valley
INIS	island
LAG	hollow
LLAN	land, ground
MAINISTIR	monastery
MAR	sea
MOIN	bog
MOR	great, big
MUIR	sea, large lake
MULLACH	summit
PORT	bank, promontory, platform
RI	king
SCRIN	shrine
SEN	old
SLAN	health
TIGERNA	ruler
TIR	country, territory, land

Ancient Welsh (Brittonic)

ABATY	abbey
ABER	estuary, confluence
ADWY	gap, pass
AEL	brow of a hill
AFON	river
ALLT	hill, slope
ANWEN	very beautiful
ARAN	mountain ridge
BACH/FACH	small
BARR	top, head
BEDD	grave
BERTH	copse, hedge
BLAEN	head of a valley, river source
BOD	dwelling

Common Celtic Place Name Elements

BONT	bridge
BRAEN	rain, moisture
BRAN	raven
BRO	area
BRYN	hill
CAD	battle
CAE	field
CAER	fort, castle
CAPEL	chapel
CARREG/CERRIG	stone
CASTELL	castle
COCH/GOCH	red
COAD	trees
COED	wood, forest
CWM	narrow valley
DIN/DINAS	hillfort
DU	black
DYFFRYN	valley
EGLWYS	church
FFIN	border, boundary
FFORDD	road
FFYNNON	well, spring
GARTH/ARTH	headland, promontory
GLAN	bank or shore
GLYN	deep valley, glen
HEN	old
LLAN	parish
LLE	place
LLWYN	bush
LLYN	lake
MAES	field
MAUR	big
MOEL	bare hill, bald
MOR	sea
MYNYDD	mountain
NANT	stream, brook
NEWYDD	new
PANT	a hollow
PEN	top, end
PONT	bridge
PORTH	gate
PRIDD	soil

Celtic Places and Placenames

RHOS	moorland
RHYD	ford
TIR	land, territory
TRAETH	beach, shore
TREF	town
TYDDYN	farmstead
UCHEL	high
WAUN/GWAUN	heath, moor
YSGOL	school
YSGUBOR	barn
YNYS	island, water meadow

Manx (Goidelic/Gaelic)

ARD	high, high ground
ALT	brook, stream
AWIN	river
BAIE/BAIH	bay
BALLEY	farmstead
BEG	small
BROOGH	bank, brow of a hill
BWOALLEE	field, fold
CARN	heap of stones
CARRICK	rock, crag
CLAG	stone
COAN/COUAN	valley
COON	narrow
CROIT	croft
CRUINN	round
CRONK	hill
CURRAGH	bog
DOO	black
EAS	waterfall
FODDEY	long
GLACK	hollow
GOB	headland
INNIS	island
KEEILL	church
KEYLL	forest
KIONE	promontory
LHEEANEE	meadow
LOGH	lake, pool
MAGHER	field

Common Celtic Place Name Elements

MOOAR	big
MOOIR	sea
PEELEY	tower, fortress
POOYL	pool
PURT	port, harbour
RAAD	road
RATH	fort
SILEAU	mountain
SLOGH	pit
THIE	house
TRAIE	shore
TRAIE	sea shore
USHTEY	water

Scottish (Brittonic Gaelic)

ABER	mouth, confluence
ABH	river
ABOUR	marsh
ALLT	brook, stream
AN	of
ARD	high, upper
ATH	ford
BARR	hill, height
BEINN/BEN	mountain
BLAR/BLAIR	plain
BRAIG	upper part
BURGH	fortified settlement
CAOL	straits
CARR/CRAEG	rock
CRUACH	pile, stack
CRUMB	crooked
CAU	hollow, ravine
CEANN/CINN	head
COET	wood, forest
DAIL/DAEL	meadow, dale
DUN	fort, stronghold
EGLES	church
FALH	fallow land
GALL	stranger, foreigner
GLEANN/GLEN	valley
GORN	marsh
HOH	ridge, hill spur

INBHIR	mouth, estuary, confluence
INNIS	island
LANG	long
LEARG	hill-slope
LYN	lake
KIRK	church
MAC	son of
MARK	horse
MUC	pig, sow
MUIR	sea
PASGIL	pasture
PETT	standing stone, sentinel
RAA	roe deer
RIGHE	slope
ROS	headland, promontory
RUIM	spacious, roomy
STRATH	valley
TAIN	water, waters
TOM	knoll, hillock
TREF	town, settlement

Part Two

Cornwall, the South East & the Isles of Scilly

The People, their Language & Cornish Nationalism
Cornwall proudly asserts its unique identity and separateness from the rest of Britain by flying the black and white flag of the sixth century monk St Piran. The flag itself stems directly from the fifteenth century arms of the Saint-Peran family, (sometimes Saint-Pezran), who originated in Cornouaille, Brittany. Cornwall's geographical detachment is possible because the county is effectively cut off from the rest of mainland Britain by the River Tamar, a boundary set by King Athelstan in 936 AD, which goes some way to explain the Cornish sense of separateness.

History repeatedly demonstrates the efforts made by Cornishmen to assert their independence. As early as 1479, some fifteen thousand Cornishmen from the Lizard marched to London in revolt against the imposition of punitive English taxes. In the sixteenth century there was another uprising against the imposition of a new *English Book of Common Prayer*.

Men-an-Tol standing stones near Madron, Cornwall.

The Cornish language has been threatened with extinction many times. In the fifteenth and sixteenth centuries the Tudors prohibited the teaching of the Cornish language and some of the more outspoken speakers were executed and common use of the language went into decline. It is only in recent years that it has been clawed back from total extinction, as the Church of England began publishing the scriptures in Cornish, a few schools began teaching the language, and road signs began to appear in English and in Cornish. Since 2004, Cornish school children have been able to officially record their ethnicity as Cornish. As of 2020 it is estimated that Cornish is only spoken by a few thousand people, of which three or four hundred people speak it fluently.

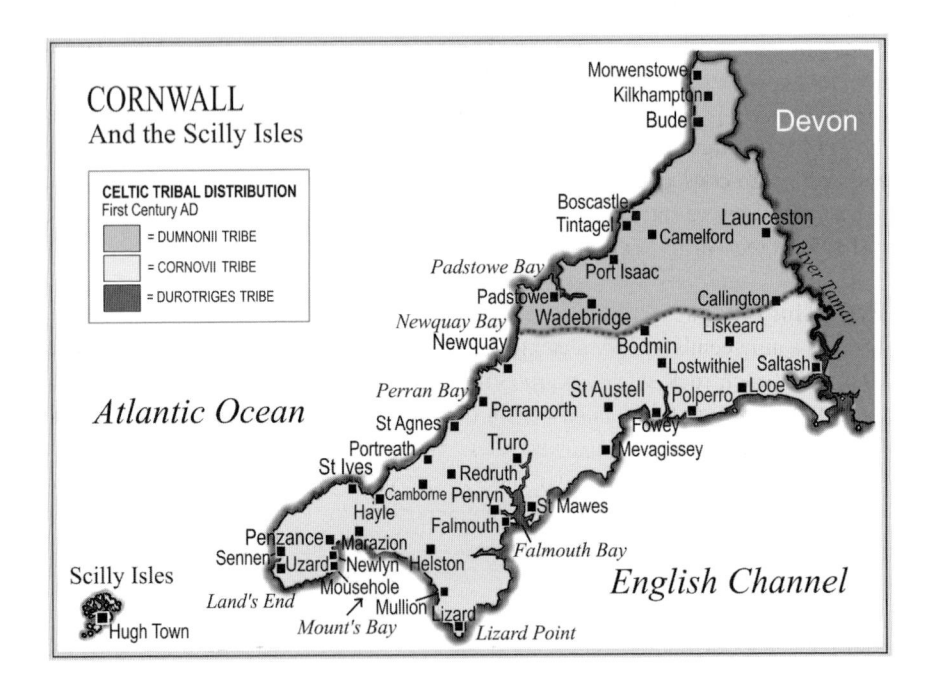

Cornish & Isles of Scilly Place Names

Advent
Advent is a small rural parish on Bodmin Moor whose name in Cornish is 'Pluwadwyn' (or sometimes 'Sen Adhwynn' and in Welsh, 'Santes Dwynwen'), and derives its name from St Adhwnn or Adwenna, one of the daughters of the Welsh King Brychan of Brycheiniog. The Grade I Listed parish church which stands at the village centre is dedicated to her. Actually, there is no village called Advent as such, and apart from sparsely populated moorland and a few farms, the Parish of Advent only comprises the small hamlets of Pencarrow, Tresinney and Treclagoe.

Altarnun
The village of Altarnun, situated on Bodmin Moor on the North Cornish coast, is named after the Celtic saint, St Nonna, a female holy woman, and the mother of the Patron Saint of Cornwall, St Piran or Pyran (in Cornish, 'Peran', and in Latin, 'Piranus'), and an altar dedicated to her in the sixth century. Hence, the name means 'altar (of the church) of Nonna'. In the Cornish language the village is known as 'Pluwnonn'. The *Domesday Book* listed the place as 'Penpont' in 1086, as it stands on Penpont Water, which is a tributary of the River Inney. The nearby Holy Well of St Nonna is traditionally believed to possess miraculous curative properties.

Annet
Annet, or in Cornish 'Anet', meaning 'Kittywake' is one of the Scilly Isles' largest uninhabited islands and is both a Scheduled Ancient Monument on account of its two prehistoric granite cairns, and a designated Site of Special Scientific Interest (SSSI) for its large seasonal seabird colonies of Manx Sheerwater, Storm Petrels and Puffins. In consequence, the island is closed to the public. The place name has undergone many variations over time, including its first as 'Anet' in 1302, 'Anete' in 1305, 'Agnet' in 1570 and as 'Agnet iland alias Annett' in 1650.

Bedruthan Steps
There is a nineteenth century Cornish legend which tells of a giant called Bedruthan who used beach rock stacks as stepping stones in order to take a shortcut across the bay during high tides. The steps in question go down from Bedruthan farm to the sandy beach below. The place name is more likely to have originated with a man called Rudhynn, and his dwelling (in Cornish, a 'bod', related to the modern English word 'abode'). Hence, the place name means 'Rudhynn's dwelling'. Who he was is not known but the place was recorded as Boduthyn in 1335.

Bishop Rock
This rock is located at the extreme south-west of the Scilly archipelago, and derives its name on account of its silhouette which some say resembles a Bishop's mitre. It is surrounded by other small rocks who took their name from its lead – these included Maenenescop in 1302 (from the Cornish words 'men', meaning 'stone', 'an', meaning 'the' and 'escop', meaning 'bishop', as well as the 'Bishops and his Clerks Rock' in 1779.

Bodmin
Bodmin town lies on the edge of Bodmin Moor, a somewhat desolate area of heathland covering around eighty square miles. The town derives its place name from the Old Cornish words 'bod', a dwelling, and 'meneghi', signifying land belonging to a monastery or a church. Hence, 'a dwelling on church land' or 'dwelling by the sanctuary of churchmen or monks'. The name was recorded as 'Bodmine' in the *Domesday Book*, held by the Church of St Petroc. Tradition has it that in the sixth century St Petroc came to Bodmin and took over the monastic

settlement that had been founded earlier by St Guron. By 1086, it was an important centre for religious pilgrimages to see the relics in St Petroc's shrine. The place name has had many variants over the centuries, including 'Botmenei' in 1100, 'Bodmen' in 1253, 'Bodman' in 1377 and 'Bodmyn' in 1522.

Bolingey
This village is now known as Bolingey (or in Cornish, 'Melinji'), and lies within the Parish of Perranzabuloe in north Cornwall. Its original name came from the Cornish 'melin', meaning 'mill', and 'chi', a house. Hence, 'mill house'. The name was recorded as 'Velingey' in 1566 and as 'Melinge' in 1650.

Breage
This Cornish village derived its place name from the church which was established in the village in 1170 to honour St Breage, an Irish-born nun of the fifth or sixth century. The name of the church was adopted as the name of the village that grew up around it. At the time of the church foundation, the place name was 'Egglosbrec', the Cornish word 'eglos', meaning 'church', having been added to it. Hence, '(place at the) church of St Breage'. The village boasts two Cornish crosses, one of which stands in the local churchyard and the other at a junction a mile distant.

Brean
The name of the village of Brean in Somerset identifies it as having Celtic origins, as the Brittonic word 'bryn', as with the Welsh word 'bre', signifies a hill. In simple terms the place name means '(place by the) hill'. The hill in question is known as Brean Down. *Domesday* recorded the name as 'Brien' in 1086.

Bryher
The island of Bryher, in the Isles of Scilly, gets its name from the Cornish word 'bre', meaning 'hill', and 'yer' which makes it a plural. Hence, '(place of the) hills'. It is one of the hilliest parts of the archipelago as well as one of the smaller of the inhabited islands in the island group. It was recorded in 1319 as 'Braer'.

Bude
This small north-east Cornish seaside town on the River Neet (also known locally as the River Strat), was formerly known as Bude Haven (in Cornish, 'Porthbud'), on account of its sheltered harbour in a bay off the Bristol Channel. The origin of the place name is uncertain, but possibly taken from a river name, or may even be a corruption of the Old Saxon 'bede', a word for a prayer or bidding.

Budock Water
This village was named after St Budoc (also known as St Beuzec or St Buzoc), the fifth century Bishop of Dol in Brittany, where his relics are preserved. The name

Buzoc means 'saved from the waters' from the Breton word 'beuzin', meaning 'drowned'. The saint was especially venerated in Brittany and in Cornwall. The 'Water' element was added when the village was established around the church in the nineteenth century and refers to the local stream. In Cornish the place name is 'Dowr Budhek', which means 'St Budock's church beside a stream'.

Calstock
Calstock is a small village, located on the River Tamar on the Devon border with Cornwall. Its Cornish name is spelled 'Kalstok'. There is an Iron Age hillfort in the parish and a Roman fort has been unearthed beside the village church. Two possibilities have been suggested for the meaning of the place name: first that the name element, 'Cal' is an abbreviated form of Callington, while 'stoc' is an Old English expression referring to an outlying or remote settlement. This suggests that Calstock might have been such a district of Callington. Alternatively, some maintain it refers to a Saxon man called Cal, whose settlement it was. *Domesday* recorded the place name as 'Kalestoc' in 1086.

Camborne
Camborne's place name is spelled 'Kammbronn' in Cornish and comes from the words 'kamm' and 'bronn', which together mean 'crooked hill'. By the late-twelfth century, the name had been recorded as 'Camberon'. In earlier times it was known as Camborne Churchtown. The word 'kamm' is the same in the Breton language, while the Welsh, Gaelic and Irish Gaelic words differ slightly as 'cam'.

Cannalidgey
Cannalidgey is a Cornish hamlet in the Parish of St Issey, located a few miles south of Padstow and is known in Cornish as 'Egloskrug', which means 'the church on the tumulus'.

Caradon Hill
Caradon Hill, or in the Cornish language, 'Bre Garn', is located on Bodmin Moor in the former Caradon district of Cornwall. The name comes from the Cornish word 'carn', which represented a tor or a cairn, and the Old English word 'dun', meaning 'hill'. The second word 'Hill' of the place name is essentially redundant.

Cardinham
The name of this Cornish village hits the nail on its head twice, as it is derived from the two Cornish words, 'ker' and 'dinan', both of which mean 'fort'. Therefore, technically, the place name means 'fort fort'. It is thought that its original name might simply have been 'Dinan', and that the 'ker' element was added later, possibly in reference to the nearby Bury Castle Iron Age hillfort in Exmoor, just across the border in Somerset. The name was recorded as 'Cardinan' in about 1180.

Carharrack
There are several views as to the meaning of the name of the village of Carharrack in Cornwall. One maintains that it is a corruption of the Cornish 'ker', meaning 'fort', along with a reference to a man called Ardhek or Arthroc. In which case, the name may be taken to mean 'Arthroc's fort'. Who Arthroc may have been is unknown. Another view is that the second element of the place name may have come from 'harrack', which could signify a camp or settlement near a rock or cairn – hence, 'fort near a rock'. A third offers the possibility that the second element could derive from 'ardh', meaning 'high place'. In this case the name could be interpreted as 'fort in a high place', and might refer to Carn Marth, an ancient hill south-east of Redruth.

Carthew
Carthew, in the Parish of St Austell, is an ancient name, probably of Celtic origin, and is comprised of two Old Cornish words: 'ker', meaning 'fort' and 'du', meaning 'dark' or 'black'. The place name was recorded as 'Carduf' in 1327 and as 'Carthu' in 1367. The name means 'black (or dark) fort'.

Castle-an-Dinas
In Cornish, the word 'castell' signifies a fort, and in this case it refers specifically to the Iron Age hillfort at the summit of Castle Downs near St Columb Major, which dates from the third century BC. Reputedly, it is the largest and most impressive of its kind in Cornwall. Dinas is the name of a nearby farm.

Cawsand/Cawsand Bay
See: 'Kingsand'.

Chapel Amble
Chapel Amble, in the Parish of St Kew, was begun by sixth century Celtic monks from Ireland and Wales who established chapels throughout Cornwall. It is located on the River Amble, which is the origin of the place name. In Cornish it is known as 'Amaleglos', meaning 'church on the River Amble'. The river name itself comes from 'amal', meaning 'edge' or 'boundary'. It was recorded by *Domesday* as 'Amal', and by 1284 it had acquired its present name.

Chacewater
The Cornish parish and village of Chacewater near Truro is derived from 'chace', a hunting ground, and a local stream (a 'water'). Hence, 'hunting ground near a stream'. In Cornish, the place is called 'Dowr an Chas'. It was a favoured place to hunt by the early kings of Cornwall. The stream in question continued to provide the villagers with drinking water until relatively recent times.

Chysauster
Chysauster began as an ancient Romano-British settlement almost 2,000 years ago. Its Cornish name is 'Chisylvester', meaning 'Sylvester's cottage'. It was then an unfortified settlement, probably occupied by members of the Celtic Dumnonii tribe. The place name derives from 'chi', meaning 'cottage'. Who Sylvester was is not known, but by the beginning of the fourteenth century the place was already known as 'Chisalwester'.

Clovelly
The village of Clovelly in Devon has decidedly Celtic origins. Its Cornish name is 'Cleath', meaning 'dyke' (or 'ditch'), on account of the Iron Age fort known as Clovelly Dykes. Its current name includes a corruption of the personal name Fele, who is associated with the fort. The complete place name translates as 'fort (or earthworks) of Fele'.

Clyst Honiton
The first element of this Devonshire village place name comes from the River Clyst, a Brittonic name related to the Welsh word 'clust', which technically means 'ear', but in this case it refers to the sea inlet or upper reaches of the river. The village is close to the town of Honiton, whose name comes from the Old English 'hiwan', which referred to a community of monks, and 'tun', a farmstead. Hence, the name translates as 'farmstead of the community of monks on the River Clyst'. By the beginning of the twelfth century, it was recorded as 'Hinatune' and by the end of the thirteenth it had become known as 'Clysthynetone'.

Colyton
The ancient village of Colyton is located in Devon on the River Coly, and first appeared in written records around 946 AD as 'Culintona'. The name derives from the river with the addition of the Old English suffix 'tun', signifying a farmstead. The place name means 'farmstead on the River Coly'. The river name is thought to come from a Celtic source and probably meant 'narrow'. The place was recorded in the *Domesday Book* as 'Culitone'.

Cornwall
Cornwall gets its name from the ancient Celtic tribe known as the Cornovii and the Old English word 'walh', meaning 'foreigner' or 'ancient Briton'. Hence, the county name means 'territory of the Cornovii Britons'. The word 'Cornovii' meant 'horn people', a reference to the horn-shaped geography of Cornwall. In Cornish, the county name is 'Kernow', a probable corruption of Cornovii. In the early eighth century the county name was known as 'Cornubia', by the end of the ninth it had been recorded as 'Cornwalas', and the Great Survey of 1086 listed it as 'Cornualia'.

Countisbury
This hamlet on Exmoor derived its place name from the nearby hill, anciently known as Cunet Hill, which is of Celtic origin, though the meaning is unknown.

The present-day Countisbury Hill is also the site of an Iron Age hillfort which is thought to have been where the Battle of Cynuit (or Cynwit) took place between the West Saxons and Vikings in the year 878. The 'bury' element of the name is from the Old English 'burh', signifying a stronghold or fortified place. Hence, the name means 'stronghold on Cunet Hill'.

Crantock
The village of Crantock was earlier known as 'Langurroc', which meant the 'dwelling of the monks'. Crantock was founded in the fifth century by St Carantacus, the son of a Welsh chieftain who is said to have studied with St Patrick. He established a church in Cornwall, where he was later venerated as St Carantoc. *Domesday* recorded the place name in Latin as 'Sanctus Carentoch'.

Crediton
Crediton is situated in the valley of the River Creedy in Devon, from which it gets its name. The river name is of Celtic origin and probably means 'slow flowing one'; this is thought to be a comparison to the fast-flowing River Yeo, of which it is a tributary. The Old English affix 'tun' signified a farmstead or estate. Hence, the place name means 'farmstead (or estate) on the (River) Creedy'. The town was known as 'Cridantune' in 930 AD and was recorded in the *Domesday Book* as 'Chritetona'.

Creech St Michael
The name of the Somerset village of Creech St Michael near Taunton derives the first part of its place name from the Celtic word 'crug', meaning 'hill', identical to the Welsh word 'crug', meaning 'hillock'. It has been suggested that it refers to Creech Barrow Hill. The second element relates to the dedication of the local church of St Michael and this was only added in the nineteenth century to distinguish it from nearby Creech Heathfield. At the time of the *Domesday Book* it was recorded simply as 'Crice'.

Cubert
The Cornish name for the village of Cubert is 'Egloskubert', from the word 'eglos', meaning 'church'. The place was formerly known as St Cubert, after the Welsh missionary who accompanied St Carantoc in bringing Christianity to Cornish Celtic tribes. It is thought that the former 'Saint' element of the place name was dropped during the Reformation as it was regarded as Catholic and thereby controversial. An alternative view is that the name is an abbreviation of St Cuthbert, the Bishop of Lindisfarne. In 1269 the place name was recorded as 'Sanctus Cubertus'.

Cullompton
It is thought that the River Culm, after which this Devon township gets its name, comes from a Celtic word meaning 'winding (or leisurely) stream', similar to the Welsh word 'clwm', meaning 'knot'. In around 880 AD, the name was recorded as 'Columtune', the Old English word 'tun', having been added, indicating a

farmstead or estate. Therefore, the place name means 'farmstead (or settlement) on the River Culm'. In *Domesday* it was entered simply as 'Colump'.

Devon
The name of the County of Devon translates as '(territory of the) Devonians', after the Dumnonii tribe whose tribelands included parts of present-day Dorset and Somerset. There are at least two possible explanations as to the origin of the tribal name. 'Dumnonii' might mean 'deep valley dwellers' from the proto-Celtic word 'dubnos' meaning 'deep'. According to other accounts, it is thought to mean 'worshippers of the God Dumonos', whose name in turn meant 'mysterious, dark or gloomy one'. In Brittonic Welsh, Devon is known as 'Dyfnaint', in Breton as 'Devnent' and in Cornish as 'Dewnens', each meaning 'deep valleys'. It has been argued that the Cornovii of Cornwall may have been a sub-division of the Dumnonii tribe.

Dunterton
The name of the village of Dunterton in Devon combines early Celtic and Old English. The Brittonic name elements 'din' and 'tre' respectively suggest 'fort' and 'village' and the Old English suffix 'tun' indicates a farmstead or farming settlement. Therefore a fair interpretation of the place name might be 'farming village with (or near) a fort'. The place was recorded as 'Dondritone' in the Great Survey of 1086.

Egloskerry
This Cornish village near Launceston derives its place name from two sources. The first, 'eglos', an old Cornish word for 'church', and the second element refers to St Keri, to whom the church was dedicated in the mid-sixteenth century. Keri, along with his many siblings, of which St Petroc was one, was the son of King Brychan of Brecknockshire in Wales. The full place name therefore means 'the church of St Keri'.

Exeter
Exeter is a major Devon city whose name means 'Roman town on the River Exe'. In fact, the Romans called the military fortress settlement 'Isca Dumnoniorum' (meaning 'water of the Dumnonii'), incorporating the name of the Celtic tribe. The word 'isca' represents the 'water' in question, later corrupted simply to 'Exe', the present-day river name. The Roman appellation is reflected in the Welsh name for Exeter, 'Caerwysg', meaning 'fortified settlement on the River Uisc'. Later, the Roman fort element had been recorded in the place name, which was written as 'Exanceaster', indicating a military fort or encampment. Hence, the 'fort of the River Exe'.

Feniton
The name of this village in Devon stems from Vine Water, a stream which flows through it. The original name for the stream was a Celtic word, something similar to the Welsh 'ffin', meaning 'boundary' or 'end' (as in the Latin word 'finis'). The

stream is a tributary of the River Otter and marks the boundary of the parish. The Old English affix 'tun' (indicating a farmstead or settlement), was added sometime before the Conquest, as *Domesday* recorded it as 'Finetone'. The place name may be taken to mean 'farmstead by Vine Water'.

Feock
The village and Parish of Feock (in Cornish, 'Lannfiek'), is situated in the Fal Estuary, and its place name is based on St Fioc (sometimes Feoca), whom local tradition maintains lived in a small hut near a well in a place called La Feock. Nothing else is known about him for certain. There was a St Fiac in Brittany, who might have been the same person, though this is entirely supposition. The village has the church of St Feoca at its centre, which dates back to the twelfth century.

Garras
A small hamlet whose Cornish spelling is 'Garros', a name that comes from the word 'garow', meaning 'rough', and 'ros', moorland. Hence, the name means '(place in) rough moorland'. Around the end of the seventeenth century the place name was being recorded as 'Garrows Common'.

Gerrans
The village of Gerrans (sometimes 'St Gerrans'), stretches along the eastern side of the Roseland Peninsula. The place name derives from Gerent, an eighth century Cornish king, and latter-day saint. Early scribes wrote his name in Latin as 'Gerontius', and the name survives today in the Welsh name Geraint. Geoffrey of Monmouth, the medieval English chronicler and bishop of St Asaph (1152), included Geraint as a knight of King Arthur's court at Caerleon in his major work, *Historia Regum Britanniae* (History of the Kings of Britain), and Alfred Lord Tennyson used the ancient Welsh *Mabinogion* to include 'The Marriage of Geraint' among his poems. Ninth century documents held by Canterbury Cathedral reveal that the Parish of Gerrans was once the seat of the Bishopric of the Celtic Church in Cornwall.

Glastonbury
'Glaston' is a Celtic word which probably means 'place of woad'. Woad was a plant-based blue dye which many Britons and later Celtic peoples painted on themselves as body decoration or before battle, presumably to strike fear into the opposition. The site dates from Neolithic times, but during the seventh century the name was recorded as 'Glastonia' and by the mid-eighth it had become 'Glestingaburg'. The Old English element 'burh' was added to this Somerset place name to produce the meaning, 'stronghold of the people of Glaston' and it may once have been a fortified monastic settlement. It has also been suggested that Glason may have been the personal name of a Celtic chieftain. In the seventh century, the place was sometimes known as 'Ineswytrin', a derivation of a similar Welsh name for

the place, 'Ynys Gwydrin', which literally translates as 'island of blue, green or glass'. The island in question would have been Glastonbury Tor, and 'glass' was a misinterpretation that referred not to glass but to woad. Confusingly, the Latin word 'vitrum', as used by Roman colonists, could mean either 'glass' or 'woad'. Before land drainage was undertaken in relatively modern times, the Tor would have stood out as an island above the flooded Somerset Levels during the rainy season. It was almost certainly a pagan religious site or small settlement well before Christianity came to the shores of Britain, and it was not until the tenth or eleventh century that a stone church was built on its summit. The winding zig-zag path that ascends through its terraces is thought to have been created for pilgrims making their way to the top. The Tor continues to be surrounded by ancient tales, legend and folklore.

Grampound
The Romans built the first bridge over the River Fal here, and the Normans referred to the bridge as the 'Grand Pont', from which the village gets its present name. The place name means '(place by the) great bridge'. The name is 'Ponsmeur' in Cornish.

Gugh
This is one of the smallest of the inhabited islands in the Isles of Scilly at just over half a mile in length, and is usually grouped with neighbouring St Agnes, to whom it is connected by a sand bar which is exposed during low tides. Its Cornish name is 'Keow', which translates as 'hedge bank'. The place name is frequently pronounced as 'Goo', 'Guff' and 'Gogh'. The island contains Bronze Age cairns and a standing stone below Kittern Hill known as The Old Man of Gugh, providing evidence of ancient occupation, with pottery remains dated to the late Neolithic or early Bronze Age. There are also five entrance graves containing human bones. Over succeeding centuries it has been used by St Agnes farmers for animal grazing. It has been designated as an Area of Outstanding Natural Beauty and is managed by the Isles of Scilly Wildlife Trust.

Gulval
This Cornish village overlooking Mounts Bay, gets its name from the church dedicated to the sixth century saint, St Gulval (sometimes St Gwelvel, or St Gudwal, scholars seem unable to agree). Consequently, little is known about the saint except that her feast day is celebrated every 12 November. The village was originally called Lanisley (or 'Lannystli'), derived from the old Cornish words 'lan', meaning church, and 'ishei', meaning 'low' (or lower). Hence, 'lower church'.

Gunwalloe
The coastal village of Gunwalloe, or in Cornish, 'Gwynnwalow', is situated on the Lizard Peninsula. It was included within the Manor of Winnianton (Winetone) in the first entry in the 1086 Survey for Cornwall. The village is named after its thirteenth century church which is dedicated to the Breton saint, St Winwaloe, illustrating the connection which Cornwall has long had with Brittany.

Gwinear

The Parish of Gwinear (in Cornish, 'Sen Gwynnyer', also known as St Winierus, or in Irish, St Fingar), after whom the church and village is named, was a sixth century Celtic martyr and missionary who is said to have been murdered nearby by the Cornish pagan king Theodoric.

Harrowbarrow

The village of Harrowbarrow (in Cornish, 'Kelliskovarnek') in east Cornwall, derives its name from the Old English 'har', meaning 'boundary' and 'bearu', a grove, wood or copse. The place name therefore translates as '(place by the) boundary wood'. A Celtic Bronze Age cist, complete with decorated clay pot from around 2,000 BC was unearthed during house renovations in the village in 1989, and is thought to have been the burial place of a child.

Hayle

The south-west Cornish coastal village of Hayle (in earlier records sometimes written as 'Heyl'), located across the bay from St Ives, is named after the river which flows through it and comes from a Celtic word which means 'estuary'. Evidence has been found for Bronze Age occupation of the area as well as an Iron Age hillfort above Carnsew Pool. The discovery of Greek and Roman pottery also indicates that it was an important trading port at that time, and a rudimentary tin industry may have already existed there long before Hayle emerged as an important industrial centre for copper and iron production in Cornwall.

Helland

The meaning of the name Helland is uncertain, though most cite the Cornish words 'hen', meaning 'old' and 'lan' or 'lann', indicating a church or church site, to produce a place name that means '(place at the site of an) old church'. The church is dedicated to St Helena, who was the mother of the Roman emperor, Constantine the Great. The village is referred to in the *Domesday Book* as 'Henland'.

Hendraburnick

The Manor of Hendraburnick, along with Halwell, historically belonged to Launceston Castle and the Manor of Tremeal. It was partly located in the Parish of Davidstow and partly in St Juliot, which had belonged to the Grenville family before 1620. The name Hendraburnick (in Cornish, 'Hendra Bronnik'), means 'rushy home farm', and began as a small farmstead near Davidstow. North-east of the manorial estate is Hendraburnick Quoit, a Late Neolithic dolmen, one of the most decorated prehistoric stones in southern Britain.

Hugh Town

Also spelled as one word, 'Hughtown', the settlement and port in St Mary's in the Isles of Scilly was known in the sixteenth century as 'Hew Hill', most likely derived from the Old English 'hoh', signifying a promontory or spur of land. The promontory was the site of a military garrison ('The Garrison'), historically known as 'The Hugh', where a Roman altar was discovered in the nineteenth century. However, there is evidence of human activity on the island going back at least four thousand years. The earliest form of the present-day name appeared in the seventeenth century, and by 1868 the name had been spelled 'Heugh Town'.

Illogan
Located a few miles from Redruth, the name of this Cornish village is 'Egloshalow'. The place is named after a parish church dedicated to the Celtic saint, St Illogan (sometimes known as 'Ylloganus' or 'Euluganus'), of whom little is known. The village was referred to in 1235 by the Latin name of 'Ecclesia of Eglossalau', and later in 1291 as 'Sanctus Ilganu's'. The place name means 'Church of St Illogan'.

Isles of Scilly
The Isles of Scilly are an archipelago comprising a hundred and forty islands, of which just five are inhabited. They are located off the coast of the ancient Celtic kingdom of Dumnonia, now modern Cornwall. Several possible explanations have been offered as to the origin of their name: first, they are thought to have been a pilgrimage centre during Roman times, and were dedicated to a sea goddess or to the Sun God Sulis or Sulina. Hence, they knew them as Sillinae and Silurae Insulae which probably meant '(place of the) sun islands'. The Greeks knew the island group as Hesperides and Cassiterides (meaning 'Tin Isles'), and the Danes later knew the islands as 'Syllorgar'. On old maps they were called 'Sorlingus', which could be a corruption of 'salt ling' (the fish found around its shores). The islands are named 'Les Sorlingues' in French and 'Las Sorlingas' in Spanish.

Kerrier
Kerrier is a Cornish council district whose name derives from the Cornish words 'ker' and 'hyr', which taken together mean 'long fort', a reference to an ancient Iron Age hillfort, possibly Castle Pencaire on Tregonning Hill.

Ladock
The village of Ladock near Truro is named after the church at its centre that was dedicated to the female saint, St Ladock (sometimes 'St Ladoca'). Its Cornish name is 'Egloslajek', which means 'church of (St) Ladock'. The place was known by its Latin name of 'Sancta Ladoca' in the mid-thirteenth century, but little is known about the saint or her life.

Lamorna
The name of this village on the Penwith Peninsula in Cornish is 'Nansmornow', and means '(place in the) valley of the River Mornow'. The first name element,

'nans' is the Cornish word for a valley and the second, 'mor' means 'sea'. It has been suggested that the river name could also have come from a Celtic word related to the Welsh 'mwrn', meaning 'sultry'. The river flows into Lamorna Cove.

Land's End
As the name suggests this marks the southernmost place where Cornwall, England and Great Britain end. The Cornish name for Land's End is Penwith (sometimes 'Pennwedh'), which translates as 'end district'. The name was recorded as 'Londeseynde' in 1337. The Breton town of Finistère in north-west France also has a name that translates from the original Latin as 'land's end'.

Lellizzick
Lellizzick, located on the tidal inlet of the River Camel near Padstow in Cornwall, was the site of a Bronze Age and later Romano-British settlement. The place has undergone a series of slight name changes over the centuries: the earliest documented reference dates to 1284 when the settlement was known as 'Lanwoledec'; it was recorded as 'Lanwoegyk' in 1302 and 'Lannwoledik' in 1334. By 1348 it was known as 'Launledeke' and by 1540 as 'Lanlesyke'. The place name combines the Cornish elements of 'lann' (meaning 'enclosed cemetery' or 'church site') and possibly 'gwlesyk' (meaning 'leader'). Hence, the name means 'enclosed cemetery (or church land) of the leader'.

Lezant
The village of Lezant (or in Cornish, 'Lannsant'), probably means 'holy church site', based on 'lann' indicating a church site or grounds and 'sant', meaning 'holy'. The parish church is dedicated to St Briochus, a Celtic saint who founded a religious settlement in the area.

Looe
The south-east coastal Cornish township of Looe is thought to have been an inhabited settlement for the best part of three thousand years. Until relatively modern times it was divided into two separate towns – East Looe and West Looe. They are joined by a bridge across the East Looe River (sometimes simply called the River Looe). The place name derives from the old Cornish 'loo', which meant 'pool' or 'inlet', in reference to the body of water known locally as the Mill Pool. Nearby is Looe Island, also known as St George's Island, which was settled by monks from Glastonbury Abbey from 1144. Its original Cornish name was 'Enys Lann-Managh', which translates as 'island of the monk's settlement'.

Ludgvan
The origin of this village place name is comprised of two Cornish words, 'lusow', meaning 'ashes' along with the suffix 'an', meaning 'the place of'. Hence, 'the place of ashes'. The significance of the place name is open to interpretation, but it is

argued that there may have been a Celtic cremation or burial site here in its distant past. The village is entered in the Great Survey of 1086 as 'Luduham'.

Marazion
The village of Marazion, located in Mount's Bay in west Cornwall derives its name from two Cornish words: 'marghas', signifying a market, and 'byghan', possibly meaning small or little. Opinions differ and the place name has been variously translated as 'Little Market' and as 'Thursday Market'. Whatever the true meaning, the Romans knew the place as 'Ictis', suggesting some form of market or Celtic trading post existed there long before their arrival in Britain. It was recorded as 'Marghasbigan' in the mid-thirteenth century, and claims to be one of the oldest townships in Britain. Marazion has a man-made causeway linking it at low tide to St Michael's Mount.

Marhamchurch
The ancient Parish of Marhamchurch derives its name from the village church dedication to the Celtic saint, St Marwenne (also known as St Morwenna), who founded a hermitage here in the fifth century. She is thought by some to have been a daughter of St Brychan, a Welsh saint and king; others believe her to have been Merewenna, the tenth century Abbess of Romsey in Kent. The village was recorded as 'Maronecine' in the Great Survey of 1086.

Mawgan
Bronze and Iron Age settlements have been have been excavated in various parts of the Parish of Mawgan (or more properly, 'St Mawgan-in-Pydar'). The village probably dates from the sixth century, when the Welsh missionary, St Mauganus (also known as 'Meugan' or 'Mawgan'), arrived at what is now Mawgan Porth, accompanied by St Breoc and St Cadoc on missionary journeys to convert the pagan Celtic tribes of Cornwall to Christianity. The village and its church are located on the River Menalhyl in the Vale of Lanherne. Both are named after the saint.

Minions
Reputedly, the village of Minions on Bodmin Moor, part of Linkinhorne Parish, was known in Cornish as 'Menyon' (probably meaning 'stone'), and is the highest in the county at almost one thousand feet above sea level. The place gets its name from the nearby Celtic Iron Age barrow known as Minions Mound, or Minions Barrow; the derivation of the name is unknown but it was recorded in 1613 as 'Mimiens Borroughe'.

Morwenstow
In 1201, the coastal Cornish village of Morwenstow was called 'Morwestewe', referring to the early sixth century Irish saint, St Morwenna, along with the Old English affix 'stowe', indicating a holy place. The village name may therefore be interpreted as 'holy place of St Morwenna'. The most northerly parish and village

in the county, it was known in Cornish as 'Logmorwenna'. The Norman church of around 1296 stands on an original Saxon site and is dedicated to St Morwenna and St John the Baptist.

Mullion
The village of Mullion (in Cornish, 'Eglosvelyan'), is a civil parish on the Lizard Peninsula of south Cornwall. The name has evolved over the years, but local parish records list the name variously as St Mullyon, St Mullian, Mullian, Mullyan, Mulion, Mullyon and St Mullion. In the church valuation carried out in 1535 the village name is recorded as Melyan. The name derives from St Melaine (in Latin, 'St Melanius'), who was the Breton Bishop of Rennes in France in the early sixth century.

Mylor Bridge
In Cornish the village of Mylor Bridge is known as 'Ponsnowyth' and is located at the head of Mylor Creek, a few miles north of Falmouth. The name derives from the dedication of the village church to the martyred saint, St Melorus, who was reputedly a Cornish prince and son of Melianus, the Duke of Cornouaille in Brittany. The dead body of Melorus was said to have been responsible for many miracles. The translation of the Cornish place name comes from 'pons', a bridge, and 'nowydh', meaning 'new'. Hence, '(place by the) new bridge'. In 1562 it was still known by its Cornish name, and it was not until 1697 that it appeared in an English form as New Bridge. In the mid-eighteenth century it had emerged under its current name as Mylor Bridge.

Nanstallon
Nanstallon is located in the valley of the present-day River Camel, which was formerly known as the River Alan. Added to this is the old Cornish word 'nans' (or 'nant'), meaning 'valley' and the result is a place name meaning '(place in the) valley of the (River) Alan'. The river name, Alan, is of Celtic origin, but its meaning is unknown.

Padstow
This fishing village was known in Cornish as 'Lanwenehoc', and by the eleventh century by its Latin name, 'Sancte Petroces Stow', where 'stow' indicated a holy place, in this case dedicated to St Petroc. According to legend, St Petroc arrived from Ireland around 520 AD and built a monastery on the hill above the harbour. The monks of St Petroc went on to own extensive lands, stretching from Portreath to Tintagel. In 1318, the place was known as 'Patristowe', and by the early sixteenth century had been recorded as 'Padstowe', something approaching its present name.

Pelynt
Known in Cornish as 'Pluwnennys' and 'Pluwnonna', this village has a name originally incorporating the word 'plu', meaning 'parish', and 'Nennyd', the fourth

century Celtic Welsh female saint, better known as St Nonn (or Nonna). Hence, 'Parish of St Nonna'. The saint is said to have been the mother of St David, and the parish church is dedicated to her memory. The village was listed as 'Plunent' in the *Domesday Book* in 1086.

Pentreath

In the Cornish language the name of this village near Praa Sands on the Lizard Peninsula is spelled 'Penntreth', representing 'penn', meaning 'headland', 'an' meaning 'the', and 'treth' meaning 'beach'. Hence, '(place at the) head (of) the beach'. It comprises the two hamlets of Higher Pentreath and Lower Pentreath. A woman called Dorothy Pentreath (1692–1777) known as Dolly, was recorded as the last known native speaker of the Cornish language in the eighteenth century. A contemporary writer remarked that before she died at the age of eighty-two she 'could speak Cornish very fluently'. However several other native speakers were identified in Cornwall in the nineteenth century. Happily, the language has undergone a significant revival in recent years, and an upcoming generation of young Cornish speakers are emerging.

Perranarworthal

In Cornwall, the 'Perran' element of place names generally refers to the fifth century monk, St Piran, patron saint of Cornwall, and this village is typical. The final element in the name reflects its location within the ancient Manor of Arwothel, itself made up of two Cornish words: 'ar', meaning 'beside', and 'goethel', which means 'marsh' or 'bog'. The Cornish name for the village is 'Peran ar Wodhel', which means, '(the church of) St Piran in Arwothel'.

Perranporth

Perranporth is a relatively new settlement, having been known at the latter end of the sixteenth century as St Perin's Creek, after St Piran (or Pyran, in Cornish, St Peran), who was originally the patron saint of Cornish tin miners. It is his flag, a white cross on a black background, which has become the county flag of Cornwall. It was not until the nineteenth century that the village became known as Perran Porth. 'Porth' is an old word for a port or harbour. Hence, the 'Port of St Piran'. Every March, St Piran's Day is celebrated when hundreds of people make a pilgrimage to Perranporth.

Perranzabuloe

Probably one of the most unusual and least English-sounding place names, the Cornish township of Perranzabuloe, like many others in Cornwall, derives from St Piran, the county's patron saint. The place name relies on the Cornish word 'Peran', the saint's name in Cornish, the affix 'lann', indicating the site of a church, and the Latin suffix 'in sabulo', which translates into English as 'in the sands'. Hence, the place name may be interpreted as 'Parish of St Piran's Church in the sands'. *Domesday* named the place as 'Lanpiran'. In 1535, the place was recorded as 'Peran in Zabulo' and by the mid-nineteenth century was commonly known as 'Perran-in-the-Sands'.

Phillack
This village was originally built around the church dedicated to St Felicity, and this was thought to be the origin of its place name. In 1259, the place was recorded in Latin as 'Sancta Felicitas'. However, the discovery of a tenth century document which mentions St Felec of Cornwall, resulted in the dedication being re-attributed to St Felek, a Celtic saint about whom little is known. In Cornish the place name is 'Eglosheyl'. In 1388, the name 'Felok' appears and by the early seventeenth century it was being recorded as 'Phillacke'.

Porthleven
Porthleven grew at the mouth of a small stream called Leven, which translates from Cornish as 'smooth' and 'porth', meaning harbour. Hence 'smooth harbour'. It may also be related to St Elvan of Avalon, who was known to have preached Christianity to kings of the Britons. In this case, the place name may represent 'the harbour of St Elvan'.

Porthloo
Porthloo (sometimes spelled and often pronounced 'Porthlow'), is known in Cornish as 'Porth Logh', meaning 'cove of the deep water inlet', and is also known as Little Porth. It is a coastal settlement on the island of St Mary's in the Isles of Scilly, situated about half a mile north-east of Hugh Town. This small hamlet comprises no more than two dozen properties, mainly surrounding Porthloo Green, facing Porthloo beach and the sea, flanked on one side by Newford Island and the other by Taylor's Island.

Praze-an-Beeble
An unusual village place name, Praze-an-Beeble, or in Cornish, 'Pras an Bibel', comes directly from the Cornish language, where 'pras', means 'meadow', 'an' simply means 'the', and 'pibell' signifies a pipe or conduit, although some cite 'Beeble' as a direct reference to the River Beeble, on which the village stands. The place name may therefore translate as either 'meadow with a conduit', or more likely, 'meadow on the River Beeble'. The Beeble is a tributary of the River Hayle, which runs at the bottom of the village.

Probus
The village of Probus (in Cornish, 'Lannbrobus'), is a civil parish located about four miles east of Truro, and boasting the tallest church tower in Cornwall. The place name originates from the church's dedication to the fifth century British Christian St Probus. A monastery existed there before the Norman Conquest, established by King Athelstan, with the expressed intention of converting the Celtic tribes of Cornwall to Christianity. However, during the reign of Henry I, the church was given to Exeter Cathedral.

Quethiock

Quethiock, pronounced 'Gwithick' (in Cornish, 'Koosek', and in Old Cornish 'Cuidoc' or 'Cruetheke'), is a place name meaning 'forested (or wooded) place'. It is located about five miles east of Liskeard and situated in the Parish of St Germans, within the Deanery and Hundred of East. The ancient parish church is dedicated to St Hugh. A Celtic cross which stands in the churchyard is arguably the tallest in the county.

Quies

Quies is a group of islands off the north-west coast of Cornwall. The name is a corruption of the Cornish word 'gwis', meaning 'sow' (a female pig). It is thought that its rocks resembled a sow's head, and this was the origin of the place name.

Rame

Little is known about Rame, except that in 981 AD Earl Ordulf, uncle of King Ethelred, gave it to Tavistock Abbey for their sustenance and upkeep. In Cornish its name is 'Penn an Hordh', and it is located at the extreme south-east of Cornwall, on a peninsula to the west of Plymouth Sound. The meaning and origin of the place name remain unknown. There is an ancient Iron Age fort, known as Cliff Castle on Rame Head and it has a medieval parish church dedicated to St Germanus.

Roseland

Roseland, in Cornish known simply as 'Ros', meaning 'headland' or 'promontory', is a district in west Cornwall. It is not a village as such, but a peninsula that includes the villages of St Mawes, St Just and Gerrans. Another interpretation of the place name is that it comes from the Cornish 'rhos', an old Celtic name for gorse or heather. There is a local dispute concerning which villages are technically included in the Roseland district, with Veryan, Ruan Lanihorne and Philleigh all claiming to be part of it.

Samson

Nowadays this island, part of the Isles of Scilly archipelago, is completely uninhabited. Its name emerged as a dedication to a chapel on the island commemorating the sixth century saint, St Samson, Bishop of Dol-de-Bretagne in Brittany. In fact, no chapel now exists on the island, nor is there a record of one ever having been there, so apart from a reference in his biography, *Vita Sancti Samsonis* (Life of Saint Samson), assembled from earlier sources sometime between the seventh and ninth centuries, the attribution is a mystery. In 1160, the island was recorded as 'Sanctus Sampson'.

Sancreed

Sancreed can trace its foundation to St Credan (in Latin, 'Sancredus'), a follower of St Petroc of Bodmin and Padstow. However, there is evidence of much earlier settlements in the area with fragments of timber huts dating from 200 BC and both Neolithic and Iron Age archaeological finds. Sancreed Parish encompasses the settlements of Bejouans, Bosvennen, Botreah, Drift, Sancreed Churchtown, Trenuggo, and Tregonnebris. In 1176 the place was recorded as 'Eglossant', and in the thirteenth century by its Latin name 'Sanctus Sancretus'.

Scilly Isles
See: 'Isles of Scilly'.

Seaton
Seaton is a village whose name in Cornish is 'Sethyn', meaning '(place on the) River Seaton'. The origin of the river name is unknown, but possibly came originally from an ancient Celtic word which over time has been Anglicised as 'sea town'. In 1601 the place was recorded as 'Seythen'.

Sennen
Sennen was named after St Senana, the patron saint of the local church; it was first dedicated in 1441 and recorded in its Latin form, as 'Sancta Senana', though the building is on a site that has been in use since the sixth century. St Senana was an Irish missionary, known to have established many churches along the Cornish coast, and thought to have founded the early Celtic church sometime between 410 AD and 1066 at Sennen, just one mile from Land's End.

St Agnes
There are two places in Cornwall called St Agnes. The first is a village that lies on the north coast of Cornwall and is named after the church dedicated to St Agnes ('Sancta Agnes'). She was a Roman martyr who refused to marry the governor of Rome's son and was killed in 304 AD. The second is the most outlying of all the islands in the Scilly archipelago. It is separated from the main island group by a deep water channel. Archaeologists have revealed Bronze Age occupation, and even today St Agnes is home to less than a hundred permanent residents as well as colonies of rare bird species.

St Blazey
The village is named after St Blaise and known simply as 'Blaze' or 'Blayze' in the mid-fifteenth century (in Latin, 'Sanctus Blasius'). This Cornish township is located three miles from St Austell, and is known as 'Landrayth' or 'Llandreth' in Cornish, which translates as 'sanctuary on the sands'. According to *Wilson's Imperial Gazetteer* of 1870, St Blaise was Bishop of Sebaste in Armenia and is thought to have landed at Par in Cornwall in the third century, before he was tortured and martyred by beheading in 316 AD. The place received no entry as such in the *Domesday Book*, but was probably included in the Manor of Towington, Trenance, or Treverbyn.

St Breward
St Breward (in Cornish, 'St Bruwerd') is a civil parish and village located about six miles north of Bodmin. The parish name derives from the ancient Breton saint and monk, St Branwalader, whose remains are kept at Milton Abbas in Dorset. Until the nineteenth century the village was commonly known by the corrupt pronunciation of the name, as 'Simonward'. St Breward has one of two churches that claim to be the highest in Cornwall. The saint also gave his name to St Brelade in the Channel Island of Jersey.

St Buryan
The Church of Sancta Beriana in the Parish of Penzance was first recorded in the early tenth century. In the *Domesday Book* it was listed as 'Eglosberrie'. At that time the estate belonged to the Augustine Canons of the Collegiate Church St Buryan. It took its place name from the sixth century Irish missionary saint, St Buriena. She was buried in St Buryan after her death, having been kidnapped by a local tribal king, despite Cornwall's patron Saint Piran's attempts to save her.

St Germans
In 1086, the township known as 'Ecclesia Sancti Germani' was the Latin name recorded in the *Domesday Book* as belonging to the Bishop of Exeter and the Priory of Augustinian Canons. The village name in Cornish is 'Lannaled' and translates as 'Church of St Germans', after St Germanus (c.378–c.448), the Bishop of Auxerre, who reputedly confronted local pagan tribes with his message of Christian salvation and led native Britons to victory against warring Scottish Picts and Saxons in North Wales. The church at St Germans, was dedicated to the saint when it was established as Cornwall's cathedral by King Athelstan in 926 AD.

St Helen's
St Helen's, or in Cornish, 'Enys Elidius' (meaning 'the Isle of Elidus'), in the Isles of Scilly, is best known for the remains of a Pest House, an isolation hospital built in 1764 to quarantine plague victims arriving on visiting ships. It contains the remains of the eighth century St Elidius Hermitage which was inhabited by the reclusive St Lide (also known as Elid or Elidius).

St Ives
Three townships in England are known by the name St Ives: in Cornwall, Cambridgeshire and Dorset. St Ives in Cornwall derived its name from St Ya (sometimes St La), a female saint, the daughter to an Irish chieftain who, according to tradition, floated over the sea on a leaf and landed in Cornwall. What is certain is that she founded an oratory here in the mid-fifth century, which is now the local church that is dedicated to her. By 1284 it had been recorded as 'Sancta Ya'. In Cornish the name was 'Porth la', or 'Porthia',

meaning 'St La's Cove'. In the thirteenth century, locals referred to the town as 'Saynt Lyes'.

St Keverne
According to the *Domesday Book*, the coastal Parish of St Keverne was known by its Latin name, 'Sanctus Lannachebran', after the patron saint of the church, St Aghevran (sometimes 'Achebran'). In Cornish, the place name is 'Lannaghevran', after the saint, who may have been otherwise known as St Kevin (498–618 AD), an Irish missionary saint, the first abbot of Glendalough in modern day County Wicklow. He was probably a pupil of St Petroc.

St Martin's
This northernmost of the Isles of Scilly was dedicated to the French saint, St Martin, Bishop of Tours and patron saint of France, who died in either 371 AD or 397 AD. Initially the name was given to the local church but was eventually applied to the whole island. Around 1540, the place name was recorded in Cornish as 'Seynt Martyns', and appeared at the same time in English as 'St Martines Isle'.

St Mawes
The small fishing village of St Mawes is located on the Roseland Peninsula overlooking the River Fal and lies within the old St Just-in-Roseland Parish. Evidence exists for the human occupation of St Mawes for more than two thousand years. The Welsh missionary St Mawes (sometimes St Maudez, St Maudetus, St Machutus or St Maudyth), came to Cornwall sometime around 550 AD and built a hermitage cell and chapel at what is now Church Hill. He later lived in Ireland before moving to live in Brittany where he was martyred for his faith. The chapel was in use throughout the Middle Ages, before being abandoned in the sixteenth century and subsequently falling into decay.

St Michael's Mount
St Michael's Mount is a small tidal island in Mount's Bay offshore from the Cornish town of Marazion to which it is joined by a man-made tidal causeway. Its Cornish name is 'Karrek Loos yn Koos', which translates as 'hoar (or grey) rock in woodland'. The name probably dates from ancient Neolithic occupation, before rising sea levels isolated the island from the British mainland, when it would have been surrounded by woodland. This argument is supported by remnants of decayed wood that have been found during low tides. The mount is dedicated to St Michael the Archangel who, according to legend, appeared to a group of Cornish fishermen here in 495 AD. The conical rock is dominated by an eighth century monastery which was gifted in the eleventh century by Edward the Confessor to the Benedictine order of Mont Saint-Michel in France, with whom it retains a degree of symbolic affinity as well as visual similarity, albeit on a much smaller scale.

Talland
This small hamlet derives its name from its church which is dedicated to the fifth century saint, St Tallanus (sometimes 'St Tallan'). The saint's name is interesting because it contains the Cornish word elements 'tal', indicating a ridge or hill brow, and 'lann' which specifically refers to a church site or grounds. Hence, his name means 'church grounds on the brow of a hill'. The church had been earlier dedicated to St Catherine.

Teän
Teän (or Tean) is located just west of St Martins in the Scilly Isles and is known in Cornish as 'Enys Tian'. It is one of the archipelago's many uninhabited islands and has an early Christian chapel, possibly dedicated to St Theon of Alexandria. The origin of the place name is obscure, but may conceivably have been a corruption of the saint's name. Tean was certainly occupied during the Romano-British period and several stone cairns are evidence of a much earlier Bronze Age settlement. The island was still used for animal grazing at the end of the Second World War. In the mid-twelfth century, it was known by the Latin name of 'Sancta Teona'.

Tintagel
In his *Historia Regum Britanniae* (History of the Kings of Britain), probably completed around 1138, Welsh cleric Geoffrey of Monmouth cited Tintagel as the place where King Arthur was conceived. The place name may have come from two old Cornish words, 'din' meaning fort or stronghold, and 'tagell', a promontory or neck of land. Hence, 'fort on a neck of land or promontory'. Alternatively, there is an opinion that its alternative name of Trevena (in Cornish, 'Tre war Venydh'), would indicate that the name means 'settlement, or village on a mountain'. Another source has proposed 'dun (or din) tagell' as meaning in the Celtic language, 'a narrow place'. Given its location, either would seem appropriate. The site had almost certainly existed earlier as a stronghold of Devonian and Cornish rulers of the Dumnonia tribe of Celtic peoples. Tintagel received no mention in the *Domesday Book* in its own right, but was part of the Manor of Bossiney.

Towednack
The church at Towednack (in Cornish, 'Tewydnek'), is dedicated to the sixth-century Breton hermit, St Winwaloe. His name had the prefix 'to', meaning 'thy' added for some reason, so that the name means '(parish of) thy St Winwaloe'. The church was built on the site of a Celtic hermitage. In 1327 the place name was recorded as 'Sanctus Tewennocus'.

Tresco
The small island of Tresco in the Scilly Isles derives its name from two old Cornish words, 'tre' and 'scaw', which together translate as 'farmstead of the elder trees'.

The township was given by Henry I to Tavistock Abbey who established the Benedictine Priory of St Nicholas. Its prior, Alan of Cornwall, became Abbot of Tavistock in 1233. The original Cornish place name was 'Ryn Tewyn', meaning 'promontory among the dunes'; later it was known as 'St Nicholas's Island' and in 1305 as 'Trescau'.

Trevone
This Cornish coastal village near Padstow is known as 'Treavon', meaning 'river farm'. The second element, 'avon', reflects a Celtic word which is a common river name in Britain, and usually means 'river', but in this case probably refers to the sea. Hence, it may be taken to mean 'farm (by the) sea'.

Truro
There are three schools of thought concerning the origin of Truro's place name: one has it derived from the Cornish 'tri veru', where 'tri' means 'three' and 'run' means 'roads'. Hence 'three roads'. Some have it as meaning 'three rivers'; another suggests 'tre uro', signifying '(the) settlement by the river', where the 'uro' element means 'river'; Truro does indeed have three major roads leading into its centre, and three rivers can be seen from certain places around the city. A third explanation cites 'Triueru', the name given to the town around 1174, as meaning '(place of) great water turbulence'.

Uny Lelant
Lelant (in Cornish, 'Lannanta'), is a village in west Cornwall whose place name is derived from the Cornish word 'lann', referring to the site of a church, and St Anta. The last element of the place name means 'church site of Anta'. The earliest known spelling of the name occurs around 1170 as 'Lananta'. Lelant parish church is actually dedicated to St Uny, the patron saint of Lelant and of Redruth. However, the church in nearby Carbis Bay is dedicated to St Anta. Little is known about the saint, but she was thought to have established a small chapel on the rocks at the entrance to the River Hayle.

Veryan
A small hamlet in Cornwall, known in 1281 by its Latin name, 'Sanctus Symphorianus', after the church was dedicated to St Symphorian, a second or third century French martyr. Over time Symphorian became corrupted to Severian and then Saint Veryan. Veryan was recorded in the *Domesday Book* as the Manor of Elerchi (or Elerky), owned by the Bishop of Exeter in 1086. The manor name was derived from 'elerch', the Cornish word for a swan, a swannery or a swan's house.

Warbstow
The Old English word 'stow' indicated a church or religious site, and this village takes its name from the dedication of the local church to the Saxon saint, St Warburgh,

the daughter of King Wolpher (sometimes 'Wulfhere') of Mercia, who was the son of King Penda. The place name was recorded as 'Sancta Werburga' in 1282 but in the early fourteenth century had become known as 'Warberstowe'. The Warbstow Bury Iron Age hillfort is one of the largest and best-preserved in Cornwall. (See also: 'Warbstow Bury Hillfort'.)

Zennor
Located on Cornwall's Atlantic coast, three miles south-west of St Ives in the Parish of Penzance, the village of Zennor was named after its patron and Cornish saint, St Senara, and recorded around 1170 in Latin as 'Sanctus Sinar'. The saint is thought to have been the Breton Princess Azenor of Brest, the mother of St Budock, Bishop of Dol in Brittany. The twelfth century Norman church is dedicated to her and stands on the site of an earlier sixth century Celtic church.

Part Three

Ireland
Northern Ireland (Ulster) & the Republic of Ireland (Eire)

Ireland in the Roman Iron Age
There is evidence of the importation of trade goods between the indigenous Celtic peoples of Ireland and the Roman world in the first century AD, a period known as the Late Iron Age (sometimes called the Roman Iron Age). Unlike mainland Britain, the Romans never invaded Ireland, although according to the contemporary Roman historian Tacitus, such an invasion had been planned. Julius Agricola, the Roman Governor of Britain, boasted that he could conquer it with just a single legion and a few auxiliaries, but in the event, given their problematic experience in quelling Scotland's Pictish tribes, it was not considered worth the effort. Nevertheless, many hordes of Roman coins have been found in Ireland. At that time there were possibly two hundred or so petty Irish kingdoms, and with typical pragmatism, Rome opted for trade and peaceful co-existence, rather than conquest.

As a result, with few exceptions, Ireland's Celtic people remained mainly uninfluenced by the Latin culture that Rome had spread across its European

Kilclooney Dolmen, County Donegal.

Ireland Northern Ireland (Ulster) & the Republic of Ireland (Eire)

empire. Irish tribes retained a form of language called Goidelic (also known as Q-Celtic), which is the root of modern Irish and Scottish Gaelic, unlike the Brittonic (Brythonic) form of Celtic which formed the basis of Welsh, Cornish and Breton.

There had been other foreign invasions of Ireland, including repeated Viking incursions between 800 and 1200 AD and the Anglo-Norman invasion of the eleventh and twelfth centuries, as well as the so-called 'Plantation of Ulster' in the seventeenth century. Consequently, for a time, many places shared both Gaelic and English names, of which some survive to this day; Londonderry (or Derry) in the Province of Ulster is a perfect example. The old Irish language barely survived among the underclass, although, unlike Manx and Cornish Gaelic, significant numbers of Irish men and women speak it as their first language and what remains is arguably the purest of the Celtic languages that have survived to the present.

The Plantation of Ulster

Following the Nine Years' War against English rule and the defeat of Irish 'rebels' in 1609, in what came to be known as Tyrone's Rebellion (1593 to 1603), a period called 'The Plantation', the English Crown decided to exert tighter control over Ireland. There followed a period of organised colonisation, when the traditional lands of Gaelic tribes like the O'Neills and O'Donnells were confiscated and ceded to imported English and Scottish settlers. These new 'planters' began to build new towns like Belfast and Bangor and develop places like Derry, Omagh and Enniskillen, which hitherto had been little more than small military outposts.

Presbyterian Scots and Anglican Englishmen gradually established a new order in Ulster, where English dominated and the speaking of the Irish language went into decline. These British colonists were required to be English-speaking, Protestant, and loyal to the king. Further, the majority of British immigrants during the Plantation period were Lowland Scots, which led to the emergence of a distinct Irish-Scots-English dialect that became known as 'Ulster Scots', which accounts for the discernible difference between the spoken dialect of Ulster compared to that of Eire.

The Plantation created an inevitable north-south divide, with Protestants predominantly living in the north and Catholics in the south, a state of affairs which many believe was a major factor in leading to the Partition of Ireland in 1921.

The Partition of Ireland

The Republic of Ireland accounts for around four-fifths of the island of Ireland's land mass. As from the Act of Union on 1 January 1801, it was part of the United Kingdom of Great Britain and Ireland, with the status of a Dominion. Following the armed insurrection against British rule in Dublin in 1916, an event known as the Easter Rising (in Irish, 'Eiri Amach na Casca'), in 1922 it became the Irish Free State. As a result of the Anglo-Irish Treaty, the island was partitioned in 1937, when a new constitution was adopted. On 17 April 1949, it became the Republic of Ireland (or in Gaelic, Eire), as a fully independent nation in its own right.

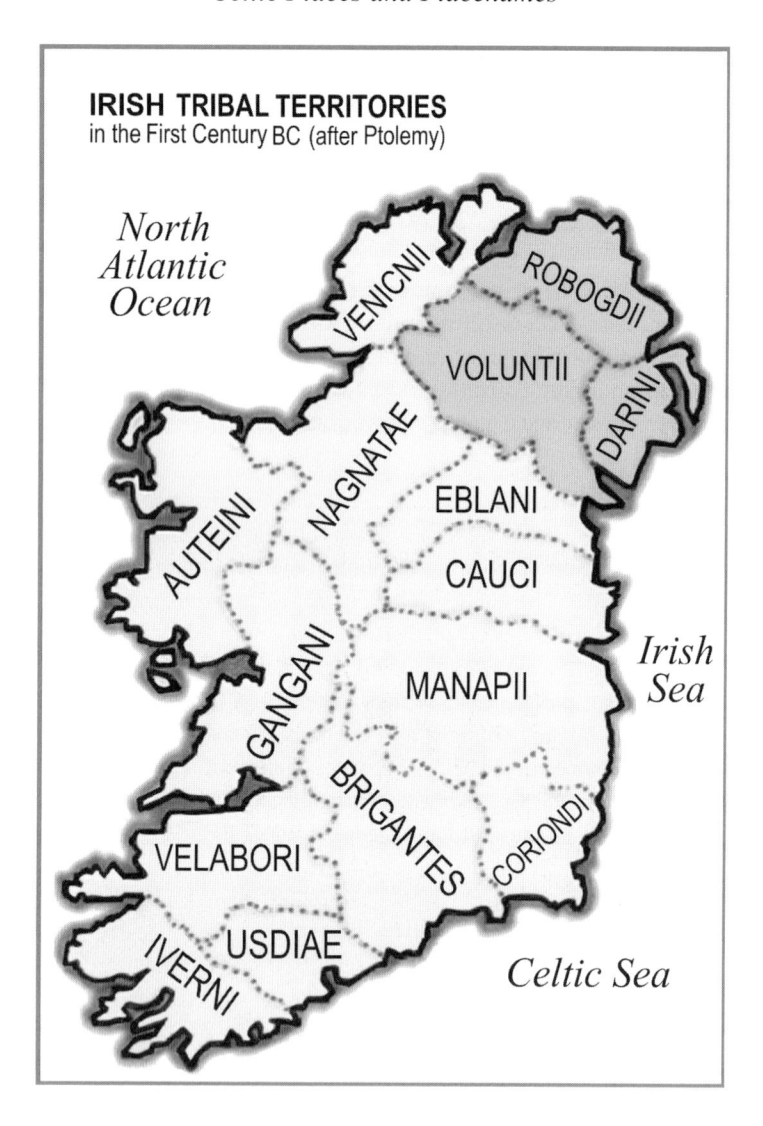

IRISH TRIBAL TERRITORIES
in the First Century BC (after Ptolemy)

(Map showing tribal territories: VENICNII, ROBOGDII, VOLUNTII, DARINI, NAGNATAE, EBLANI, AUTEINI, CAUCI, GANGANI, MANAPII, BRIGANTES, CORIONDI, VELABORI, IVERNI, USDIAE; labelled with North Atlantic Ocean, Irish Sea, Celtic Sea)

The Vikings in Ireland

In about 795 AD, the Vikings arrived on Irish shores and attacked St Cuthbert's remote monastery on the island of Iona. They had come initially as hit-and-run opportunists, pillaging and looting monasteries, with around twenty-five such raids recorded in the next few years, but eventually they began establishing their own settlements and building fortified settlements. By the mid-ninth century, Norse had begun to appear as village place names and by the late-tenth century many Norsemen had effectively become assimilated with the local population through intermarriage.

Ireland Northern Ireland (Ulster) & the Republic of Ireland (Eire)

Despite this, Viking incursions continued unabated with only token Irish resistance until 848 AD, when an army of Ui O'Neill, the self-styled High King of Ireland, fought off a sustained attack and Viking aggression more or less ceased. Soon, large tracts of Ireland became Viking enclaves, including Dublin, and subsequent Scandinavian visitors came as traders. The tenth century also saw many Viking leaders converted to Christianity by missionary monks, and their integration was complete.

Their historic presence in Irish history still survives in some of the place names they left behind. However, the present-day order bears little resemblance to the traditional Celtic tribelands, and what follows represents the political status of the island at a time before partition, when the whole of Ireland was unified, and townships in both Ulster and Eire are equally represented in what follows.

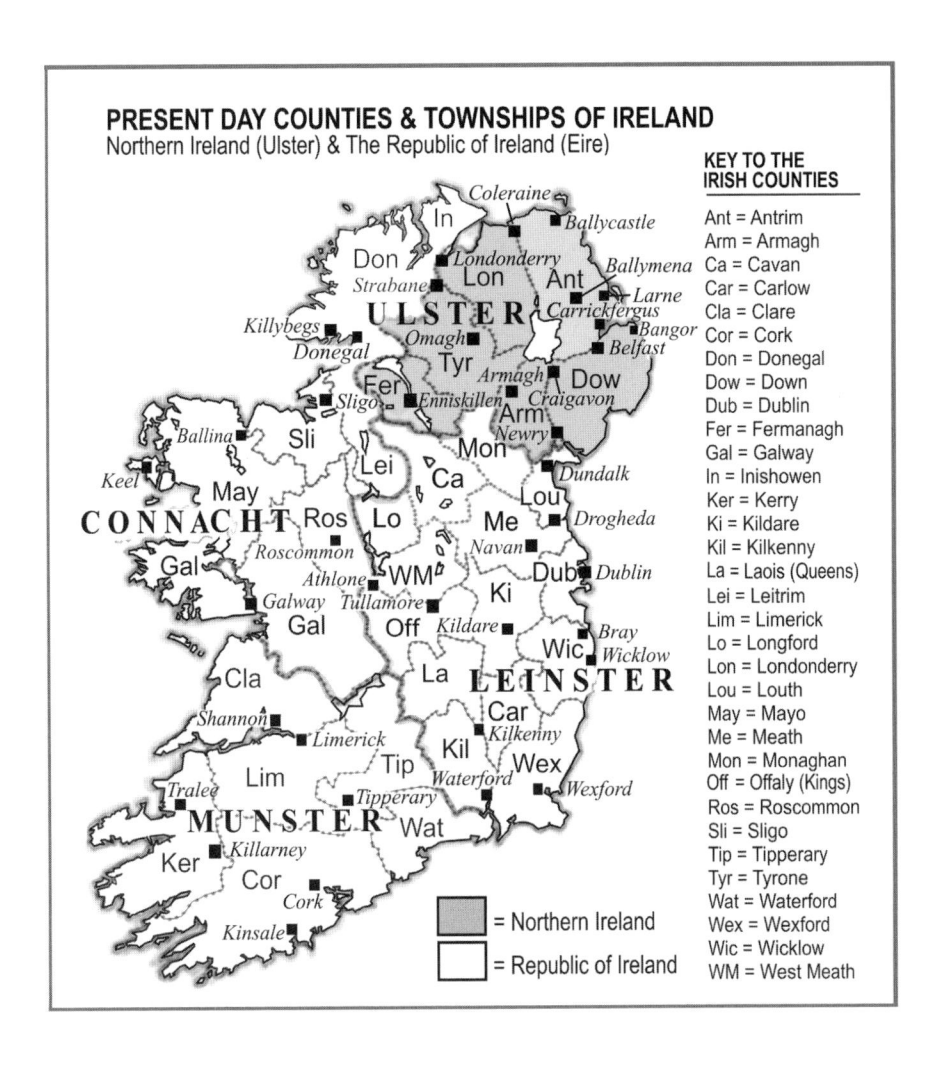

PRESENT DAY COUNTIES & TOWNSHIPS OF IRELAND
Northern Ireland (Ulster) & The Republic of Ireland (Eire)

KEY TO THE IRISH COUNTIES

Ant = Antrim
Arm = Armagh
Ca = Cavan
Car = Carlow
Cla = Clare
Cor = Cork
Don = Donegal
Dow = Down
Dub = Dublin
Fer = Fermanagh
Gal = Galway
In = Inishowen
Ker = Kerry
Ki = Kildare
Kil = Kilkenny
La = Laois (Queens)
Lei = Leitrim
Lim = Limerick
Lo = Longford
Lon = Londonderry
Lou = Louth
May = Mayo
Me = Meath
Mon = Monaghan
Off = Offaly (Kings)
Ros = Roscommon
Sli = Sligo
Tip = Tipperary
Tyr = Tyrone
Wat = Waterford
Wex = Wexford
Wic = Wicklow
WM = West Meath

The Irish Place Names

Achonry
The name of the township of Achonry in County Sligo is 'Achadh Conaire', formerly also known earlier in Gaelic as 'Achad Cain Conairi', which translates as 'Conaire's field'. The name comes from the sixth century Irish saint, St Nath I, who founded a monastery in the village, which was granted to the Conaire Clan.

Adare
The village of Adare is located on the banks of the River Maigue in County Limerick. It is the site of a shallow river crossing, and this is the source of its Gaelic place name, 'Ath Dara', which means '(place that the) ford by the oak tree'. The oak tree in question may have been 'The Tree of Mag Adar', referred to in the *Annals of Inisfallen*, a chronicle of medieval Irish history covering the years from the fourth to the fifteenth century.

Agha- (prefix)
The prefix 'agha' appears in many Irish place names and in general terms means 'field'. This tends to be followed by a qualifying element based on local topography. Examples include Aghadoe in County Kerry ('Achadh Da Eo', meaning 'field of two yews'), Aghalane in County Cavan ('Achadh Leathan', meaning 'wide, or broad, field'), Aghinver in County Fermanagh ('Achadh Inbir', meaning 'field of the estuary'), and Aghagower in County Mayo ('Achadh Ghobhair', meaning 'field of the well').

Aghadowey
The township of Aghadowey in County Derry is part of the Causeway Coast and Glens district. In Irish the name is 'Achadh Dubhthaigh', which means 'Dubhthach's field'. The 'dubh' element means 'black', producing a place name that translates as 'black field'. However, 'Dufaigh', which is a variant on the name, is often translated as 'Duffy', a fairly widespread Irish family name. The village was established on the site of an earlier monastery dedicated to St Guaire, also known as St Goar, St Guarius or Guaire Mor.

Aghagallon
The village of Aghagallon (sometimes 'Aughagallon') in County Antrim, is known in modern Irish as 'Achadh Gallan', which translates as 'field of standing stones'. It had earlier been known as 'Eanach Gallanach', meaning 'moorland (or field) of standing stones'. The aforesaid stones no longer exist but a large cairn was recorded there as recently as 1835.

Alt- (or Allt-) (prefix)
This is a common Irish Gaelic prefix which represents the modern word 'glen' (a deep pastoral valley). Several dozen places throughout Ireland carry this prefix;

Ireland Northern Ireland (Ulster) & the Republic of Ireland (Eire)

among them are Altachullion in County Cavan ('Allt an Chuilinn', meaning 'glen of the holly'), Altamooskan in County Tyrone ('Allt an Mhuscain', meaning 'glen of the spongy ground'), and Altnahinch in County Antrim ('Allt na hUinse', meaning 'glen of the ash tree').

Annaclone
The Irish name of the County Down village of Annaclone is 'Eanach Luain', which means 'marsh of the haunch-like hill'. The marsh in question is in the Ardbrin area, where several Celtic artefacts have been unearthed, including the so-called Ardbrin Horn. The village is located in the Mourne Mountains, within the traditional territory of the Magennis clan.

Annaghdown
This village is located on Annaghdown Bay which is an inlet of Lough Corrib in County Galway and its name in Gaelic is 'Eanach Dhuin', which means 'the marsh of the fort'. The modern Irish word 'dun' often refers to a ring-fort or other stronghold, probably an earlier construction than the ruined castle which now exists on the site.

Annacotty
This is a town in Limerick whose Gaelic name is 'Ath na Choite'. The initial place name element should more properly be 'ath', which signifies a ford or a shallow river crossing, in this case across the River Mulkear. The entire name translates as 'ford of the small boat', indicating that the river may once have been navigable up to this point or even been a ferry crossing.

Annadorn
Annadorn is a village in County Down and has the Irish name 'Ath na nDorn', which is taken generally to mean 'ford of the fists', although there is an argument that it could more properly be translated as 'ford of the stones'. The word element 'dorn' or 'dor' does in fact literally mean 'fist', but it has been widely interpreted to mean 'fist-shaped stones (or pebbles)'. The term is often used to describe a rocky causeway and could easily apply to a stony or pebbly river crossing or ford such as here across the River Blackstaff. The 'dor' name element is also found in the English county of Dorset and its county town, Dorchester.

Antrim, County
The County of Antrim in the Province of Ulster was part of the territory of Dalaradiae (or Ulidia) in ancient times. These early Celtic inhabitants were designated by Ptolemy as 'Darnii' or 'Darini'. The medieval historian Nennius also wrote of the regions of people he called the 'Dalrieda'. The county's Irish name is 'Aontreibh', which translates as 'single house', a probable reference to an early monastery that existed north of the town. It is believed that its founder was Aodh, a

pupil of St Patrick in the late fifth century; it was eventually destroyed by the Danes. In the sixth and seventh centuries it was part of the O'Lynch clan's Kingdom of Dal Riada. The town itself was known as 'Entrium', 'Entrum' or 'Aontroim', which translates as 'habitation upon the waters'. This explains its location on the Bay of Belfast, near Lough Neagh, the River Bann and the River Lagan, which separates it from County Down.

Aran Islands
The Gaelic name for the Aran Islands of County Galway is 'Oileain Arann', meaning 'islands of the ridge'. The word 'aran' derives from the Irish 'ara' or 'arainn', which technically means 'kidney' or 'loin', but in this particular case might be better translated as 'arched back', a description of the islands' typical geography. The group of three islands include Inishmore ('Arainn Mhor', meaning 'big island'), Inishmaan ('Inis Meain', meaning 'middle island'), and Inisheer ('Inis Oirr' or 'Inis Thiar', possibly meaning 'rear' or 'back island').

Ard- (prefix)
The prefix 'Ard' is found in several Irish place names, and translates as 'height' or 'high ground', and generally denotes a feature of the local geography.

Ardara
This small town in County Donegal has the Irish name, 'Ard an Ratha', from 'ard', meaning 'high' or 'height', and 'rath' referring to a ring-fort. The name translates as '(place near the) height of the fort'. Ardara actually lies in a valley, and an ancient ring-fort stands on cliffs overlooking the town.

Ardee
In Irish this town in County Louth is 'Baile Atha Fhirdhia', which translates as 'town of the ford of Fear-Diadh'. The names 'Fhirdhia' and 'Fear-Diadh' refer to the legendary Connacht warrior more commonly known as Ferdia, who died in battle here in the first century AD while trying to prevent the army of Queen Maeve from entering Ulster. The site was originally at a ford crossing of the River Dee, and a bridge now stands there bearing a plaque commemorating the event.

Ardfinnan
Sometime in the seventh century, an Augustine monastery and leper colony was established by St Fionan (or 'Finian Lobhar', known as 'the Leper') beside the River Suir in this small Tipperary township. Its Irish name is 'Ard Fhionain', which means 'St Foinan's height'. Fionan founded the abbey in the early seventh century. It was plundered by the Normans and a castle built on the site following their invasion of Ireland in 1178.

Ireland Northern Ireland (Ulster) & the Republic of Ireland (Eire)

Ardnaree
Ardnaree is a suburb of Ballina in County Mayo whose Irish place name is 'Ard na Ria', which means 'the place of execution'. The name commemorates an event when four men named Mael mac Deoraidh, Maelcroin, Maeldalua, and Maelseanaigh, conspired to kill Bishop Ceallach of Kilmoremoy, the son of Eoghan Bel, King of Connaught, in the late sixth century. They were all hanged, and the place of execution was permanently marked by a dolmen known as 'Four Maols'. (See also: 'Four Maols Dolmen'.)

Ards Peninsula
The Ards Peninsula on the coast of County Down has the Irish name 'Aird Uladh', which means 'headland of the Ulstermen'. It had originally been known as 'Aird Ua nEchach' ('peninsula of the Ui Echach'), after the Ui Echach tribe whose name meant 'the descendants of Echu', and who made up the ancient kingdom of Ulaid in eastern Ulster before they were conquered by the Vikings in the ninth century. Thereafter their tribal name was replaced by 'Uladh', meaning 'of the Ulstermen'. The name forms the final element in the name of the town of Newtownards.

Armagh
The City of Armagh was known as 'Ard Macha', which translates as 'Macha's height' in Old Irish, after the ancient goddess Macha. Others give the name as 'Mag Macha', meaning 'the plain of Macha'. The name traditionally refers to Queen Macha ('of the golden hair'), an ancient Irish war goddess. In time the place name was Anglicised as 'Ardmagh', and eventually its present name of Armagh. The original name dates back to at least the fifth century, when St Patrick founded a church which was to become Armagh Cathedral, and the settlement that grew up around it for a time was the capital of Ireland. It was here that the famous illuminated manuscript of *Codex Ardmachanus* (the 'Book of Armagh'), was compiled by its monks in the ninth century; it contains the oldest known examples of the New Testament in the Old Irish language. Ptolemy recorded the Armagh region as the territory of the Celtic Vinderii and Voluntii tribes.

Arvagh
In Irish, this County Cavan village, which is located at the south-west corner of Lough Garty, is known as 'Armhach', which is commonly translated as 'place of slaughter' or simply 'battlefield'. The significance is uncertain, but it has been argued that lying as it does on the border of the three provinces of Connacht, Leinster and Ulster, it may have been the site of serious and ongoing tribal border disputes in ancient times, where ferocious battles may have taken place, earning it the macabre place name.

Athleague
Athleague is a town in County Roscommon whose Gaelic name is 'Ard Liag', which translates as 'ford of the stone (or flagstones)'. The ford was at a crossing

point in the River Suck between the kingdoms of the U' Maine and U' Briuin, two royal dynasties of Connacht. The stone in question is a large mid-stream boulder which prompted an ancient local legend that if it were ever to be removed the whole town would be flooded and disaster would ensue.

Athlone
The earliest reference to this township, which stands on an old ford on the River Shannon in Westmeath, was way back in the Bronze Age when it was called 'An Sean Ath Mor', which means 'the great old ford'. Later in the tenth century it was known as 'Baile Ath Luain', which means 'the town at Luan's ford', probably after an early founder or landowner. It is known that sometime around 1000 AD there was a causeway across the river, which had been built by the kings of Connacht. In the year 1129, King Turlough O'Connor (in Irish, 'Toirdelbach Ua Conchobair'), built a bridge across the Shannon at this point to provide him with access to the County of Meath. A new bridge replaced the earlier one in 1210, built under the auspices of King John's Irish Justicar, the Norman Bishop of Norwich, John de Grey.

Aughrim
In Old Irish, this town in County Wicklow is known as 'Eachroim', which means 'horse-shaped ridge'. It was the scene of a battle in July 1691, between Irish Jacobites and the forces of William of Orange. The Jacobite defeat marked an important turning point in Irish history, which has been cited by some as the main cause of the partition of Ireland.

Avoka
In Irish this place name is 'Abhoca' (formerly 'Abhainn Mhor'), meaning 'great river', and was earlier known as 'An Droichead Nua', meaning 'new bridge'. It is a small town near Arklow, in County Wicklow situated on the River Avoca. It is thought that the name may have been a corruption of 'Oboka', a term which Ptolemy used of this part of the nearby confluence of the Avonmore River.

Balla
'Balla' simply means 'wall' in Irish. However, the wall referred to in this township in County Mayo encloses the so-called 'Blessed Well' ('Tobar Mhuire'), which was dedicated in the seventh century to St Mochua, who founded a monastery nearby.

Ballinalack
This Westmeath village and townland (known as 'Beal Atha na Leac' in Irish), is located on the River Inny and has a place name that means 'mouth of the ford of flagstones'. The original ford across the Inny was covered by flagstones or stepping stones, which have since been replaced by a bridge.

Ireland Northern Ireland (Ulster) & the Republic of Ireland (Eire)

Ballinasloe
Ballinasloe is a town in eastern Galway in Connacht Province. Its Irish name is 'Beal Atha na Sluaighe', meaning 'mouth of the ford of the crowds (or gathering)'. The town grew up around a shallow river crossing on the River Suck, which is a tributary of the River Shannon. The ford in question is thought to have been a place where horse fairs were held, attracting large gatherings. At such fairs it remains customary to run horses through shallow rivers to show them off. The Appleby Horse Fair held on the River Eden in Cumbria, still continues this same age-old tradition.

Bally-/Balli-/Baill- (prefix)
The prefix 'Bally-' ('Baill-', 'Ball-', or 'Balli-') is found in many dozens of Irish place names. In general terms it stands for 'townland', a word that describes small divisions of land or districts of a town. The system pre-dates the Norman Conquest. The term is also found in the Western Isles of Scotland. Many of these prefixes are followed by a personal name, usually of the founder, chieftain or owner of the original settlement. Examples include Ballysheerin in Donegal (meaning 'O Sirin's townland'), Ballygorey in Kilkenny (meaning 'Guaire's townland'), Ballyhale in Kilkenny (meaning 'Howell's townland'), and Ballyandreen in Cork (meaning 'Aindrin's townland'). Others tend to describe locations or topographical features such as woods, streams and fords; examples include Ballinglen in Wicklow (meaning 'townland of the glen'), Ballynure in Antrim (meaning 'townland of the Yew Tree'), Ballintemple in Cork (meaning 'townland of the church'), and Ballycarra in Mayo (meaning 'townland of the weir').

Ballybetagh
In the seventeenth century, the Province of Ulster was divided by the English into thirty 'hundreds' (an old Saxon unit of land measurement), and each of these were further sub-divided into about twenty-eight or thirty 'biadhtaighs' (defined as 'lands of a food-provider' or 'ballybetaghs'). This is the origin of this Dublin district (or 'townland'). The area approximated to around four hundred and eighty Irish acres (195 hectares).

Ballyclare
The township of Ballyclare in County Antrim in Northern Ireland is known in Irish as 'Bealach Clair', which means 'the pass on (or of) the plain'. It is located on the River Six Mile Water, which was originally called the River Ollar.

Ballyconnell
The County Cavan town of Ballyconnell has the Irish name 'Beal Atha Conaill', which means 'mouth of the ford of Conall'. The ford in question was a shallow crossing over the River Grainne, which formed the ancient border between Ulster

and Connacht. It was around this river crossing that the original settlement of Ballyconnell was established as early as five thousand years ago. Its original name may have been 'Ath na Mianna', which means 'ford of the miners'. The 'connell' element of the place name represents Conall Cearnach, a mythical Ulster warrior who was killed by soldiers of Queen Maeve of Connacht to avenge the slaying of her husband Ailill by Conall, who is said to be buried somewhere nearby.

Ballymena
Ballymena's recorded history dates from the fifth century when a church and monastery were founded a few miles from the modern town. It derived its place name from the Irish 'an baile meanach', meaning 'the middle town', reflecting its location in the virtual centre of County Antrim. The modern town dates from 1626, when land in 'Ballymeanagh' was granted by Charles I to a Scotsman, William Adair of Kinhult. It became known locally as the 'City of Seven Towers', given the profusion of them in the place; these included towers at Ballymena Castle, the water mill, several churches and the town hall.

Ballymoney
Bronze Age and Iron Age artefacts have been unearthed in Ballymoney on the Causeway Coast of County Antrim, suggesting settlements of some kind dating back at least nine thousand years. However, historical records of the district began in 460 AD, when the church at Derrykeighan was established by St Colman. The Old Irish name for the place, according to some, was 'Baile Monaid', meaning 'homestead (townland or settlement) of the moor', while others have it as 'Baile Muine', meaning 'townland of the thicket'.

Ballynahinch
Ballynahinch lies beside the Twelve Bens mountain range in Connemara. Some translate 'Baile na hlnse', the Irish name of Ballynahinch, as 'household of the island', while others assert that it means 'townland of the river meadow'. The first reference may refer to O'Flaherty Castle, which was built on an island in the middle of the lake, one of many owned by their family. The O'Flaherty clan (in Middle Irish, 'O Flaithbheartaigh', and in Modern Irish, 'O Flaithearta'), were Lords of Connacht and virtual rulers of Ballynahinch in the fourteenth century. In 1546, Grace O'Malley, known as 'the pirate queen of Connaught', took over the role of head of the O'Flaherty family when her husband was murdered by a rival clan, and distinguished herself as a fierce leader of men, taking part in many inter-clan battles. She is said to have had an audience with Elizabeth I at Greenwich Palace, where she refused to bow or to acknowledge her as the rightful Queen of Ireland.

Bangor
By the mid-sixteenth century, Bangor was known as 'Bennchuir' (from the Irish, 'Beannchar'), meaning 'place of points', probably in reference to a

Ireland Northern Ireland (Ulster) & the Republic of Ireland (Eire)

thorny enclosure that would have formed a protective perimeter around the early settlement. However, another suggestion is that it derives from the Gaelic and means 'horned curve', referring to the topography of Bangor Bay, which it overlooks. There are other explanations: one has it called 'Inver Beg', named after the stream which ran past the abbey. Another names the place as the Vale of Angels, as St Patrick reputedly slept there and had a vision of angels. The original settlement was founded around an abbey monastery built by St Comgall in the year 555 AD. Following his death sometime around 602 AD, his body was buried in the abbey and over time a school of learning grew up around it.

Bantry

In Irish this township in County Cork is 'Beanntrai', named after Beann, the son of Conor MacNessa who was King of Ulster in the first century AD. There are two possible interpretations of the place name: one suggests '(place of) Beann's people', while another has it derived from the word 'beann', meaning 'hill' or 'headland', and 'traigh', a strip or strand of land or shore. Hence, 'hilly strip (of land)'.

Bel- (prefix)

The prefix 'bel' (sometimes 'bale' or 'beul') translates from Irish as meaning 'ford-mouth' or 'ford entrance'. A dozen or so coastal villages and townships in Ireland follow this convention, including Belcoo in County Fermanagh ('Beal Cu', meaning 'ford-mouth of the narrow'), Bellananagh in County Cavan ('Beal Atha na nEach', meaning 'ford-mouth of the horses'), and Bellanamullia in County Roscommon ('Beal Atha na Muille', meaning 'ford-mouth of the hill').

Belfast

Belfast is located at the western end of Belfast Lough and the mouth of the River Logan in County Antrim, Ulster. Its place name comes directly from the Gaelic 'beal feirste', meaning '(place at the) mouth of the sandy ford (or sandbank)'. Evidence of Stone and Bronze Age occupation of the area exists in the Iron Age fort, known as McArt's Fort whose remains survive on Cavehill, north of the city, and the five thousand year old stone circle called The Giant's Ring located nearby.

Bellanamallard

This village and townland, located a few miles north of Enniskillen in County Fermanagh, (sometimes spelled 'Ballinamallard'), has the Irish name 'Beal Atha na Mallacht', which means 'ford mouth of the curses'. The ford mouth in question was across the River Ballinamallard. For some inexplicable reason, according to a legend, St Columcille (also known as St Columba, one of Ireland's three patron saints), placed a curse on roosters, ducks or mallards here in the sixth century.

Celtic Places and Placenames

Benbo
Benbo is a mountain in County Leitrim, whose Irish name is 'Beanna Bo', meaning 'peaks of the cow', after its double peaks which some thought resembled the horns of a cow.

Benburb
The original settlement which was to become Benburb was established near a clifftop overlooking the River Blackwater in County Tyrone. The Irish name 'An Bhinn Bhorb' translates as 'the rough peak', a description given to its location within the local landscape.

Boho
The place name of the Fermanagh village of Boho is an Anglicisation of the Irish 'botha' (or in its plural form 'both'), which is an ancient word for a hut or booth. The reference is likely to have been to monastic cells, though none still exist. However, a ninth century Celtic cross in the local church graveyard is thought to mark the site of an early monastery.

Boyne
The River Boyne flows through the Counties of Kildare, Offaly and Meath and is named after the Celtic river goddess Boand (or 'bo bhan', meaning 'white cow'). The Irish name for the river is 'An Bhoinn', meaning 'river of the white cow'. The reference may be related to wild Auroch, white cattle which were the dominant breed in Celtic Britain at that time.

Bray
In Irish, this County Wicklow coastal township is known as 'Bré', meaning simply 'hill', probably after the nearby Bray Head. Until the mid-twentieth century it had been known as 'Bri' and 'Bri Chualann', but Bré was formally adopted in 1975.

Bruree
Bruree is a town on the River Maigue in County Limerick, whose place name comes from 'Bru Ri', meaning either 'the king's fort' or 'the dwelling of the king'. The appellation refers to Oillill Olum, the second century king of Munster (who died in the year 234 AD), and whose fortress and ancient capital it was, as it continued to be during the reigns of several subsequent monarchs.

Carlow
The County Town of Carlow in the Republic of Ireland has the Old Irish name 'Ceatherlach', which means '(place near) four lakes'. The River Barrow, which forms the historic boundary between County Laois and County Carlow, runs through the town, but there remains no trace of four lakes. It is thought they may

Ireland Northern Ireland (Ulster) & the Republic of Ireland (Eire)

have been where the Barrow meets the River Burren. The place name has been spelled 'Caherlagh', 'Caterlagh' and 'Catherlagh' over the centuries. The region was the ancient Celtic territory of the Brigantes and Cauci tribes.

Carnfree
Carnfree is a distinctive and prominent hill in Roscommon, and was the traditional site for the inauguration of the kings of Connacht. The place is still identified by a stone marker, or cairn, which is reflected in the place name. In Irish the place is called 'Carn Fraoich', meaning 'Fraoch's (or Fraech's) cairn'. Fraech was a Connacht hero who featured in the *Ulster Cycle of Irish Mythology*, and is said to have been the lover of Queen Medb's (or Maeve's) daughter Findabair, who is believed to reside in the mound, and whose grave is marked by Fraech's Cairn.

Carrick- (prefix)
Several places in Ireland either go by the name of Carrick, or contain it as an initial prefix to their place name. The word comes from the Irish Gaelic 'carraig' or 'charraig', meaning 'rock'. Some examples are Carrickbeg in County Galway ('An Charraigh Bheag', meaning 'the little rock'), Carrickboy in County Longford ('An Charraigh Bhui', meaning 'the yellow rock'), and Carrickcarnan in County Louth ('Carraigh Charnain', meaning 'rock of the little cairn').

Carrickfergus
This place name is derived from 'carraig', meaning 'rock', and 'Fhearghais', a personal name. Hence it might translate into English as 'Rock of Fergus'. By the beginning of the thirteenth century it had been recorded as 'Carraic Fergusa'. It had also been known as 'Dunsobarky', where 'dun' indicated a rock, and 'sobarky' translates as 'powerful' or 'strong'. Hence, 'strong rock (or hill)'. In the sixth century, the name of Irish King Fergus Mor mac Eirc of Dal Riata (c.426–c.501 AD, later King of Scotland, known as Fergus the Great), was appended to the place name. Little reliable information is available concerning him, though there are several popular myths in existence, one of which maintains that he brought the Stone of Scone to Scotland from Ireland. Reputedly he was drowned on his return from Scotland and is buried at Monkstown in Newtownabbey. Over time, the town has been known by several place name variants, including 'Cragfergus' and 'Kragfargus'; in the time of Elizabeth I it was recorded as 'Knockfergus'.

Carrickmore
In Irish the name of this village in Tyrone is 'An Charraig Mhor', which translates into English as 'the big rock'. The rock in question is a natural feature south-west of the village where St Columba's well is located. The settlement was established many years before the Christian era and is connected to myths and legends related to the many cairns, stone circles and standing stones found in the area.

Carryduff
Carryduff is a small town in County Down, about six miles south of Belfast, whose Old Irish name is 'Ceathru Aodha Dhuibh'. It appeared in 1622 in the Anglicised form of 'Carrow-Hugh-Duffe', which translates as 'Black Hugh's (or Black-haired Hugh's) quarter'. The original settlement was established at a place where a river and six roads met, at the site of an ancient ring-fort known as Queen's Fort Rath. It is not known who the aforesaid Black Hugh was.

Cavan
In Old Irish, Cavan's place name is 'An Cabhan', which means 'the hollow', a perfect description of this town, which does indeed lie within a grassy hollow. The town grew up around a medieval castle and friary, neither of which still survives. County Cavan took its name from this place. During the Iron and Bronze Ages, the region was occupied by the Erdini tribe (in the Irish language, 'Ernaigh'). Traces of their name survive in places like Lough Erne and the River Erne, which form much of the district's border.

Clandyboy/Clandeboy
Clandyboy is a district south-west of the town of Bangor in County Down, whose Old Irish name is 'Clann Aodha Bui', which translates as 'clan of Yellow-haired Hugh'. The Clandeboy clan of Hugh of Tyrone (known as 'Hugh the yellow-haired' or 'Clanaboy'), were a branch of the O'Neills of Tyrone, who controlled large territories in County Antrim and County Down in the fourteenth century.

Clare, County
The Celtic tribes who inhabited present-day County Clare (in Irish, 'Contae an Chlair') at the time of Ptolemy were the Gangani, or in the Irish language the 'Siol Gangain'. They are thought to have been descended originally from the Concani, one of the eleven tribes of the Cantabria in the northern part of the Iberian Peninsula, who migrated here in the second or third centuries BC. The county name did not come from the de Clare family, as some might suppose, but it was named as such long before their arrival in Ireland. It actually comes from the Irish word 'Clar' or 'Chlair', which means 'plank' or 'board' and derives from an event where a board was placed across the River Fergus outside Ennis, at a place which became known as Clare (now known as Clarecastle town). The county was originally known as 'Tuath-Mumhan' (or 'Thomond'), signifying 'North Munster', despite the fact that its boundaries were only fixed in 1569 by the Lord Deputy, Sir Henry Sydney, who subdivided the existing region of Connacht into the counties of Clare, Galway, Mayo and Sligo. County Clare was returned to Munster Province in 1639.

Clifden
Clifden is a town in Galway whose Irish name is 'An Clochan', meaning 'stepping stones'. The word 'cloch' signifies a stone or stones, which in this case probably

Ireland Northern Ireland (Ulster) & the Republic of Ireland (Eire)

enabled foot passage across the River Owenglin. The Anglicisation of the place name clearly lost a great deal in translation, as its present-day name bears scant resemblance to the original.

Cloghfin

The Irish Gaelic name for this townland near Sixmilecross in County Tyrone is 'An Chloch Fhionn', which means 'the white stone'. The reference is to the remains of one of the three megalithic standing stones nearby. The townland of Cloghfin is five miles long and stretches from Sixmilecross to the River Cloghfin.

Coleraine

In the seventh century, this place located on the River Bann in County Londonderry (formerly known as County Coleraine), was known as 'Cuil Raithin', which translates as 'nook (or corner) where ferns grow'. Reputedly, Mountsandel Fort, about a mile south of the town centre, is the site of the earliest known settlement in Ireland, dating from the seventh century BC. However, Coleraine as it is today was begun with the Plantation period, when migrant Englishmen and Lowland Scots began to rule Ulster. They effectively expanded and fortified the township, as well as building a bridge on the former ford on the River Bann and established the castle. Coleraine was under the control of the London Society of the Governor & Assistants, and later renamed The Honourable Irish Society. According to popular legend, St Patrick passed through sometime around 450 AD and was given land by the local chieftain on which to build a church. In the late ninth century, St MacEvin wrote the *Vita tripartita Sancti Patricii* (The Tripartite Life of Saint Patrick), a bilingual life of the saint, written in Irish and in Latin, which is the only evidence for the tradition. The gifted ground was apparently covered with ferns, and Patrick called it 'Cuil Raithin', the 'nook of ferns'.

Comber

Comber's Irish name is 'An Comar', meaning 'the confluence'. It is a town in County Down, located at the northern end of Strangford Lough. The confluence in question is that of the Glen River and the Enler River which meet here and gave the town its name. It is thought that there had been a church in the settlement since the time of St Patrick. Sometime around 1200 a Cistercian abbey was founded on the site of the present Church of Ireland church.

Connacht, Province of

The Province of Connacht in the Republic of Ireland (formerly spelled 'Connaught'), or in Irish, 'Cuige Chonnacht', derived its name from the Connachta, a group of medieval Irish ruling families who were descended from the legendary second century High King Conn Cetchathach (known as 'Conn of the Hundred Battles'). Connachta means 'descendants of Conn'.

Connemara
In Old Irish Connemara is 'Conamara', a name that derives from a Celtic tribal name 'Conmacne Mara', that translates as 'the coastal territory of Conmac'. Conmac was the son of Fergus mac Roich, a legendary Ulster hero who claimed coastal territory as 'sea-coast' (from the Irish 'muir', meaning 'sea', or 'mara', meaning 'of the sea') to distinguish it from other tribal territories. The origin of the place name is also said to come from 'Cuain na Mara', meaning 'harbours of the sea'.

Corcomroe
This County Clare township gets its name from the Irish, 'Corca Mrua', meaning '(place of the) descendants of Modhruadh'. Legend has it that Modhruadh was one of the three sons of the mythical Queen Maeve (also known as Meabh and Medb of Connacht, often described as the 'fair-haired wolf-queen'), by her lover Fearghus mac Roich.

Cork
The City of Cork was first recorded in 682 AD, when Suibne, abbot of the Monastery of Cork, died. The location of the monastery is thought to have been on the site of the present-day St Fin Barre's (sometimes 'Finbarre's') Cathedral. Finbarre may have been the founder of the monastic settlement, though many doubt this, citing St Finian of Moville as its most likely founder. Cork's place name derives from the Irish 'Corcach (or Corcaigh) Mor Mumhan', which means the 'great marsh of Munster', referring to the city's location on the islands of the River Lee and its propensity for flooding. The earliest inhabitants of the south-western part of the region were designated by Ptolemy as the 'Uterni' or 'Uterini', and by other writers as the 'Iberni' and 'Iberi'. They are thought to have migrated to Ireland from the Iberian Peninsula of Spain, and given it the designation 'Hibernia', the Latin name commonly used by the Romans for the island of Ireland.

Craigavad
Craigavad is a County Down village and townland lying on the south shore of Belfast Lough. Its Irish name is 'Creig an Bhada', which means 'the rock of the boat', a reference to a boat-shaped outcrop offshore, although the word 'Mhada', meaning 'dog' has been suggested as a replacement for the last element of the place name, a possible reference to the local seal population. The place was referred to around 1306 as 'Cragger', in 1623 as 'Cregevada' and in 1645 as 'Cragyvadda'.

Crumlin
Crumlin is a village a few miles south of Antrim, located at the head of a wooded glen on the Camlin (sometimes 'Crumlin') River, near Lough Neagh. Its Irish name is 'Cromghlinn', meaning 'crooked glen', which described the natural landscape and winding valley of the River Crumlin. Crumlin has the distinction of having introduced the Irish language in pre-school and primary school education.

Ireland Northern Ireland (Ulster) & the Republic of Ireland (Eire)

Culmore
In Old Irish this townland at the mouth of the River Foyle in County Londonderry is 'An Cuil Mhor', meaning 'the great corner or peninsula'. The word 'cuil' signifies a corner or an angle and probably refers here to Culmore Point on the west bank of the Foyle.

Daingean
In Irish this small town in east County Offaly is known as 'An Daingean', simply meaning 'the fort'. From 1556 until 1920 the place was called Philipstown, after Philip II of Spain. Historically, the town was the seat of the O'Connor Faly clan, who were chieftains of the surrounding area of Offaly. The fortress was known as 'Daingean Ua bhFailghe', meaning 'fortress of the Ui Failghe clan'. King Philip also gave his name to King's County, the former name of County Offaly.

Derry- (prefix)
Derry is a common prefix in many Irish place names. It comes from the Irish Gaelic word 'doire', which means 'oak grove'.

Derry/Londonderry
The City of Derry (sometimes expressed in English as 'Londonderry'), stands on the River Foyle at the head of Lough Foyle, and has the Irish name 'Doire', meaning 'oak wood' or 'oak grove'. The place was known in the seventh century as 'Daire-Galgach', meaning 'Calgach's oak wood'. Calgach was an ancient warrior chieftain who controlled territory in this part of north-west Ulster. Later the town was named 'Doire Choile Chille', meaning 'St Columba's oak wood', after the saint who had established a monastery here in the sixth century. The prefix 'London' was attached to the place name when it was granted a market charter by James I in 1609, during the Plantation period. The original oak wood has long since disappeared. County Derry took its name from the city.

Derrynacreeve
The name of this townland and parish in County Cavan is 'Doire na Craoibhe (or Craidh)', meaning 'the oak glade or wood of large branching trees'. The name comes from 'doire', meaning 'oak wood' and 'craidh', meaning 'densely wooded' or 'densely leafed'. In February 1610, during the Plantation period, King James granted the land to William O'Shereden, the chief of the Sheridan Clan in County Cavan.

Dingle
This isolated township on the Dingle Peninsula of County Kerry has the Irish name 'An Daingean', which means 'the fortress'. This is an abbreviated form of an older name, 'Daingean Ui Chuise', which replaced the place name 'Dingle' in March 2005, and may have referred to a chieftain named 'O Cuis' who anciently ruled the region and had his principal fortress here. Others have translated the name as meaning 'the fortress of the Husseys', after a Norman family who arrived in Dingle shortly after the Norman invasion of 1169.

Donagh- (prefix)
The prefix 'donagh' is a common element in Irish place names and generally means 'church'. A few examples include Donaghcumper in County Kildare ('Domhnach Coimir', meaning 'church of the confluence'), Donaghmoyne in County Monaghan ('Domhnach Maighean', meaning 'church of the little plain'), and Donaghcloney in County Down ('Domhnach Cluana', meaning 'church of the meadow').

Donaghmore
There are at least two places in Ireland called Donaghmore: one is a hamlet in County Down and the other a village in County Tyrone. Both come from the same source, from the Irish Gaelic 'Domhnach Mor', which means 'great church'. Coincidentally, they both also have ninth or tenth century high crosses in their churchyards. The example in County Down marks the site of an early monastery and was formerly known as 'Tulaigh na Croise', meaning 'hillock of the cross'.

Donegal
Celtic warrior tribes had probably arrived here in the third century BC. According to Ptolemy's *Geographia*, the earliest inhabitants of the region around Donegal were the Vennicnii and the Rhobogdii tribes. These peoples were commonly known as the Gaels (which came to mean 'foreigner'). They divided their conquered Irish territories into at least five kingdoms. The place name in Gaelic is 'Dun na nGall', which translates as 'fort of the foreigner', which would appear to be an early reference to a stronghold or fortified settlement which they may have established. In the ninth century, Scandinavians were known to occupy the estuary of the River Eske around Donegal. There is a record of an early Viking fortress being destroyed in the town in 1159 by Murtagh mac Lochlainn, High King of Ireland. Whichever is the true derivation, several earth hillforts overlook the town. An even older name for the place is 'Tyrconnell', meaning 'land of Conall', commemorating a monarchy founded in the fifth century by Conall Gulban. Tyrconnell was ruled by the O'Donnell family, one of the two major branches of the O'Neills of Tyrone that had dominated Ulster for more than a thousand years. Donegal's population remained largely Gaelic-speaking well into the nineteenth century. To this day, the districts of Gweedore and Cloughaneely are officially classified as 'Gaeltacht', or Irish-speaking areas.

Down, County
County Down, along with a small part of County Antrim, was anciently known by the name Ulagh or Ullagh (in Latin, 'Ulidia'), which according to Ptolemy was inhabited by the Voluntii or Uluntii tribes in the first century AD. It is one of six counties of Northern Ireland, and its Irish name is 'Contae an Duin'. The name 'Down' is derived from 'An Dun', meaning 'the fort', referring to the one at Downpatrick, which gave its name to the county.

Ireland Northern Ireland (Ulster) & the Republic of Ireland (Eire)

Downpatrick
Known in Irish as 'Dun Padraig', this place name was first recorded in the seventeenth century, and translates into English as 'Patrick's fort'. The fort in question was an Iron Age hillfort which formerly stood on Cathedral Hill. St Patrick is said to have established one of Ireland's oldest abbeys here in the year 493 AD. A later fort in the township was held by the MacDunleary family before the Anglo-Norman knight Sir John de Courci (sometimes de Courcy) took possession in 1177 and it became his headquarters until 1203. The original name for Downpatrick in Irish was 'Dun Lethglaise', which probably translates as 'fort at the side of the stream', referring to the River Quoile located at the foot of Cathedral Hill.

Drogheda
Drogheda is located at the mouth of the River Boyne, and derives its name from the Irish 'Droichead Atha', meaning 'bridge of the ford'. It was originally founded on either side of the river, part in Louth and part in Meath, as Drogheda-in-Meath and Drogheda-in-Oriel, each with its own separate administration, and a ford crossing existed where a bridge now stands. Nowadays, Drogheda straddles the mouth of the Boyne and is the most southern town administratively located in County Louth. It was not until November 1412, when Henry IV granted a charter unifying the two settlements, that they became the single township of Drogheda.

Drum- (prefix)
The prefix 'Drum' or 'Drom' is found in several Irish townlands and villages, and means 'the ridge', invariably a term descriptive of its geographical location. Among others, examples include Drum in County Monaghan, Dromineer in County Tipperary ('Drom Inbhir', meaning 'ridge of the estuary'), Drumahoe in County Derry ('Droim na hUamba', meaning 'ridge of the cave'), Drumbeg in County Down ('Drom Beag', meaning 'little ridge'), and the Parish of Drumcree in County Westmeath ('Drion Cria', meaning 'ridge of cattle').

Drumcannon
Drumcannon is a parish in Waterford in County Donegal, located on the Bay of Tramore. Its name in Gaelic is 'Droim Ceanannain', which translates as 'ridge of the white'. The last element of the name comes from 'ceann-fhionn', meaning 'white-faced'. The term usually refers to a cow.

Drumcroon
This small hamlet in County Derry has the Irish name 'Droim Cruithean' (or in Middle Irish, 'Cruithnig' or 'Cruithni'), which translates as 'ridge of the Cruithin'. The Cruithin were an early Celtic tribe who occupied lands in present-day Counties of Antrim, Down and Derry and were thought to be related to the Pictish tribes of Scotland. Their name may relate to the Irish word 'cruth', meaning 'form' or 'shape', although the significance is lost to us. Cruithin may

not have been the name which they called themselves, but was probably a name given to them by others.

Dublin

The earliest inhabitants of the region around present-day Dublin were a native people designated by Ptolemy as the Blanii (or 'Eblani'), whose territorial tribeland it remained until the arrival of Scandinavians in the eighth century. Officially, the capital city of Dublin is known by the name of its first settlement which in Irish was, 'Baile Atha Cliath', which translates into English as 'the town of the hurdle ford', referring to an early crossing place on the River Liffey. The significance of the 'hurdle' element of the translation has been much debated, without resolution. Its more commonly known name dates from the sixth century when the Monastery of Duiblinn was founded a little way south of the tidal pool in the River Poddle, which is a tributary of the Liffey. The name 'Duiblinn' means 'black pool', and over time it was transformed by its Gaelic name into 'Dyflinn', and in the eighth and ninth centuries via the Vikings the Gaelic name was corrupted to Dublin. In 1949, Ireland became an independent Republic, and Dublin remained its capital.

Duleek

Duleek is a village in County Meath whose Irish name is 'Damhliag', meaning 'stone house'. This is thought to be a reference to St Cianan's Church which was a very early stone building, and reputedly the first stone-built church ever constructed in Ireland. A monastic settlement had been established here by St Patrick around 450 AD, and was placed in the care of St Cianan in 489. The original church was over-built later by the Augustinian monks.

Dun- (prefix)

The modern Irish prefix 'dun' invariably refers to a fort or fortified stronghold, of which there are scores in Ulster and in the Republic. Among many others too numerous to include here, are Dundrum in County Down ('Dun Droma', meaning 'fort of the ridge'), Dunluce in County Antrim ('Dunlios', meaning 'fortified dwelling'), Dunmoyle in County Tyrone ('An Dun Maol', meaning 'the bald (or dilapidated) fort'), and Dungiven in County Derry ('Dun Geimhin', meaning 'Gevin's fort').

Dunaff

The village of Dunaff is located in the Urris Valley on the Inishowen Peninsula of County Donegal. Its Irish name is 'Dun Danh', which translates as 'fort of oxen'. The remains of the fort in question are to be found near the south-west boundary of the village, but the reference to the oxen is obscure.

Dundalk

Dundalk in County Louth began as a prehistoric fortress known as 'Dun Dealgan' (the fort of Dealgan), and is said to be the birthplace of the mythological first

Ireland Northern Ireland (Ulster) & the Republic of Ireland (Eire)

century Celtic warrior hero, Cuchulainn Dealgan (or 'Dealga'), after whom the fort was named. He was chief of the Fir Bolg tribe and is said to have built the fort. Dundalk had been earlier known as 'Sraidbaille' (which translates as 'street-town'), signifying a settlement with just one street or thoroughfare running through it.

Dungannon
By tradition, the town of Dungannon in County Tyrone is named after Geanann, the son of an ancient Druid named Cathbadh. Consequently, the place name is 'Dun Geanann' in Irish, which means 'fort of Geanann'. The ruins of the fort in question were a former medieval fortress of the O'Neills located on Castle Hill in the town. The place was known as 'Duin-genainn' in 1505.

Edenderry
In Irish, the name of this hill in County Offaly is 'Eadan Doire', meaning 'hill brow (or ridge) of the oak grove'. The hill referred to is thought to be either the one on which Blundell's Castle now stands, to the south of the village, or Carrick Hill to its north. The place was known as 'Coolestown' in the sixteenth century, named after the Cooley family, who held the castle at that time.

Eire
The name 'Eire' probably means 'western', describing its geographical location in the British archipelago. The name probably evolved from the Old Irish word 'Eiu', an early Celtic goddess. Unlike England or Scotland which were named after their people (the English and the Scots), the Irish people got their name from the country's name. The term 'Ireland' is a largely English appellation. The name 'Eire' distinguishes it as a separate entity from Northern Ireland (Ulster). Eire was adopted by its government in 1937 as the official name for the Republic of Ireland.

Emly
In Old Irish this Tipperary place name is 'Imleach Iobhair', which means 'lakeland of the yew tree'. Its later name was modified to just 'Imleach', meaning 'borderland', a probable reference to its location at the edge of a former lake. The original settlement was established in the fifth century by St Ailbhe of Emly (known in English as St Elvis), who was a pupil of St Patrick.

Ennis
The name of Ennis in County Clare is a corruption of the Irish word 'inis', signifying an island. Actually, its location on the River Fergus contains several small islands, of which this is but one.

Enniscrone
Debates continue as to the exact meaning of this town in County Sligo, where even the original Gaelic source is open to question. The place name is also contentious:

while most have it as 'Enniscrone', many historians and academics insist it should more properly be 'Inishcrone'. Officially, its Irish name is 'Inis Crabhann', but some have it derived from 'Inis Eascar Abhann', meaning 'island on the esker in the river'. The word 'esker' comes from the Old Irish word 'escir', which is a long, winding ridge of stratified sand and gravel, which in this case referred to a sandbank. The first element of the place name means 'island'.

Enniskillen
Known by its Irish name as 'Inis Ceithleann', the town of Enniskillen is sometimes spelled 'Inniskillin'. It is located on Cethlin's Island, in the Fermanagh and Omagh district, and was a strategic crossing point of Lough Erne. In 1439, the place name was recorded as 'Inis Ceithlenn', which translates into English as 'Ceithleann's island', after Ceithleann, a mythological Irish goddess. Enniskillen Castle was the stronghold of the Maguire chieftains, who ruled Fermanagh for more than three hundred years, before it was sequestered by the English Crown and granted to English settlers during the Plantation of Ulster. Later, it became the garrison of the British army regiments of the Royal Inniskilling Fusiliers and the 6th Inniskilling Dragoons.

Erne, Lough
In Old Irish, this lake in Fermanagh is called 'Loch Eirne', which translates as 'lake of the Erni'. The name 'Erni' (or 'Ernai') was applied to the early tribe of Fir Bolg, who are said to have lived there before the lake formed over it.

Fahan
This village and parish in Donegal has the Irish name 'Fathain', meaning 'burial place'. The present graveyard marks the place where St Columcille established a monastery in the late sixth century, although there may have been a pre-Christian burial site already in place long before that time.

Fenagh
Fenagh, or in Irish, 'Fiodhnach' (or 'Fionacha'), is a village in County Leitrim in the west of Ireland, whose name means 'woody place'. However, as densely wooded as the place may have been when the Celtic monk St Caillin founded Feragh Abbey sometime in the fifth century, its trees have long since gone, possibly cleared for farmland in the Middle Ages.

Fermanagh, County
The County of Fermanagh (in Irish, 'Contae Fhear Manach'), is one of the six counties of Ulster. The Irish word 'fhear', meant 'men', so the place name may be taken to mean 'men of Manaigh'. Its name relates back to the first century Celtic tribe, who Ptolemy called 'Menapii' who settled around the Lough Erne area. The Manaigh were an offshoot of the Menappii, better known as the 'Fir Manach', from which the county

Ireland Northern Ireland (Ulster) & the Republic of Ireland (Eire)

gets its name. The tribe are thought to have spread across all Ireland, and their émigrés were instrumental in establishing some of the eventual Scottish and Manx clans.

Finglas
Finglas is an outer suburb of Dublin whose name in Irish is 'Fionnghlas', which means 'clear stream'. The name is derived from the River Finglas. According to popular tradition, the original settlement grew around an early abbey founded by the missionary St Cainnech in the sixth century. The saint was known as St Kenneth in Scotland, and preached Christianity throughout Ireland and to the Pictish tribes of Scotland. The original place name is thought to have referred to a holy well which was said to cure eye diseases.

Finn, River
The Finn (or in Irish, 'An Fhinn'), rises in Lough Finn and flows through the Counties of Donegal and Tyrone before becoming the River Foyle south of Lifford. The name means 'holy one' and probably referred to an early Celtic river goddess.

Foyle, River
The name of the River Foyle is derived from Lough Foyle into which it flows. Its name in Irish is 'An Feabhal', which refers to Febail, an eighth century mythological figure of Irish folklore. The Foyle is formed by the confluence of the River Finn and the River Mourne, south of Lifford and flows through the Counties of Donegal and Tyrone before entering Lough Foyle near Derry in the Province of Ulster.

Gallen
The County Offaly settlement of Gallen derives its name from the priory which was founded by St Canoc in the fifth century. Sometimes called Gallen Abbey or Gallen Priory, its Irish Gaelic name is 'Mainistir Ghaillin', which translates as 'monastery of the garden'. What little remains of the building has been designated as a National Monument. Its name is said to have originally derived from a local chieftain called Gallen of the Britons ('Galline na nBretan').

Galway
The ancient origin of a settlement in Galway is borne out by a granite stone decorated with Celtic art dating from around 200 BC. At that time the region was inhabited by the Auteri, who also occupied areas of the adjoining counties of Mayo and Roscommon. Galway was known in Gaelic as 'Gaillimh' and means 'stony', as in a river, referring to the River Corrib that flows through the town into Galway Bay. From the earliest times, as a small fishing village, Galway was subjected to many Viking raids in the eighth and ninth centuries. The first written record of Galway was in 1124 with the establishment of a fort. The English arrived in Ireland in 1170 and in 1232 the Norman Baron Richard de Burgh (sometimes de Burgo), took over the entire Kingdom of Connacht, including Galway, where he established the town.

Giant's Causeway
This iconic geographical feature of Ulster's northern Antrim coast was formed by ancient volcanic fissure eruptions and has been designated as a World Heritage Site by UNESCO, and has long been the subject of myths and folklore. Its most common name in Irish is 'Clochan an Aifir', meaning 'stepping stones of the giant'. However, an alternative name of 'Clochan na Formorach' refers to Finn MacCumaill, an Irish popular hero who took on the giant sea rovers from Scotland and is said to have built the causeway across the sea to Scotland to defeat them.

Glenavy
The 'glen' element of this village in Antrim is actually a corruption of 'llan', an alternative Old Irish name for a church, and not as might be supposed, a valley (or glen). The Irish place name is 'Lann Abhaigh', which translates as 'church of the dwarf'. Legend has it that St Patrick built a church here and left his disciple Daniel (apparently a very short man who was nicknamed 'the dwarf'), in charge during his absence. The site is now occupied by the graveyard of the Church of Ireland church in the village.

Gorticashel
In Irish this association of two neighbouring hamlets in County Tyrone is called 'Gort an Chaisil', which means 'field of the stone ring-fort'; this despite no stone fort ever having been found in the district. The 'fort' that actually exists is an earthen mound and a single standing stone. The place name Gorticashel (sometimes 'Gorticastle') encompasses the two townlands of Gorticashel Upper and Gorticashel Lower, which are separated by a stream known as Gorticashel Burn. The name was recorded in 1666 as 'Gorte-Castell'.

Gougane Barra
Gougane Barra is a mountain lake in County Cork whose name comes from St Finbarr (the Bishop of Cork, whose name is often abbreviated to 'Barra'). He is said to have built a monastery on an island in the middle of the lake nearby during the sixth century. In Gaelic, the name is 'Guagan Barra', which means 'the rock of Barra'.

Inish-/Inis- (prefix)
The prefix 'inish' or 'inis' in any Irish place name generally refers to an island, and is found in dozens of hamlets and villages on both sides of the border. They include Inishannon in County Cork ('inis Eonain', meaning 'Eonan's riverside land'), several places called Inishbeg meaning 'little island', Inisheer in County Galway ('Inis Oirr', meaning 'eastern island'), Inishfree in County Donegal ('Inis Fraoigh', meaning 'island of heather').

Ireland Northern Ireland (Ulster) & the Republic of Ireland (Eire)

Inishbofin
The island of Inishbofin in County Donegal has exactly the same root and meaning as Inchbofin in Galway. The name in Irish is 'Inis Bo Finne', meaning 'island of the white cow'. Like many other Irish islands, the name is somewhat shrouded in mystery and nobody really knows what the name signifies, even though legends of mystical cows abound in national folklore. However, it may be a reference to the Auroch wild white cattle which were the dominant breed in the Bronze Age, before others were imported into the British Isles by the Normans. The islands are sometimes known simply as 'Boffin' or 'Bophin island'.

Inishmore
This is a fairly common place name in Ireland with examples in the Aran Islands of Galway and beside Upper Lough Erne in County Fermanagh. The Irish name is spelled 'Inis Mhor', which translates as 'big island'.

Inishowen
In Irish, this County Donegal area is known as 'Inis Eoghain' (the Island of Eoghan) after Eogan MacNeill (also known as Owen). The present-day place name is understood to mean 'Owen's peninsula'. Inishowen is the largest peninsula in Ireland. Legend has it that the Owen in question was the son of Niall Naoighiallach (known as 'Niall of the Nine Hostages'), who ruled Ireland in the fifth century, and is said to be buried on the peninsula.

Ireland, The Republic of
See: 'Eire'.

Keady
The place name of the County Armagh town of Keady is both the name of the town and the old name of the river. Its Gaelic name is 'An Ceide', which means 'flat-topped hill', a reference to its location on high ground near the border with County Monaghan and the Republic of Ireland. The River Clea, which runs through the middle of the village once powered the waterwheels of the town's bleaching and linen mills.

Kells
This County Antrim village is universally celebrated for *The Book of Kells*, the illuminated gospel manuscript (also known as *The Book of Columba*), produced in the monastery which was founded in the village in around 500 AD. The Irish name for Kells is 'Na Cealla', which means 'the monastic cells'. The place was originally known as 'Ceannanas' (or 'Ceannanus'), and was a royal site inhabited by the High King Cormac MacAirt. Over time the name of the settlement was referred to in English and Anglo-Norman in its shortened form as Kenenus, Kenlis, Kellis and finally Kells.

Kerry, County

County Kerry (in Irish, 'Contae Chiarrai') is located in the south-west region of the Province of Munster, which according to Ptolemy, was inhabited by a Celtic tribe known as the Velabri (or 'Vellibori') in the first century AD. They are thought to have been descended from the Iberi of Spain (natives of the Iberian Peninsula). Others identify them as the Lugadii (or 'Luceni') who settled in the area around Dingle Bay. Later the area became the territory of the Ciarraige, an ancient group whose name meant 'the people of Ciar' (who was the son of King Fergus of Ulster). A branch known as the 'Ciarraige Luachra', gave their name to County Kerry.

Kil-/Kill- (prefix)

The prefix 'kil' or 'kill' comes from the Gaelic word 'cill', meaning 'church', and there are several villages, hamlets and townlands whose place names begin with it. Most church names tend to include the personal name of the saint to whom they are dedicated. Examples are Kilcar in County Donegal ('Cill Charthaigh', meaning 'Carthach's church', after the sixth century saint), Kilcronaghan in County Derry ('Cill Chruithneachain', meaning 'St Cronaghan's church'), Killadeas in County Fermanagh ('Cill CheileDe', meaning 'church of the Culdee', after a group of monastic reformers), Killcullan in County Kildare ('Cill Chuilinn', meaning 'church of the holly') and Killevy in County Armagh ('Cill Shleibhe', meaning 'church of the mountain').

Kilbride

There are several places called Kilbride in Ireland, including in the counties of Antrim, Cavan, Waterford, Westmeath and Wicklow, as well as a place of that name in Scotland. In Irish, the name is 'Cill Bhride', meaning 'St Brigid's church'. Early pagan tribes knew Brigid as the goddess of poetry, and as St Brigid of Kildare she was one of the important saints adopted into the Roman Catholic Church. Places of this name generally reflect the dedication of local churches to her.

Kilcock

This place in County Kildare was named after the church dedicated to St Coca. She is thought to have been the aunt of St Patrick and was the head of the late-fifth century monastery here. In Irish the name is 'Cill Choca', simply meaning 'St Coca's church'.

Kildare, County

The earliest known settlement in County Kildare has been found on the Curragh plain, where more than forty-four prehistoric sites have been identified, many dating from the Neolithic period, including a number of circular earthwork mounds and ditches, of which the largest is the Gibbet Rath. This was the territory of the Celtic Coriundi tribe. The Kildare place name is derived from the Gaelic Irish 'Cill Dara', which translates as 'the church of the oak tree'. Little else is known of Kildare before the ninth century, when *The Annals of Ireland* made references to Viking raids on its church. The church in question is said to have been built beneath

Ireland Northern Ireland (Ulster) & the Republic of Ireland (Eire)

an oak tree and contained the shrine to the Celtic goddess Brigid; this became the Monastery of St Brigid, Kildare's patron saint.

Kilfenora
This village on the west coast of County Clare has the name 'Cill Fhionnurach', possibly meaning 'church of Fionnuir'. In legend, Fionnuir was the daughter of Oilill Olum, an early king of Muster and Maeve, the queen of Connacht. Alternatively, there is a suggestion that the place name should more properly be interpreted as 'church on a fertile hillside' – but the former explanation is the more widely held.

Kilfullert
Kilfullert is a township in County Down whose name in Old Irish is 'Coill Fulachta', which means 'wood of the cooking place', The term 'fulacht' (or 'fulacht fiadh') refers to a primitive field kitchen, typically an open pit filled with heated stones for cooking, of the type in common use during the Bronze Age. The word 'fiadh', means 'wild'. Hence, 'wild cooking'.

Kilkenny
The Gaelic name of the Leinster township of Kilkenny is 'Cill Chainnigh', which means 'the church of Cainneach (or Canice)'; *The Annals of the Four Masters* recorded Kilkenny by that name in 1085. The county was originally inhabited by the Celtic tribes of the Brigantes and the Caucoi and was later recorded as Osraighe (the Kingdom of Ossory). The settlement became known for a time as 'Irishtown' and later as 'Hightown'. Sometime after the Norman invasion of Ireland in 1169 (which was led by Richard FitzGilbert de Clare, known as 'Strongbow'), Kilkenny Castle was begun on a hill overlooking the ford on the River Nore. Thirty years later, Strongbow's son-in-law, the Earl of Pembroke, replaced the original wooden castle in stone. In 1301 it was bought by the third Earl of Ormonde, James Butler, whose family remained powerful overlords for the following five centuries. Under the Ormonde earls, the township developed a thriving market economy and the wealth it gained fostered the town's growth, so much so that from 1366 the Irish parliament was based in Kilkenny.

Kill
The village of Kill in County Cavan derives from the Irish Gaelic word for a church. The present-day place name is a truncation of 'Kildrumsheridan', based on 'Cill Dhroim Shirideain', meaning 'the church on Siridean's ridge'. This is itself derived from the 'O Siridean' surname, which has evolved into English as O'Sheridan or simply 'Sheridan'. Grants of land in Cavan were given by James VI to William Sheridan, who was chief of the Sheridan clan in 1610, but no trace of the church in question still exists.

Killashandra
The village of Killeshandra (sometimes Killashandra) in County Cavan, has the Irish name 'Cill na Seanratha', meaning 'church of the old fort'. This came about when

the old Church of Rath was established in the fourteenth century inside an old ring-fort, fragments of which survive to the present day in the church graveyard. The town itself was created as a Protestant community by the Scot Sir Alexander Hamilton of Innerwick who had been granted lands in 1610 as part of the Ulster Plantation.

Killarney

In Old Irish, the name of the County Kerry township of Killarney is 'Cill Airne', which means 'the church of the sloes'. The town and its wider region (which includes Killarney National Park), has many sites of prehistoric and archaeological interest, including Bronze Age stone circles, standing stones, cooking sites ('fulachta fiadh'), as well as ring-forts dating from the Iron Age and monastic establishments from early Christian times.

Kinsale

The County Cork market town of Kinsale (sometimes spelled 'Kingsale'), probably derived its place name either from the Irish 'Cean Taile', meaning 'headland in the sea', in reference to the nearby Old Head promontory, or from 'Cuin Saila', which translates as 'smooth sea (or basin)'. The promontory is the site of the ruins of a twelfth century castle established by the Anglo-Norman Baron, John de Courci (sometimes de Courcy), the first Lord of Kinsale. Edward II granted a royal charter in 1334, after which Kinsale became a major port trading in wine and salt as well as supplying provisions to the English navy. Kinsale has the distinction of being the place where the father of the Quaker, William Penn, founder of the State of Pennsylvania in America, held office in the town.

Knock- (prefix)

The prefix 'knock' derives from the Old Irish word 'cnoc', meaning 'hill'. There are dozens of Irish place names bearing this prefix. They tend to fall into two main categories: on the one hand as descriptive of their location, or on the other, after the people who settled them or to whom they are dedicated. Examples of the former include places like Knockaderry in County Limerick ('Cnoc an Doire', meaning 'hill of the oak wood'), Knockglass in County Waterford ('Cnoc Glas', meaning 'the green hill'), Knockalough in County Clare ('Cnoc an Locha', meaning 'hill by the lake'), Knockduff in County Cavan ('An Cnoc Dubh', meaning 'the black hill'). Examples of the latter include Knockmaroon in County Dublin ('Cnoc Mhaolruain', meaning 'Maolruan's hill'), Knockninny in County Fermanagh ('Cnoc Ninnidh', meaning 'St Ninnidh's hill'), Knockainy in County Limerick ('Cnoc Aine', meaning 'Aine's hill'), and Knockmoy in County Galway ('Cnoc Muaidhe', meaning 'Muaidh's hill').

Knock

The district of Knock in County Down (in Irish, 'An Cnoc') was originally a town in its own right, but was amalgamated with Breda in the mid-seventeenth century

Ireland Northern Ireland (Ulster) & the Republic of Ireland (Eire)

to form the civil Parish of Knock-Breda. As it stands, the place name simply means 'hill', but is an abbreviation of its fuller early name 'Cnoc Cholm Cille', which translates as 'St Colmcille's hill'. St Colmcille is better known outside Ireland as St Columba, a missionary and evangelist who was the patron saint of Derry. He was venerated by the Gaels of Dal Riata and the Picts of Scotland, and as a Catholic saint he is celebrated as one of the Twelve Apostles of Ireland.

Knockcroghery
The village of Knockcroghery lies on the River Shannon in County Roscommon and has the Irish name 'Cnoc an Chrochaine', which means 'the hill of the hangman'. The original name of the village was 'An Creagan', meaning 'the stony hill', but at some time in its history the hill east of the village must have been a place of execution as it became commonly known as Hangman's Hill.

Lagan, River
The River Lagan largely forms the border between County Down and Antrim, having risen a few miles south-east of Dromara before flowing into the sea at Belfast. Its Irish name is 'Abhainn an Lagain', which means 'river of the low-lying district'. It was earlier known as 'Lao' (meaning 'calf'), referring to the bovine goddess of the river.

Laois, County
County Laois (in Irish, is 'Contae Laoise', and formerly Anglicised to 'Leix'), is located in the south midlands of the Province of Leinster in the Republic of Ireland. It was formerly known as Queen's County and takes its present name from an Celtic Irish tribe known as the Loigis (also known as the 'Laoighis' or 'Laeighis', after the tribe's first chieftain, Laigseach), who first settled the area in the third century and ruled it until the beginning of the seventeenth century. The county had for some time been named in honour of the English queen, Mary Tudor, who issued orders for the Plantation of Laois by English settlers.

Larne
The Northern Irish port of Larne is thought to have derived its place name from Lathar, who was the son of Hugony the Great (also known as 'Ugaine Mor'), High King of Ireland in the fifth century BC. His father granted lands to him on the Antrim coast, stretching from Glenarm to the River Inver, known in Gaelic as 'Latharna', which translates as 'the descendants of Lathar'. It has the alternative Irish name 'Inbhear an Latharna', which means 'river mouth (or estuary)', and is sometimes shortened simply to 'Inbhear' or 'Ollarbha'. In the ninth and tenth centuries Vikings made many raids upon the settlement as well as finding shelter in Larne Lough; for a time the Lough was known by its Viking name of 'Ulfreksfjord' after the Norse King Ulfric, later Anglicised as 'Wulfrickford'.

Leinster, Province of

Leinster (in Irish, 'Laighin'or 'Cuige Laighean') is a province in the east of Ireland which formerly combined the ancient Kingdoms of Meath, Leinster and Osraige. The place name translates as '(place or territory of the) Lagin people'. The Lagin were a third century BC Celtic tribe whose name is thought to derive from the Irish word 'laighean', meaning 'spear'. Later, 'staor' was added from Old Norse (meaning 'territory'), and 'tir', the Irish word for 'land'. Hence, these elements taken together produce a place name that means 'the land (or territory) of the Lagin'.

Leitrim, County

According to the geographer Ptolemy's first century map, this county, along with substantial parts of the counties of Fermanagh and Cavan, was occupied by the Erdini tribe (in Irish, 'Ernaigh'). The county name is derived from the village by the River Shannon (which marks the county border), whose name in Irish is 'Liatroim', meaning 'grey ridge', a reference to rising ground to the east of the village.

Letterkenny

Letterkenny is located on the River Swilly and is the largest town in County Donegal. It has the Irish name 'Leitir Ceanainn', but there is a dispute as to the exact meaning of the place name. Some have it as 'hillside of the white top', based on the Old Irish 'ceann', meaning 'head' or 'top', and 'fionn' meaning 'white' or 'fair'. Others prefer 'hillside of the O'Cannons', whose medieval stronghold was based at Conwal, about one mile outside Letterkenny. The O'Cannons where the ancient chieftains of the Kingdom of Tir Conaill, the old name for County Donegal.

Limavady

There was once a castle overlooking a valley of the River Roe on the site of present-day Limavady in County Derry. The place name in Irish is 'Leim an Mhadaidh', which translates as 'leap of the dog'. The precise meaning is much speculated, but it is thought to refer to a legend concerning a dog belonging to the chief of the O'Kane clan. The animal is said to have jumped a wide gorge to carry a message of danger to O'Cahan Castle which once stood on the east bank of the Roe.

Limerick

In Old Irish, Limerick was known as 'Luimneach', a name that translates as 'bare area'. The first settlement was founded by the Vikings at the southern tip of what became King's Island on the River Shannon sometime around 922 AD. Early sources refer to a place called 'Inis Sibtonn' or 'Luimneach', as an island in the River Shannon. When Donal Mor O'Brien (c.1155–94, sometimes known as Domnall Mor mac Toirrdelbaig Ui Briain), King of Munster, died in 1194, the Normans

Ireland Northern Ireland (Ulster) & the Republic of Ireland (Eire)

took control of Limerick and created the administrative County of Limerick soon afterwards. The city gives its name to the ubiquitous five-line humorous verse, the Limerick, thought to be derived from the eighteenth century, Maigue Poets of Croom in County Limerick.

Lis- (prefix)
The Irish prefix 'lis' stands for 'ring-fort', and occasionally represents a stronghold or fortified enclosure. There are several dozen places which contain it, as well as other descriptive elements, either of its locational topography or by the names of early founders, owners or chieftains. Examples of the former include places like Lisnacree in County Down ('Lios na Cri', meaning 'the fort on the boundary'), Lislea in County Antrim ('Lios Liath', meaning 'the grey fort'), Liscloon in County Tyrone ('Lios Claon', meaning 'the crooked fort'), and Lisduff in County Laois ('An Lios Dubh', meaning 'the black ring-fort'). Among examples of personal name inclusions are Lisfinny in County Waterford ('Lios Finin', meaning 'Finin's ring-fort'), Lispole in County Kerry ('Lios Poil', meaning 'Paul's ring-fort'), and Lisrodden in County Antrim ('Lios Rodain', meaning 'Rodan's fort').

Liscolman
In Irish Gaelic, this County Wicklow parish in the barony of Shillelagh in the Province of Leinster, has the name 'Lios Cholmain', which translates as 'Coleman's ring-fort'. It was earlier known as 'Lismacolman', which more properly translates as 'ring-fort of the sons of Colman'.

Lismore
In Irish, 'Lois Mor' as this township in Waterford is known, has a literal meaning of 'big-ring-fort', though in this case it probably represented the word 'enclosure', in reference to that built around the monastery which was founded here by St Carthach in the seventh century. The remains of the monastery can still be seen on a flat-topped earth mound about a mile outside the town.

Londonderry
See: 'Derry'.

Lough- (prefix)
Lough is the Irish Gaelic word for a lake, and as well as the many lakes that carry the 'Lough' prefix, a number of lakeside villages and hamlets also share it as an element in their place name. Some of these lakes include Lough Derg in County Donegal ('Loch Dearg', meaning 'red lake'), Lough Beg in County Antrim ('Loch Beag', meaning 'little lake'), Lough Mourne in County Monaghan ('Loch Murn', meaning 'lake of the Murna tribe'), and Lough Ramor in County Cavan ('Loch Ramhar', meaning 'broad lake').

Lough Erne

The two connected lakes of Lough Erne Lower and Lough Erne Upper are actually widened parts of the River Erne in County Fermanagh. Their Irish name is 'Loch Eirne', meaning 'Erann's lake', or as some prefer 'lake (of the goddess) Erann'. Ancient mythology maintains that it is named after a mythical woman named Erne, Queen Meabh's lady-in-waiting at Cruachan. Erne and her maidens fled northward to avoid a rampaging giant and were drowned in a river, where their bodies dissolved into the water to become Lough Erne. It has also been suggested that the name may have its root in the personification of Ireland as 'Eriu', of which 'Eire' or 'Erin' are modern derivations.

Loughros

The Loughros Peninsula in County Donegal is actually a combination of a headland (or promontory) and two bays, Loughros More Bay to the north and Loughros Beg Bay to the south. They derive their names from Loughros Point. The Irish word 'mor' means 'big' and 'beg' means 'small', and the suffix 'rhos' translates as 'rushes' or 'rushy'. Hence, the place name means 'headland of rushes'.

Louth, County

Louth is a county in the Province of Leinster, named after village of Louth, which in turn is named after Lugh, a god of the ancient Irish. There have been various spellings of the place name over time, including 'Lugmad', 'Lughmhaigh', and 'Lughmhadh', which is commonly abbreviated to 'Lu', which in Irish signifies a plain. County Louth was a predominantly Irish-speaking region until the early twentieth century, and an Ulster Irish dialect existed well into the 1930s. That particular dialect became almost extinct, but some thirty-four percent of the county's population are still Irish speakers. In the first century AD, Louth formed part of the territorial tribelands of the Voluntii tribe.

Lusk

Lusk is located in Fingal, around ten miles north of the City of Dublin and since the earliest days of its settlement, it has been associated with St MacCullin, who founded a monastery here in the mid-fifth century. Tradition has it that the saint may have been buried in a local cave and that the name 'Lusk' derives from an old Irish word 'lusca' meaning 'cave' or 'underground chamber'.

Maghera- (prefix)

Several places in Ireland are either called Maghera or include it as part of their place name. The word derives from the Irish 'machaire', signifying a plain or low-lying flat land. Maghera in County Derry is a good example; its full name in Irish is 'Machaire Ratha', meaning 'plain of the ring-fort'. Others include Magheracloone in County Monaghan, ('Machaire Cluana', meaning 'plain of the meadow'),

Ireland Northern Ireland (Ulster) & the Republic of Ireland (Eire)

Magheramena in County Down ('Machaire Meadhonach', meaning 'middle plain'), Magheramore in County Wicklow ('Machaire Mor', meaning 'great plain'), and Magheralin in County Down ('Machaire Lainne', meaning 'plain of the church').

Malin
The village of Malin in County Donegal has the Irish name 'Malainn'. Malin Head (in Irish, 'Cionn Mhalanna'), which is located on the Inishowen Peninsula, a few miles north of the village, is the most northerly point of the island of Ireland. The Malin place name translates as 'the brow', and 'cionne' signifies a headland. Hence, 'headland of the brow'.

Mayo, County
The original full name of County Mayo in the Irish Republic was 'Maigheo na Sacsan', which meant 'the yew tree plain of the Saxons', a reference to the English monks who settled here in the seventh century. Later the name was shortened to 'Maigh Eo', which translates as 'plain of the yew trees'. In the first century AD, the Nagnatae tribe had been the inhabitants of the whole county, except for a small area in the south where the Auterii tribe had settled. Less than ten per cent of the population of County Mayo live in its Irish-speaking region, known as 'the Gaeltacht'.

Meath, County
The Irish name of County Meath in the Province of Leinster is 'Contae na Mi' or simply 'an Mhi'. Its name is derived from 'midhe', meaning 'middle' or 'centre'. It was known in the ninth century as 'Mide', indicating its location, bordered by seven other counties. The Hill of Tara, located near the Rover Boyne, which flows through Meath, was the seat of the High Kings of Ireland. The present county name has existed since the thirteenth century.

Moate
The village of Moate in County Westmeath derives its name from the raised earth ring-fort that once stood south of the present-day village. When the Normans arrived in the British Isles they introduced a form of defensive fortification, a system known as 'motte and bailey'. The word 'motte' signified a raised earth mound on which a wooden stockade was constructed. The 'bailey' was an enclosed reinforced area surrounding the motte. This was later replaced by a stone fortification, with a stone keep replacing the temporary wooden structure. The present-day earth mound is called Moatgrange, meaning 'little Grace's mound', a reference to a one-time Princess of Munster.

Monaghan, County
According to some accounts, County Monaghan, along with all the inland parts of Ireland, was inhabited at the time of Ptolemy by the Scoti (or 'Scotii') tribe,

although this is often used as a general term for the Celtic tribes who may have migrated to Ireland from Scotland. However, on his map of Ireland made in the year 150 AD, Ptolemy identifies the area as territory of the Menapii Celtic tribe. The county name comes from the town of Monaghan, or in Irish, 'Muineachan', which means 'place of little thickets' in reference to a thickly overgrown area. Some (including Monaghan County Council), prefer an interpretation of 'land of the little hills'.

Mountrath

It is thought that Mountrath in County Laois probably gets its place name from an ancient fort in nearby Redcastle. The Irish name for the place is 'Moin Ratha', meaning 'the ring-fort in the bog'. Others cite the name 'Maighean Ratha', meaning 'homestead (or village) of the ring-fort'. However, the prevailing opinion seems to prefer the first interpretation, insomuch as the Irish word 'moin' represents 'bog'. The word was misinterpreted by English settlers who erroneously inserted the word 'Mount' into the place name.

Mulla- (prefix)

The prefix 'mulla' is present in thirty or more Irish place names, and means 'hilltop'. In general terms it is accompanied by a defining or descriptive term based on its local landscape. Examples include such places as Mullagh in County Cavan ('An Mullach', meaning simply 'the hilltop'), Mullaghcarn in County Tyrone ('Mullach Cairn', meaning 'hilltop of the cairn'), Mullaghanee in County Monaghan ('Mullach an Fhia', meaning 'hilltop of the deer'), Mullaghroe in County Sligo ('An Mullach Rua', meaning 'the red hilltop'), and Mullaghglass in County Armagh ('An Mullach Glas', meaning 'the green hilltop').

Munster, Province of

The Province of Munster in the Republic of Ireland is known in Irish as 'an Mhumhain' (or 'Cuige Mumhan', and sometimes in Old Irish as 'Muma'). It was historically the Kingdom of Munster, one of the 'Five-Fifths' ('cuige') or ancient provinces and Gaelic kingdoms. In the first century, Ptolemy described in his *Geographia* the Celtic tribe of the Iverni occupying the lands in southern Ireland, in the region now called Munster. The Nordic suffix 'tir', meaning 'land' completed the name, 'Muma-tir' or 'Mumhan-tir', which over time emerged as Munster.

Naas

Naas, or in Irish 'Nas na Riogh' or 'An Nas', was historically the county seat and is now the administration centre of County Kildare; it was one of the royal seats of the ancient Province of Leinster. The place name translates as 'the assembly place of kings', and until the tenth century it was an important meeting place for state assemblies.

Navan
Navan is the county town of County Meath, located at the confluence of the River Boyne and its tributary, the River Blackwater. The place name is thought to come from Irish 'An Uamhain' (sometimes 'An Uaimh'), meaning 'the cave' or 'the cavern'. In 1922, 'An Uaimh' was adopted as the town's official name, but it proved unpopular and in 1971 it reverted to the English name of Navan, the only palindromic place name in Ireland.

Newry
According to legend, St Patrick is supposed to have founded a monastery here in the fifth century and planted a yew tree at the head of the strand of Carlingford Lough. Consequently, the early Irish name for this city in County Down, 'Iobhar Chind Trachta', means 'yew tree at the head of the strand'. Its present-day name in Irish is the shorter version, 'An Iuraigh', meaning 'the grove of yew trees', and sometimes even simpler as 'An tIur', meaning 'the yew tree'.

Newtownards
The first record of the township of Newtownards (known locally as 'Ards'), occurs in 1177 when the Norman knight, Sir John de Courcy arrived in the Ards area and immediately divided it into small counties, one of which was the 'County of Blaethwyc of the Ardes'. It was in this newly created county that the New Town of the Ardes was built. In Gaelic, this County Down township is 'Baile Nua na hAirde', referring to the Arde Peninsula, but was originally known as 'Ul Bhlathmhaic', which translates as '(town of the) descendants of Blathmhac'. Blathmhac means 'famous son'; his father was Aed Slaine, the son of Diarmait MacCerbaill, an ancestor of the O'Neill clan who dominated Ireland from the late sixth century until the rise of High King Brian Boruma (sometimes 'Boru'), in the tenth century. Even earlier evidence has been unearthed of a settlement dating from the Bronze Age, between 2000 and 300 BC, around Scrabo Golf Club, which overlooks Newtownards itself. The hill is also the site of an Iron Age fort which dates from around 500 BC. The 'Newtown' element of the place name dates from 1613, when James I incorporated the township under the designation of the 'Provost, Free Burgesses and Commonalty of the Borough of Newtowne'.

Offaly, County
County Offaly (formerly known as King's County), lies within the Province of Leinster, in the Republic of Ireland. Its Irish name is 'Contae Uibh Fhaili', which translates as '(place of the) descendants of Failge'. Failge was the son of Cathair Mar, the legendary leader of the Ui Failge, which became known as the Offaly people, after which the county is named. It had been named King's County in tribute to Queen Mary's husband, Philip of Spain, but reverted to its original Irish

name, following the Irish War of Independence and the establishment of the Irish Free State in 1922.

Omagh
Located on the River Strule in County Tyrone, and in the Fermanagh and Omagh district of south-west Ulster, Omagh is represented in Irish as 'An Omaigh' or 'An Oghmaigh', which translates as 'the virgin plain'. A monastery is believed to have been established on the site of the town about 792 AD, and a Franciscan friary was founded in 1464. But Omagh township really began in 1430 when the O'Neills of Dungannon included it as part of their territory, and MacArt O'Neill established its castle, reputedly the oldest building in the township. The place name that was applied at that time was 'Oigh Rath', meaning 'seat of the chiefs'. By the time of the rebellion of 1641, the demography of Ulster was irrevocably changed and the English language had gradually begun to supplant Gaelic, from which time the present form of the place name began to appear.

Oxmantown
The name of the City of Dublin district of Oxmantown (or Oxmanstown) is a corruption of the original Viking name, 'Austmannatun', meaning 'settlement (or homestead) of the Eastmen'. These Scandinavian 'Eastmen' or 'Ostmen' established a fortified settlement just north of the city near the River Liffey. The Irish name for the district is 'Baile Lochlannach', meaning 'Scandinavian settlement'. Over time the place has been known as 'Ostmantown' and 'Ostmaneby'.

Ra-/Rath- (prefix)
In many Irish place names the prefix 'ra', 'rat' or 'rath' refers to an ancient Celtic ring-fort or early defensive earthwork. There are a hundred or more such place names in Ulster and Eire, including Ratallan in County Roscommon ('Rath tSailainn', meaning 'ring-fort of the salt'), Ratass in County Kerry ('Rath Teas', meaning 'southern ring-fort'), Rathgar in Dublin ('Rath Garbh', meaning 'rough ring-fort'), Rathmoyle in County Kilkenny ('An Rath Mhoal', meaning 'the bald ring-fort'), and Rathnure in County Wexford ('Rath an Iuir', meaning 'fort of the yew tree').

Rahugh
This is a civil parish in County Westmeath, sometimes known as 'Bathue' or 'Rathue', which was an early Christian site founded inside a ring-fort (or 'rath') in the sixth century by Aed mac Bricc, also known as St Aed and as St Hugh of Rahugh. Its Irish name is 'Rath Aodha' or 'Raith Aeda Meic Bric', meaning 'the ring-fort of St Aed'. St Aed was related to the ruling dynasty of the O'Neills.

Raphoe
The County Donegal town of Raphoe (sometimes 'Raffoe'), derives its place name from the Irish words 'rath', meaning 'ring-fort' and 'bhoth' meaning 'hut'. This

Ireland Northern Ireland (Ulster) & the Republic of Ireland (Eire)

is thought to refer to early wattle and daub huts surrounding a fortified mound probably built by monks in the sixth century when St Columba (also known as St Colmcille), founded a monastery settlement here.

Rathconrath
The village of Rathconrath in County Westmeath in the Province of Leinster has the Irish name 'Rath Conarta', which translates as 'ring-fort of the covenant'. It is thought that Scandinavian settlers built a fort here having made a treaty or pact with its indigenous Celtic tribes.

Ros-/Ross- (prefix)
More than forty places in Ireland begin their names with the prefix 'Ros', which generally translates as 'wood' or 'woodland', but may also indicate a headland or promontory. They tend to be followed either by the personal name of the owner, chieftain or founder of the original settlement or else descriptions of the local geography. A few examples of the former include Roscrea in County Tipperary ('Ros Cre', meaning 'Cre's wood'), and Ross Carbery in County Cork ('Ros O gCairbre', meaning 'wood of the O'Cairbre family'). Examples of the latter type include Roscor in County Fermanagh ('Ros Corr', meaning 'round promontory'), Rossglass in County Down ('Ros Glas', meaning 'green headland') and Rossbeigh in County Kerry ('Ros Beithe', meaning 'headland of the birch trees').

Roscommon, County
Roscommon is one of the five counties of the Province of Connacht. It is thought that St Comain founded a religious settlement in Roscommon in the eighth century and the Irish name, 'Ros Comain', meaning 'St Comain's wood' reflects his residence there. He became the abbot of the monastery and Bishop of the emergent township of Roscommon.

Saul
Saul is a village in County Down, whose Irish name is 'Sabhall', meaning 'barn'. The name emerged when St Patrick arrived in Ireland in 432 AD and converted a local chieftain called Diochu mac Trichim (known as 'Diochu of Sabhall') to Christianity, said to be his first convert in Ireland. Reputedly, Diochu donated his barn to the saint for holding services. According to tradition, St Patrick died in Saul in March 461 and St Patrick's Memorial Church now stands on the spot where the barn is thought to have stood.

Skerries
The Skerries is a coastal township and fishing port in Fingal, Dublin County, whose place name is Norse in origin and combines the words 'skere', meaning 'rocky', and 'ey', meaning 'island(s)'. In Irish the name is 'Na Sceiri' which translates as

'the reefs' or 'rocky islands', a reference to the rocky coast and the offshore islands of Red Island, Colt Island and St Patrick's Island.

Slieve- (prefix)
There are around thirty places in Ireland that begin their names with the prefix 'slieve'. The element comes from the Irish Gaelic word 'sliabh', meaning 'mountain'. This is generally followed by a second name element which is descriptive of the mountain, or identifies the name of the person who owned it or was an early leader or chieftain of the territory in which it lies. Examples include Slieve Ban in County Down ('Sliabh Ban', meaning 'white mountain'), Slieve Gallion in County Derry ('Sliabh gCallan', meaning 'mountain of the heights'), Slievemore in County Tyrone ('An Sliabh Mor', meaning 'the big mountain'), Slieve Donard in County Down ('Sliabh Donairt', meaning 'Donart's mountain'), and Slemish in County Antrim ('Sliabh Mis', meaning 'Mis's mountain').

Sligo, County
The town and county of Sligo in the Province of Connacht derive their name from the River Garavogue, whose Irish name is 'Sligeach', meaning '(place with an) abundance of shells' or 'shelly place'. The River Garavogue is known for the shellfish in its estuary, large quantities of which have been found dumped in its waters. The original Irish name for the river was 'An Gharbhog', meaning 'little rough one'. In the first century, the county was part of the territory of the Nagnatae tribe, and their main settlement was at a place called Nagnata, reputedly somewhere near the present-day town of Sligo.

Strabane
The village of Strabane (sometimes spelled 'Straban'), in County Tyrone, gets its place name from the Irish 'An Srath Ban', meaning 'the white strath', or 'the white water-meadow'. A strath is a large valley that is wide and shallow – most often a river valley, and in this case specifically the Mourne River. The area was originally territory of a northern Celtic tribe known as the Orighella.

Tallaght
Tallaght is a large suburb of Dublin and was the site of a monastic settlement founded by St Maolruain sometime around the eighth century. An early Irish name for the place was 'Tamhlacht Maolruain'. 'Tamh' is an old Gaelic word for the plague and 'tamh-leacht' meant 'plague pit' or 'plague graveyard', a reference to the more than nine hundred plague victims who were buried here in the Middle Ages.

Tipperary, County
County Tipperary was named after the town of Tipperary, whose Irish name is 'Tiobraid Arann', meaning 'well of the Ara'. The well in question lay in the town's

Ireland Northern Ireland (Ulster) & the Republic of Ireland (Eire)

Main Street but is now covered over, and the Ara is the name of the river that flows through the town. The ancient well is thought to have been important to the Celtic tribes of the Crotraighe, Eoghanacht and Artraighe, who settled the region before the territory was taken over by the Deise in the fifth century.

Tobereendoney
The small village of Tobereendoney in the north of County Clare is an ancient site of significant religious importance on account of its so-called 'healing well' ('an Tobar'). In Irish the place name is 'Tobar Ri an Domhnaigh', meaning 'the king of Sunday's well'. The town name is often shortened to 'Tubber'.

Tralee
Tralee is the capital town and administrative centre of County Kerry. It takes its name from the River Lee, which flows into Tralee Bay. Its Irish spelling is 'Tra Li', and was formerly 'Traigh Li', meaning 'strand of the River Lee'. The strand in question is the three mile stretch of sandy sea shore. The earliest recorded people to inhabit the Tralee area were the Ciarraige, a Pictish tribe from what is now Sligo and Roscommon. The Celtic Fir Bolg arrived some years later and settled in North Kerry where they eventually became known as the Corcu Dùibne.

Tull-/Tully- (prefix)
The Irish prefix 'tull' or 'tully' translates as 'hillock'. There are a few dozen towns and villages in Ireland which include one or the other of them into their place names. These include the likes of Tullintrain in County Derry ('Tulaigh an Trein', meaning 'hillock of the warrior'), Tullycarnet in County Down ('Tulaigh Charnain', meaning 'hillock of the little cairn'), Tullaherin in County Kilkenny ('Tulach Iarainn', meaning 'hillock of iron'), and Tulloha in County Kerry ('Tulach Atha', meaning 'hillock of the ford').

Tullamore
The town of Tullamore in County Offaly has the Irish name 'Tulach Mhor', which means 'big hillock' or 'great mound'. The hillock in question refers to the one on which the Church of St Catherine currently stands, and was at one time part of the ancient Kingdom of Meath.

Tullyhogue
The small village of Tullyhogue (also spelled spelt 'Tullaghoge' or 'Tullahoge') in County Tyrone was the ceremonial place where the ancient kings of Ulster, the 'Cenel nEogain', were crowned as 'The O'Neill'. Its Irish name is 'Tulaigh Og', which translates as 'hillock of the youths (or young warriors)', a reference to the young men who participated in the sports and games that were once held there. The date of the construction of Tullyhogue Fort is not known, but it is thought to have been in existence long before it became important for the investiture of the O'Neills. The site was abandoned in the sixteenth century.

Tyrone

According to some accounts, at the time of Ptolemy the area around Tyrone was inhabited by the Celtic Scoti tribes. The term 'Scoti' referred to all Gaelic people, whether Scottish or Irish, so the term was somewhat loosely used. The present-day name of the town and the county comes from the Irish, 'Tir Eoghain', meaning 'land of Eoghan'. Tyrone was the traditional seat of the O'Neill clans, who were probably the most powerful of the Gaelic Irish families in Ulster until the seventeenth century.

Ulster, Province of

The Province of Ulster derived its name from a time when the region was known by the ancient name of Ulaid, whose capital was at Emain Macha, near Armagh, the former seat of the ancient kings that ruled over most of the north of Ireland in pre-Norman times. In common with Munster and Leinster, the last element of the original Gaelic place name, 'ster' comes from the Irish word 'stair', meaning 'province'. Therefore the present day name translates as 'land (or province) of the Ulaidh'. Ulster is divided into six counties: Antrim, Armagh, Down, Fermanagh, Derry (or Londonderry) and Tyrone.

Ushnagh

Ushnagh is a hill in County Westmeath whose Irish name is 'Uisneagh' or 'Uishneach', which means 'place of fawns', though the reference remains obscure. In ancient times the Hill of Uishneach was regarded as the centre of the island of Ireland where annual Gaelic May Day ceremonies, including the so-called 'fire festival of Bealtaine' were held. The hill is now regarded as a National Monument.

Vartry, River

The River Vartry in County Wicklow, or in Irish 'Abha bhFear Tire' (sometimes 'Abhainn Fheartrai'), has a name that means 'river of the men of the district'. The river runs from the Wicklow Mountains to the Broad Lough Bird Sanctuary at the Irish Sea, and since the passing of the Dublin Waterways Act in 1861 it has been an important source of water for the City of Dublin. According to J B Bury's *The Life of St Patrick and His Place in History*, the saint landed in Ireland at Inverdea, at the mouth of the River Vartry.

Waterford

According to Ptolemy, writing at the turn of the first century, the Celtic Menapii tribe had occupied the present-day County of Wexford for several centuries before the Romans arrived. That said, the town and port were effectively established by Viking settlers in the eighth century. Consequently, the Waterford place name originated in the Norse word 'Vadrefjord', which means 'wether inlet', a reference to the place where castrated rams, (known as wethers) were loaded aboard ships for export. Its present-day Irish name is 'Port Lairge', which translates as 'bank of the haunch', is a description of the river bank here. Much earlier its Irish name had been 'Cuan na Greine', meaning 'harbour of the sun'.

Westmeath, County
County Westmeath once formed part of the ancient Kingdom of Meath when the island of Ireland was divided into five provincial dynasties, and was then known by the name 'Eircamhoin', or 'the Western Division'. The Irish name is 'An Iarmhi', meaning 'western Meath', where the word 'meath' derives from 'midhe' and means 'middle district (or province)', on account of its location in the geographical centre of Ireland. The county was formerly created as part of the Province of Leinster in 1542.

Wexford, County
In the first century, at the time of Ptolemy, the greater portion of what is now County Wexford was the territorial tribeland of the Menapii, which bordered the former River Modonus, now called the River Slaney. Their chief town was Menapia, which is thought to have occupied the site of the town of what is now Wexford. The present place name came into being when Vikings established it as a colony in the ninth century; they called it 'esker fjord', meaning 'inlet by the sandbank'. The contemporary Irish name for the town is 'Loch Garman', meaning 'lake of the (River) Garman', a reference to a pool in the Slaney estuary at the narrow approach to Wexford Harbour, which was earlier known as the Garma (an Irish word meaning 'headland'). The town gave its name to the county.

Wicklow
According to Ptolemy, writing in the year 130 AD, the inhabitants of the present County of Kildare were Celtic tribes of Belgic-Gaulish extraction. However, the place name probably comes from the old Viking word 'Vykyngrlo', which means 'meadow of the Vikings', given that Norsemen had settled in the River Vardy estuary region in the early ninth century. The Irish name for Wicklow is 'Cill Mhantain', which translates into English as 'church of St Mantan'. Mantan is thought to have been a disciple of St Patrick who arrived here in the year 432 AD.

Part Four

The Isle of Man

Manx, Old Norse & Celtic Place Names
When Ned Maddrell died in 1974, he was thought to have been the last surviving native speaker of Manx, and it was widely held that the language was entirely lost. However, proactive efforts have been made to resuscitate its written and spoken forms since then, so that by 2015 it is estimated that almost two thousand people spoke it as a second language. Manx is now being taught in many primary schools and has begun to appear on road signage.

The Manx language is a Goidelic form of the Celtic language family, related to both Irish and Scottish Gaelic, having been brought to the island by Irish monks in the fourth century. It is now regarded as a 'heritage language' of cultural significance. In Manx the language is known as 'Gaelg' or 'Gailck', meaning 'Gaelic'.

St Patrick's Chair, near Marown, Isle of Man.

The Isle of Man

In the first years of the ninth century, invasions by Norsemen added a Scandinavian element to many of the island's place names. It was they who established the island's first parliament, the Tynwald, in 979 AD, at which time it came under the rule of Magnis III, King of Norway. It was not until the 1266 Treaty of Perth that Norway effectively ceded the island to Scotland. Thirty years later, Edward I of England took possession, and in 1313 it fell to Robert Bruce after he laid siege to Castle Rushen, at which time it returned to being a Scottish possession. It would be another six hundred years before the Isle of Man would gain a degree of home rule when its own Legislative Council was appointed by the English Crown in 1866.

Celtic Places and Placenames

The Manx Place Names

Andreas
Andreas, or Kirk Andreas, is a small village and historic parish located in the north of the Isle of Man, one of the island's seventeen parishes. The place name in Manx is 'Skeerey Andreas'. Its church is dedicated to St Andrew, after whom it derives its name. In the churchyard there are a number of ancient and distinctive Celtic crosses.

Arbory
The Isle of Man Parish of Arbory (or in Manx, 'Cairbre'), is located in the south of the island in the sheading of Rushen. Its Manx name comes from the dedication of the parish to the Irish saint, St Cairbre (sometimes 'Corbre' or 'Cairpre'), about whom little is known. The parish was recorded at the end of the thirteenth century by its Latin name, 'Ecclesia Sancti Carber', reflecting the aforesaid saint, thereafter becoming 'Kirk Carbery' and 'Kirk Arbory' and finally, simply Arbory.

Ballabeg
Ballabeg is a small village in the Parish of Arbory in the sheading of Rushen, in the south of the Isle of Man whose Manx name is 'Balley Beg', which simply means 'small homestead (or village)'. This is related to the Irish words 'bally', meaning 'village' or 'settlement' and 'beg', meaning 'small', both name elements being very closely related to Irish Gaelic.

Ballaugh
The name of the village of Ballaugh lies within the sheading of Michael. 'Ballaugh' derives from the Manx 'Balley-ny-Loghey' (or 'Balla Lough'), meaning 'place of the lake'. The lake in question once occupied the land depression now known as Ballaugh Curragh, which was drained around three hundred years ago.

Ballasalla
The village of Ballasalla is located on the Silver Burn in the Parish of Malew a few miles north of Castletown in the south-east of the island. Its name in Manx Gaelic is 'Balley Sallagh', (sometimes 'Balley ny Shellee'), meaning 'place of willows'.

Barregarrow
In the Manx language, Barregarrow, in the Parish of Kirk Michael, is known as 'bayr garroo', meaning 'rough road'. The area was a former mountain common, rough pasture or grazing land, which gave the district its name.

Braaid
Sometimes called 'The Braaid', this Iron Age roundhouse and the two nearby Viking long houses in the Parish of Marown were occupied well into the eleventh century. The apparent integration of styles suggests that the site may have been

originally a Celtic farm which was taken over or inherited by a Scandinavian settler. The site is now under the care and protection of Manx National Heritage. Thus far it has proved impossible to find an explanation as to the meaning of the place name.

Braddan
The Isle of Man Parish of Braddan as it is known today began around 1876 when its local church (the 'Old Kirk') was dedicated to St Brendan (or Braddan), from whom the parish gets its name. A church is known to have existed on this site for more than fourteen centuries, as evidenced by stones that survive from the earliest Celtic chapel. There are a total of nine runic crosses in the parish including Celtic and Scandinavian crosses of which the earliest is from around 600 AD.

Castletown
The name of the island settlement of Castletown is 'Balley Chashtal' in the Manx language. It is located within the historical Parish of Malew, and was the Manx capital until 1869. In 1370 it was known as 'Villa Castelli', which translates as 'village of the castle'. The present-day place name began to appear when the Middle English words 'castel' and 'toun' were combined to form Castletown. The castle in question, Castle Rushen, had originally been built in 1265 by Norse settlers in the town centre, and was reinforced and extended in the fourteenth century.

Colby
The village of Colby in the Parish of Arbory is thought to have derived its place name from two Viking words, 'col', meaning 'hill', and 'byr' meaning 'farm'. Hence, 'farm (on the) hill' or 'hill-farm'. Colby Glen is one of seventeen designated National Manx Glens.

Cregneash
Cregneash ('Creneash' or 'Cregneish') is a small village located on Mull Hill, a plateau overlooking the Calf of Man, in the extreme south-west of the Isle of Man. Much of the village forms the so-called 'Living Museum', which is dedicated to the preservation of the traditional Manx ways of life and is claimed to be 'one of the last strongholds of the Manx language'. The place name is from the Scandinavian 'krcikuness', which translates as 'crow ness' or 'kraka's ness'. This was the former name of the promontory forming Spanish Head and Black Head, and is now applied to the village. It is locally pronounced 'Greg n' Eash', which literally means 'rock of ages'.

Dalby
Dalby is a small hamlet in the Kirk-Patrick Parish near Dalby Mountain on the western coast of the Isle of Man. The origin of the place name is uncertain, but it may be derived from the Old Norse 'dalr', meaning 'valley' and 'byr', a farm or

settlement, so the name may be taken to mean 'farm (or settlement) in the valley'. In the Manx language the name is 'Ta Delbee'.

Douglas
Douglas, or in the Manx language 'Doolish', is the capital of the Isle of Man, having replaced Castletown as the island's seat of government in 1874. It is located at the confluence of the Dhoo and Glas rivers to form the River Douglas, which accounts for its place name. The outflow of the river forms the town's harbour. The settlement was first recorded in 1192 by the monks of St Mary's Abbey. It appeared again, as 'Dufglas' in 1257, the name having derived from the old Gaelic words 'dub' and 'glais', or the Celtic 'duboglassio', which roughly translate as 'black stream' or 'dark water'.

Glen Maye
Glen Maye (sometimes spelled as one word, 'Glenmaye'), has the Manx name 'Glion Muigh' or 'Glion Meay', which means 'luxuriant glen'. This small village is located three miles south of Peel, and celebrated for its spectacular bridged gorge and waterfall. The place name eminently describes the green fern-filled nature of the glen and its surrounding woodland.

Isle of Man
The Crown Dependency of the Isle of Man (or in the Manx language, 'Ellan Vannin'), is often referred to simply as 'Mann'. The word 'ellan' is derived from 'mannin' and simply means 'island'. It was known to the Romans as 'Mona', and an early form the name was written as 'Manu'. However, local tradition has it that it was Manannan, the Brittonic (Brythonic) and Gaelic sea god, who once ruled the island and gave it its name.

Jurby
Jurby, in the sheading of Michael, is one of the seventeen parishes of the Isle of Man. Its name in Old Norse is 'djura-by', meaning 'deer settlement' or 'animal park'. Early records show that a church dedicated to St Cecilia was already in existence when the Vikings arrived in the eighth century. A number of Viking burial mounds have been found in the parish as well as Manx crosses dating back to the sixth century.

Laxley
Laxley, or in the Manx language, 'Laksaa' (or 'Laxa'), is a village on the east coast of the Isle of Man. Its name derives from the Old Norse 'lax', meaning 'salmon' and 'a', which represents 'river'. Hence, taken together, these elements produce the word 'laxa' meaning 'salmon river', a reference to the Laxley River. The village is the site of the Great Laxley Wheel, known as 'The Lady Isabella', the largest surviving waterwheel of its kind in the world, and probably the island's biggest tourist attraction.

Lezayre
One of the Isle of Man's seventeen parishes, Lezayre is located in the north of the island (part of the so-called North Side Division) in the sheading of Ayre. The Isle of Man was historically divided into six sheadings, known in the Manx language as 'sheadinyn', areas which were subdivided into parishes. The name Lezayre means 'of the Ayre'. It is now part of the town of Ramsey.

Lonan
The Parish of Lonan lies on the River Laxey in the east of the island and is part of the historical South Side Division, in the sheading of Garff. The place name comes from St Adamnan (also known as Onan or Lonan), the Abbot of Iona who died in 704 AD; he is thought to have been the biographer of St Columba. Following his death, the church that was dedicated to his memory went by the name 'Kill Onan', that is 'church of St Onan'. Over time, the name was condensed to form Lonan, which became the name of the whole parish.

Malew
The Isle of Man Parish of Malew, in the sheading of Rushen, gets its name from the Celtic patron saint of the district, St Malew, who was also known as St Moluag. Kirk Malew Church has what is claimed to be the largest churchyard on the island, leading it to become known as 'the Westminster Abbey of the Isle of Man'.

Marown
The historic Parish of Marown (in Manx, 'Marooney'), is one of seventeen of the Isle of Man, and is located in the centre of the island. The parish name is dedicated to St Runius (sometimes known as St Ronan, or in Manx, 'Ma-Ronan'), and this is the origin of the name. Who Runius was is open to argument, but some have it as the so-called Bishop Ronan 'the Kingly', an ancient Christian martyr about whom little is known. Others prefer the Scottish Abbot, Ronan of Kingarth, who died in Bute in 737 AD. Yet a third offering suggests that he may have been a minor local holy man, whose name has been erroneously attached to other more celebrated persons.

Maughold
The Parish of Maughold is dedicated to St Maughold, who is associated with the early Celtic Church and venerated as the patron saint of the island. Traditionally, he was said by some to have been converted to Christianity by St Patrick, while others claim he had been expelled from Ireland by St Patrick himself. Whatever the truth of it, following his conversion, he retired to the Isle of Man to avoid worldly temptation and founded the church in Maughold in 447 AD, after which he was accepted as bishop by the Manx people.

Celtic Places and Placenames

Nairbyl

Niarbyl is a rocky promontory on the south-west coast of the Isle of Man, and is located between Port Erin and Peel. Its name in Manx is 'Yn Arbyl', which means 'the tail' for the way it extends as a long reef from the shoreline out into the Irish Sea.

Onchan

The name of the village and Parish of Onchan is 'Kione Droghad' in the Manx language, which means 'bridge head'. The name relates to the village location on a headland at the north side of Douglas Bay. Six Celtic slab crosses dated from the seventh to the twelfth centuries stand in the grounds of St Peter's church in Onchan, The church was a religious site in the Dark Ages, but the earliest known building was dedicated to St Conchan (sometimes Connachan) in the twelfth century when it was called 'Kirk Conachan'.

Peel

There are just over a thousand people on the Isle of Man who can speak the Manx language and often refer to Peel as 'Purt ny Hinshey', which means 'the harbour (or port) of the island'. The original Viking settlement was called 'Holmtown', from the Old Norse word 'holm' or 'hulm', meaning 'island' and the Middle English 'toun', a settlement. This name remained in use until the late seventeenth century. In 1392, a pele tower was built opposite the harbour, and the place was known in 1399 as 'Pelam'. The name derived from the Anglo-Norman word 'pel', meaning a palisade or fortified enclosure. Thereafter, it was known as 'Peeltown', which by the mid-nineteenth century had simply become Peel.

Port Erin

Port Erin is a former coastal fishing village in the south-west of the Isle of Man, in the ancient Parish of Rushen. Its Manx name is 'Purt Chiarn', meaning 'lord's port'. The 'Lord' element of the place name might refer to the Parish of the Holy Trinity, but it has also been suggested that the name might be interpreted as 'iron port'. Present-day Port Erin owes much of its existence to the Victorian tourists, who came for its sandy beach set in an enclosed harbour.

Port Soderick

The small hamlet of Port Soderick lies about three miles south of Douglas at a place where the River Crogga enters the sea. Its name in Manx is 'Purt Soderick'. The place became a Manx National Glen in 1975, and is a registered Dark Sky Discovery Site, well placed to observe the Northern Lights (Aurora Borealis).

Port St Mary

Port St Mary is a fishing village in the south-west of the island that takes its name from the former Chapel of St Mary (in Manx, 'Keeill Moirrey'), which once overlooked Chapel Bay. The village name in Manx is 'Purt le Moirrey' or 'Purt-noo-Moirrey'.

Ramsey
The township of Ramsey is located in the Parish of Kirk Maughold at the mouth of the River Sulby, backed by the North Barrule Hills, on the north-east coast of the Isle of Man, and is the second largest town on the island. The place name stems from the Old Norse word 'hramsa', which was the name for wild garlic and translates as 'the stream where wild garlic grows'. It was known in Manx in the mid-thirteenth century as 'Ramsa' or 'Rhumsaa'.

Santon
St Sanctain's Church in the village of Santon stands on the site of an ancient church (or in Manx, a 'keeill'), which was established around fifteen hundred years ago. St Sanctain, after whom the place is named, was an Irish saint, a bishop and disciple of St Patrick. The place name has undergone many different spellings over the centuries and has been recorded as 'Sanctain', 'Santain' and 'Santan', before emerging in its present form as Santon.

Snaefell
At more than two thousand feet above sea level, Snaefell (in Manx, 'Sniaull') is the highest mountain on the Isle of Man. Its name means 'the snow mountain'.

Sulby
The name of the village and river of Sulby is of Scandinavian origin and reflects the Viking influence on the place names of the Isle of Man. In Old Norse the place was called 'Sola-bor' or 'Solabyr', meaning 'Soli's farm'. It has also been suggested that the name comes from a combination of 'Sula' and 'by', meaning 'cleft', a possible reference to a fork in the River Sulby.

Talkin
Talkin comes from Celtic words, similar to the Modern Welsh words 'tat', meaning 'head', 'brow' or 'forehead' and occasionally 'end', and 'can', meaning 'white'. Hence, 'white brow'. This is a reference to nearby Talkin Fell.

Part Five

Scotland & the English Borders

Picts and Scots

The British Isles were occupied long before Celtic-speaking peoples arrived in Scotland, a land which they may have called Albion. The term probably derived from the Latin word 'albus', meaning 'white', as these migrant peoples of continental Gaul referred to the 'White-land', that is, the land beyond the white chalk cliffs of southern England.

There are several ancient references to 'Albiones', the two islands of Great Britain and Ireland. The Greek philosopher Aristotle described two very large islands lying north of Gibraltar, which he called Albion and Ierne. The Roman author and philosopher Pliny the Elder described the islands as 'Bretannic Isles' and its people a 'Britanniae' (the Britons).

Scotland was sometimes also known as Pictavia or Pictland. However, people of the northern part of the British mainland continued to use the name 'Alba', an abbreviated form of Albion. Later accounts distinguish between what were called 'Fir Alban' (the men of Britain) and 'Scotii (or Scoti) Britanniae' (the Scots or Gaels of Britain).

The Callanish Stones, Isle of Lewis, Outer Hebrides.

Originally, 'Scotia' was a Latin term which the Romans often used for Ireland (though Tacitus referred to it as 'Hibernia'). Later, the name was specifically applied to Scotland, since the Scoti (or Scotii) peoples had originated in Ireland before migrating and resettling in Scotland. It was inevitable that sooner or later, the land of the Scoti became known as Scotia, 'the land of the Scoti', and eventually would emerge as Scotland.

The Caledonians, or 'Picti' (the Picts, or 'painted people') as the Romans sometimes called them, on account of the blue wode with which they painted their bodies, and their love of body tattoos, often went into battle naked, and were regarded as barbarians. These Picti were described by the Roman historian Tacitus in his *De Vita et Moribus Iulli Agricolae* (On the Life and Character of Julius Agricola) around 98 AD. He wrote: 'The physique of the people presents many varieties...the red hair and large limbs and dark complexion of the Britons, their unusually curly hair'. He went on to describe their way of fighting: 'Their strength lies in their infantry, but certain tribes also fight from chariots. Our greatest advantage in coping with tribes so powerful is that they do not act in concert. Seldom is it that two or three meet together to ward off a common danger. Thus, while they fight singly, all are conquered'.

Scotland and the Romans

Despite the power of the Roman war machine which had already overrun most of southern England, indigenous Caledonian tribes mounted fierce resistance. In 83 AD, ahead of a large military force, Agricola, invaded southern Scotland, lands that were dominated by the Caledonii tribe (sometimes known as the Caledones or Calidones), whose territory became commonly known as Caledonia. Agricola had already conquered the tribes of the Lowlands and at a place known as Mons Graupius in the Grampian Hills, 30,000 Caledonian tribesmen, led by Calgacus, confronted the legions and a ferocious battle took place in which 10,000 were slain. According to Tacitus, only 350 legionaries died in the battle and it was a resounding defeat for the Caledonians.

Notwithstanding this initial defeat, the Caledonian tribes of Highland Scotland were never completely vanquished; they continued to raid and harry Roman encampments in guerrilla-type raids so that their continual aggressive resistance eventually proved too costly for the Romans to contain. Faced with eastern European threats to Rome itself, troops were withdrawn, including a substantial cohort of the Ninth Spanish Legion (the Legio VIIII Hispana), so that the occupation of Scotland was effectively aborted.

According to popular legend, the withdrawn legionaries were the lucky ones: the remainder of the Ninth Legion seems to have disappeared completely, some say in the Scottish Lowlands, wiped out in battle against the Picts. Others maintain it more likely that it was transferred to the Middle East.

Two further expeditions were made to conquer the Highlands. Both failed on account of the insufficiency of Roman resources on the ground. Thus, the legions were withdrawn back to the Solway-Tyne region and the English borderlands. In 84 AD, Agricola himself was recalled to Rome.

Celtic Places and Placenames

The Roman legions had met their match in Scotland after which both the emperor Hadrian and later Antoninus built walls to mark the limit of the empire on the English border, deeming Scotland not worth the effort. As a result, the old Iron Age culture, its Gaelic language and religion continued more or less unhindered and unmodified by the Latin which Rome imposed upon all of its conquered territories.

Scottish Gaelic

Following the Act of Union between England and Scotland in 1707, the English increasingly dominated every aspect of Scottish life. First came the so-called Highland Clearances, where English landlords evicted Scottish crofters from their homes and lands to make way for more profitable sheep pasture. This inevitably saw the disintegration of the clan system, as well as rural depopulation, food riots and forced mass migration to America, Australia and Canada, especially to Nova Scotia ('New Scotland').

The Clearances saw Scotland become a divided nation. While the Lowlands were more aligned and integrated with England and adopted English as their primary language, the northern Highlands clung on to what they could of a traditional Gaelic culture and language. This division intensified to a point where Scottish Highlanders took up arms in support of Charles Edward Stuart ('Bonnie Prince Charlie', sometimes known as 'the Young Pretender'), in his claim to the English throne in a period known as the 'Glorious Revolution'. In the event, Charles and the Jacobite cause were roundly defeated at the Battle of Culloden in 1746 and Highland forces were decimated, its survivors forced to flee. Those Jacobites that were caught were imprisoned or executed, their lands and estates confiscated.

There followed a period which saw the draconian repression of all traces of 'Scottishness' and the dismantling of Scottish Gaelic culture. Bagpipes and plaid kilts were banned by law, as the speaking of Gaelic had so been since outlawed by the Crown in 1616. English became the language of education, trade, business and law, while the vestiges of Gaelic that survived were relegated to a peasant underclass as a virtual underground language.

Thankfully, things have moved on. Today, active efforts are being made to revive Gaelic, and a survey in 2015 revealed that around 60,000 Scots were estimated to be speaking it, especially in the far north and outer island groups. Scots Gaelic is increasingly found in schools and in dedicated television and other media channels. Roads and railway signage is now commonly seen in both English and Gaelic. Organisations like 'Feisean nan Gaidheal' have actively raised awareness of traditional Gaelic music. Further, the Scottish Government set up 'Bord na Gaidhlig' (The Gaelic Board) in 2005 to promote the use of the Gaelic language and culture around the world. The Board was empowered to require public bodies to formulate Gaelic Language Plans for their region. Also in 2005, the Scottish Parliament passed the Gaelic Language (Scotland) Act to secure the Gaelic language as an official language of Scotland with equal status to English.

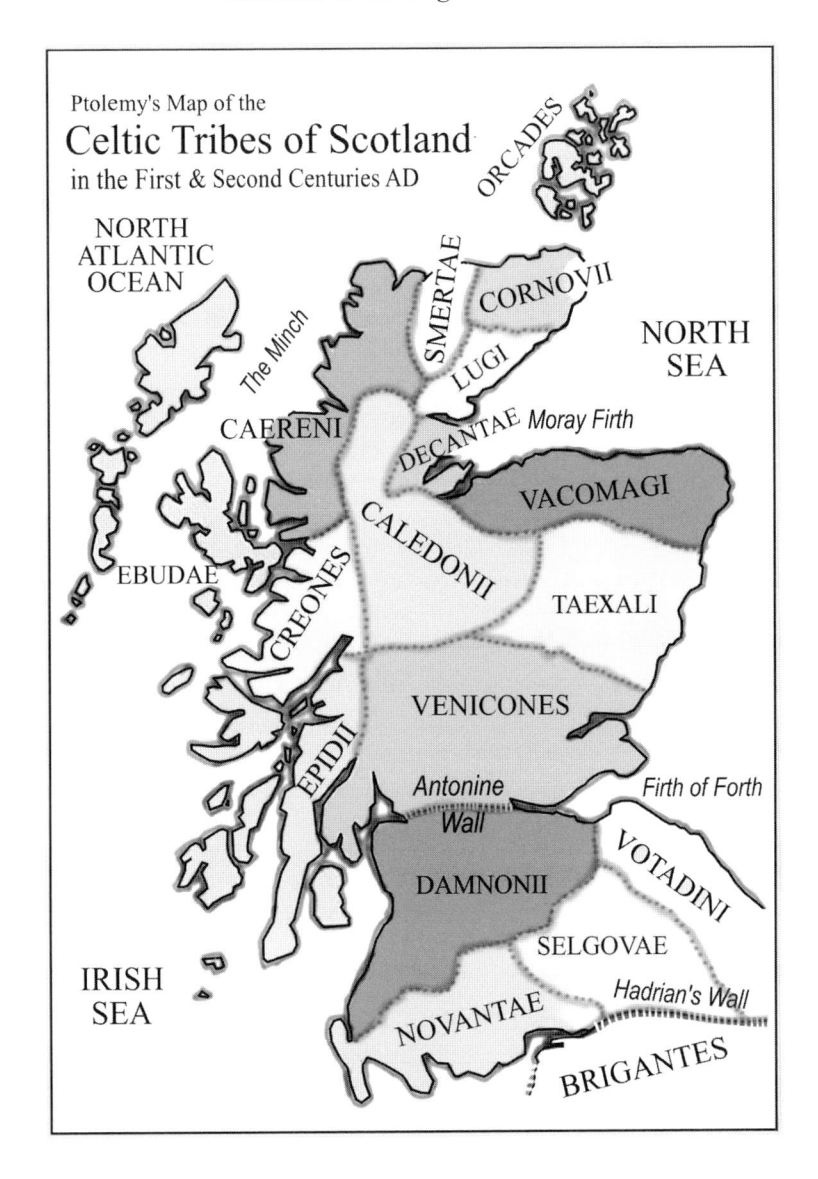

Scotland and the Vikings

The Celtic roots of Scottish Gaelic are still to be found in place names but significant modifications came to Scots and Gaelic when in the early ninth century, Vikings from Norway arrived in northern Britain. In what became known as 'the Viking Age', many Norsemen settled and established viable communities, especially in outer island groups like the Hebrides, Orkney and Shetland, and the names which they gave to their settlements reflect their occupation and domination of Scotland

Celtic Places and Placenames

for the next three hundred years. As a former Viking colony, studies have shown that today some twenty per cent of Orcadians possess Scandinavian DNA.

The end of the age of the Vikings began in the eleventh century, following the Norman Conquest, but the final blow came in October 1263 at the Battle of Largs, when victorious Scots defeated the army of King Haakon IV and finally drove the last Vikings from Scotland. But the Viking legacy persists and a significant number of Scottish place names still show Scandinavian influence, while some are entirely of Old Norse origin.

Meantime, the border and lowland regions of Scotland saw far less Nordic influence, due to their geographic proximity to England. Given that the borders have been fluid throughout the centuries, many of the towns and villages of southern Scotland have been part of England for some of that time, and place names have been Anglicised or contain partial Old English elements, as some of the townships that follow demonstrate.

The Scottish Place Names

Aber- (prefix)
This is a common prefix in Scottish Gaelic place names, which relates to the mouth, confluence or estuary of a river. Scotland shares this word prefix in common with other Celtic nations, especially with Wales. There are other examples than have been listed here, but as a general rule, 'aber' is followed by the name of a river which identifies its location. For example: Aberlour in Moray (at the confluence of the River Lour) and Abernethey in Perthshire (at the confluence of the River Nethy).

Abercorn
Abercorn is a settlement in West Lothian whose place name has two possible explanations. One has it named after the Cornie (or 'Curnig' in Gaelic), a stream that runs through it, plus 'aber', meaning 'mouth' or 'estuary', in which case it may be taken to mean 'mouth of the Cornie stream'. Another cites 'curn', meaning 'cone-shaped hill', similar to the Cornish word 'kernan'. Taken together, a realistic translation of the place name might be 'estuary or river mouth by a cone-shaped hill'.

Abercrombie
The name of the Fife village of Abercrombie (or in Gaelic, 'Obar Chrombaidh' – anciently known as 'Abercrumbin'), translates as 'mouth of the Crombadh stream'. As currently no such stream of that name exists, and as the only possible candidate is Inverie Burn (also known as St Monan's Burn), it is a reasonable supposition that Crombadh may have been an earlier name for that stream.

Scotland & the English Borders

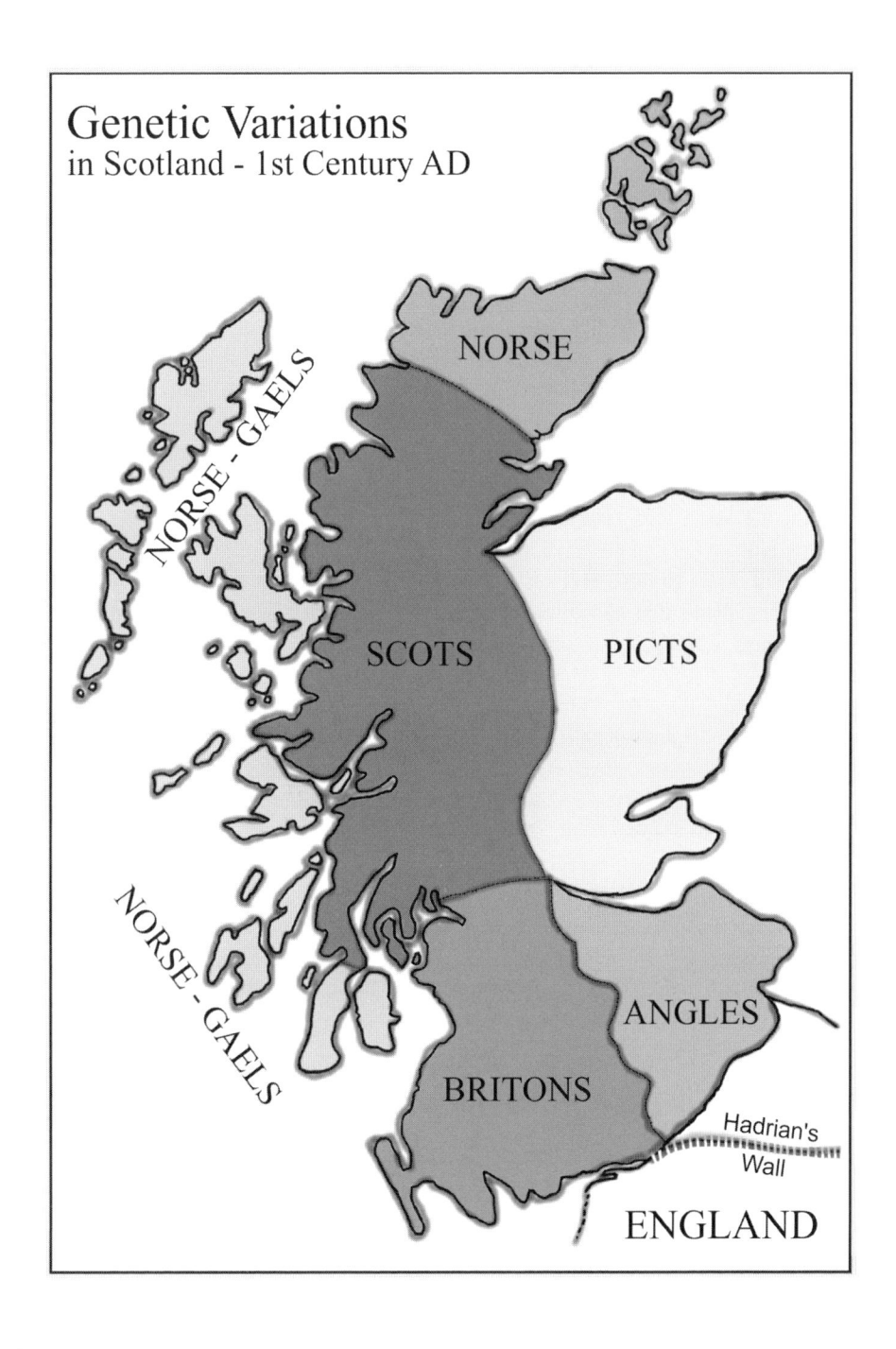

Genetic Variations
in Scotland - 1st Century AD

NORSE-GAELS

NORSE

NORSE-GAELS

SCOTS

PICTS

ANGLES

BRITONS

Hadrian's Wall

ENGLAND

Aberdeen

The City of Aberdeen has ancient roots. Its name translates as 'mouth of the River Don'. This early river name is thought to have derived its name from the Celtic goddess Devona, and, though contemporary Aberdeen lies on the River Dee, Old Aberdeen lies at the mouth of the Don. In the late-twelfth century the place name was spelled 'Aberdon', and around 1214 it was recorded as 'Aberden'.

Aberfeldy

In Scottish Gaelic, this highland township in Perth and Kinross, located on the River Tay is known as 'Obar Pheallaidh'. The name stems from a combination of the Scots word 'aber', with the Brittonic Gaelic word 'phellaidh' a reference to the fifth century missionary St Paldoc (sometimes known as St Pallidius) who was sent to convert the Pictish tribes to Christianity. Alternatively, some prefer it named after Peallaidh, a water sprite that tradition has it haunts the place.

Aberfoyle

The Pictish word 'aber', refers to the confluence of the River Foyle. The river name is derived from the Gaelic word, 'poll' or 'phuill', which generally indicates a pool, but in this case a stream. The settlement is located in Stirling and marks the place where the Forth's two headstreams meet and converge. Consequently, the place name means 'confluence of the streams'.

Aberlady

There is some dispute over the interpretation of the place name of the East Lothian township of Aberlady (in Scots, 'Aiberleddy', and in Gaelic, 'Obar Lobhaite'). One version has the first element 'aber' as meaning 'estuary' and another has it derived from the Gaelic word 'abar', indicating a marsh. On balance, the former engenders most support, especially since the town has been a major harbour centre for fishing, sealing, and whaling since the Middle Ages. Aberlady has undergone many variations to its name over the centuries: it was known as 'Aberlessic' in the twelfth century, as 'Abirleuedi' and 'Aberlefti' in the thirteenth and in the fifteenth as 'Abirladye', 'Aberladye' and 'Abirlathie'. The second element of the place name derives from the Peffer Burn stream (historically known as 'the Leddie') that outflows into Aberlady Bay.

Aberlour

This Highland town in Moray derives its name from the Celtic word 'aber' and the River Lour, It means 'confluence of the River Lour', which flows into the River Spey at this point. The river name translates as 'talkative (or babbling) brook'. The town name was formally changed to Charlestown of Aberlour in 1812, after the son of Charles Grant, who laid out the original village.

HISTORIC COUNTIES & SHIRES OF SCOTLAND
Before 1974

KEY TO COUNTIES

ABERDE = Aberdeenshire
ANG = Angus
ARG = Argyl
AYR = Ayrshire
BANF = Banffshire
BER = Berwickshire
BUT = Bute
CAITH = Caithness
CLA = Clackmannanshire
CRO = Cromartyshire
DUM = Dumfriesshire
DUN = Dunbartonshire
E = East Lothian
ELG = Elginshire
FIF = Fife
INVER = Inverness-shire
KINCA = Kincardineshire
KINROS = Kinross-shire
KIRK = Kirkcudbrightshire
LAN = Lanarkshire
MID = Midlothian
MOR = Moray
NA = Nairnshire
PEE = Peeblesshire
PERT = Perthshire
REN = Renfrewshire
RO = Ross-shire
ROX = Roxburghshire
SELK = Selkirkshire
STIR = Stirlingshire
SUTH = Sutherland
W = West Lothian
WIG = Wigtownshire

Abernethy
This village in Perth & Kinross is located at the mouth of the Nethy Burn (River) and has the Scottish Gaelic name, 'Obar Neithich'. The name was 'Aburnethige' in the tenth century, where it had been the religious centre of the Southern Picts. The river name comes from the Pictish word 'nectona', meaning 'pure', after the Celtic river goddess Nectonos. The remains of a hillfort lie just outside the village and a Roman camp was located nearby in the river valley.

Aboyne
In Scots this Highland village, located on the River Dee in Aberdeenshire is known as 'Abyne', and in Gaelic as 'Abeidh'. The place name is thought to derive from the Gaelic 'abh', meaning 'river', 'bo', a 'cow', and 'fionn', meaning 'white', which translates as '(place by the) white cow river', a possible reference to the Auroch, wild white cattle which were widespread across the British Isles during the Bronze Age. The full place name is Charleton of Aboyne, after Charles Gordon, 1st Earl of Aboyne, who established the township in 1670.

Acharacle
Acharacle is a small village in Ardnamurchan in Argyle County. In Gaelic, the place name is 'Ath Tharracail' which comprises two elements: 'ath', signifying a shallow river crossing and the name of a Norseman called Tarracal, who may have been the founder of the original settlement. Hence, 'Tarracal's ford'.

Achnashellach
Achnashellach in Glen Carron, Wester Ross in the Scottish Highlands has the Gaelic name 'Achadh nan Seileach', which translates as 'field of the willows'. Achnashellach was the site of an inter-clan battle between the Camerons and the Mackay and Muno clans, said to have taken place in 1505.

Ailsa Craig
The South Ayrshire island of Ailsa Craig (or in Gaelic, 'Creag Ealasaid'), is located in the Firth of Clyde. In the sixteenth century the place was known as 'Elsay', from a Gaelic word 'aillse', meaning 'fairy' and with the affix 'creag', meaning 'rock', it later became 'Aillse Creag', meaning 'fairy rock'. There is a small limited number who prefer the name as 'Creag Alasdair', meaning 'Alasdair's rock', but this seems less credible.

Airdrie
Airdrie's name comes from the Gaelic words 'ard', meaning 'high', and 'ruighe', a slope. Hence, '(place on a) high slope'. The town is located on a plateau spur of the Pentland Hills, some four hundred feet above sea level in North Lanarkshire.

Alness
Alness, or in Scottish Gaelic, 'Alanais', is a town on the River Averon (also historically known as the River Alness), where it meets the north shore of Cromarty Firth in Ross & Cromarty. It was a major port on the firth by the end of the seventeenth century. The river name is pre-Celtic and is thought to mean 'flowing water'. The name was recorded as 'Alenes' in 1226.

Angus
The Unitary Authority of Angus is one of the thirty-two local government council areas of Scotland. It was officially known as Forfarshire until 1928. The name 'Angus' derives from the eighth century Pictish king of that name, whose territory it was.

Annan
Annan is a town in Dumfries & Galloway, whose name in Scottish Gaelic is 'Inbhir Anainn', and means '(place by the) River Annan'. In the seventh century it was called 'Anava'. The town was the original seat of the de Brus family, of which its most famous member was Robert the Bruce. The river name is Celtic (or even older), and simply means 'water'. Later versions of the place name include 'Annandesdale' in 1179, the Old English word 'dael' being appended to mean 'valley'. It was recorded as 'Estrahanent' in 1124.

Anstruther
Anstruther is located on the Firth of Forth in the East Neuk of Fife, south of St Andrews, and the parish comprises Anstruther Easter and Wester, the fishing village of Cellardyke and the settlement of Kilrenny. Locally the place is known as 'Ainster' and in Scottish Gaelic the place name is spelled 'Ansruthair'. As to the meaning of the name, the first element is obscure, but it has been suggested that it might refer either to the Gaelic word 'an' or 'ain' which means 'driving', or 'aon', meaning 'one'. The second element is simpler and derives from 'sruthair', meaning 'burn' or 'stream'. The complete place name therefore means either 'driving (raging) current or burn', or 'place of (or on a) burn'.

Antonine Wall
The Antonine Wall runs east–west across Scotland from Bo'ness on the Firth of Forth to Old Kilpatrick on the Forth of Clyde. It was known to the Romans as 'Vallum Antonini' (the wall of Antoninus). Unlike the more substantial Hadrian's Wall to the south, Antonine's was a turf fortification on stone foundations. Construction began in 142 AD at the order of Roman Emperor Antoninus Pius, and took about six years to complete. Within twenty years it was virtually abandoned as the Roman legions were withdrawn to Hadrian's Wall as it proved an ineffective defence against the warring Pictish tribes of the region. For many years it was known as the Devil's Dyke, because people could not believe that it was man-made. Little now remains other than a shallow depression, though parts are sufficiently maintained by the Scottish Government to have earned it World Heritage Site status in 2003.

Applecross
The Highland coastal village of Applecross ('Obar Crosain' in modern Gaelic), was founded in the year 673 by St Maelrubha (sometimes St Maelrubai, or in Old Irish Gaelic, 'Mael Ruba'), an Irish monk, and is claimed to be the second oldest Christian settlement in Scotland. The place name comes from the Celtic words 'aber' and 'Crosan', the original name for the River Cross. Hence, '(place at the) mouth of the River Cross'. The name 'Crosan' actually meant 'little cross'. In 1080 the name was recorded as 'Aporcrosan'.

Arbroath
Arbroath has an ancient history dating back to its foundation as a small Pictish village in Angus, but the modern township as we know it began in 1178 when King William ('the Lion') founded the abbey around which the settlement would grow up and dedicated it to the martyred Archbishop Thomas Becket. The place name is derived from two elements: the first from the Celtic word 'aber', signifying a river mouth and the second from the Gaelic 'brothach', meaning 'seething' or 'boiling', which became the name of the river on which it stands. Arbroath, in its earlier name form of 'Aberbrothock', translates as '(place at the) mouth of the Brothock Burn'. It has been known by several variations over time, including 'Berbrothock', 'Aberbrothik', 'Aberbrothick' and 'Aberbrothwick'. The present-day version of the name, Arbroath, only dates from the mid-nineteenth century.

Ardnamurchan
Ardnamurchan is located on a peninsula in the Highland region where it has been inhabited for more than four thousand years, and many of its place names are predominantly Norse in origin, revealing historic Viking dominance of the region. That said, the name of the peninsula is entirely Gaelic and comprises the words 'ard', 'na', 'muir' and 'chon', which taken together respectively translate as 'height of the sea dogs'. The latter word is often taken to refer to sea otters, and this is the usual and preferred interpretation. However, it has been suggested that 'sea dogs' could also be a reference to pirates.

Ardrishaig
Ardrishaig is a coastal village on Loch Gilp, at the south-eastern entrance to the Crinan Canal in Argyll & Bute. Its name in Scottish Gaelic is 'Aird Driseig' (sometimes 'Rubha Aird Driseig'), meaning 'height (or promontory) of small brambles', based on 'ard' meaning 'height' and 'dris' meaning 'bramble'.

Ardrossan
The North Ayrshire town and port of Ardrossan's place name comes from three Scottish Gaelic words, 'ard', meaning 'height', 'ros', a 'headland', and the suffix 'an', meaning 'little'. Hence, 'height of the little headland'. The 'height' element distinguishes the place from the lower land on which

Saltcoats is now located. The settlement really began with the construction of the castle on Cannon Hill by the Norman knight Simon de Morville sometime around 1140.

Argyll
The Scottish Gaelic name of this county and district in western Scotland, sometimes called Argyllshire, is 'Oithir-Ghaidheal' (sometimes in Old Gaelic 'airer Goideland'), means 'coastal (or border) land of the Gaels', and was once part of the ancient Kingdom of Dal Riata. The Gaels (a word that translates as 'strangers' or 'foreigners') referred to in the place name began to arrive and settle in the area from the ninth century onwards, and were predominantly Old Norse-speaking migrants.

Arran
See: 'Isle of Arran'.

Auchinleck
Auchinleck is a town in East Ayrshire whose place name comes from the Gaelic words 'achadh', meaning 'field' and 'leac' meaning 'flat stone'. Hence, 'Achadh na Leac' ('field of flat stones'). These may possibly have been tombstones or the remains of ancient cairns. According to the Clan Auchinleck website, 'Auchinleck appears to have been one of those places where the ancient Celts held conventions and performed acts of worship'. The place name was recorded as 'Auechinlec' in 1239.

Auchterarder
Auchterarder is a small town located on high ground north of the Ochil Hills beside the River Ruthven in Perth & Kinross. Its place name reflects the topographical features of the local landscape in Scottish Gaelic as 'Uachdar Ard dobair', meaning 'upland of high water'. Its mile-and-a-half long High Street has given the town the popular name, 'The Lang Toun' (The Long Town). The town's name was recorded around 1200 as 'Ucherardouere'.

Auchtermuchty
The township of Auchtermuchty in Fife (in Gaelic, 'Uachdar Mucadaidh' and in Scots, 'Achad na Muic'), has a place name that means 'upland (or heights) of pigs'. Evidently the place was used in the past for rearing or grazing pigs or boars. In 1210 the name was recorded as 'Uchtermuckethin'.

Aultbea
The small fishing village of Aultbea in the North-West Highlands (in Gaelic, 'An t-Allt Beithe'), gets its name from two Gaelic words: 'allt', signifying a brook or a stream, and 'beithe', meaning 'birch'. Hence, '(place by the) stream where birch trees grow'.

Aviemore
The popular skiing resort of Aviemore in Strathspey is located about thirty miles south-east of Inverness. The Gaelic form of the name is 'An Aghaidh Mhor'. The 'Aghaidh' element is shrouded in mystery but may have devolved from an early Pictish word meaning 'cleft'. The antiquity of the original settlement is evidenced by the prehistoric stone circle situated in the town. Others have suggested that the name more properly translates as 'the big (mountain) face'.

Ayr
The township of Ayr is located where the River Ayr outflows into the Firth of Clyde, around forty miles south-west of Glasgow. The place name derives from an ancient Celtic word meaning 'watercourse'. The place was previously known as 'Inverair' (or 'Inverayr'), which meant 'mouth of the River Ayr', later shortened simply to 'Ayr'. In Scottish Gaelic the place name is 'Inbhir Air'.

Badenoch
The Highland district of Badenoch (in Gaelic, 'Baideanach') has a name taken from 'baithte', meaning 'drowned', and translates as 'drowned (or submerged) land'. It is located south of the River Spey in an area that is prone to frequent flooding – hence the place name.

Ballachulish
The name of this Highland village comes from the Gaelic and translates as 'homestead (or village) of the straits (or narrows)'. The Gaelic word 'baile' signified a townland or village settlement, similar to the Irish Gaelic word, and 'chaolais' indicated a place where a river narrows. Its location is at the point where Loch Leven enters Loch Linnhe through a narrow strait – hence the place name.

Ballantrae
This village and former fishing port of Ballantrae is located at the mouth of the River Stinchar in the district of Carrick, South Ayrshire. The place is known in Gaelic as 'Baile na Traigh', from 'baille', meaning 'village' and 'traigh', meaning 'shore'. Hence, 'village on the shore'. The present place name was created in 1617.

Ballater
Ballater is a township in Aberdeenshire, whose place name originally comprised two Gaelic elements: 'bealach', meaning 'pass' and 'dobhar' which referred to water. The Batter Burn stream flows through a mountain pass at this point which explains the place name. It was spelled 'Balader' and 'Ballader' in the early eighteenth century.

Balmoral
The Aberdeenshire estate of Balmoral has been owned by the Royal Family since Prince Albert purchased it for Queen Victoria in 1852. The place was first recorded as 'Bouchmorale' in 1451. The first element of the place name comes from the Gaelic word 'baile' signifying a dwelling or homestead. The second is from 'mor', meaning 'large', and the final suffix, 'ial', refers to an open space or clearing. Therefore the full name translates as 'dwelling in a large clearing'.

Banchory
This Aberdeenshire township, located on the north bank of the River Dee, about eighteen miles from Aberdeen, is surrounded by mountains, a fact that is reflected in its place name. It derives its meaning from the Gaelic word 'beannachar', meaning 'mountainous'. In Scots the place name is 'Banchry' and in Scottish Gaelic, 'Beannchar'.

Banff
The ancient Royal Burgh of Banff in Aberdeenshire (formerly Banffshire), stands on the River Deveron that was historically known as 'The Banff', which comes from the Gaelic word 'banbh', meaning 'piglet', or possibly 'buinne', simply 'a stream'. Another view suggests an early importation of the word 'banbha' into Scotland by Irish settlers. Then, as the Banff coat of arms shows the Virgin Mary carrying the Christ child; this last version suggests the name comes from 'bean-naomh', meaning 'holy woman'.

Bannockburn
This historic village in Stirling is known in Gaelic as 'Allt a' Bhonnaich' after the Bannock Burn, a stream that runs through the village to outflow into the River Forth. The first element of the place name comes from a Celtic word, similar to the Welsh 'bannog', meaning 'horn-shaped' or 'peaked', which describes the hill on which the source is located. The second is the Old English 'burna', meaning 'brook' or 'stream'. The place name literally means '(place at the) Bannock stream'. The name has also been spelled as 'Bannokburne'.

Barra
Barra's place name illustrates the synthesis of early Brittonic and Scandinavian cultures and languages in that the first element of the name, 'barr', is a Celtic word meaning 'hill' or 'hilly' and the second comes from the Old Norse 'ey', meaning 'island'. Barra is located in the Western Isles and its name means 'hilly island'. The place was known in the eleventh century as 'Barru', and was recorded around 1200 as 'Barrey'.

Barrhead
Barrhead is a town in East Renfrewshire, whose Scottish name is 'Baurheid', and in Gaelic is known as 'Ceann a' Bharra'. It is effectively tautological in that both

elements of the place name have the same meaning, but in different languages. In Gaelic, the word 'barr' means 'head' or 'top', as does the modern English word 'head'. Strictly translated therefore, the place name means 'head head'. It is presumed that, unable to understand Gaelic, some well-meaning person added the English word later, in the misapprehension that it somehow made the name simpler to understand and its meaning clearer, while the reverse is actually the case.

Bathgate
The West Lothian town of Bathgate gets its name from a Celtic word similar to the Welsh 'baedd', meaning 'wild boar', and 'coed', signifying a wood, forest or woodland. Hence, '(place in a) boar wood'. In Scots the name is 'Bathket' or 'Bathkit', and in Gaelic, 'Both Cheit'.

Bearsden
Despite what the name might imply, this East Dunbartonshire township located on the north-western edge of Glasgow, has a place name more related to wild boars than to bears. The name comes from the Old English words 'bar', meaning 'boar' and 'denu', meaning 'valley'. Hence, 'valley (where) boars (live)'. The earliest date for the place was when it was created as a Roman fort in the second century to billet legionaries who worked on the construction of the Antonine Wall.

Beith
Beith is a town in the Garnock Valley of North Ayrshire whose name descends directly from the Gaelic word 'beith', meaning 'birch'. Hence, '(place of the) birches'. The town was once known as the 'Hill of Beith'. Evidently, the hill in question was at one time densely covered with birch trees, although few if any still remain.

Benbecula
Benbecula in the Outer Hebrides has a Gaelic name of 'Beinn na Faoghla', which means 'hill of the ford' on account of the causeway crossing between Benbecula and the islands of North and South Uist. Apart from modestly high Ruabhal Hill, the island is otherwise quite flat, and the first element of the name is somewhat misleading. The last element of the Gaelic name comes from a Norse word for a ford.

Ben Cruachan
The Gaelic word 'beinn' (or 'ben' in modern Scottish), means 'mountain' and the mountain known as Ben Cruachan in Argyll & Bute has the Gaelic name 'Cruach na Beinne'. It means 'mountain of the stacks', from 'cruach', meaning 'pile' or 'stack'. This descriptive term refers to the various rugged peaks of differing heights which are its predominant visible feature. The name was recorded as 'Crechanben' in 1375.

Ben Vorlich

Located between Loch Lomond and Loch Sloy, the mountain of Ben Vorlich (in Gaelic, 'Beinn Mhurlaig'), is part of the Arrochar Alps in the former historic County of Dumbartonshire (which changed its name to Dunbartonshire in 1914). The Gaelic word 'mhurlaig' comes from two elements: 'mur' or 'muir', meaning 'sea', and 'lag', a bag or a sack. Hence, the 'sea bag' is a reference to the sack-shaped inlet at the head of Loch Lomond.

Biggar

The Scottish border town of Biggar was originally in South Lanarkshire before the old county ceased to exist in 1974. It derived its name from two Old Norse words, 'bygg', meaning 'barley', and 'geiri' which signified a triangular plot of land. Viking settlements were not uncommon during the Middle Ages; hence, this Scandinavian place name means 'triangular plot of land where barley is grown'. In 1170 the name was spelled 'Bigir'.

Blackwaterfoot

The small and ancient North Ayrshire village of Blackwaterfoot is located at the mouth of the Black Water (also known in its upper reaches as 'Clauchan Water') overlooking Drumadoon Bay, on the west coast of the Isle of Arran. The place name in Scottish Gaelic is 'Bun na Dubh Abhainn', which translates as 'bottom of the dark (or black) river'.

Blair Atholl

The name of this village in Perth & Kinross in Gaelic is 'Blar Athall' (and earlier, 'Blar Ath Fhodla'). The first name element, 'Blar' means 'plain', and the second translates as 'New Ireland'. The Irish connection came about when Irish Gaels settled in the region. Nowadays the place is universally celebrated for its malt whisky production.

Blairgowrie

Blairgowrie is a town in Perthshire which was simply known as 'Blare' in the thirteenth century. In Scottish Gaelic the name is 'Blar Ghobharaidh' or 'Blar Ghobhraidh'. This derives from the Gaelic word 'blar', meaning 'plain' (referring to the geographical feature). The second place name element, 'gowrie' is a corruption of 'Gabran', named after a sixth century Gaelic king. Hence, the full name translates as 'plain (or territory) of Gabran'. In 1604 the place was recorded as 'Blair in Gowrie'. Locals still refer to the place as 'Blair'.

Blantyre

In Gaelic this South Lanarkshire town's name is 'Baile an t-Saoir', and its exact meaning is obscure, though some relate the first element to the Welsh word 'blaen', meaning 'front'. The second element derives from 'tir', a Gaelic word meaning 'land'. The place name is therefore thought to represent 'front land' or 'edge land', possibly denoting land at the edge or foot of hilly or higher ground, but this is somewhat speculative. In 1289 the name was recorded as 'Blantir'.

Boat of Garten
This village in the Highland region has the Gaelic name 'Coit Ghairtean', which translates into English as 'ferry boat by the (River) Garten'. The ferry boat in question once crossed the River Spey at the point where it met the Garten at Gartenmore. The name 'Garten' itself derives from the Gaelic word 'gairtean', meaning 'cornfield' or 'standing corn'. In 1600, the place was recorded as 'Gart'. It is also known to some as 'Osprey Village', on account of the resident population of Ospreys.

Bonhill
In Gaelic, the West Dunbartonshire township of Bonhill is 'bot an uillt', which translates respectively as 'house', 'the' and 'stream'. Hence, 'house (beside) the stream'. The stream in question ran into the nearby River Leven. The place name has been spelled variously as 'Buchlul' in 1225, as 'Buthelulle' in 1270 and as 'Buchnwl' in around 1320.

Bonnybridge
The small town of Bonnybridge is situated close to the Forth & Clyde Canal near Falkirk, beside Bonny Water, which is a tributary of the River Carron. In Gaelic the place name is 'Drochaid a'Bhuinne' and in Scots, 'Bonniebrig'. The name translates as 'bonny' (a word still commonly used in Scotland), meaning 'beautiful'. Hence, '(place by the) bridge over Bonny Water'. It was recorded as 'Aqua de Boine', meaning 'beautiful water' in 1682.

Bonnyrigg
The precise meaning of the Midlothian village of Bonnyrigg's place name is obscure. The problem is compounded by the many different spellings it has undergone over the years. It was called 'Bonnebrig' in 1750, 'Bannockrigg' in 1766, as 'Bannocrig' in 1815. It was not until 1855 that the name was finally fixed, as a result of signage at the newly opened railway station where it was spelled Bonnyrigg. The name is commonly taken to mean '(place by the) bannock-shaped ridge', either from 'bannock', a flat oat bread, or something like the Welsh word 'bannog', meaning 'horn-shaped' or 'peaked', which is thought to be descriptive of the land ridge. Over time the word has been corrupted to 'bonny', meaning beautiful, handsome or pretty, and some maintain that the place name might thereby be more properly interpreted as '(place by the) bonny bridge'.

Bothwell

There are several theories as to the origin of the name of the North Lanarkshire village of Bothwell, but it is thought to be that it comes from the Gaelic or from the Middle English words 'bothe', meaning 'hut' or 'shelter' and the Old English 'wella', meaning 'well' or 'spring'. Therefore, possibly, 'hut by the well (or spring)'.

Braemar

This Aberdeenshire village on the River Dee has a name which in Scottish Gaelic is 'Braigh Mharr' and translates as 'the upland of Mar'. 'Braigh' is a Gaelic word meaning 'upper part' and the second element reflects its possession by the Jacobite Earls of Mar. The Earldom of Mar is one of the seven original Scottish earldoms, and is possibly the oldest peerage in Britain. The earls were the hereditary Chiefs of Clan Erskine and the Countess of Mar is the hereditary Chief of Clan Mar. In 1560 the place name was recorded as 'The Bray of Marre'.

Brechin

Brechin is a town and former Royal burgh in Angus. Its earliest record was in a charter by William the Lion, who reigned between 1165 and 1214. Later in 1296 it was the place where John Baliol handed over lordship of Scotland to the Bishop of Durham as the representative of Edward I of England. Brechin became a royal burgh in 1641. The town's place name in Scottish Gaelic is 'Breichinn', which translates as '(place of) Brychan', which some think is named after the Celtic druidical leader Briochan. Little is known about him, as the only mention of the aforementioned Druid is in Adomnan's *Life of Saint Columba*. Others cite the Gaelic words 'Bri-achan', meaning 'place of the slopes (or braes)'. This might be a reference to a sloping river bank on which the original settlement was built.

Bressay

Bressay, in the Shetland archipelago, derived its name from the Vikings who settled it. The name comes from the Old Scandinavian words 'brjost' meaning 'breast' and 'ey', meaning 'island'. Hence, 'breast island' – a reference to the island's distinctive shape.

Bridge of Allan

In Scots the name of this town in Stirling is spelled 'Brig Allan' and in Gaelic, 'Drochaid Ailein'. It is located north of the City of Stirling on the Allan Water, which is a tributary of the River Forth. The tribe of the Maetae occupied the territory and constructed the nearby hillfort during the Iron Age. Self-evidently, the place name means 'bridge over the (River) Allan', referring to that built in 1520 as a crossing of the road from Stirling to Perth. The name of Allan Water itself is thought to be of Celtic origin and might mean 'holy one'.

Brodick
In Gaelic, the name of this North Ayrshire township is 'Traigh a' Chaisteil' and in Scots, 'Breadhaig', which means 'castle beach'. It is the main village and ferry terminal on the Isle of Arran in the Firth of Clyde, The name is derived from the Scandinavian elements 'breithr', meaning 'broad' and 'vik', meaning 'bay', evidence of widespread Viking settlements in the area. The meaning of the resultant place name is '(place by the) broad bay'. It was known in the early fourteenth century as 'Brathwik' and by the mid-fifteenth as 'Bradewik'.

Brora
More evidence of the Scandinavian influence on Highland Scotland is the village of Brora (in Scottish Gaelic, 'Brura') in the east of Sutherland, which has a name derived from an Old Norse word meaning 'river with a bridge'. The name comes from the Scandinavian 'bru' (or 'bruar'), plus 'a', indicating the river, in this case the River Brora.

Broxburn
The West Lothian township of Broxburn (in Gaelic, 'Srath Bhroch'), gets its name from two Old English words, 'brocc', meaning 'badger', and 'burna', a brook or stream. Hence, 'stream where badgers live'.

Buckie
The former coastal fishing town of Buckie lies on the coast of the Moray Firth, and was formerly within the historic county of Banffshire. Its Scottish name is 'Bucaidh', which is derived from the Gaelic word 'boc', meaning 'buck', a male deer. The place name therefore means '(place where) male deer (are found)'. The name was taken from Buckie Burn, the local stream, which is also known as 'Buckpool'.

Burntisland
Unsurprisingly, the name of this coastal fishing town in Fife is thought to mean 'burnt island'. From the twelfth century the place was known as Wester Kinghorn, but it was renamed Burntisland in 1586, possibly on account of a fire which burned down fishermen's huts in the locality. Other sources suggest that it might have resulted from land cleared by fire for cultivation purposes. However, it has also been argued that it might be a corruption of 'Burnet's Land' after the personal name of its one-time owner. In 1540 the name was recorded as 'Bryant Iland' and at the beginning of the seventeenth century the name was spelled 'Bruntisland'.

Bute
In Gaelic the island of Bute in the Firth of Clyde is 'Eilean Bhoid' or 'An t-Eilean Bodach', and derived its modern name from the Gaelic or possibly Old Irish word

'bod', meaning 'fire'. The place name is taken to mean '(island of) fire'. This may have been a reference to signal fires or beacons lit to warn of Viking approaches. In 1093 the name was recorded as 'Bot' and in 1292 as 'Boot'.

Caithness
The Highland district of Caithness is the most northerly county of mainland Scotland. Its name in Gaelic is 'Gallaibh', and in Scots, 'Caitnes'. The name derives from the Gaelic name 'Cattey' or 'Cattadh', possibly from a Celtic tribe who were known as 'Cats', plus the Old Scandinavian suffix 'nes', meaning 'headland'. Hence, 'headland of the Cats'. In Old Norse the county was called 'Katanes' or 'Kataness', which means 'the nose of Cattey'.

Callander
The name Callander was recorded as 'Kallandrech' in 1438; the Romans had named the place 'Bochastle' when they built a fort beside the River Teith here in the first century AD. The origin of the place name is obscure, but some think it to be a derivation of the Gaelic 'calasraid', meaning 'harbour (or ferry) street'. Others have suggested that Callander may be of Brittonic origin, similar to the Welsh 'caled-dwr', meaning 'hard-water', a possible reference to the River Teith on which the town stands. A Neolithic settlement was excavated just south of the river in 2001, and the remains of a timber building measuring eighty feet long was discovered along with shards of prehistoric pottery. Historically, the town lies within the ancient County of Perthshire.

Cambuslang
The South Lanarkshire township of Cambuslang's name may derive from its location on a bend in the River Clyde south-east of Glasgow. 'Cambus' (or 'camas') is a Scottish Gaelic word signifying a bend in a river, and 'lang' means long.

Campsie Fells
Sometimes known as 'the Campsies', this range of fells is located a few miles north of Glasgow. The name in Scottish Gaelic is 'Monadh Chamaisidh', and while the meaning of the name is contentious, there is a view that 'Campsie' means 'crooked fairy hill', based on the Gaelic word 'cam', meaning 'crooked', and 'sìth' meaning 'seat'. The word 'fell' originates from the Old Norse word 'fjall', meaning 'hill'. The nearby geological fault known as Campsie Fault resulted from about thirty lava flows over sixty million years ago during the Carboniferous period.

Cape Wrath
Cape Wrath is a Highland promontory which is located at the extreme north-west of the British mainland. The name comes from the Old Scandinavian word

'hvarf', meaning 'corner', 'bend' or 'turning point'. The Vikings used the place as a navigational landmark where longships would alter course to follow the coastline.

Carluke
Despite several early interpretations, the name of the South Lanarkshire town of Carluke would appear to have nothing to do with the Christian apostle St Luke, since its local church is dedicated to St Andrew, but is more probably related to the pre-Christian Celtic god Lugh (Lugus or Lugg). The first element of the name signifies 'caer', meaning 'stronghold', in which case the entire place name could be interpreted as 'stronghold of Lugus'. The name has been written in many variant forms and spellings over time, including 'Carneluk', 'Carlowck', 'Carlowk', 'Carluk', 'Carlook' and 'Carlouk'. Its Scottish Gaelic form is 'Cathair MoLuaig'.

Carnoustie
In Gaelic, the town of Carnoustie in Angus is known as 'Carn Ustaidh', but the precise meaning of the place name is contentious. It has been suggested that the first part could be derived from 'cairn', (a pile of stones laid as a way marker) or 'cathair', referring to a fort, but it is the last element that remains obscure.

Carstairs
The name of this South Lanarkshire village in Gaelic is 'Caisteal Tarrais', and appears to be comprised of a Middle English word 'castel' and the name of a Celtic person, probably called Tarres, though exactly who he or she was is unknown. The place name is generally taken to mean 'Tarres's castle'. By the end of the twelfth century the place had already been called 'Casteltarres'.

Coatbridge
Although the name of this North Lanarkshire town translates as '(place by the) bridge of coats', it would be a mistake to think that it refers to any item of clothing. The 'coats' element of the name actually comes from the Old English word 'cot', meaning 'cottage' and the place name should more properly be interpreted as 'cottages (near a) bridge'. The cottages referred to are those alongside the Monkland Canal. In 1584 the place was known as 'Coittis'.

Coldstream
On the face of it, although the cold stream to which this name refers might appear to be the River Tweed, it actually seems more probable that it originally referred to Leet Water, which joins the Tweed at this point. The town is located in the Scottish Borders and was known in the late twelfth century as 'Kaldestrem'. By the end of the thirteenth it had been recorded as 'Coldstreme'. The name means '(place beside a) cold stream'. However, why the stream in question was regarded as especially cold is uncertain as it could be argued that most Scorrish streams share that same characteristic. In Gaelic the name is 'An Sruthan Fuar' and in Scots, 'Caustrim'.

Colonsay
The remote island of Colonsay (or in Scottish Gaelic, 'Colbhasa'), is located within the Inner Hebrides, in the council area of Argyl & Bute. It is the ancestral home of the Macfie Clan. Scalasaig is its main settlement, and the island is linked by a tidal causeway to Oronsay. The place name reflects a Nordic personal name, probably of a man called Kolbein, and the Old Scandinavian word 'ey', meaning 'island'. Hence, it means 'Kolbein's island'. By the fourteenth century the name had already been identified as 'Coluynsay'.

Coupar Angus
The Perth & Kinross town of Coupar Angus has a place name that means 'the community in Angus'. Its Scottish name is 'Cubar Aonghais'. The first part of the name comes from the older Gaelic expression 'comh-phairt', meaning 'community'. The boundary between Perthshire to the west and Angus to the east was once delineated by the local stream, and although the boundary changes of 1891 moved the town administratively from Angus into Perthshire, the town preferred to retain the Angus element of its place name to distinguish it from the township of Coupar in Fife.

Cowdenbeath
Cowdenbeath is a town in Fife whose name contains two distinct elements: the first comes from the personal name of a man called Colden or Cowden, and the second derives from the Gaelic word 'beith', which means 'birch tree'. Hence, 'Cowden's (place among the) birch trees'.

Crail
The name of this town in Fife is comprised of two Gaelic elements: 'carr', meaning 'rock', and 'all', which also means 'rock'. However, both elements seem to have coalesced over time into one single entity to indicate a 'rocky place', probably referring to its rocky coastline and particularly the nearby Carr Rocks. The place was known as both 'Cherel' and 'Caraile' during the twelfth century.

Crawford
A village in South Lanarkshire whose place name comes from the Old English words 'crawe', meaning 'crow', and 'ford', a shallow river crossing. Hence, the name means 'river crossing where crows are seen'. The ford in question was across the River Clyde. In around 1150, the name was recorded as 'Crauford'.

Cromarty
This Highland town and former royal burgh is located at the entrance to the Cromarty Firth, a coastline which is so rugged and irregular that this is thought to be the source of the name. It comes from the Gaelic word 'crumb', which means 'crooked' and either 'bati', meaning 'bay', or possibly the Old Irish word 'bath', meaning 'sea'. In Gaelic, the name is 'Cromba', and the interpretation of the place

name is thought to mean 'crooked (place by the) bay (or sea)'. The former County of Cromarty was named after the town, and was combined with Ross in 1975 to form the new County of Ross & Cromarty.

Culross
The town of Culross (locally pronounced 'Coo-Ross'), overlooks the Firth of Forth in Fife, and has the Gaelic name 'Cuileann Ros', which means 'ridge point or promontory', based on the Gaelic 'cul', a ridge and 'ros', a promontory. Tradition has it that Culross was founded in the sixth century by St Serf, a Scottish saint also known as St Serban (in Latin, 'Sancte Servanus', c.500–c.583), who was especially venerated in western Fife.

Cults
Cults is a suburb of Aberdeen whose place name derives from the Gaelic 'coillte', meaning 'woods' or 'woodland'. The name means 'place in the woods'. In the mid-fifteenth century, the place name was recorded as 'Qhylt', and 'Cuyltis'.

Cumbernauld
A relatively recent town in North Lanarkshire, Cumbernauld has the name 'Cummernaud' in Scots, and in Gaelic is known as 'Comar nan Allt'. The name means 'the meeting of the waters (or streams)', referring to Luggie Water and Red Burn which come close to the village as they flow westwards to the River Clyde. The original settlement dates from Roman times when it was a fort on the Antonine Wall.

Cumbrae
The Scottish island of Cumbrae, earlier known in English as Great or Greater Cumray, has the Gaelic name 'Cumaradh', which means '(place of the) Cymric people'. This is a reference to the Brittonic-speaking Celtic inhabitants of the ancient Kingdom of Strathclyde. They have been identified as the 'Kumreyiar' in the Norse Saga of Haakon Haakonarson. In the year 714 AD, *The Annals of Ulster*, the first book ever to be written in the Irish language, referred to the islands as 'The Isles of the Virgins'. Legend has it that St Mirin came to Cumbrae in about 710 and miraculously expelled all of the island's snakes, before going on to found a religious community in Paisley. The island is the larger of two which are collectively known as 'The Cumbreas'; they are located in the Firth of Clyde a mile and a half off the coast of North Ayrshire, and historically lay within the ancient County of Buteshire.

Cumnock
There are many conflicting arguments regarding the meaning of the place name of this town in East Ayrshire. It has been suggested that it might derive from 'Com-cnoc' (meaning 'hollow in the hills'), 'Com-oich' (meaning 'confluence of the

waters'), 'Cam-cnoc' (meaning 'crooked hill'), and 'Cumanag' (meaning 'little shrine'). Nobody can quite decide which. The name emerged around the turn of the thirteenth century, first as 'Comnocke' in 1297, then as 'Comenok' in 1298, and finally in its present for as 'Cumnock' in 1300.

Dalbeattie
The first element of this Dumfries & Galloway town's place name comes from the Gaelic word 'dail', meaning 'field' or 'water meadow'. The second element, 'beith', referred to birch trees. This produces an overall place name that means 'water meadow with (or among the) birch trees'. It was recorded as 'Dalbaty' in 1469.

Dalkeith
The Midlothian town of Dalkeith has a Celtic name which is comprised of two elements, but as the Celtic languages were never written down, we have to rely on Welsh as the nearest approximation available. In Welsh the words 'dol' or 'ddol', indicate a meadow or a field, and 'coed', indicates woodland or forest. Hence, '(place in a) field (by a) wood'. In Gaelic the place name is 'Dail Cheith'. In 1144 the name was recorded as 'Dolchet'.

Dallas
The name of this small village of Dallas in Moray in Scottish Gaelic is spelled 'Dalais'. It derives from two Celtic words, related to the modern Welsh 'dol', meaning 'meadow', and 'gwas', a dwelling or homestead. Hence, 'dwelling in a meadow'. In 1232 the name was spelled 'Dolays'.

Dalry
There is evidence that the township now called Dalry may have begun as an Iron Age fort on Rye Water in present-day North Ayrshire. In Gaelic, the name is 'Dail Ruighe', derived from 'dail', meaning 'meadow', and a second element from 'fhraoich' (heather). Hence '(place in a) heather meadow'. Others have suggested that the place name might come from 'dail an righ', which would translate as 'meadow of the king'.

Dalwhinnie
The small hamlet of Dalwhinnie is backed by a dramatic mountain landscape within the Cairngorms National Park in the Scottish Highlands. The place name in Gaelic is 'Dail Chuinnidh', which some maintain translates as 'meeting place (in the valley)', while others prefer 'valley of the champions', based on 'dael', meaning 'valley', and 'cuingid' meaning 'champion'. Whichever is true, it seems that this valley location (Glen Truim), was once the site of some sort of contest or gathering.

Celtic Places and Placenames

Dalziel
This town in North Lanarkshire is well known nowadays as a family surname with various spellings, including Dalzell and Dalyell. It comes from the Scottish Gaelic 'Dail-ghil', meaning 'bright dale' or 'white meadow'. The place name originates from the former barony of Dalzell in Lanarkshire, and was first recorded in 1259, when Thomas de Dalzell fought at Bannockburn. According to Clan Dalziel, the name also appears in Shetland as 'Yell', derived from the island of that name.

Dingwall
The Highland township of Dingwall had the distinction of being once a Scandinavian council meeting place or parliament for Vikings who settled in the area. The place name comes from the Old Norse 'thing-vollr' meaning '(place of) assembly'. In 1297 the name was spelled 'Dingwell'. The Scots name is spelled 'Dingwal', and in Gaelic it is 'Inbhir Pheofharain', which translates as 'mouth of the (River) Peffery', on which the town stands.

Dornoch
The town of Dornoch was a former royal burgh in the County of Sutherland in the Highlands. Its name comes from the Gaelic word 'dorn', meaning 'fist', in this instance applied to fist-shaped stones, most likely pebbles, given its location on the shore of Dornoch Firth. Such stones may have been collected here as weapons, perhaps for use in slingshots, or simply as hand-thrown missiles. The place name is generally taken to mean '(place of) fist-shaped stones (or pebbles)'.

Doune
In Gaelic the village of Doune is 'An Dun', which means 'the fort', based on the word 'dun', a term often applied to ancient hillforts. The appellation comes from Doune Castle, which overlooks the village on the site of a much earlier Roman fort, one of many established by Agricola to quell local opposition to Roman occupation and subdue native Britons. The settlement is located on a thin peninsula at the confluence of the River Teith and Ardoch Burn, about eight miles north-west of Stirling in Perthshire.

Drumnadrochit
The Highland village of Drumnadrochit is located beside the River Enrick and close to the western shore of Loch Ness. In Gaelic, the name is 'Druim na Drochaid', and means 'the ridge of the bridge (over the River Enrick)'.

Dryburgh
Dryburgh is a village in the Scottish Borders region lying within the old County of Berwickshire. Due to its close proximity to England, it is little wonder that the place name comes entirely from Old English, specifically 'dryge', meaning 'dry', and 'burh', a fortified place or stronghold. Hence, the name translates simply as 'dry fortress'. The use of the word 'dry' most probably refers to a dried up stream

or watercourse at the place. In the mid-twelfth century its name was recorded as 'Drieburh'.

Dumbarton
In Scottish Gaelic, the town of Dumbarton in Strathclyde is known as 'Dun Breatann' or 'Dun Breatainn', which means 'fort of the Britons'. The name derives from the fact that by the year 870, Dumbarton Rock had become the fortified base of a British settlement. Until 1450 the place was called 'Dunbretane'. However, the original settlement is known to have been established at least as far back as the Iron Age and probably much earlier, and was the site of a strategically important Roman settlement known as 'Alcluith' which translates as 'Hill of the Clyde'. Dumbarton was formerly known as 'Dunbarton'. How the 'n' in the original place name became transformed into an 'm' remains an ongoing Scottish mystery, but the change seems to have taken place in the early 1900s. To confuse matters further, the town of Dumbarton is in the historic County of Dunbartonshire.

Dunbar
The early settlement of Dunbar was part of the Anglo-Saxon Kingdom of Northumbria due to its proximity to the English border and over the centuries has been on either side of it. However, nowadays, it sits fairly and squarely in East Lothian. The place name in Gaelic is 'Dun Barra' probably derived from the Celtic 'din-bar'. The two name elements, 'dun' refers to a fortified stronghold, and 'barr' means 'height'. Hence, 'stronghold on the height'. This is a reference to the site on a rocky ledge, where the ruins of Dunbar Castle are now located.

Dunblane
The small town of Dunblane is known in Scottish Gaelic as 'Dun Bhlathain'. The Gaelic word 'dun' refers to a fortified stronghold so that the place name should translate as 'stronghold of Blane'. However, some have it as 'meadow of Blane' and others as 'Blane's hill'; this latter might make sense if the word was taken to signify a hillfort. Dunblane was first established by monks from St Blane's (in Old Irish, 'Blan'). He lived in the late sixth and early seventh centuries and had his base at Kingarth on the Isle of Bute. The place name was first recorded in the tenth century as 'Dulblaan', and later around 1200 as 'Dumblann'. Before 1975, the town was part of Perthshire, but afterwards came under the authority of Stirling Council.

Dundee
Located in the historic County of Angus, beside the Firth of Tay, the name of the City of Dundee (in Gaelic, 'Dun Deagh') is derived from two words: 'dun', a hillfort, plus Deagh, Daig or Daigh, which was probably a person's name. Hence, 'hillfort of Deagh'. It is an old settlement, with fragmentary archaeological finds unearthed dating from the Mesolithic period as well as a Neolithic stone circle

north-west of the city. The city as we know it today began in 1191, when it was granted a charter by William the Lion.

Dunfermline
Apart from the first element of the place name, 'dun' (in this case meaning 'hillfort'), the interpretation of the name of this township and former Royal Burgh in Fife is unknown. It was already called 'Dumfermelyn' in the eleventh century and by 1124 had been recorded as 'Dumferlin'. In Scots the place is spelled 'Dunfaurlin' and in Gaelic, 'Dun Pharlain'. The hillfort alluded to may have been a Neolithic reinforcement to the rocky outcrop in Pittencrieff Park, where numerous stone and flint implements have been discovered.

Dunkeld
The original settlement of Dunkeld (earlier known as 'Duncalden'), may have been established by Caustantin, son of Fergus, king of the Picts sometime in the early ninth century. Its Gaelic name, 'Dun Chailleann', means 'fort of the Caledonii' (the Caledonians, early Celtic tribes of the region). The contemporary historian Tacitus recorded that the Caledonii had 'red hair and large limbs…(and that) they were a fierce people that were quick to fight'. The site is thought to have been the hillfort north of the town at King's Seat.

Dunoon
Dunoon derived its place name from the Scottish Gaelic 'Dun Omhain' and means 'Fort by the river'. The river in question is the Clyde. It is located on the Cowal Peninsula in the south of Argyll & Bute, on the western shore of the Firth of Clyde. The town was known as 'Dunnon' in the mid-thirteenth century and by 1270 as 'Dunhoven'.

Duns
The town of Duns, or in Scots, 'Dunse', lies in the Scottish Borders region and was formerly part of the historic County of Berwickshire. The Old English word 'dun' signified a fortified hill, making the place name here mean '(the place by the) hill'. Originally, it was known as Duns Law, having taken on the name of the Iron Age hillfort, at the foot of which it is located.

Durness
Durness is a village in the North-West Highlands, formerly in the historic county of Sutherland. Prevailing opinion suggests that the name could be a corruption of the Old Norse word 'dyr-nes', meaning 'deer-headland', indicating a promontory frequented by deer. Its Gaelic name is 'Diuranais'.

Easter Ardross
The Highlands district of Ardross has the Gaelic name 'Aird Rois', which translates as 'height (or high-point) of (Easter) Ross'. From the sixth to the tenth century the

region was held by Pictish tribes and the remains of several of their roundhouses have been discovered in the Easter Ross area.

East Linton
The village of East Linton is located on the River Tyne in East Lothian. The name comes from the Old English word 'lin', meaning 'flax' and 'tun' a farmstead. Hence, 'Eastern flax farm'. 'East' was added to the original 'Linton' in order to distinguish it from West Linton in Peebleshire. There has been an alternative suggestion offered in that the first name element may derive from 'linn', meaning 'waterfall', in which case 'eastern farmstead by a waterfall'.

East Wemyss
East Wemyss is a coastal village in Fife, whose name comes from the Gaelic word 'uamh', meaning 'cave', plus the English plural 's', a reference to the eleven nearby caves, several of which contain Pictish wall carvings. The place name may be interpreted as 'Eastern (place by the) caves'.

Ecclefechan
The place name of the township of Ecclefechan (in Gaelic, 'Eaglais Fheichein'), in modern-day Dumfries & Galloway, is rooted in the ancient Brittonic Celtic language, where the first element, 'egles', meant 'church' (similar to the Welsh word 'eglwys' or the Latin word 'ecclesia'), and the second refers to St Fechin (or Feichín, also known as Mo-Ecca), a seventh century missionary Irish monk from County Sligo.

Edinburgh
The Romans called the Iron Age Celtic tribes who occupied central Scotland the 'Votadini', and they knew their territory by the Brittonic Celtic name, 'Eiydin'. Its meaning is unknown, but it was to form the basis of the modern name of the city. By the sixth century the Old English word 'burh' had been appended and it was recorded as 'Edenburge', indicating a fortified settlement or stronghold. Hence, 'Stronghold at Eidyn'. An alternative explanation is given by Adrian Room in his *Penguin Dictionary of British Place Names,* where he suggests that the name may refer to Edwin, a seventh century King of Northumbria, and might be translated as 'Edwin's fort'. Edinburgh is often nicknamed 'Auld Reekie', a Scots expression meaning 'Old Smoky'.

Eilean Donnan
Eilean Donnan is an island in the western Highlands located at a place where three sea lochs meet: Loch Duich, Loch Long and Loch Alsh. The place name simply means 'island of Donnan'. St Donnan (of Eigg) was an Irish priest who brought Christianity to the Picts of north-western Scotland during the Early Middle Ages. It is thought that an early monastic cell dedicated to Donnan (who was martyred

on Eigg in 617) was founded on the island in the sixth or seventh century, although no trace of it remains.

Elgin
The origin of the Moray town of Elgin's place name is uncertain, though at least two hypotheses exist as to the derivation. One interpretation is that it derives from 'Eig', an early Gaelic name for Ireland, and the suffix 'in', meaning 'little' or 'diminutive'. Hence, the name could mean 'little Ireland', possibly after an unknown Irish migrant who was nostalgic for his mother country. Another cites a legend around the Latin motto on the town's corporation seal, 'Sigillum commune civitatis de Helgyn' (meaning 'The Common Seal of Helgyn'), and that 'Helgyn' is a corruption of Helgy, a general in the army of Sigurd, the Norwegian Earl of Orkney, who may have founded the original settlement.

Eriskay
The small island of Eriskay in the Outer Hebrides (also known as the Western Isles) has the Gaelic name 'Eirisgeigh', taken from the Old Norse meaning 'Erikr's Island'. In 1549, the place was known as 'Eriskeray'. The island is connected to South Uist by a causeway road.

Erskine
In Gaelic, this Renfrewshire town, located on the banks of the River Clyde in the West Central Lowlands, is known as 'Arasgain'. The exact meaning of the place name is uncertain, but it is thought it may possibly derive from Brittonic Celtic words similar to the Welsh 'ir', meaning 'green', and 'esgyn', meaning 'to climb' or 'ascend' – perhaps a reference to a green or grassy slope or hillside, which eminently describes the town's location. The place name has varied over time, as 'Erskin', 'Yrskin', 'Ireskin' and 'Harskin'.

Fair Isle
Lying midway between the Orkney and Shetland, Fair Isle is known in Gaelic as 'Fara', and by its Old Norse name of 'Fridarey'. Its meaning in Gaelic is 'isle of sheep' and in Norse, 'calm or peaceful island'. The island has been occupied since the Iron Age with several forts and houses discovered here in recent years. It was a Norwegian possession until 1469, when Shetland and Orkney were ceded to Scotland as part of a royal marriage dowry.

Falkirk
The earliest recorded name for the town of Falkirk, located historically within the county of Stirlingshire in the Central Lowlands, comes from the Brittonic Celtic, 'Ecclesbrith'. In Scots the place is referred to as 'The Fawkirk', and in Gaelic the place name is 'An Eaglais Bhreac'. The name translates as '(a place with a) speckled church', in reference to one built in mottled or variegated stone or flint. Over time

the place name has been recorded respectively in Gaelic, Latin and Old French, as 'Egglesbreth' in 1065, as 'Varia Capella' in 1166, and 'Varie Capelle' in 1253. By the close of the thirteenth century the name had been written as 'Faukirke'.

Falkland
The meaning of the first element of the place name of this village in Fife is somewhat obscure, though some think it could be derived from the Gaelic word 'falach', meaning 'hidden'. The second element may come from the Scottish Gaelic word 'lann', meaning 'enclosure'. A speculative interpretation of the place name therefore might be 'hidden enclosure'. It seems probable that there was a settlement of some kind there before the twelfth century, but the village itself came into being with the construction of Falkland Castle sometime after 1160. The earliest known forms of this name include 'Falecklen' around the year 1160 and 'Falleland' in about 1128.

Fannich
The name of the village of Fannich is thought to have come from the Gaelic 'fainich', which itself originated as an early Pictish name, similar to the Welsh word 'gwaneg', meaning 'wave'. Fannich is located in the Highland region and formerly lay within the historic County of Ross-shire. The village and the nearby hills are named from Loch Fannich, which was dammed between 1946 and 1960 to create a hydro-electric generating power station.

Fauldhouse
Fauldhouse is a village in West Lothian whose place name in Scots is 'Fauldhoose' and in Gaelic, 'Falas'. The name means 'house on fallow land' and comes from the Old English word 'falh' (fallow), and 'hus' (house). The place was known in 1523 as 'Fawlhous', in 1540 as 'Falhous' and in 1559 as 'Faldhous'.

Fettercairn
The small village of Fettercairn is located at the base of the Grampian Mountains in Aberdeenshire. Its name in Scottish Gaelic is 'Fothair Chardain' which is derived from the Gaelic word 'foithir', meaning 'slope' or 'terrace', and the Pictish word 'carden', meaning 'copse' or 'thicket', which taken together produce a place name that means 'slope by a thicket', or according to some, 'terraced slope by a copse'. The name appeared as 'Fotherkern' around the year 970 AD and had appeared in its present form by the mid-fourteenth century.

Fife
The present-day Unitary Authority of Fife, anciently known as the Kingdom of Fife (or in Gaelic, 'Fiobha'), is a peninsula that lies between the Firth of Forth and the Firth of Tay. By the twelfth century it was known as 'Fib' and 'Fif', traditionally derived from the name of Fib, one of the sons of Cruithe, leader of the Pictish tribes in east-central Scotland. However, the name is thought by some to be much older,

and its real source is obscure. A nearby hillfort is known to have been an important Pictish stronghold between the sixth and eighth centuries.

Fingal's Cave
This internationally famous sea cave on the uninhabited island of Staffa in the Inner Hebrides, owes its notoriety to the composer Felix Mendelssohn who visited the cave in 1829 and wrote *The Hebrides Overture*, nowadays better known as *Fingal's Cave*, thereby creating a world-beating tourist attraction. In folklore, Fingal was the legendary giant and hunter-warrior, Fionn Mac Cumhall (also known as Finn McCool), a figure of Irish and Isle of Man mythology. The Gaelic name of the cave is 'An Uamh Binn', which translates as 'the melodious cave', a characteristic attributed to the often eerie and melodic sounds and reverberations which the sea currents and waves make against the cave's basalt wall pillars.

Firth of Forth
This estuary which flows between Fife on its northern bank and East Lothian on its southern was known in the tenth century as 'Forthin' and its Scottish Gaelic name is 'Linne Foirthe'. This translates as 'estuary of the River Forth'. The river name itself is of Celtic origin and some argue that it probably means 'fast flowing one'; others disagree and prefer 'slow flowing one'. What is certain is that the word 'firth' derives from the Old Norse word 'fjord', meaning 'narrow inlet'.

Flotta
Located in Scapa Flow, the small Orkney island of Flotta is another territory that was at one time part of the Nordic kingdom. This fact is borne out by its place name, which is based on the Old Scandinavian words 'flatr' and 'ey', together meaning 'flat island'.

Fochabers
In Gaelic this village in Moray beside the River Spey is called 'Fachabair' (or 'Fothabair'). There are two differing opinions as to the meaning of the place name. Once has it coming from the Gaelic words 'fothach', meaning 'lake' and 'abor', a marsh – hence, 'marshy lake', while another prefers a Pictish origin whose first element is unknown but the second might be 'aber', meaning 'confluence'.

Forres
The burgh of Forres on the Moray coast received an entry in Ptolemy's *Geographia*, and a fortified castle is known to have existed here from the tenth century. In Scottish Gaelic, the name is written as 'Farrais', based on the words 'fo', meaning 'below', and 'ras', meaning 'shrubbery' or 'undergrowth'. In this case the place name translates as '(place) below an undergrowth'.

Forteviot
Forteviot is a village in Strathearn, located on the River Earn in Perth & Kinross. Its Gaelic name is 'Fothair Tabhaicht'. The word 'Foithuir' could mean 'terrace' or may even derive from the pre-Celtic 'uotir', meaning 'territory'. It is assumed the Tobacht was a personal name, implying that the place name means 'Tobacht's territory (or terrace)'. The town was the first capital of the ninth century Pictish kingdom of King Cinaed macAilpin (also known as Kenneth I).

Fortrose
The Highland township of Fortrose, formerly in Ross-shire, is located on the Inner Moray Firth and has a place name that means '(place) beneath the headland', based on the Gaelic words 'foter', meaning 'lower' and 'ros', a headland. The place name was recorded as 'Forterose' in 1455.

Foula
The remote Shetland island of Foula is commonly known as Bird Island on account of its substantial sea bird cliff colonies. The name comes from the Old Scandinavian word 'fugl' (related to the English word 'fowl'), together with 'ey', meaning 'island'.

Gairloch
The name of the village of Gairloch comes from the Gaelic words 'gearr' and 'loch' which taken together mean 'short loch or sea inlet'. The village is located beside Loch Gairloch in Wester Ross, in the North-West Highlands. The place name was recorded as 'Gerloth' in 1275 and as 'Gerloch' by the mid-fourteenth century.

Galashiels
Evidence of early Pictish settlements have been found near Galashiels, with an Iron Age hillfort and an ancient earthwork known as the 'Picts' Work Ditch'. The Galashiels place name is known in Gaelic as 'An Geal Ath', which translates as 'huts beside Gala Water'. The origin and meaning of the river name is unknown, but the 'shiels' element comes from the Middle English word signifying shepherd's huts or night shelters. The town is located in the Scottish Border region, and was known in 1237 as 'Galuschel'.

Galloway
The earliest Celtic inhabitants of Galloway were the Novantae tribe. However, the place name came later in the ninth century, when Irish and Scandinavian settlers moved into South-West Scotland. The place name comes from 'gall', meaning 'stranger' or 'foreigner' and 'Ghaidel', signifying Gaels. Hence, '(territory of the) foreign or stranger Gaels'. In Gaelic the place is known as 'Gall-Ghaidhealaibh' or 'Gallobha', and in Scots, as 'Gallowa'.

Galston
The East Ayrshire township of Galston (in Scottish Gaelic, 'Baile nan Gall'), gets its name from the Gaelic word 'gall', meaning 'foreigner', and the Old English word 'tun', signifying a village or farmstead. Hence, 'the village of foreigners', a reference to settlers from Ireland or Scandinavia.

Gigha
The island of Gigha, located off the west coast of Kintyre in Argyll & Bute, derives from the Old Norse 'guth' or 'gothr', meaning 'god' (or 'good') and 'ey', an island. Hence, 'God's island'. In Scottish Gaelic the name is spelled 'Giogha'. It has been inhabited since prehistoric times and in the fifth century it was part of the Irish Kingdom of Dalriada (or Dal Riata). Gigha is also the ancestral seat of Clan MacNeill. In the thirteenth century the place name was spelled 'Guthey' and 'Gudey'.

Girvan
The original Gaelic name of Girvan in Carrick, South Ayrshire, is 'Inbhir Gharbhain', which literally translates as 'mouth of the River Girvan'. However, its present-day name is more likely to have come from the Gaelic word 'gar', meaning 'thicket', whereby the place name might translate as '(place of the) thicket'.

Glamis
Glamis is a village in Angus, best known for its castle, as the birthplace of the Queen Mother. the Dowager Queen Elizabeth (Bowes-Lyon), and for its reference in Shakespeare's play *Macbeth*. The place name is thought to come from the Gaelic word 'glamhus', meaning 'wide gap' or 'open country', in description of the local landscape at the foot of the Sidlaw Hills.

Glasgow
The City of Glasgow is known in Scots as 'Glesca' or 'Glesga', and in Gaelic as 'Glaschu'. The place name is from the Brittonic language, and was known as 'Cathures'. The modern name was first recorded in the twelfth century as 'Glasgu'. The first element of the place name, 'glas', means 'grey-green', and the second comes from 'cau', signifying a hollow, which together produce an overall meaning of 'grey-green hollow'. Tradition has it that the original Christian settlement was founded in the sixth century by St Mungo, when he established a church beside the River Clyde, thought to be on the site of present-day Glasgow Cathedral.

Glen Affric
Glen Affric is a township in the Highland region whose Gaelic name is 'Gleann Afraig', meaning 'valley of the River Affric'. The river flows into Loch Affric, and

its name comes from the expression 'ath-breac', meaning 'dappled', probably due to the thick woodland of Scots Pine that border the middle part of the glen through which it flows.

Glencoe
The name of the Highland town of Glencoe comes from the Gaelic word 'gleann', meaning 'valley', and the River Coe that runs through it. The meaning of the river name is unknown, but the entire place name is commonly held to mean 'narrow valley of the (River) Coe'. The village is historically remembered for the Massacre of Glencoe in 1692.

Gleneagles
This valley in Perth and Kinross has the Gaelic name 'Gleann na h-Eaglais', and has little to do with eagles. The name is comprised of two Gaelic words: 'gleann' (valley), and 'eaglais', derived from the Latin word 'ecclesia' and meaning 'church'. Hence the place name means 'valley of the church'. The church in question was founded here by St Mungo in the seventh century.

Glenelg
As with all Scottish settlements bearing a 'glen' element, this Highland village is located in a valley. Its Gaelic name is 'Gleann Eilg'. The second element, 'ealg' (or 'eilg'), is an ancient name for Ireland, which was given to the place by Irish immigrant settlers. The name therefore means 'valley of Ireland'.

Gourock
The town of Gourock has the Scottish Gaelic place name 'Guireag' and was previously a burgh of the County of Renfrew. In 1661 the place was known as 'Ouir et Nether Gowrockis', which translates as '(place by the) hillock', and comes from the Gaelic 'guireag', strictly meaning 'pimple', but in this instance referring to a hillock. The hillock in question may be the local Kempock Point.

Greenock
Greenock's location on a hilly rise overlooking the Firth of Clyde in the former County of Renfrewshire, gives the clue to its place name. In Gaelic its name is 'Grianaig', and means 'hillock'. The name is taken to mean '(place on the) sunny hillock'. In 1395 the place name was recorded as 'Grenok', and in 1717 it was spelled 'Greenoak'.

Gretna
The modern township of Gretna, in contemporary Dumfries & Galloway, is located on the border of Scotland, but the name is decidedly English, coming as it does from the Old English words 'greoten', meaning 'grit', 'gravel' or 'gravelly', and

Celtic Places and Placenames

'hoh', a hill. Hence, 'Green by the gravelly hill'. In Scottish Gaelic the place is known as 'Greatna'. It had been known as 'Gretenho' ('gravelly hill'), since 1223, with several later variations, including 'Gretenhou' in 1240 and 'Gratnay' in 1576.

Hamilton
The town of Hamilton in South Lanarkshire was originally known as 'Cadzow', before adopting the name of the local ruling Hamilton family following the Battle of Bannockburn during the Wars of Scottish Independence, and (eventually) supporting Robert de Brus ('the Bruce'). Hamilton is an Old English name comprising 'hamel', meaning 'broken', and 'tun', a village settlement or farmstead. Hence, 'settlement in broken country'. The term 'broken country' refers to lands ravaged by years of continuous warfare.

Harris
See: 'Isle of Harris'.

Heanish
Heanish (sometimes 'Heaness') on the Isle of Tiree in the Western Isles, most likely derived its name from the Old Norse words 'hey', meaning 'grass', and 'nes', meaning 'headland'. Such grassy promontories, known as 'machairs', are fertile grassy plains typically found on the north-west coastlines of Ireland and Scotland, and particularly in the Outer Hebrides. The Machair at Heanish has an ancient stone and turf dyke of unknown date running north–south across it.

Hebrides
The Hebrides are an island group in the west of Scotland. Their Scottish Gaelic name is 'Innse Gall', meaning 'islands of the strangers or foreigners', and in Old Norse, 'Sudreyjar' or 'Suthreyar'. Sometime around 77 AD, the Roman author Pliny the Elder described some thirty islands in his *Naturalis Historia* (Natural History), which he called the 'Hebudes'. Later Latin writers called them 'Haebudes', 'Ebudae' and 'Ebudes'. The meaning of these names remains a mystery, although some have suggested a connection to the ancient Irish Ulaid tribe. The archipelago of over forty inhabited islands is divided into two groups, separated by the narrow channel called The Minch: the Outer Hebrides which include Lewis and Harris, Barra, North and South Uist and Vatersay, and the Inner Hebrides which include Islay, Jura, Rhum, Raasay, Skye and Muck.

Heddon-on-the-Wall
Heddon-on-the-Wall is located in Northumberland near Hadrian's Wall on the main road from Newcastle to Hexham. The place name was first recorded as 'Hedun' in the 1175 Pipe Rolls, as 'Heddun' in 1262 and by its Latin form as 'Hedon super murum' (Heddon above the wall) in 1242. The name is derived from the Old English 'haeth-dun', meaning 'hill where heather grows'. The village was the location of the original Roman milecastle number twelve.

Highland
The historic region of Highlands (or in Scottish Gaelic, 'a' Ghaidhealtachd', meaning 'the place of the Gaels'), is the largest local government area and Unitary Authority in the United Kingdom, covering nearly 10,000 square miles in northern Scotland. Its area encompasses three language groups: English, Scots and Gaelic. The region was known as 'The Heland' in 1529 and by the early seventeenth century had been designated as 'The High-Lands of Scotland'. It is now designated as the Highland Unitary Authority.

Holywood
Formerly located in the historic County of Dumfries-shire, the village of Holywood derives its name from two Old English words, 'halig', meaning 'holy, and 'wudu', meaning 'oak wood' or 'oak copse'. Hence, 'holy (or sacred) oak wood'. It was the site of a twelfth century abbey, and was previously known as 'Dercongal' (meaning 'Congal's oak-copse'). The name Congal is thought to refer to St Convallus, who was a disciple of St Mungo. The churchyard has an ancient stone circle called 'The Twelve Apostles'.

Hoy
Hoy is the second largest of the islands that form Orkney. Its place name comes from the Old Norse word 'haey', meaning 'lofty island', based on its highest peak, Ward Hill, which rises to almost 1,600 feet above sea level.

Huna
Huna lies on the north coast of Caithness in the Highland Council Area of Scotland. It was an important sheltered port for the Vikings when it was known as 'Hofn', a name based on the Old Scandinavian 'hafn-a', possibly meaning 'harbour river'. However, others connect the name 'Hofn' to the burial place of Hlodvar Thorfinnsson, who was the Norse Jarl (Earl) of Orkney in 980 AD.

Inchcolm
The island of Inchcolm in the Firth of Forth derives it place name from the Gaelic 'Innis Choluim'. In Gaelic, 'innis' means 'island', and 'Choluim' is an old name for St Columba, an Irish missionary evangelist who arrived in Scotland in the sixth century to convert the Pictish tribes to Christianity. The place name came into being sometime in the twelfth century and translates as 'Columba's island'. Before that time, it was known as 'Emona' or 'Aemonia'. The abbey on the island is dedicated to him. In 1123 the place was known by the Latin name of 'Insula Sancti Columbae', and in 1605 the name was recorded as 'St Colmes Ynch'.

Inchkeith
This island in the Firth of Forth has a name that combines Gaelic with Celtic. The modern form of the Gaelic is 'Innis Cheith'. The first element, 'innis', means

'island' and the second is related to the Welsh word 'coed', meaning 'woodland'. Hence, mysteriously, the name is widely held to mean 'wooded island', despite the fact that, in the present time the island is rocky and exposed and it is hard to see how it could ever have supported a woodland.

Innerleithen
Innerleithen, or in Gaelic, 'Inbhir Leitheann', is a small town in Tweeddale in the Scottish Borders, and was formerly in the historic County of Peeblesshire. The first name element is a corruption of the Scottish Gaelic 'Inver', meaning 'mouth' or 'confluence', and 'Leithen', the name of the river here, at a point where it joins the River Tweed. Hence, 'the confluence of Leithen Water'.

Inver- (prefix)
Many Scottish place names begin with the prefix 'inver-', which comes from the Gaelic word 'inbhir', meaning 'estuary' or 'river mouth'. As a rule, the word element which follows will be the name of an associated river. These include places like Inveraray in Argyl (mouth of the River Aray), Inverurie in Aberdeenshire (mouth of the River Urie), the Unitary Authority of Inverclyde (mouth of the River Clyde), Inverleith in Edinburgh (mouth of the River Leith), among many others.

Invergordon
Until the mid-eighteenth century, this Highland town on the Cromarty Firth in Easter Ross, was known as 'Inverbreckie', derived from two Gaelic words, 'inbhir', signifying a river mouth or estuary, and 'breac', meaning 'speckled', after the name of the local river. Then at sometime around 1760 Alexander Gordon took over land ownership and the place was renamed Invergordon, or 'Gordon's (place at the) river mouth'. In Gaelic, the modern place name is 'Inbhir Ghordain' (or 'An Rubha').

Inverkeithing
In Gaelic this settlement is known as 'Inbhir Ceitein', combining 'inbhir' with the name of the River Keithing that runs through the town. Hence 'mouth of the River Keithing'. The river name is thought to come from the Brittonic Pictish word 'coet', which means 'wood' or 'woodland'.

Inverness
This place name signifies the mouth of the River Ness. Opinions differ as to the precise meaning of the river name; some have it simply meaning 'moist' or 'wet', and others cite 'rushing' or 'roaring' as more likely. Its Gaelic name is 'Inbhir Nis', meaning 'mouth of the River Ness', and in Scots the name is frequently said and written as 'Innerness'. It was a major Pictish stronghold.

Scotland & the English Borders

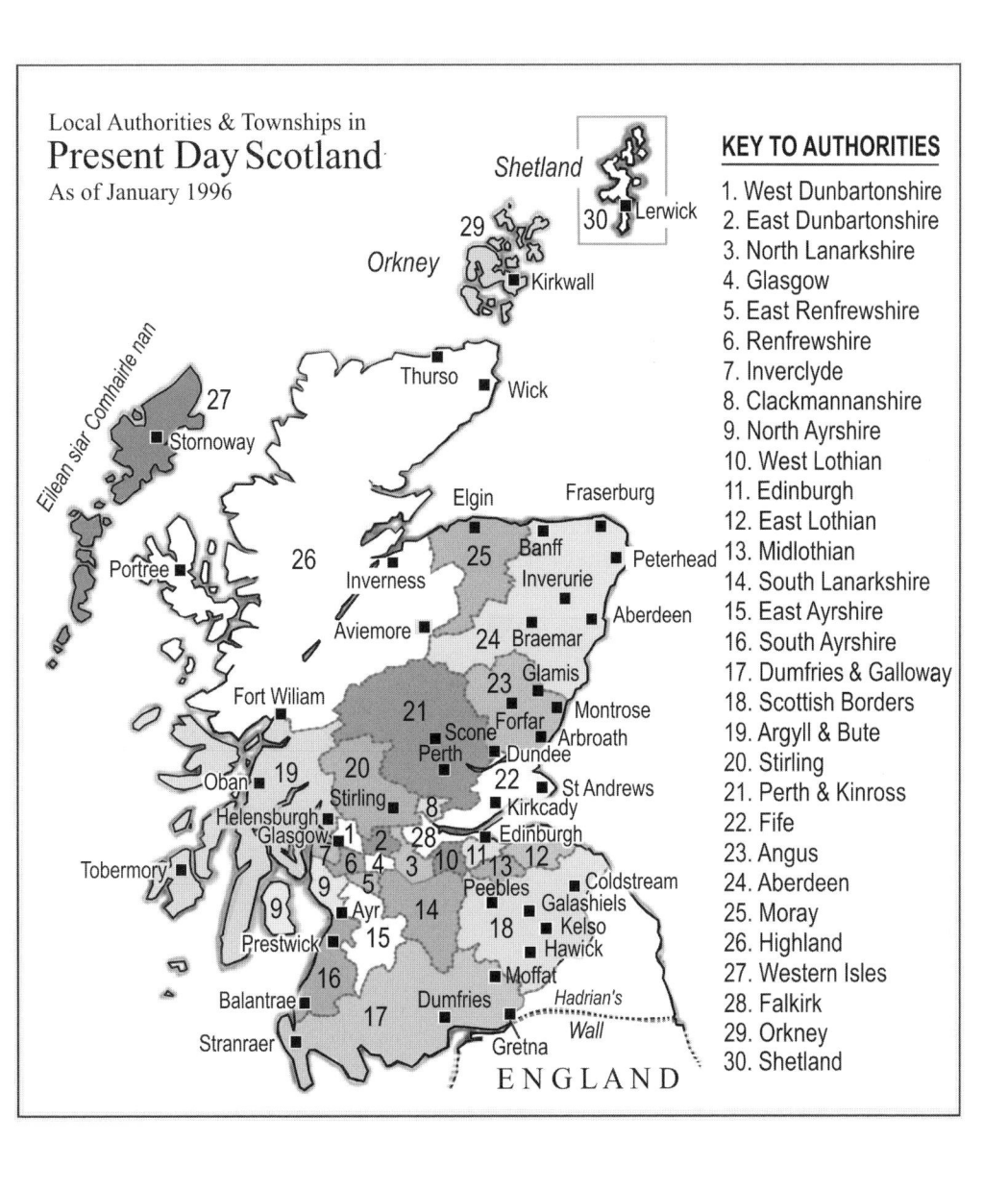

Local Authorities & Townships in Present Day Scotland
As of January 1996

KEY TO AUTHORITIES

1. West Dunbartonshire
2. East Dunbartonshire
3. North Lanarkshire
4. Glasgow
5. East Renfrewshire
6. Renfrewshire
7. Inverclyde
8. Clackmannanshire
9. North Ayrshire
10. West Lothian
11. Edinburgh
12. East Lothian
13. Midlothian
14. South Lanarkshire
15. East Ayrshire
16. South Ayrshire
17. Dumfries & Galloway
18. Scottish Borders
19. Argyll & Bute
20. Stirling
21. Perth & Kinross
22. Fife
23. Angus
24. Aberdeen
25. Moray
26. Highland
27. Western Isles
28. Falkirk
29. Orkney
30. Shetland

Iona
See: 'Isle of Iona'.

Irvine
The name of the North Ayrshire coastal town of Irvine derives from two Brittonic Celtic words which are thought to approximate to the Welsh 'ir', meaning 'green' or 'fresh', and 'afon', meaning 'river', which relates to the River Irvine which joins the Firth of Clyde here. The place name in Gaelic is 'Irbhinn'. Irvine is the site of an ancient Mesolithic settlement and was once a royal burgh.

Islay
This island of the Inner Hebrides is known in Scottish Gaelic as 'Ile' and was recorded as 'Epidion' by Ptolemy in the first century AD. The meaning of the Celtic word 'ili' is the likely derivation of the island's name, and may have meant 'swelling island'. Later, the 's' was added, as was the final element 'ey', meaning 'island' by Scandinavian arrivals. For much of its early history, Islay was part of the Gaelic Irish Kingdom of Dal Riata.

Isle of Arran
Arran is an island located in the Firth of Clyde. Its name in Scottish Gaelic is 'Eilean Arainn' which comes from a Brittonic word meaning 'high place' (similar to the Middle Welsh word 'aran'). The island saw Viking immigrants arriving around the ninth century and many places have Norse elements in their place names. The Scandinavian name for the island may have been 'Herrey' or 'Hersey'.

Isle of Harris
Ptolemy referred to the island as 'Adru' on his map of the British Isles (thought to mean 'thick', 'stout' or 'bulky'). In Old Norse, the island was known as 'Herao' (from 'herath', a word meaning 'district'). In Scottish Gaelic the place name is 'Na Heararadh'. A literal translation of the name would be '(the island) which is higher', no doubt in direct comparison with the lower and flatter land of Lewis to the north.

Isle of Iona
Iona is a tiny island in the Inner Hebrides. In Gaelic, the name is 'I Chaluim Chille', which is thought to mean either 'Calum's Iona' or 'island of Calum's monastery'. Calum was a Latin form of St Columba. The Gaelic place name is frequently shortened simply to 'I'. In its time it has also been known as 'I nam ban boidheach', which translates as 'the isle of beautiful women'.

Isle of Lewis
Lewis is the largest island of the Outer Hebrides archipelago, sometimes known as the Western Isles. The name in Gaelic is 'Eilean Leodhais' or simply 'Leodhas'. Some

argue that the name may be derived from Old Norse word 'ljodahus', meaning 'song house', while others refer to the Scottish Gaelic word 'leogach', meaning 'boggy' or 'marshy'. The existence of prehistoric Iron Age forts, stone circles and standing stones bear witness to the fact that Lewis has been inhabited for at least five thousand years.

Isle of Mull

Mull has seen human occupation for more than eight thousand years, with successive settlements by Mesolithic hunter-gatherers as well as later Iron Age Celtic tribes, as evidenced by the many standing stones and circles that exist on the island. In Gaelic, Mull is known as 'An t-Eilean Muileach', and in Scots simply as 'Muile'. It is the second largest island of the Inner Hebrides (after Skye). There are at least three possible explanations for the meaning of its place name. First, the Gaelic word 'muileach' meaning 'dear' or 'beloved' has been proposed, indicating that some early inhabitant was particularly fond of the place. Second, the Old Norse word 'muli' signified a headland, and thirdly it has been suggested that the name comes from a Celtic word whose meaning is entirely lost to us. On balance the most likely explanation is that it means '(island of the) headland'. The Norse word 'muli', could also refer to a jutting crag, or snout. Other variants on the Norse name were 'Myl', 'Mowyl', 'Mulle' and 'Mwll'.

Isle of Skye

Skye has been occupied since prehistoric times and was settled by Gaelic-speaking people from Ireland during the first century BC. Later, from the ninth to the twelfth century, the island was ruled by Norsemen. Skye is located on the north-west coast of the Scottish Highlands and is the largest and most northerly of the Inner Hebrides. The origins of the place name may have been derived from the Old Norse words 'ski', meaning 'cloud' and 'ey', meaning 'island'. In Gaelic it is called 'An t-Eilean Sgitheanach' or 'Eilean a' Cheo', and in Norse 'Skío', and these translate as 'island of the mist (or clouds)'.

Jedburgh

Given its location near to the Scottish-English border, it is no surprise that Jedburgh has both Celtic and English elements to its place name. In the ninth century its name was 'Gedwearde', based on the River Jed and the Old English word 'wrthe', signifying an enclosure (a field, paddock or yard). Hence, the original meaning of the place name was 'enclosure by the River Jed'. For some unexplained reason, the Old English word was changed for the Middle English 'burgh', meaning 'town'. The river name is thought to be Celtic, but its meaning is unknown. In Gaelic, the place name is 'Deadard', and in Scots, 'Jeddart' or 'Jethart'.

John O' Groats

This iconic Highland village at mainland Britain's northernmost edge takes its name from Jan de Groot (or de Grot), a Dutchman who was bailee to the Earls of

Caithness and once ran a ferry from the Scottish mainland to Orkney. Tradition has it that he charged the sum of one groat for passengers to use his ferry, and that this is the origin of the 'O' Groats' element of the place name. However, it more likely derives from the Dutch 'de groot', meaning 'the large', possibly a description of his physical appearance. People from John O' Groats are known as 'Groaters'.

Jura
Jura is an island in the Inner Hebrides whose name in Gaelic is 'Diura', and in Norse, 'Dyroy'. According to some, the name came about in the seventh century when Vikings called it 'deer island', from the Old Scandinavian words 'dyr' and 'ey.' Others claim a quite different devolution, based on the personal name of a man called Doraid, in which case the place name could be taken to mean 'Doraid's island'. In Gaelic the name was 'Doirad Eilinn', but by the early fourteenth century the name had been abbreviated to 'Dure'.

Keith
In Scottish Gaelic, this small Moray township in North-East Scotland is called 'Baile Cheith', or 'Ceith Mhaol Rubha', derived from a Celtic word, similar to the Brittonic Welsh 'coed', and simply meaning 'wood'. Hence, the place name simply means '(place by the) wood'. Keith was historically in the County of Bamffshire.

Kelso
Kelso is a small township in the Scottish Borders, located beside the River Tweed and historically lying within the County of Roxburghshire in South-East Scotland. In Scots, the place is known as 'Kelsae', and in Gaelic it is 'Cealsaidh'. The town came into being with the establishment of Kelso Abbey in 1128 and its place name reflects the original settlement's location on a chalky outcrop, which gave the town the name of 'Calkou' or 'Calcehou'. This comes from two Old English words: 'calc', meaning 'chalk' and 'hoh', a hill spur, producing an overall meaning of '(place on a) chalky hill spur'.

Kennoway
The meaning of this village name in the district of Kirkcaldy derives from the Scottish Gaelic 'ceann', meaning 'head', 'top' or 'end'. The second element of the place name may derive from 'uaigh', meaning 'den', a reference to an overhanging ravine or den, producing a place name that could either mean 'place at the top or (end)' or '(place at the) head of the den'. The name has been spelled variously over the years, including 'Kennachin' in 1183, 'Kennachyn' in 1250 and 'Kennoquhy' in 1510.

Kilmacolm
Kilmacolm is a village parish formerly in the historic county of Renfrewshire. Its name comes from the Gaelic 'cill mo Colm', meaning 'church of my Columba',

a dedication to St Columba of Iona who is generally associated with the monastic cell established on the site of the current parish church in the sixth or seventh century. 'Colm' is a popular diminutive form of Columba. The insertion of the word 'my' in the name reveals a personal affection in the dedication. The village name was recorded as 'Kilmacolme' in the early thirteenth century.

Kilmarnock

In simple terms, the East Ayrshire town of Kilmarnock's place name means 'the Church of St Marnoch (or Mernoc)', sometimes referred to by the diminutive form, 'Mo'. In Scottish Gaelic the place name is 'Cille Mhearnaig'. The word 'cill' refers to a church and 'oc' means 'my'. Mernoc is a contraction of the Celtic words 'Mo-Ernin-occ', which translates directly as 'my little Ernene', an alternative name for the Irish saint, St Ernin, who died in 634 AD.

Kilsyth

Kilsyth is a town in North Lanarkshire which has known human habitation since Neolithic times and its proximity to the Antonine Wall made it an important Roman settlement. Its name in Scottish Gaelic is 'Cill saidhe', and possibly referred to a church dedicated to St Syth, although this assertion is disputed. Over the centuries the name was recorded as 'Kelvesyth', 'Kelnasydhe' before finally evolving into its present form. This later 'kel' element in the town's early place name tends to strengthen the case for its more likely relationship to the River Kelvin whose source is nearby.

Kilwinning

In the mid-twelfth century this North Ayrshire town name was recorded as 'Killvinin'. The name comes from the Gaelic word 'cill', meaning 'church', and St Finnian, to whom it was dedicated. St Finnian, the Abbot of Clonard, was a sixth century Irish saint and missionary to the Pictish tribes. The place name means '(place by the) church of St Finnian'. It was known by the end of the twelfth century by its Latin name, 'Ecclesia Sancti Vinini', and by the fourteenth was being recorded as 'Kykvynnyne'.

Kincardine

Kincardine, or Kincardineshire, was a former historic county in eastern Scotland which took its name from Kincardine Castle in Aberdeenshire. The name comprises the Gaelic element 'cinn' or 'ceann', meaning 'head' or 'top', along with a Celtic word related to the modern Welsh 'cardden', meaning 'thicket' or 'copse'. Hence, '(place at the) head of a copse'. Several other places in Scotland have the same name: Kincardine on the coast of Fife, more properly Kincardine-on-Forth is one, while others exist in Perth & Kinross and in the Highland region – all have the same root and meaning. There is a suggestion that the original form of the name might have been 'Pencarden'. Kincardineshire marked the northern limit of the brief Roman advance into Scotland, at which time it was part of the kingdom of the Picts.

Kinghorn

This township in Fife gets its name from its geographical location, and is based on two Gaelic words, 'cinn', meaning 'head' (the top of), and 'gorn', a marsh. As the settlement was established on higher firmer ground overlooking marshes, Kinghorn was logically named as being 'at the top (or head) of the marsh'. In Scottish Gaelic the township is called 'Ceann Gronna'.

Kinross

The town of Kinross on the River Dee estuary has been located within the administrative county of Perth & Kinross in South-West Scotland since the 1930s, but was historically in Kinross-shire. Its name in Gaelic is 'Ceann Rois', where 'ceann' means 'head' or 'end' and 'ros' indicates a headland or promontory. Hence, the place name means '(place at the) end of the promontory'. As Kinross is a landlocked county, the promontory in question projects not into the sea, but into Loch Leven. In the mid-twelfth century the place name was recorded as 'Kynros'.

Kintyre

In Scottish Gaelic, Kintyre is known as 'Cinn Tire', which means 'end of the land', a feature that defines this peninsula in south-west Argyll & Bute. The place name comes from the Gaelic 'ceann', meaning 'head' or 'end', and 'tire', meaning 'land'. Its southern extremity, the 'Mull', gets its name from 'maol', meaning 'bare' or 'bald'. The place was known in the early ninth century as 'Ciunntire'. The Roman name for the Mull of Kintyre was 'Epidium Promontorium', meaning 'headland of the horse people', a probable reference to a local cult of a Celtic horse deity. In the year 807 the place name was recorded as 'Ciunntire'.

Kirkcaldy

The 'kirk' element of the Kirkcaldy place name is misleading, as it does not refer to a church as might be supposed, but is more closely related to the Welsh word 'caer', meaning 'fort' or the Pictish 'caled', meaning 'hard'. Its Scottish Gaelic name, 'Cair Chaladain', translates as 'fort at Caledin (or Caled)', or 'place of the hard fort', referring to a fortified stronghold on a hill, which was probably built of stone. The township lies on a long curved stretch of the north shore of the Firth of Forth in Fife, and is sometimes known as the 'lang toun', or 'long town'.

Kirkcudbright

The town of Kirkcudbright now lies within the County Authority of Dumfries & Galloway, but from the mid-fifteenth century was a Royal Burgh in the former ancient County of Kirkcudbrightshire. The first element of the name comes from Old Norse word 'kirkja', meaning 'church' (or chapel), and 'cudbright' is a corruption of St Cuthbert. Hence, 'church of St Cuthbert'. In Gaelic the place name is 'Cille

Chuithbeirt'. In earlier times the place was called 'Kilcudbrit', in the twelfth and thirteenth centuries the name was written 'Cudbright' and 'Kircuthbright', and in the fourteenth century it appeared as 'Kirkubry'.

Kirkintillock
The first element of the East Dunbartonshire town of Kirkintillock's place name might mislead one to think it relates to the Norse word 'kirkja', meaning 'church', but in this case the derivation is quite different. It comes from a Celtic word meaning 'fort'. The remaining place name elements are two Gaelic words: 'ceann', meaning 'head' or 'at the top of', and 'tulach', signifying a hillock or small hill. Hence, the place name means 'fort at the top of a small hill'. The fort in question refers to a Roman fort on the nearby Antonine Wall. One of the earliest spellings of the name dates from the beginning of the thirteenth century when it was recorded as 'Kirkintulach'. In Gaelic the place is known as 'Cair Cheann Tulaich'.

Kirkwall
The Vikings who founded this settlement in Orkney in the ninth century called it 'Kirkjuvagr', from the Old Norse words 'kirkja' (church), and 'vagr' (bay). Hence, 'church on the bay'. Over time the place name changed to 'Kirkvoe' and 'Kirkwaa' before finally emerging as Kirkwall. The place name in Gaelic is 'Bagh na h-Eaglaise'. For no apparent or logical reason the meaning of 'bay' seems to have undergone a transformation over the centuries into 'wall'.

Kirriemuir
This Angus township sometimes goes by the shortened version of name, 'Kirrie'. It has been settled since the earliest times as evidenced by the decorated Pictish standing stones known as the Kirriemuir Sculptured Stones. The place name comes from two Gaelic words, 'ceathramh', meaning 'quarter', an area of land measurement similar to a quarter of an old English 'hide' (known as a 'dabhach'), and 'mor', meaning 'big', signifying an area that was considered sufficient to support a family. Hence the place name may be taken to mean 'big quarter'.

Knoydart
Knoydart is a peninsula in the Lochaber district, situated between Loch Nevis and Loch Hourn on the west coast of the Scottish Highlands. Its Gaelic name is 'Cnoidear' and is often referred to as 'the last wilderness'. The place name comes from an Old Scandinavian personal name of a man called Knut, plus the word 'fjorthr', meaning 'inlet'. Hence, 'Knut's inlet'. It has been suggested that it might be a reference to the Danish King Cnut (sometimes known as Canute), who invaded Scotland in the year 1031.

Kyleakin
Kyleakin is a Highland village situated on the east coast of the Isle of Skye in the Inner Hebrides. Its name in Scottish Gaelic is 'Caol Acain' (or 'Kyle Akin'). The meaning is frequently disputed. Many claim it means 'strait of Haakon', as 'caol' is a Gaelic word meaning 'strait', and King Haakon IV of Norway is said to have moored his battle fleet here in 1263. Others cite the mythological Celtic hero, Acunn, as more likely – in which case the place name could mean 'strait of Acunn'.

Kyle of Lochalsh
In Gaelic 'Loch Aillse' (from the Gaelic word 'aillseach', meaning 'foaming lake'), is a sea inlet between the North-West Highlands and the Isle of Skye. Kyle, from the Gaelic 'caol' means 'strait'. Hence Kyle of Lochalsh translates as '(place by the) strait of the foaming loch'. The village was historically in the old County of Ross-shire.

Lairg
The Highland village of Lairg gets its name directly from the Gaelic word 'lorg', meaning 'shank'. It is located at the south-eastern end of the man-made Loch Shin, and formerly lay within the historic County of Sutherland. Its Scottish Gaelic name is 'An Luirg', which means 'the leg (shank or shin)'. The place name was known before 300 AD as 'Larg' and 'Largge'.

Lammermuir
The Lammermuir hills in the Border region of Scotland (in Gaelic, 'An Lomair Mor'), have a name which is fairly straightforward: it means 'lamb's moor'. The place name comes from the Old English, 'lambra', meaning 'lamb' and 'mor', a moor. The place was of low agricultural value, suitable only to support sheep and grazing lambs. There have been several variations of the place name over the years, including 'Lombormore', 'Lambremore', 'Lambermora' and 'Lambirmor'.

Lanark
After King David I made this small town in the central belt of Scotland a Royal Burgh in 1140, Lanark became the historic county town of Lanarkshire. The place name in Scottish Gaelic is 'Lannraig', and in Scots, 'Lanrik'. It is thought to derive from the Cumbric Welsh word 'llanerch' meaning 'woodland clearing' or 'glade'. Hence, '(place in the) woodland glade'.

Langholm
This town, formerly in East Dumfries-shire, has a name comprised of the Old English word 'lang', meaning 'long' and the Old Norse 'holmr', signifying an island. In fact, there is no island as such, but the location is a narrow strip of land beside the River Esk. The place is referred to locally as 'Muckle Toon' and is the traditional seat of the Armstrong Clan.

Larbert
Larbert, in the Forth Valley, has a place name that comes from the Gaelic word 'larach', meaning 'farm', and a Celtic word, 'pert', meaning 'thicket'. In Scottish Gaelic the name is spelled 'Leirbert' or 'Leth-pheairt', and in Scots, 'Lairbert'. Hence, 'farm by a thicket'. In the twelfth century the name was recorded as 'Lethberth'.

Largs
The place name derives directly from the Gaelic word 'learg', meaning 'hill-slope'. The plural form (with an 's') is a later English addition. Formerly a district of North Cunninghame on the Firth of Clyde, it now lies within the administrative County of North Ayrshire. Its name in Scottish Gaelic is 'An Leargaidh Ghallda'.

Lasswade
There are two possible explanations as to the meaning of the Midlothian village of Lasswade's place name. The first cites the Old English words 'laeswe', meaning 'pasture', and 'waed', a ford, in which case the name means '(place by a) pasture ford'. The second suggests that it may be derived from the Brittonic 'lis', meaning 'court' or 'administrative centre', and 'wudu', a forest or a wood. Hence, 'the court in the forest'. The place name was spelled 'Leswade' in 1150 and in 1750 it appeared as 'Laswaid'.

Lauder
Possibly based on an ancient Celtic river name, 'lou' and 'dubro', and meaning 'cleansing river', Lauder (or in Gaelic, 'Labhdar'), lies within the Scottish Borders region, having previously been part of Berwickshire. Other accounts cite a Celtic word meaning 'wash', referring to a river that overflows onto river plains or washes away embankments.

Laurencekirk
Laurencekirk in Aberdeenshire has a name which contains the Old Scandinavian element 'kirkja', which evolved into the Scottish word 'kirk' meaning 'church', combined with the name of St Laurence of Canterbury, after whom the village church is dedicated. Earlier the place had been known as 'Kirkton', containing the Old English word 'tun', signifying a village or settlement. Hence, 'village with a church'. Later it became known as 'Kirkton of St Laurence' and since about 1770 by its present name of Laurencekirk.

Laxford
The village of Laxford in the Sutherland region of the Scottish Highlands, derived its name from the Old Norse words 'lax' meaning 'salmon' and 'fjiord', a bay or an inlet. Hence, 'inlet where salmon are found'. Laxford Bay is a large shallow inlet with a sea loch (known as Laxford Loch). The River Laxford still retains plentiful shoals of salmon and brown trout, as it did when the Vikings named it.

Lerwick
The origin of Lerwick's place name is decidedly Scandinavian. It comes from the Old Norse word 'leirr', meaning 'mud', and 'vik', meaning 'bay'. Hence, '(place by the) muddy bay'. Situated on Bressay Sound on the east coast of Shetland, Lerwick is the capital town of the archipelago.

Leslie
In the twelfth century this place in the Leven Valley of Fife was known as 'Lesslyn', a name of Celtic origin, similar to the Welsh words 'llys' and 'celyn', which translate as 'holly', and 'court' or 'enclosure'. Hence, 'enclosure where holly is found'. There is an alternative argument that the place name may come from the Leslie family who are said to have settled in the area in the years preceding the Norman Conquest.

Lesmahagow
This village on the River Nethan in South Lanarkshire is known as 'Lismahagie' and 'Lesmahagae' in Scots and in Gaelic as 'Lios MoChuda'. The Gaelic word 'leas' signified an enclosure and the second element of the place name refers to the sixth century Welsh saint, St Machutus, who may have been the founder of Saint-Malo in Brittany. He was also known as 'Mahagw' and 'Mo Fhegu' ('mo' is a Gaelic word meaning 'my'). Hence, the name means 'enclosure of my St Machutus', possibly referring to an enclosed monastery. In the sixth century Lesmahagow was known as 'Abbeygreen'.

Leuchars
The small town of Leuchars on the north-east coast of Fife derives its place name from the Gaelic word 'luachar', meaning 'rushes'. The name is taken to mean '(place of the) rushes' and was known in 1300 as 'Locres'.

Leven
The coastal sea-port of Leven, historically lay within Scoonie Parish in the Kirkcaldy district of Fife, some twenty-six miles north-east of Edinburgh. The origin of the place name is Pictish and means 'flood', after the river on which it stands and the frequent flooding outflow from Loch Leven. In Gaelic the place name is 'Inbhir Liobhann', meaning '(place at the) mouth of the River Leven'. The river name comes from the Gaelic 'leamhain', meaning 'elm river', no doubt a reference to the trees that would have lined the river banks in earlier times.

Lewis
See: 'Isle of Lewis'.

Liddesdale
The Scottish Borders town of Liddesdale is located in the valley of the Liddel Water, in the former historic County of Roxburghshire. The place name means 'valley of the River Lid'. The river name itself derives from two Old English words,

'hlyde' and 'dael' which taken together mean 'loud one', and it forms the Scottish border with England for about seven miles.

Linlithgow
The name of the West Lothian town of Linlithgow is of Celtic origin, and comprises several words similar to the Welsh 'lyn', meaning 'lake', 'llaith', meaning 'damp', 'moist' or 'wet' and 'cau', a field. Hence, the name means '(place by a) lake in a damp field'. The site was first occupied as far back as Roman times and it was established as a royal residence by David I (1124–53), who founded the town that grew up around it. The name was recorded as 'Linlidcu' in 1138.

Little Minch
See: 'Minch'.

Lochaber
There are two opinions as to the origin of this place name, which in Scottish Gaelic is 'Loch Abar'. The word 'abar' may have been Pictish, similar to the Welsh word 'aber', signifying a river mouth, and would have referred to the confluence of the River Lochy and the River Nevis as they flow into Loch Linnhe (in Gaelic called 'an Linne Dhubh'). Alternatively, 'abar' could be a corruption of the Gaelic 'eabar', meaning 'muddy (or swampy) place'. Hence Lochaber could mean '(place by a) lake of swamps', a characteristic of local topography,

Lockerbie
There is some evidence of a Roman camp here but it was not until the tenth century that Lockerbie was established as a Viking settlement in the present-day Dumfries & Galloway region. Its name is of Old Norse origin; the first element probably reflected its chieftain, a Viking known as Loc-hard; the second element, 'by', is Norse for 'village' or 'settlement'. Hence, 'Loc-hard's settlement'. In 1306 the name appears as 'Lokardebi'.

Lochgelly
In Scottish Gaelic this town in Fife is located between Lochs Ore and Gelly, and is known as 'Loch Gheallaidh', which means '(place by the) shining lake'.

Lochgilphead
Lochgilphead is a town in Argyll and Bute, whose name in Scottish Gaelic is 'Ceann Loch Gilb'. The 'gilp' element of the place name added to 'loch' means 'chisel-shaped lake'.

Lochinvar
In Gaelic, this loch in the Parish of Dalry, lies within Dumfries & Galloway in southern Scotland. Its Gaelic name is 'loch an barrha', from 'barr' meaning 'top',

'height' or 'summit'. It translates as 'lake on the height', a reference to its location among the hills.

Lochinver
The port of Lochinver, is a district of Sutherland in the Highland region, and the largest settlement on the west coast of Scotland north of Ullapool. The town lies at the head of Loch Inver. The name means '(place at the) mouth of Loch Inver'. The River Inver takes its name from the lake.

Loch Lomond
In Gaelic this freshwater Scottish lake in Argyl is known as 'Loch Laomainn', meaning 'lake by the River Leven'. The river name means 'of the elm trees'. It is located across the Highland Boundary Fault, which traditionally separates the lowlands of Central Scotland from the Highlands. The place name was recorded as 'Lochlomond' in about 1340.

Loch Ness
Loch Ness in the Scottish Highlands is named for the River Ness which flows from the loch's northern end. It is thought that the river name derives from an old Celtic word meaning 'roaring one'. In Gaelic the name is 'Loch Nis'.

Lossiemouth
Lossiemouth is a small coastal town in the ancient Royal Burgh of Elgin, located at the mouth of the River Lossie (known to the Romans as 'ostium Loxa Fluvius'), and its location is directly reflected in the place name. The river name comes from the Gaelic 'uisge lossa', which means 'water of herbs'.

Luss
The village of Luss in Argyl has an indelible association with a legend. It is said that the Irish missionary from Munster, St Kessog (sometimes 'Kessoc' or 'MacKessog', c.460–520), arrived in the Loch Lomond region to bring Christianity to the Pictish tribes in the sixth century. At that time the settlement was called 'Clachan Dhu', meaning 'dark village' on account of its location overshadowed by surrounding hills. Kessog was martyred and his body embalmed with sweet herbs which gradually grew to envelop his grave, and the name for the village was set – 'Lus', the Gaelic word for 'herb'. The town's name means '(place of) herbs'.

Machars
Also known as 'The Machars', this is a peninsula in the historical County of Wigtownshire in present-day Dumfries & Galloway. The name comes from the Gaelic 'machair', meaning low-lying grassland. These are sometimes known as 'links' (as in 'golf links'). The place name in Scottish Gaelic is 'Ghallghaidhealaibh', which literally translates as 'the Plains of Galloway'.

Mallaig
According to one interpretation, the Highland port of Mallaig (in Scottish Gaelic, 'Malaig'), derived its name from the Old Scandinavian words 'mel' and 'vik', which taken together mean 'sand dune bay'. Another view suggests the name stems from 'mar', which refers to a gull, and 'vagr', a bay or cove. Hence, 'bay of gulls'. Sea birds retain a persistent presence in this and other nearby bays.

Markinch
In Gaelic, this Fife village name is 'Marc Innis', which comes from the words 'marc', meaning 'horse', and 'innis', meaning 'island'. Hence, the name means 'horse island' or possibly 'horse meadow'. In 1055 the name was known as 'Marchinke', and by the end of the thirteenth century it had been recorded a 'Markynchs'.

Maybole
This town in South Ayrshire has a name which almost certainly came from its exposed location in a wide open landscape and the consequential lack of protection or security. In Gaelic the name is 'Am Magh Baoghail', where 'magh' meant 'plain' or 'open country', and 'baoghail' signified 'danger'. Hence, '(place on a) dangerous plain'. Others have suggested the origin of the place name came from the Old English words 'maege' and 'bothl', which taken together translate as 'kinswoman's dwelling'. Another hypothesis has it derived from the Gaelic 'magh-baile', meaning 'town of the plain'. Over time the place has been variously called 'Maiboil', 'Mayboill' and 'Minnybole'.

Mearns
The ancient historic County of Mearns (now East Renfrewshire), derived its name from the twelfth century Gaelic 'An Mhaoirne', which translates as 'the Stewartry'. This was a title that originally derived from a Pictish word similar to 'mormaer', which was a name for a regional or provincial ruler or a great steward who ruled in place of the monarch.

Megdale
The Dumfries & Galloway town of Megdale has a place name comprised of two elements: 'dale', derived from the Pictish word 'dol', meaning 'meadow' or signifying a low-lying area by a river, and 'mig', meaning 'marshy' or 'swampy'. Hence '(place in a) marshy meadow'.

Melrose
This small burgh of Melrose is located on the banks of the River Tweed in the Scottish Borders. It was originally known as Fordel, but became known as Old Melrose in 1136, around the time of the foundation of Melrose Abbey by David I. The place name comes from the Brittonic words 'mailo', meaning 'bald' (featureless), and 'ros', signifying a promontory or headland. A monastery had been established here

in the sixth century, possibly by St Cuthbert, and the name has been in place since around 700 AD, having been mentioned in the writings of Bede as well as *The Anglo-Saxon Chronicles*.

Midlothian
The ancient region and historic County of Lothian, according to the anonymous and incomplete *Life of St Kentigern*, took its name from Leudon (sometimes 'Leudonus'), the pagan king of Leudonia, which was Latin for Lothian, or 'Llewddyn' in Welsh, and in Scottish Gaelic, Midlothian is 'Meadhan Lodainn'. Before the Roman era, the region was populated by the Celtic Gododdin tribe, who descended from the Votadini. In the late tenth century the region was known as 'Loonia', and around 1200 was recorded as 'Louthion'.

Milngavie
The Glasgow suburb of Milngavie in East Dunbartonshire has the Gaelic place name 'Muileann-Gaoithe', meaning, '(place by a) windmill' or 'Meall na Gaoithe', meaning 'windswept hill', and in Scots is known as 'Mulguye'. Over the centuries there have been several variants on the place name, including 'Mylnedavie', 'Mylnegaivie', 'Milnegaivie' and 'Milngaivie'.

Minch, The
The Minch is a sea strait between the the Outer Hebrides and the Scottish Highland region which is divided between North Minch and South Minch. The name has been variously written as 'Mynch', 'Minsh', 'Mensh' and 'Mansh'. To add to the confusion there are at least four names for the straits in Gaelic, including 'An Cuan Sgitheanach', 'An Cuan Sgìth', 'Cuan na Hearadh' and 'An Cuan Leodhasach'. Several suggestions have been offered as to the meaning of the name. One has it as a corruption of the French term 'manche' as in La Manche ('the Sleeve') the French name for the English Channel as a potential source. Another has the Old Norse words 'megin', meaning 'great', and 'nes' meaning 'headland', resulting in '(sea of) great headlands' as a likely candidate. The majority of commentators seem to plump for the French connection as the most likely.

Minginish
Minginish (or in Scottish Gaelic, 'Minginis'), is a peninsula on the Isle of Skye, located west of Glen Sligachan and south of Loch Harport. The name comes from the Old Scandinavian words 'megin' and 'nes', which taken together mean 'great headland (or promontory)'

Minto
The Borders village of Minto takes its name from nearby hills, whose name derives from the Welsh Gaelic 'mynydd', meaning 'mountain', and the Old English word 'hoh', indicating a ridge or hill spur. Hence, 'mountain ridge (or hill spur)'. In

1296 the place name was recorded as 'Myntowe'. The hill called the Long Mynd in Shropshire derives its name from the same source.

Moffat
Moffat (or in Gaelic, 'Maghfada'), is a township on the River Annan in Dumfries & Galloway. The name means '(place in the) long plain', referring to the valley of the Annan. Over time the place name has been recorded as 'Moffet' in 1179 and as 'Moffete' in 1296. An alternative has been suggested in that it is a corruption of Mowat, a Norman family name.

Montrose
The township of Montrose, historically a royal burgh in the County of Angus, is located at the mouth of the River South Esk. Two explanations have been suggested for the origin of the place name: the first is derived from the Gaelic 'moine', meaning 'moor' and 'ros', signifying a promontory. Hence, '(place in the) moor on the promontory'. The second interpretation suggests Montrose is a corruption of the Old Norse 'Mouth Hrossay', as its location is at the mouth of the River Esk near to Rossie Island (in Norse, 'horse island'). The Vikings knew Montrose as Stroma, which translates as 'tidal river'. Local tradition has the place name meaning simply 'Mount of Roses', a claim supported by the town's armorial motto, 'Mare ditat, rosa decorat'.

Monzievaird
Monzievaird is a village located about two miles west of Crieff in Perth & Kinross. The place name has two possible interpretations: one is derived from the Gaelic words 'magh' and 'bard', which translates as 'plain of the bards', while the second cites 'magh' and 'edha', meaning 'corn', together with the Old English word 'vaird', signifying an enclosure or walled yard. In the latter case the name may mean 'enclosure where corn is stored'.

Morar
The west coastal region of Morar in the Highland region derives its place name from the River Morar which flows through it into Loch Morar. Until the mid-twelfth century it was a Norwegian territory known as the Kingdom of the Isles. The name comes from the Gaelic words 'mor', meaning 'big' or 'great', and 'dobhar', meaning 'water'. Hence, '(place of) great water'.

Moray
Contemporary Moray is a Unitary Authority in North-East Scotland, and was formerly part of the Grampian Region. The name in Gaelic is 'Moireibh' (or 'Moireabh'), in Latin, 'Moravia', and in Old Norse, 'Myraefi'. It is thought that the name comes from the earlier Celtic words 'mori' and 'treb', similar to the Welsh 'mor', meaning 'sea' and 'tref', a town or settlement. Hence, 'settlement by the

sea'. The place gave its name to the Moray Firth. Over time Moray has undergone several name changes: from 'Moreb' in 970, 'Moraula' in 1124 and 'Murewe' in 1185.

Mousa
The small island of Mousa in the Shetland archipelago gets its name from the Old Norse, 'Mosey', meaning 'moss island', based on the Scandinavian 'mor' meaning 'moss' and 'ey', an island. Evidence exists of Iron Age occupation in the form of a two thousand year old fortified tower which remains standing above the rocky shoreline. The island has remained uninhabited since the nineteenth century.

Muck
Towards the end of the fourteenth century, this small island in the Inner Hebrides was known as 'Helantmok', combining the Gaelic words 'eilean', meaning 'island' and 'muc', meaning 'pig'. Hence, in Scottish Gaelic: 'Eilean nam Muc', meaning 'island of pigs'. It is assumed that at some time in its early history the island was utilised for pig grazing and over time it was abbreviated to the single word name of Muck.

Muckle Flugga
Muckle Flugga is a remote Shetland Island located north of Uist, at the virtual northernmost point of the British Isles and was formerly known as the North Uist Lighthouse. The place name comes from a combination of the Old Norse words, 'mikla-flug-ey', meaning 'steep-sided island'.

Muir of Ord
Muir of Ord in the Scottish Highlands has a name reflecting both English and Gaelic connections. The first part of its name derives from the Old English word 'mor', meaning 'moor' or 'moorland', and the last comes from the Gaelic word 'ord', which referred to a rounded hill. Hence, 'moorland on a rounded hill'. Its Scottish Gaelic name is 'Am Blar Dubh', and it was known as 'Tarradale' until 1862, when the present-day name came into being. The place is known for its Neolithic or Bronze Age henge, called the 'Muir of Ord Fort', now designated as a national monument.

Mull
See: 'Isle of Mull'.

Nairn
Nairn's place name (formerly 'Invernairn'), is thought by some to come from early Celtic as the area is known to have been originally inhabited by the Picts. The name probably means 'penetrating one', though the interpretation is obscure. Its Gaelic name is 'Inbhir Narann', which translates as '(place at the) waters of the alders',

on account of the alder trees that would once have lined its river banks. The present settlement of Nairn is said to have been founded by William the Lion, and derives its name from the River Nairn, on which it stands.

Ness, Loch
See: 'Loch Ness'.

Newstead
The Scottish Borders township of Newstead was part of the territory of the Celtic Selgovae tribe when the Roman legions arrived in the area and established the fort of Trimontium on the site of present-day Newstead. In 1189 the place name was recorded in Latin as 'Novo Loco'. The present-day name in Old English is made from 'niwe' and 'stede', respectively meaning 'new place'.

Nigg
In Scottish Gaelic this Highland township's name is 'An Neag', which according to some accounts means 'the notch', a reference to the hills that overlook the parish church. Hence, '(place by) the notch'. Others believe that it may be a corruption of the word 'Wigg', as the place name is spelled in some ancient parish records; this is thought to be a derivation of the Old English word 'wich', signifying a bay or harbour. The name was recorded as 'Nig' in 1257.

Nithsdale
Nithsdale lies in the valley of the River Nith in Dumfries & Galloway and this is the source of its place name. The river name comes from ancient Celtic and means 'new one', probably due to its ever-changing course, while the last name element comes from the Old Scandinavian word 'dalr', a valley (or a dale). It was earlier known by its name of 'Strathnith' or 'Stranith', where 'strath' was the Gaelic name for a valley.

North Berwick
North Berwick (in Scottish Gaelic, 'Bearaig a Tuath') is a harbour town located in East Lothian on the south side of the Firth of Forth. The name comes from Old English words 'bere', meaning 'barley' and 'wic', a farmstead (or 'vik' in Old Norse). The word 'North' was applied to distinguish it from Berwick-upon-Tweed, which the Scots called South Berwick in the Middle Ages. The place was recorded in 1225 as 'Beruvik' and as 'Northberwyk' in 1250.

North Ronaldsay
North Ronaldsay is one of the most isolated of the Orkney Isles, located just a few miles south of Norway, and boasts some of the earliest Iron Age settlements. Along with South Ronaldsay, the island is named after St Ronald. According to tradition, he fulfilled a pledge by building the Cathedral of St Magnus at Kirkwall, where he was later murdered and venerated as a martyr. There is an opinion that he

may actually have been St Ninian, about whom little is known, but there is no real evidence to support this.

Oban
Oban, known as 'An t-Oban' in Scottish Gaelic, and meaning '(place on the) little bay', is a coastal town in Argyll & Bute. The Gaelic word 'oban' simply means 'bay'. Its later and longer name, 'An t-Oban Latharnach' means 'little bay of Lorn', where 'Lorn' referred to the 'people of Loarn Mor'; they are thought to have been a Pictish tribe who constructed a number of Iron Age hillforts in the area.

Ochiltree
There is evidence of Stone Age and Bronze Age settlements in the East Ayrshire village of Ochiltree. The place was known as 'Uchletree' in the Middle Ages, a name derived from the Brittonic word 'uxello', meaning 'high', and a word related to the Welsh 'tref', meaning 'settlement' or 'district'. Hence, the place name means 'high homestead (or settlement)'. This refers to the commanding position of the village which offers panoramic views to its south and east. In 1232 the name was spelled 'Ouchiltre'.

Orkney
The Orkney Islands have known human habitation for at least eight thousand years, but first appear in written records as 'Orkas' in the year 330 BC. The Romans knew them as the 'Orcades' after the ancient people of that name before they came under Pictish and later Viking rule. The original Celtic name for the place probably meant 'boar', but this was misinterpreted by the Danes (who had taken control in the ninth century), to mean 'seal', based on the Old Scandinavian words 'orkn' and the suffix 'ey', meaning 'island'. The islands' name translates as 'islands of the Orcos'. In 970 AD the Vikings called the group 'Orkaneya' and they remained under Norwegian rule until 1231 when they were ceded to Scotland.

Oronsay
Oronsay is a small island south of Colonsay in the Inner Hebrides. Its Scottish Gaelic name is 'Orasaigh', sometimes spelled 'Oransay'. There are two theories for the origin of the place name: on the one hand it is thought that Oronsay derived its name from St Oran who established the original priory on the island in 563 AD, and on the other it may be from the Old Norse 'Orfirisey', meaning 'island of the ebb tide'.

Orphir
The Orkney island of Orphir apparently only appears above the waterline at low tides, and this is the source of its place name. It comes from the Old Norse words 'or', meaning 'out of', 'fjara' meaning 'low water', and 'ey', island. Hence, the

name literally translates as 'island out of low water' or in short, 'tidal island'. It was recorded as 'Orfura' in 1225 and as 'Orfiara' in 1500.

Oxnam
The Scottish Borders village and Parish of Oxnam near Jedburgh (in Scots, 'Owsenam'), lies within the historic and ancient County of Roxburghshire. It is sometimes known as Oxenham, and the Roman road from Borough Bridge to the Lothians runs through the parish. The place name comes from the Old English words 'oxa' or 'oxan', meaning 'oxen', and 'ham' a village. Therefore, a simple interpretation of the place name would be 'village where oxen are bred (or kept)'. The name was recorded as 'Oxenamm' in 1148.

Oykel, River
The Oykel is a famous salmon-fishing river in the Highland region of northern Scotland, whose name is thought to be Pictish in origin. It most likely comes from 'uxello', meaning 'high', but there is a suggestion that it could come from 'ogel' meaning 'ridge'. The river was known to the Vikings as the 'Ekkjal' and once marked the border between the Pictish territory of Cat and the province of Ross.

Paisley
The earliest records of the town of Paisley, located in the Central Lowlands of Renfrewshire, came about when the Irish monk St Mirin established a chapel here beside the River Cart in the sixth century. Over time it has been called 'Passelet', 'Passeleth' or 'Passelay'. Opinions differ as the meaning of the place name. There are three suggestions: first, it is thought to mean 'moist pasture-land', based on the Brittonic word 'pasgill', meaning 'pasture'. A second credible explanation is that it is a Celtic word for a church, and may have been a corruption of the Latin word 'basilica', or as the saint would have known it in Middle Irish, 'bislec'. On this basis the place name probably means '(place with) a church'. Finally, a third offers 'Paessa's woodland clearing' as a possibility, combining the Old English personal name of a man called Paessa with 'leah', signifying a woodland glade or clearing.

Peebles
It is thought that the name Peebles may derive from an ancient Brittonic Celtic word similar to the Welsh 'pebyli', meaning 'a place with tents', what in common parlance we might call a campsite. Its Gaelic name is 'Na Puballan', and it was at one time a royal burgh and county town in Peeblesshire, now within the Scottish Borders region. In about 1125 the place name was recorded as 'Pebles'.

Penicuik
This Midlothian township is located on the banks of the North Esk River, about ten miles south of Edinburgh. The place name originates from the Old Welsh 'Pen-

y-Cog', where 'penn' means 'hill', 'y' means 'the', and 'cog' means 'cuckoo'. Therefore the name translates from the Brittonic Celtic language as '(place by the) hill where cuckoos are heard'. In 1250 the place name was recorded as 'Penikok'.

Pentland Firth
In Scottish Gaelic this stretch of water is known as 'An Caol Arcach', meaning 'the Orcadian Strait'. It is not actually a strait, but a sea inlet which separates the Orkney Islands from Caithness in the north of Scotland. The word 'Pentland' is thought to be a corruption of the Old Norse word 'Petlandsfjord', meaning 'the fjord of the Picts'.

Perth
Perth is a city in Perth and Kinross in central Scotland, located on the banks of the River Tay and was the county town of ancient Perthshire. Its name in Gaelic is 'Peairt', a word of Celtic or Pictish origin similar to the Welsh word 'perth', which translates as 'thicket' or 'copse'. In the medieval era it was known as 'Sanct John's Toun' (St John's Town), on account of its church dedicated to St John the Baptist.

Pit- (prefix)
Several Scottish townships contain the prefix 'pit' in their place names. It derives from the Pictish word 'pett', which translates as 'portion' or 'quarter', and probably referred to a sub-divided parcel of land or a designated area of territory. The final element of these place names is generally a simple Gaelic description of the land. Such places include Pitcorthie in Fife ('pett' plus 'coirthe', meaning 'quarter of the pillar stone') and Pitglassie in the Highlands ('pett' plus 'ghlasaich', meaning 'quarter of the meadow').

Pitcaple
Pitcaple is a hamlet on the River Urie in the West Garioch district of Aberdeenshire. The name includes the Pictish word 'pett' and the Gaelic word 'capull', a horse. Hence, 'portion (or quarter) of the horse or mare'. This reference is obscure, and no reasonable explanation can be found to throw light on its meaning. The place name in Scottish Gaelic is 'Baile Chapaill'.

Pitlochry
There have been at least two suggested meanings for the name of the town of Pitlochry in Perth & Kinross. One has it coming from the Gaelic 'pit cloich aire', meaning 'place of the sentinel stone', while another cites a combination of the Pictish 'pett' and the Gaelic 'cloichreach', which taken together translate as 'portion of stones' or possibly 'stony quarter'. So, the choice is either a standing stone or a possible reference to stepping stones across the River Tummel on which the town stands. This original ancient Pictish settlement has the Gaelic name 'Baile Chloichridh' or 'Baile Chloichrigh'. In modern Gaelic the word 'baile' refers to a town or a settlement.

Pittenweem

The town and port of Pittenweem in Fife takes its name from the Celtic words for 'place, quarter or portion of the cave', referring to the ancient cave of St Fillan on Cove Wynd. The name derives from the Gaelic 'pit' or the Pictish 'pett' and the remainder of the name is the Gaelic 'na h-Uaimh', meaning 'of the caves' The cave in question was said to have been the residence of the seventh century St Fillan.

Polmadie

Polmadie is a district of Glasgow whose place name is derived from the Scottish Gaelic 'Poll Mac De'. It comes from the Gaelic word 'poll', meaning 'pool', 'stream' or 'burn', the middle element 'mac', meaning 'the son(s) of', and a third element that could be either 'Daigh', a personal name, or the Gaelic 'De' (of God). Hence, either 'pool of Daigh's son' or 'pool of the sons of God'. The latter could be a reference to an early religious establishment beside the stream. The name was recorded as 'Polmacde' in 1185, which by the early seventeenth century had evolved into Polmadie, its present name.

Portmahomack

The small fishing village of Portmahomack in Easter Ross is located on the Tarbat Peninsula of the Scottish Highlands and derives its name from the Scottish Gaelic words 'Port Mo Chalmaig', which translates as 'Harbour (or Haven) of my St Colmoc'. The saint in question could be either St Colman of Lindisfarne or St Columba. The village was the site of an early settlement three or four thousand years ago, besides being the location of a Roman military camp and of a mid-sixth century Pictish monastery dedicated to the saint.

Portree

Portree is the main township and port on the Isle of Skye whose place name's origin is disputed. First, one possibility for the name is 'Port Ruigheadh', where the words 'port', meaning 'harbour' and 'righe' signified a slope, which could be interpreted as 'harbour on (or by) a slope'. Given that there are fields rising from the port that might have been used as summer pasture for livestock, this would seem to be a reasonable explanation. However, it has also been suggested that the name comes from the Gaelic 'Port Righ', which translates as 'port of the king'. It is known that James V visited the island with a fleet of warships to drum up islander's support in 1540, which makes this an equally plausible interpretation of the place name. On balance, most authorities prefer the first option, which translates the place name as 'slope harbour'.

Quaich, River

The River Quaich in Perth & Kinross meanders its way through Glen Quaich before entering Loch Freuchie and out into the River Baan. It derives its name from the Gaelic word 'cuach', meaning 'potholes'.

Raasay
The island of Raasay is situated between the Isle of Skye and mainland Scotland, from which it is separated by the Sound of Raasay. It gets its name from the Old Scandinavian word 'raa', their name for the roe deer, 'ass', meaning 'ridge', and 'ey', an island. The complete place name translates as 'island ridge where deer live'. Its name in Gaelic is 'Ratharsair', and it was known to early Viking settlers in the eighth century as 'Suoreyjar'. A herd of roe deer still live on the island.

Rannoch Moor
Many regard Rannoch Moor (in Gaelic, 'Mointeach Raithneach'), a fifty square mile moorland located in the Highland region, as the last true wilderness in the British Isles. The Gaelic word 'raineach' or 'raithneach' means 'bracken', which is a most appropriate description of the moorland topography.

Rattray
This township in Perth & Kinross, located on the River Ericht has a place name that combines Scottish Gaelic with Pictish. The first element comes from the Gaelic, 'rath', meaning 'fortress', and the second a Brittonic word similar to the Welsh word 'tref', meaning 'farmstead' or 'settlement'. Hence, 'fort by a farm'. In 1291 the name was recorded as 'Rotrefe'.

Redgorton
Two interpretations of the Perth & Kinross township of Redgorton's place name have been suggested. One has the first element coming from the Gaelic words 'roch' or 'ruach', meaning 'red' and the second, 'gorton', meaning 'little field'. In which case the name means '(place in a) little red field'. This has also been interpreted as '(place of the) field of blood', based on its proximity to Battle of Luncarty which took place nearby in around 980 AD. A second interpretation sees the first name element as derived from the Gaelic 'rath', meaning 'fort', and the 'little field' more properly identified as an enclosure. Hence, 'fort by the little enclosure'. Around 1250 the name was recorded as 'Rothgortanan'.

Renfrew
Renfrew (in Gaelic, 'Rinn Friu'), is an ancient name which comes from a combination of two Celtic words, which relate to the Welsh words 'rhyn', meaning 'point' (as in 'place'), and 'ffrwyd', signifying a current or flow of water. Hence, the place name translates as 'point of the current'. This is thought to refer to the point at which the River Gryfe joins the River Clyde. By the twelfth century, it had already been recorded as 'Reinfry' and 'Renfriu'. The town gave its name to the historic County of Renfrewshire.

Rhins of Galloway
The Dumfries & Galloway peninsula known as the Rhins of Galloway (or in Gaelic, 'Na Rannaibh'), is sometimes referred to as the Rhins of Wigtownshire and locally

as 'The Rhins' (or 'Rhinns'). The modern name is also from the Gaelic 'rinn', meaning 'peninsula'. which reaches north to south some twenty-five miles to the Mull of Galloway, the most southern tip of Scotland. In 1460, the name was recorded as 'Le Rynnys'.

Rinns of Islay
The Rinns of Islay (or in Scottish Gaelic, 'Na Roinn Ileach'), is a peninsula on the west of the island of Islay in the Inner Hebrides that is connected to the main island by a narrow isthmus at the northern end. The word 'rinns' comes from the Gaelic word 'rann' which refers to the three districts into which Islay used to be divided. The place name means 'divisions of Islay'.

Rona
Rona (in Scottish Gaelic, 'Ronaigh'), is a small island in the Western Isles, which is often referred to as North Rona to distinguish it from South Rona, another island of the Inner Hebrides. It was formerly in the historic County of Ross-shire (now Ross & Cromarty). The name probably comes from the Old Scandinavian 'hraun', meaning 'rough', and 'ey', an island, in which case 'rough island'. However, it has been suggested that the root of the place name could come from the Gaelic 'ron' and 'oy', which taken together mean 'seal island'. It may also have been named after the Irish saint, St Ronan of Locronan, whose name means 'little seal'. Take your pick.

Ronaldsay
See: 'North Ronaldsay'.

Rosemarkie
The Scottish Highland village of Rosemarkie near Fortrose on the Moray Firth (in Scots, 'Rossmartnie') has the Gaelic name 'Ros Mhaircnidh' meaning 'promontory of the horse stream'. The name is derived from the Gaelic words 'ros', 'marc' and 'nidth'. The village is home to a collection of more than a dozen finely carved eighth and ninth century Pictish standing stones, and is reputedly the largest such site in Scotland.

Ross
Ross is a historic and former Scottish county whose name comes directly from the Gaelic word 'ros', which signified a headland, promontory or moorland. As a consequence of the Local Government (Scotland) Act of 1973, the old county was abolished and the region came under the new authority of Ross & Cromarty.

Rosyth
The meaning of Rosyth's place name is unclear. However, at least two hypotheses have been suggested. The first refers to the Gaelic word 'ros', meaning 'headland',

along with the Old English word 'hyth', signifying a landing place or a jetty; in this case the name would be taken to mean something like 'landing place on a headland'. The second cites the Gaelic 'suidhe', a word which related to a level place on a hillside (a terrace, perhaps?). However, both are suppositions and the actual interpretation of the name remains obscure. The contemporary Scottish Gaelic name for the place is 'Ros Fhìobh', which is taken to mean 'headland of Fife', which throws another ingredient into the mix.

Rousay

The name of the Orkney island of Rousay reflects its Viking history. It is named after a Norse man known as 'Hrolf' (or 'Rolf'), which along with the 'ey' suffix signifying an island, produces a name that means 'Hrolf's island'. In the thirteenth century the island was known as 'Hrolfsey', by the fourteenth it had become 'Rollesay' and 'Rolsay', and in the fifteenth, the name was recorded as 'Rowsay'. The final spelling 'Rousay' was recorded in 1549.

Rum

The Hebridean island of Rum (sometimes spelled 'Rhum') probably gets its name from 'ruim', a Gaelic word meaning 'spacious' or 'roomy'. This was in comparison to the smaller neighbouring islands of Eigg and Muck. However, the precise origin of the place name is obscure and may be pre-Celtic. In 677 AD the name was being spelled 'Ruim'.

Rutherglen

Rutherglen lies a few miles south of Glasgow and the River Clyde. Its name in Scots is 'Ruglen', and in Gaelic, 'An Ruadh-Ghleann', which on the face of it translates as 'the red valley', where the Gaelic word 'gleann' means 'valley'. However, it has been suggested that the last element of the place name might refer to 'Rydderch', an ancient king of a Welsh-speaking kingdom based at Dumbarton, whose name means 'exalted ruler'. In this case the place name could mean 'valley of the exalted ruler'.

Saltcoats

The small town of Saltcoats in North Ayrshire is known in Scottish Gaelic as 'Baile an tSalainn', which translates into English as 'buildings where salt is stored'. The present-day name comes from the Old English words 'salt' and 'cot', literally meaning 'salt cottage'. The name came about as a result of the town's earliest industry of salt harvesting from the sea in the Firth of Clyde.

Sanquhar

Sanquhar is a township in the upper Nith Valley of Dumfries & Galloway which began as an ancient Iron Age hillfort. Its Gaelic name is 'Seanchair' (or 'Seann Cathair'), meaning 'old fort', a reference to the old earthworks, known as Devil's

Dyke, just outside of the modern town. The name comes from two Gaelic words: 'sean', meaning 'old', and 'cathair', a fort.

Scapa Flow
The Orkney sea area of Scapa Flow gets its name from the Old Norse 'Skalpafloi', meaning, according to some, 'bay of the long isthmus', describing the narrow strip of land between Scapa Bay and Kirkwall. The name comprises two Norse elements: 'skalpr', meaning 'boat', 'eth', meaning 'isthmus' and 'floa', technically meant 'flood', but is nearer to the modern English word 'flow'. From the ninth century the Vikings began to use Scapa Flow as a safe and sheltered harbour, particularly as a valuable winter anchorage for their long ships.

Scone
Scone has an important place in Scottish history. It was the place where the Pictish and Scottish tribes met in 843 AD to decide the Pictish succession, following their defeat by the Vikings in 839 AD, an event that saw the merging of the Scottish and Pictish kingdoms. The actual origin of the name is obscure, but it is known to have been in use in the decades preceding the Norman Conquest. The place name is pronounced 'scoon', and is known in Gaelic as 'Sgain', and in Scots as 'Scuin'. In 1020 the name was recorded as 'Sgoinde'. Scotland itself was often shown on some old maps as the 'Kingdom of Scone'.

Selkirk
Before the Romans arrived in Britain, the land where the present-day Borders town of Selkirk stands, overlooking the river known as Ettrick Water, was a territory of the Celtic Selgovae tribe. The place name comes from two Old English words, 'sele', meaning 'hall', and 'cirice', a church. Hence, the name means 'church by a hall'. In 1120 the place was called 'Selechirche', in 1190 it was spelled 'Seleschirche', and had emerged as the present name of Selkirk by the start of the fourteenth century.

Shetland
Shetland is a northern island group and Unitary Authority in Scotland, which is known to have been inhabited by Neolithic farmers more than five thousand years ago. Initially, the archipelago, of which there are about one hundred islands, of which twenty are inhabited, would have been occupied by Pictish tribes. Then, when Viking invasions began in the early ninth century, and Norsemen began to establish settlements, the islands were to become part of a larger Norwegian empire for the next two centuries. Thereby the island's name and culture became decidedly Scandinavian. The Vikings gave it the name and established their laws and language ('Norn'), which survived well into the nineteenth century. The place name was originally known to them as 'Hjaltland', probably after an early settler chieftain named Hjalti. Later it was known as 'Zetland', which eventually emerged as its present-day name, Shetland.

Shiant Islands

The Shiant Islands, known in Scottish Gaelic as 'Na h-Eileanan Seunta', are located in the Minch, east of Harris in the Outer Hebrides. The word 'Shiant' comes from the Gaelic 'Seunta', meaning 'charmed' or 'enchanted'. Hence, 'enchanted (or holy) islands'. The islands include Garbh Eilean (rough island), Eilean an Taighe (house island), Eilean na Cille (island of the church), and Eilean Mhuire (island of the Virgin Mary). The group is also known as 'Na h-Eileanan Mora', which translates as 'the big isles'.

Skara Brae

The Neolithic settlement of Skara Brae is located on the Bay o'Skaill on the west coast of the Orkney archipelago. It was established at least five thousand years ago and is designated as a World Heritage Site. Its earliest inhabitants are known as Grooved Ware people, after their distinctive lined earthenware pottery. The name 'Skara Brae' is a corruption of the old name for the site, 'Skerrabra' or 'Styerrabrae', but the name by which the original inhabitants knew the site is unknown. The meaning of the first part of the place name (Skara) is unknown, but 'brea' means 'hill'.

Skeabost

Skeabost's name in Gaelic is 'Sgiathbost', which some believe translates as 'sheltered house or farm', while others prefer the Old Norse personal name of a man called Skithi and the word 'bolstrathr', meaning 'farmstead' or 'farming settlement', in which case, 'Skithi's farm'. It is located at the head of the Loch Snizort Beag at the southern end of the Trotternish Peninsula on the island of Skye.

Skerray

The small hamlet and fishing port of Skerray is located on the north coast of Sutherland in the Scottish Highlands. The name comes from Old Scandinavian 'sker', signifying a reef or skerry (a small rocky island), specifically the rock called Carn Mor that partially obstructs the harbour entrance, and to its location on a rocky promontory on the Atlantic. Its place name in Scottish Gaelic is 'Sgeirea', which means 'between the rocks and the sea'.

Skye

See: 'Isle of Skye'.

Slamannan

The Gaelic name of this village a few miles south of Falkirk is 'Sliabh Mhanainn', a name derived from 'sliabh', meaning 'moorland' and 'Manau', a reference to the Celtic Manaw (or Mannan) tribe, whose territory was the Kingdom of Gododdin south of the Firth of Forth. The place name translates as 'Moor of the Manaw'. References to the Mannan occur in the old County of Clackmannanshire ('Clack

Mannan'), and in Dalmeny near Edinburgh, which was formerly known as 'Dumanyn', almost certainly derived from 'Dun Manann' (the stone of Mannan). The place was known as 'Slethmanin' in 1250.

Sleat
The Sleat Peninsula on the island of Skye is the traditional homeland of the MacDonald of Sleat clan. The Scottish Gaelic name of the place is 'Sleite', which comes from the Old Norse word 'slettr' (meaning smooth or even), a description of the flatness of the peninsular when compared to the mountains of the nearby island of Rum. It is estimated that almost forty per cent of the resident population of Sleat are Gaelic speakers and the local primary school teaches much of its curriculum in Scottish Gaelic.

Soay
The island of Soay is located just off the coast of Skye in the Inner Hebrides. The place is known in Scottish Gaelic as 'Sodhaigh', which derives from the Old Norse 'sauthr' and 'ey', which means 'sheep island'. Most of its former Gaelic-speaking residents were evacuated to Mull in 1953, finally surrendering to the vagaries of ocean storms and frequently cancelled ferry services. Nowadays the resident population can be counted on the fingers of one hand.

Solway Firth
Although the name of this body of water has decidedly Scandinavian origins, its name in Scottish Gaelic is 'Trachd Romhra'. It forms part of the border between Cumbria in England and Dumfries & Galloway in Scotland. The name 'Solway' was recorded as 'Sulewad' in 1218, derived from a combination of the Old Norse words 'sul' (meaning 'pillar'), and 'vath', a ford. The pillar in question is the Lochmaben Stone which marks the original ford. Finally, 'fjorthr' means 'firth', a Scottish term meaning 'estuary'.

South Ronaldsay
See: 'North Ronaldsay'.

Stenhousemuir
In Scottish Gaelic, the town of Stenhousemuir near Falkirk in the Central Lowlands of Scotland is called 'Featha Thaigh nan Clach'. The place name is a combination of the Old English words 'stan', meaning 'stone' and 'hus', a house, with the later addition of the Scottish word 'muir', meaning 'moor'. Taken together, these produce a name that translates as 'moorland by a stone house'. In 1200, it was simply known as 'Stan house', and in the seventeenth century as 'Stenhous'.

Stenness
The Vikings referred to this promontory as 'stone headland', and in 970 AD, the name was recorded as 'Steinsness'. Nowadays the stones in question consist of four

six metre high upright monoliths in what remains of a circle that originally held twelve. They are one of a number or ancient ritual monuments that were erected some five thousand years ago in the Orkney archipelago. The site at Stenness is designated as a Neolithic Orkney World Heritage Site.

St Quivox
St Quivox is a hamlet and parish in South Ayrshire, located about two miles east of Prestwick. The parish was at one time known as 'Sanchar-in-Kyle' to distinguish it from Sanquar in Nithsdale; later it came to be called St Kevoc's, which was corrupted to St Quivox. The name of St Quivox is thought to derive from 'Santa Kennocha Virgo in Coila', a local female saint who lived during the reign of Scottish King Malcolm II (c.954–1034) and was known to be a devoted advocate of the establishment of monastic institutions. Over time the place name has been spelled variously as 'St Kevock', 'St Kenochis', 'St Cavocks' and is nowadays more commonly referred to as 'St Evox'.

Stirling
The origin and meaning of the name for the City of Stirling in Aberdeenshire is uncertain, but it is thought that it might have been an earlier name for the River Forth on which it is located. There is another opinion that the name might be a corruption of the Scots or Gaelic word 'striveling', indicating a place of battle, and meaning 'struggle' or 'strife'. This view is supported by the suggestion that Stirling Castle may have been the fortress known in Gaelic as 'Iuddeu' or 'Urbs Giudi', which suffered a siege by King Penda of Mercia in 655 AD, an event recorded by Bede. However, this is supposition, and the real meaning of the place name remains a mystery.

Stornoway
Stornoway is the capital of the Isle of Lewis in the Western Isles, and has probably been inhabited for more than six thousand years, with archaeological evidence for Neolithic activity in the area since prehistoric times. In Scottish Gaelic, the town is known as 'Steornabhagh', derived from the Old Norse name 'Sjornavagr' or 'Stjornavagr', which translates as 'steering bay'. The Scandinavian word 'stjorn' is related to the English word 'stern' (as of a boat), and 'vagr' means 'bay'. The term may have come from the necessity to make complicated steering manoeuvers by boats entering or leaving the harbour.

Stranraer
Stranraer in Dumfries & Galloway is the second largest settlement in South-West Scotland. It is located at the head of Loch Ryan on the northern side of the isthmus joining the Rhins of Galloway to the mainland. The place is known as 'An t-Sron Reamhar' in Gaelic, and is also familiarly known as 'The Toon'. The Stranraer name is derived from two Gaelic words: 'sron' and 'reamhar', respectively meaning

'promontory' and 'thick'. As Stranraer has no promontory, it is assumed that the reference is actually to the Rhins of Galloway.

Strath- (prefix)
A common Scottish place name prefix, which simply means 'valley'. It is usually accompanied by the name of a valley or most often a river with which it is associated. For example, Strathclyde (on the River Clyde) and Strathearn (on the River Earn).

Strathmiglo
The Gaelic place name of this town in Fife is 'Srath Mioglach', which means 'valley of the River Miglo', which harks back to an earlier time. In fact, the river on which it stands is now called the River Eden. The name 'Miglo' is of Celtic origin and is similar to the Welsh words 'mign', meaning 'bog' or 'quagmire', and 'llwch', meaning 'loch' or 'lake'. The river name was changed when the hitherto swampy lake became a free-flowing river in the early nineteenth century. In 1832, the waterway was called the 'Water of Miglo or Eden'.

Strathpeffer
The village of Strathpeffer (in Gaelic, 'Srath Pheofhair'), is a spa town in Ross & Cromarty, located on the upper reaches of the Cromarty Firth at Dingwall. The name contains elements of the Gaelic word 'strath' which means 'valley' and the River Peffery. Hence, 'valley of the River Peffery'. The origin of the river name is Celtic and is related to the Welsh word 'pefr', meaning 'radiant' and 'beautiful'. Locally, the river name is often referred to as 'Strat', after the town's name.

Stromness
The port and second largest town of Stromness in Mainland Orkney was named by the Vikings in reference to the powerful currents off the nearby headland. The name contains two Old Norse words: 'straumr', meaning 'stream' (or in this case, 'current'), and 'nes', meaning 'headland'. Hence, 'headland (or current) of the stream'. The Norse word 'straumr' was a specific reference to the strong rip tides that flow between the Point of Ness and Hoy Sound to the south of the town.

Sullom Voe
This sheltered inlet on the North Mainland of the Shetland coast gets its name from the Old Norse words 'sula' and 'vagr', which respectively stand for 'gannet' and 'bay', 'inlet' or 'cove'. Hence, 'bay of gannets'.

Sumburgh Head
Sumburgh Head is the location of Shetland's first Lighthouse, built by Robert Stevenson and completed in 1821. The headland's name may reflect an early Viking settler, probably called Sveinn, who established a fortified stronghold of some sort

here. Alternatively, the first element may come from 'sunn', meaning 'south'. The Old Scandinavian word 'borg' signified a fort or stronghold. Hence, the place name translates either as 'headland at Sveinn's fort' or 'southern fort'. In 1506 the name was recorded as 'Swynbrocht'.

Sutherland
Sutherland is a former historic county in northern Scotland, whose name comes from the Norse words 'suthr', meaning 'southern' and 'land'. It was a southern territory of the Vikings who had settled in Orkney and Shetland. In Scottish Gaelic its name is 'Cataibh'. In around 1250, the territory was known as 'Suthernelande'.

Tain
The name of this Highland town survives intact as a Gaelic word, 'tain', simply meaning 'water'. The name is thought to be Celtic and was probably the name for the local stream that runs through the township. It is commonly taken to mean '(place of the) river (or stream)'. In 1226, the name was recorded as 'Tene', and in 1257 as 'Thayn'.

Tarbert
Tarbert is a village in Argyll & Bute that owes its place name to an historical event. It is recorded that in the year 1263 the Norwegian Haakon Haakonsson IV had his ships dragged overland from one stretch of water to another (known as 'portage'), on this occasion from Loch Lomond to Arrochar at the head of Loch Long. In Gaelic, the word 'tairbeart', meant 'portage'. Other places with a similar name are Tarbet, also in Argyle, and Tarbet Ness in the Highlands.

Threave
Threave is located in the historical county of Kirkcudbrightshire, now in Dumfries & Galloway. The name is probably derived from the ancient Brittonic word 'tref', meaning 'homestead' or 'farmstead', suggesting that the island on the River Dee was settled before Gaelic-speaking people settled the area in the seventh century. The modern name comes from the Gaelic 'treabh', simply meaning 'farm'.

Threepwood
The name 'Threepwood' (sometimes 'Thriepwood' or 'Threppe-wood') is derived from the Old English words 'threap', meaning 'disputed' or 'debated', and 'wudu', a wood. Hence, 'disputed woodland'. The Scots term 'threaplands' referred directly to the disputed ownership of woodland on the Scottish-English border, as this place in Ayrshire must have been. In about 1230 the place name was spelled 'Trepewode'.

Thurso
Thurso stands at the mouth of the River Thurso on the extreme north coast of Highland Scotland, from which it takes its name. The river name is of Celtic origin

and meant 'bull river', itself derived from nearby Dunnet Head, known to the Romans as 'Tarvedunum', meaning 'bull fort'. The place has a history of settlement dating back at least five thousand years and came to prominence during the period of Norse rule when it developed as a major trading port and was known in 1152 as 'Thorsa'.

Tiree
The Isle of Tiree is the most westerly island in the Inner Hebrides; its Scottish Gaelic name is 'Eilean Tiriodh', from the Gaelic 'tir', meaning 'land' and the personal name of an early settler or chieftain who was probably called Ith. In which case, the name means 'Ith's land'. There is evidence of a thriving settlement on the island well before the first century, with some twenty Iron Age forts known to exist, including 'Dun Mor a' Chaolais' (the big fort of Caolas), which stands on the hill above Milton harbour.

Tobermory
Tobermory (in Gaelic, 'Tobar Mhoire'), is the chief town on the Isle of Mull in the Inner Hebrides. The name translates as 'Well (of) Mary', a reference to an ancient well by the old chapel to the west of the present-day town, which is dedicated to the Virgin Mary.

Tomintoul
This village in the Moray area has the Gaelic name, 'Tom an t-Sabhail', which means 'the barn on a knoll', from 'tom', meaning 'knoll' (or 'little hillock'), 'an', meaning 'of', and 'sabhal', a word that signifies a barn or granary.

Tranent
This East Lothian town (formerly in Haddingtonshire), is located in the south-east of Scotland. The place name is believed to be of Brittonic Celtic origin, and contains the elements 'tre' or 'tref', a farm, and 'nant', a stream or brook. Hence, 'the farm by the stream'.

Troon
The port town of Troon is thought by some to be a Celtic or Pictish word, similar to the Welsh 'trwyn', meaning 'cape' or 'headland', and that the name refers to the prominent headland in South Ayrshire on which the town stands. In 1371 the place name was recorded as 'Le Trone', and in 1464 as 'Le Trune'.

Tummel
The Tummel is a river in Perthshire that flows east from Loch Rannoch. The origin of the river name is somewhat obscure, but in Gaelic it is 'Abhain Teimheil', which translates as 'river of darkness', a possible reference to its route through heavily wooded and deep gorges. Loch Tummel, which is fed by the River Tummel, is known locally as 'Strathtummel'.

Turriff
In Scottish Gaelic, this town and civil parish on the River Deveron in Aberdeenshire, is called 'Torraibh'. The name derives from the Gaelic word 'torr', meaning 'hill' or 'mound', producing a place name that can be interpreted as 'place of the hills (or mounds)'. Over time, it has been known as 'Turrech', 'Turreth' and 'Turreff'.

Uamh Bheag
Uamh Bheag is a peak in the Glen Artney Hills range in Perth & Kinross whose name comes from the Gaelic 'uamh', meaning 'little', and 'beag' meaning 'cave' or 'cavern'. Hence the place name may be interpreted to mean '(mountain with a) little cave'.

Uig
Scotland has two places called Uig. The place name is pure Gaelic and means 'bay'. The first is in the Highland region of Skye and was known in 1512 as 'Wig'; the second is on the island of Lewis and was recorded in 1549 as 'Vie'; it may have been derived from the Old Scandinavian word 'vik', also meaning 'bay'. Both place names should be interpreted as '(place by a) bay'.

Uist
Uist (in Gaelic, 'Uibhist'), are two islands in the Outer Hebrides, separated into North and South Uist, which are linked by a causeway. The name is Scandinavian and comes from the Old Norse, comprising two elements, 'i', meaning 'in' (or 'inner'), and 'vist', meaning 'dwelling' (or 'abode'). Hence, 'inner dwelling'. The significance is somewhat obscure, but may have come from an original Celtic name.

Ulbster
The hamlet of Ulbster is located on the eastern coast of Caithness in the Scottish Highlands. The name comes from the Old Norse words 'ulfr', meaning 'wolf' and 'bolstathr', an abode or dwelling. Therefore, the place name means 'wolf's dwelling' (or in modern parlance, 'wolf's lair'), though there has been no record of wolves in the area for centuries. The place was recorded as 'Ulbister' in 1538.

Ullapool
The name of the Highland town and port of Ullapool (in Gaelic, 'Ulapul'), is yet another example of inroads made by the Vikings in northern Scotland. Its Scandinavian place name is derived from two Norse words, 'ulfr' and 'boeli', which respectively translate as 'wolf's lair (or dwelling)'. The name was recorded as 'Ullabill' in 1610.

Unst
Unst is one of the most northerly of the Shetland Islands. The name is thought to be pre-Celtic and has clear Viking associations. The place name meaning

remains unknown, though it has been suggested that it might come from the Old Norse word 'ornyst', meaning 'eagle's nest'. The island was recorded as 'Ornyst' in 1200.

Urquhart
According to one source, Urquhart, in the Scottish Highlands, derives from the Gaelic word 'aird', meaning 'headland' and the Old Welsh word 'cardden', referring to a thicket or a wood. It was recorded in the twelfth century as 'Airdchartdan', and translates as '(place by or in a) thicket on the headland'. There is another place called Urquhart in Fife, but this is thought to come from a Pictish term related to the apportionment of land or territory.

Vaternish
Vaternish (sometimes 'Waternish') is a peninsula on the north-west coast of Skye that has a Scandinavian name origin, based on the Old Norse words 'vatn' (water) and 'nes'(promontory), and means 'water promontory (or headland)', and this is the location of the present-day Vaternish Lighthouse. In Gaelic, the name is 'Bhatairnis'. In 1501 the name was spelled 'Watternes'.

Wardlaw
The meaning of the Wardlaw place name comes from the Old English 'weard', meaning to watch or keep lookout, and 'hlaw', a hill. It referred to a watch-post or fortress upon a hill, as well as those who kept watch. Hence, 'watch-post (or watchers) on a hill'. Located near Beauly (Bewley) in the former County of Inverness-shire, the name appears in 1210 as 'Wardelaue'.

Western Isles
The Western Isles, or Outer Hebrides, is a Unitary Authority, and as the name suggests, the most western islands in Scotland. Their Gaelic name is 'Na h-Eileanan an Iar', which translates as 'islands of the west'.

Westray
Westray is the most western island in north Orkney. Its name comes from the Scandinavian 'vestr' and 'ey', together meaning 'western island'. The name was recorded as 'Vesturey' in 1260. The island is known to have been inhabited for at least five thousand years, with Neolithic and Bronze Age artefacts found here during archaeological digs.

Whalsey
Whalsey, or 'whale island' in the Shetland Islands, gets its place name directly from the Scandinavian words 'hval', meaning 'whale', and 'ey', an island. The reference is not to any whaling that took place here, rather it refers to the shape of the island. The name was recorded c.1250 as 'Hvalsey'.

Whithorn

The Dumfries & Galloway township of Whithorn was known in the eighth century as 'Candida Casa', meaning 'the white house', a reference to the stone church built here by St Ninian. Its Gaelic name is 'Taigh Mhartainn', after the church dedication to St Martin of Tour. Its modern name comes from the Old English 'hwit' and 'aern', which respectively translate as 'white building'.

Wick

The burgh of Wick in Caithness is another example of a Scandinavian place name; it derives from a single Norse word, 'vik', signifying a bay or a cove. Its Scots name is 'Week', and in Gaelic it is known as 'Inbhir Uige'. The bay on which the town stands is known as Wick Bay. The place was known as 'Vik' in 1140 and as 'Weke' in 1455.

Wishaw

There are several theories as to the meaning and origin of the name of the North Lanarkshire village of Wishaw. The 'shaw' element most likely comes from the Old English word 'sceaga' meaning 'woodland', and some argue that the first name element may come from 'via', a reference to an ancient Roman road or pathway; in this case, 'road (or path) through a wood'. On the other hand, some prefer the Saxon word 'wiht', meaning 'bend' (or 'bending'), in which case 'bending (or winding path through a) wood'. Others cite the Scottish Gaelic word 'uisge', meaning 'water', which given the village's location on the banks of the River Clyde, seems eminently feasible. Yet another suggestion is 'wee wood', meaning 'small wood' in the Scottish vernacular. The township was earlier known as 'Wygateshaw', a Scots name meaning 'wicket (or willow) gate in the wood'.

Yarrow

The Scottish Borders township of Yarrow is named after the River Yarrow that flows through it. The river name derives from an ancient Celtic word similar to the Welsh 'garw', meaning 'rough one'. The place name may be taken to mean '(place by the) River Yarrow'. The name was recorded around 1120 as 'Gierwa'.

Yell

The Shetland island of Yell has a much disputed place name. Some think it dates back to a lost Pictish word, others name the Old Norse 'jala', meaning 'white island', while many cite the Norse 'gjall', meaning 'barren'. Most agree that the name is probably pre-Scandinavian, but no definitive answer to the meaning of the place name has been agreed so far. In 1250, the place was recorded as 'Yala'.

Yoker

The Glasgow suburb of Yoker dates from the twelfth century and was formerly in the historic County of Renfrewshire. It was once an important crossing point over the River Clyde to Renfrew on the south bank. The place name comes from the Scottish Gaelic 'An Eochair', which has been variously translated as '(place on) low-lying ground', and as '(place on the) river bank'.

Zetland
Zetland was the former name for Shetland. (See: 'Shetland'.)

Part Six

Wales & the Marches

Background to the Welsh Language

The Welsh language (in Welsh, 'Cymraeg'), evolved from a form of Celtic, sometimes called 'P-Celtic', and arrived in Britain in around 600 BC. A form of it was spoken throughout the British Isles long before the arrival of the Romans. Often known as Brittonic (or 'Brythonic'), it formed the basis of Welsh, Cornish and Breton and was spoken across Western Europe as far east as Turkey. This language gradually evolved into several variant dialects: in south-west Britain it developed into Cornish, while in northern England and lowland Scotland it evolved into Cumbric (or Scottish Gaelic).

Welsh became the language of storytelling, and was rarely written down until important texts like the *Mabinogion* were compiled in Middle Welsh in the twelfth and thirteenth centuries from earlier oral traditions. *The Black Book of Carmarthen* (in Welsh, 'Llyfr Du Caerfyrddin'), completed before 1250, is thought to be the earliest surviving manuscript written solely in Welsh. By this time, Welsh princes

Bryn-Celli-Ddu portal tomb mound, Anglesey.

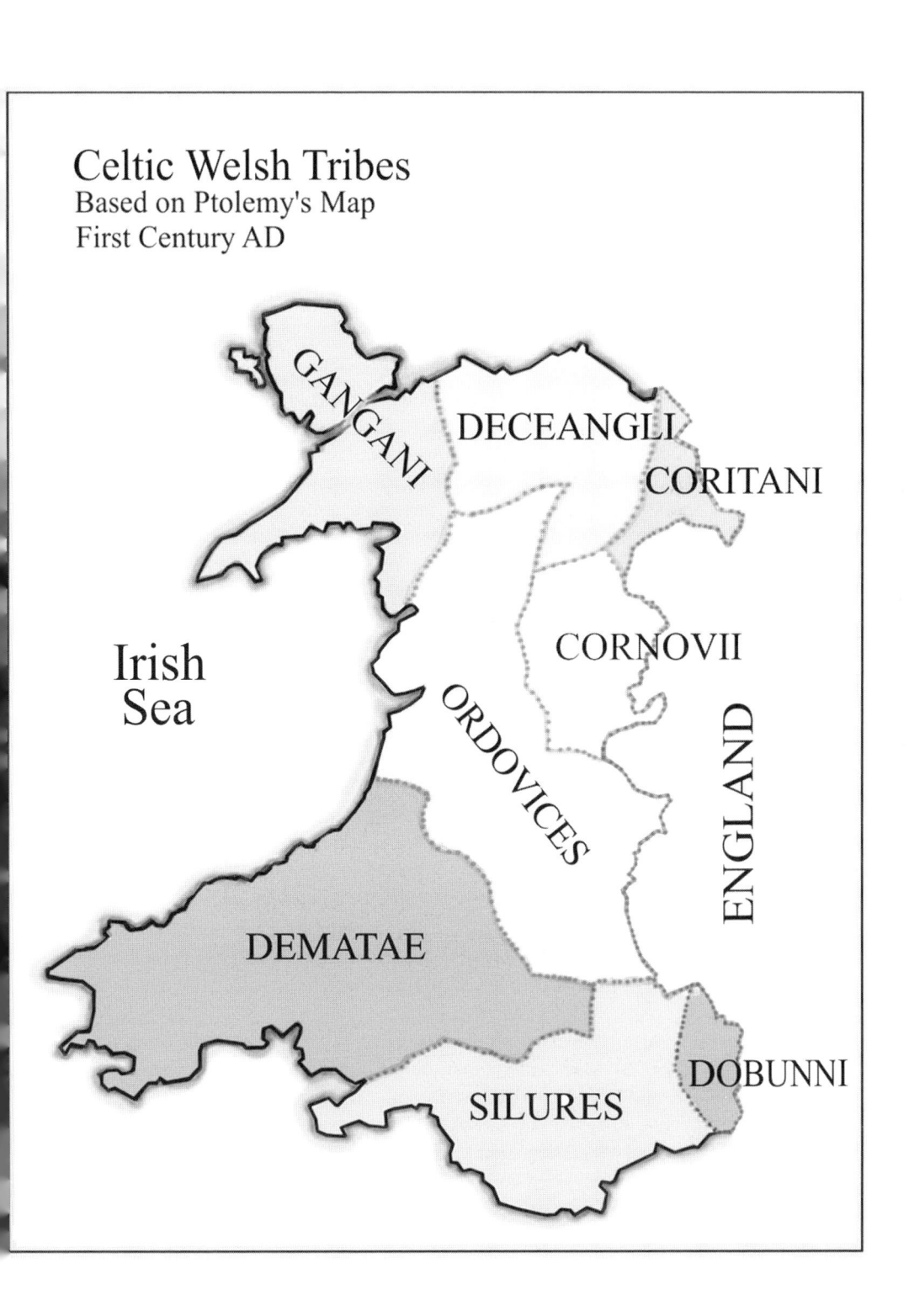

Celtic Welsh Tribes
Based on Ptolemy's Map
First Century AD

and administrators had already adopted a canon of Welsh laws known as 'Cyfraith Hywel', which had been recorded in the tenth century by Hywel ap Cadell, the King of Wales.

While the English and Cornish eventually submitted to their Norman overlords, albeit grudgingly, the subjugation of Wales proved much more protracted; it took many generations and even then it largely failed to completely eradicate the culture and language, despite whole tracts of the countryside which were ceded to Norman knights following the defeat of the Saxon army under King Harold at Hastings.

Edward I saw fit to create a whole range of heavily fortified castles around Wales, at Beaumaris, Caernarfon, Conwy and Harlech, as clear symbols of Welsh subjugation and as military establishments from which his knights and henchmen could rule.

Welsh affairs suffered a final tragic downturn with the accession of the Tudors to the English throne. In 1536, Henry VIII's Act of Union virtually banned the writing or speaking of Welsh. Laws were enacted to remove the status of the Welsh language, making English the official language of administration, law, government and trade, despite the fact that many native Welsh continued to speak it as a first language. Further, the decline was hastened by the gradual Anglicisation of Wales, which saw its upper classes opting for English and abandoning their native Welsh language.

However, there was a burgeoning undercurrent of opposition to Henry's draconian clamp-down, and in 1588, William Morgan, the Bishop of Llandaff, published *The Holy Bible* in Welsh, as well as the *Book of Common Prayer* in 1599. Morgan's work in translation is regarded as a major milestone in the history and promotion of the Welsh language. Apart from this, and despite rare, periodic and unsuccessful revolts and resurgences, little changed until the twentieth century.

It was not until the Welsh Courts Act of 1942 that defendants and plaintiffs, who hitherto had been obliged to speak English in all court proceedings, were allowed to present their cases in Welsh. Then, in 1967, supported by the Welsh Nationalist Party (Plaid Cymru), and the Welsh Language Society, the Hughes Parry Report stated that Welsh should be afforded equal legal status to English, both spoken and written, in all courts.

This saw the long-awaited and overdue reversal of Henry VIII's edict. As a consequence, Welsh began to emerge onto the public stage, with street signs appearing in both Welsh and English and its towns and cities opting for traditional Welsh spellings for their place names. For example, 'Carnarvon' became 'Caernarfon', 'Wrexham' became 'Wrecsam' and 'Caerphilly' reverted to 'Caerffilli'.

Finally, in 1999, a devolved Welsh National Assembly was created as a bilingual institution, heralding a time when the Welsh language had unequivocally come into its own.

The Marches

During the seventh century, Penda, king of the Anglo-Saxon Kingdom of Mercia, made peaceful alliances with Welsh kingdoms, who had attempted to expand their territory eastwards into Cheshire, Shropshire and Herefordshire. In the century that followed, towns like Shrewsbury and Hereford began to define the borderlands between England and Wales. In an attempt to mark the limit of his territory, King Offa of Mercia oversaw the creation of an earthwork and ditch boundary between 757 and 796 AD, which became known as Offa's Dyke (in Welsh, 'Clawdd Offa'). For centuries this was a visible, though frequently disputed frontier between Wales and England. Border towns like Oswestry, Leominster, Ludlow and Hay-on-Wye were never quite sure on which side of the frontier they were.

These borderlands became known as the 'Marches', a term derived from the Old English word 'mearc', meaning 'boundary' or 'border'. They came about when William the Conqueror sought to bring these borderlands fully under his control, but encountered stiff Welsh resistance. His reaction was to establish so-called Marcher Lordships, creating virtual petty kingdoms and granting them to over a hundred and fifty of his most valued supporters, among them his closest Norman friends and allies, Hugh d'Avranches, Roger de Montgomerie and William FitzOsbern, the earls of Hereford, Shrewsbury and Chester.

These Marcher territories stretched from Cheshire in the north to Gloucestershire in the south, and included some southern Welsh counties, from Monmouthshire in the east to Pembrokeshire in the west. The region was referred to as the 'March of Wales' in the *Domesday Book*. Marcher lords went on to build castles and fortified manor houses, to administer laws and establish towns in these autonomous borderlands.

Although nowadays, the Welsh-English border is firmly established, many English towns in the borderland still bear strong Welsh connections, retaining elements of Celtic Gaelic roots in their place names.

The Welsh Place Names

Aberaeron
The town of Aberaeron (sometimes 'Aberayron') is located in the traditional County of Cardiganshire. Its name incorporates the common Welsh element 'aber', indicating an estuary or river mouth, plus the name of the River Aeron, on which it stands. 'Aeron' comes from the Middle Welsh word 'aer', meaning 'slaughter', which relates to Aeron, an ancient Welsh god of war.

Aberavon
Also known as Aberafan, there have been many variations on this place name, including 'Abberauyn' in the early fifteenth century and 'Aberavan' by the mid-

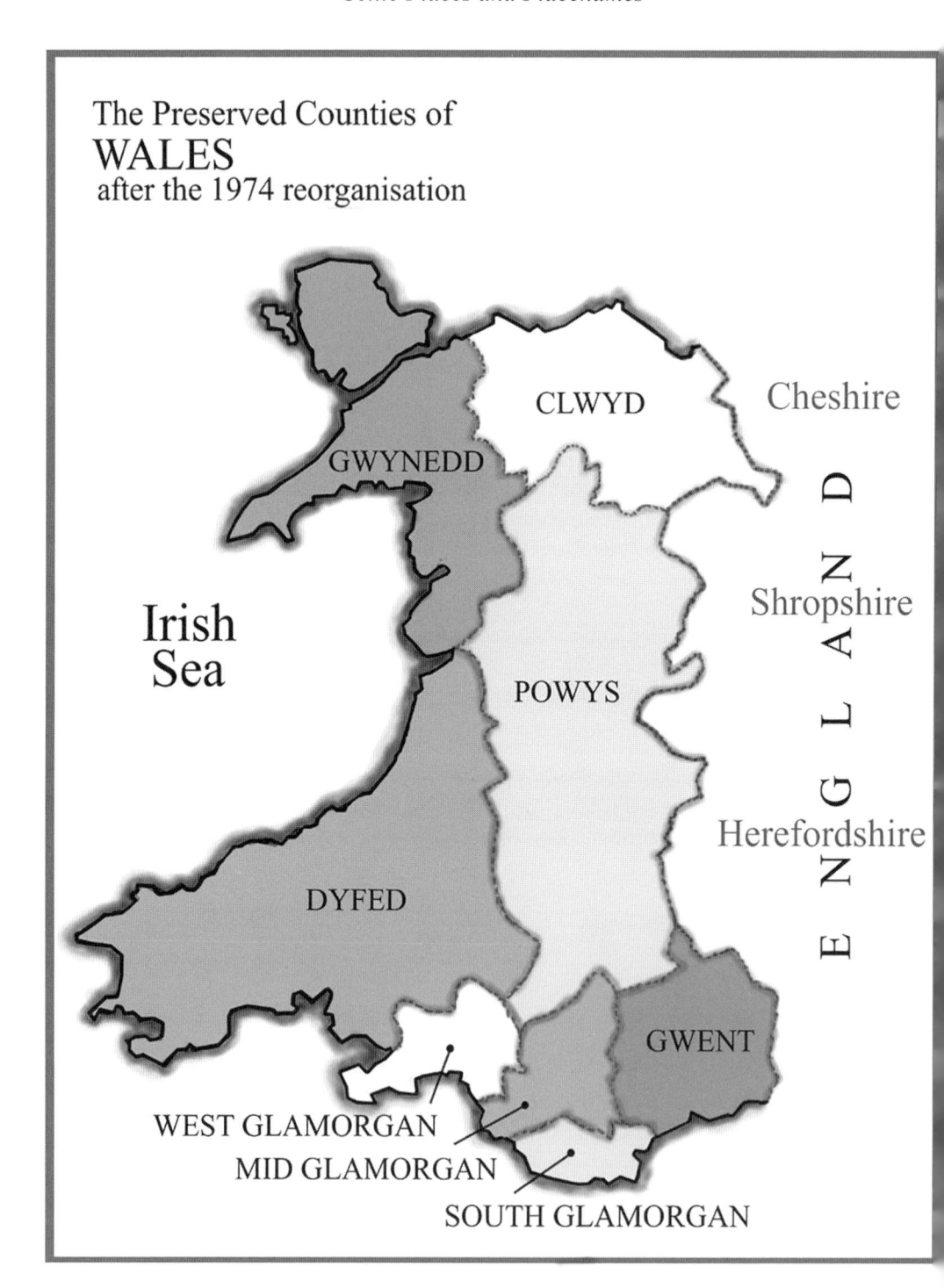

The Preserved Counties of WALES after the 1974 reorganisation

- GWYNEDD
- CLWYD
- Cheshire
- Irish Sea
- Shropshire
- POWYS
- Herefordshire
- DYFED
- ENGLAND
- GWENT
- WEST GLAMORGAN
- MID GLAMORGAN
- SOUTH GLAMORGAN

sixteenth. It is located in South Wales in the historic County of West Glamorgan. The Welsh name translates as 'mouth of the River Afan'. The origin of the river name may come from 'a-ban' meaning 'from the heights', descriptive of the river's rapid descent on its way to the sea.

Abercraf
Abercraf is located in the extreme south of Glamorgan, in the Upper Swansea Valley. The place name comes from 'craf' meaning 'stream' or 'confluence'. The stream in question is the Nant-llech Bellaf, a tributary of the River Tawe, The name of the place translates as 'mouth of the stream'.

Aberdare
In modern Welsh the name of this town in the Cynon Valley of Glamorgan is 'Aberdar', from the Gaelic 'Afon Dar', and means 'mouth of the River Dare', though it is located at the confluence of the Dar and the Cynon. The Dar gets its name the Welsh word for oak tree, and may be related to Daron, an ancient Celtic goddess of oak woods.

Abergavenny
The Romans built a fort here which they called 'Gobannum' and also worked an ironworks in the district of what would become Abergavenney. By 1175 the place was recorded as 'Abergavenni', a name derived from the Welsh 'aber', signifying the mouth of a river and Gafenni after the river name. Hence, the place name may be taken to mean '(settlement at the) mouth of the River Gafenni', which itself was derived from the Celtic, and may have meant '(place of) the blacksmith', possibly on account of the ancient ironworks.

Abergele
Abergele in the County of Conwy was known in the ninth century as 'Opergelei', and by the mid-thirteenth century had developed its modern-day spelling. It comprises, 'aber' along with the Old Welsh 'gelau', meaning 'blade', which together translate as 'mouth of the River Gele'.

Aber-soch
The village of Aber-soch (sometimes spelled as one word, 'Abersoch'), in the community of Llanengan in Gwynedd, lies at the mouth of the River Soch (in Welsh, 'Afon Soch'), and this is the meaning of the place name. The river name is probably derived from the Irish Gaelic word 'socc', which is similar to the Welsh word 'hwch', which some translate as meaning 'nosing or burrowing one', while others are more specific and cite 'sow' (a female pig). Many places in the early medieval period were named after domestic animals

Celtic Places and Placenames

Abertillery
The name of the South Wales township of Abertillery in the Ebbw Fach Valley in Blenau Gwent (sometimes 'Abertyleri' or 'Aberteleri'), means 'mouth of the River Tyleri'. It is located at the mouth of the river whose name is thought to come from the personal name of an early settler of the area. According to the Welsh Language Board, just under ten per cent of the population of Abertillery speak Welsh.

Ambleston
In the Welsh language the Pembrokeshire village of Ambleston is 'Treamlod', based on 'tre' or 'tref', meaning 'farm' and the name of an early owner or founder of the community, a man known as Amelot, which is thought to have been a Norman personal name. Finally, the Old English suffix 'tun' was added, which represents a farming settlement. Hence, the place name means 'Amelot's farm'. It was recorded as 'Amleston' in 1230.

Amesbury
Amesbury is a Wiltshire town which illustrates the fluidity and dynamically changing limits of Celtic tribelands. The name translates as 'Ambre's stronghold', based on the Iron Age hillfort overlooking the River Avon here and a man called Ambre, possibly a local chieftain or warlord. The fort became known as Vespasian's Camp. It is thought by some that the name of Amesbury may be derived from Ambrosius Aurelianus, the fifth century leader of Romano-British resistance to Saxon invasions and a figure associated with the mythical legend of King Arthur, although the name was established long before the legend. The place name was recorded as 'Ambresbyrig' in about 880 AD, and was listed in the *Domesday Book* as 'Ambresberie'.

Amlwch
The town of Amlwch on the island of Anglesey derives its name from two Welsh name elements: 'am', meaning 'near' or 'around', and 'llwch', which referred to a pool or a muddy swamp, and occasionally to an inlet. Therefore, the name translates either as '(place) near a swamp' or '(place) near an inlet'. The latter explanation is supported by the inlet which later developed into the town's harbour.

Anglesey
The Welsh name for Anglesey is 'Ynys Mon', of which the first word, 'Ynys' means 'island', while the significance of the 'Mon' element (which was 'Mona' in Latin and 'Monez' in Old English), is open to dispute, with some suggesting it may have meant 'cow'. In this case the place name would translate as 'Island of the Cow.' Others cite Old Scandinavian where in Norse, the element 'ey' referred to an island, and suggest it means 'island of the Angles'. Others cite a Viking called Ongull who may have been an early settler or chieftain; in this case the name translates as 'Ongull's island'. Alternatively, the Roman Latin word, 'mona', taken from the

Celtic language, referred to a mountain or a hill, in which case this could be a reference to Holyhead Mountain at the extreme north-west of the island.

Bala
For most of its recorded history the town of Bala in Gwynedd has included the definite article 'the' (or in Welsh, 'y') as the first element of its place name, being variously recorded as 'The Bala', 'Y Bala' and 'La Bala'. The word 'bala' represents a strip of dry land surrounded by water or wetland, generally applied to an outflow from a lake. Given that Bala Lake (in Welsh, 'Llyn Tegid'), is the largest natural lake in Wales, this might go some way to explain the place name. It has also been suggested that it may possibly be a reference to the flood plain of the River Dee.

Bangor
The Welsh word 'bangor' originally referred to a supporting crossbar that strengthened a wattled or plaited fence, and this is the simple explanation of the place name. This town in Gwynedd is thought to derive its name from just such a fence that was erected around the monastic establishment that had been established here in 525 AD. There are also towns called Bangor in Northern Ireland and Flintshire that have the same derivation; both were established by monasteries.

Bangor-on-Dee
Bangor-on-Dee is a village in Wrexham which was founded when St Deiniol established a monastery here in the sixth century. He is venerated in Brittany as St Denoual. The place name means '(place of the people of) Bangor by the (River) Dee', but paradoxically, its Welsh name is 'Bangor-is-y-Coed', which translates as 'Bangor below the wood'. Just to confuse the matter further, in 1607 it had been given the Latin name 'Bangor Monachorum', meaning 'Bangor of the monks'. In the eighth century the name was recorded simply as 'Bancor' and in 1277 as 'Bangor'.

Bargoed
The town of Bargoed in the Rhymney Valley has the Welsh name 'Bargod', which means 'border' or 'boundary'. This is a reference to the River Bargod, which is commonly known as 'Bargod Rhymni', and marks the ancient boundary between Glamorgan and Monmouthshire,

Barmouth
Barmouth in the north-western County of Gwynedd is officially known in Welsh as 'Abermaw' although it is often locally referred to as 'Y Bermo'. Its original name, 'Aber-Mawdd', derived from the estuary of the River Mawdd (now called 'Mawddach', where 'ach' means 'little'), on which the town is located. It was thanks to the dominating and pervasive English influence on Welsh culture

Celtic Places and Placenames

throughout several centuries, that the English name, Barmouth, came into being and has persisted.

Barry
In Welsh, the seaside town of Barry in the Vale of Glamorgan is 'Y Barri', named after the local hill, 'The Barr', whose name translates as 'the summit of the hill'. The place was known in the thirteenth century as 'Barren' and became attached not only to the original settlement but to the adjacent island. In Welsh, the island is called 'Ynys y Barri', meaning 'Barry Island'. In the mid-sixteenth century the place name was recorded as 'Aberbarrey' and later that same century as 'The Barry'.

Beddgelert
Despite the traditional interpretation of this place name, based on a heroic dog called Celert (or Gelert) and his apparent grave, Celert was most probably not a dog at all, but was the name of a man. The myth emerged in the sixteenth century and has persisted ever since, with a commemorative stone being erected on the site of the supposed dog's grave in the eighteenth century. The village was most likely named after a Christian missionary called Celert (or Cilert) who settled here sometime in the early eighth century. The name was first recorded in 1258 as 'Bekelert', and later in 1269 as 'Bedkelerd'. The name translates into English as 'Gelert's Grave'.

Bettws-y-Crwyn
Not untypically, like many places close to the England-Wales border, this small village in south-west Shropshire has a Welsh name that translates as 'Chapel of the Fleeces'. Originally, the first element of the name came from the Middle English word 'bedhus', meaning 'house of prayer', which became 'bettws' (or 'betws') in Welsh. The 'y-Crwyn' element means 'the fleeces'. The house of prayer in question is the village Church of St Mary.

Betws-y-Coed
As with Bettws-y-Crwyn the first element of the Conway Valley village of Betws-y-Coed's place name is exactly the same, and signifies a chapel. The last element 'coed', signifies a wood or woodland. Hence, the place name is generally taken to mean 'chapel in the wood'. In 1254 the place was simply recorded as 'Betus', and was not known by its full present-day name until the early eighteenth century.

Blaenavon
The name of this Monmouthshire town and community in Torfaen (Gwent) is spelled 'Blaenafon' in Welsh, from 'blaen', meaning 'head of the stream', and 'afon' meaning 'river'. The river in question is the Sychan which flows from its source at Blaen Sychan, to which the town name relates. In 1532 the place name was recorded as 'Blaen Avon', and was 'Blaen-Avon' or simply 'Avon' in 1868.

Wales & the Marches

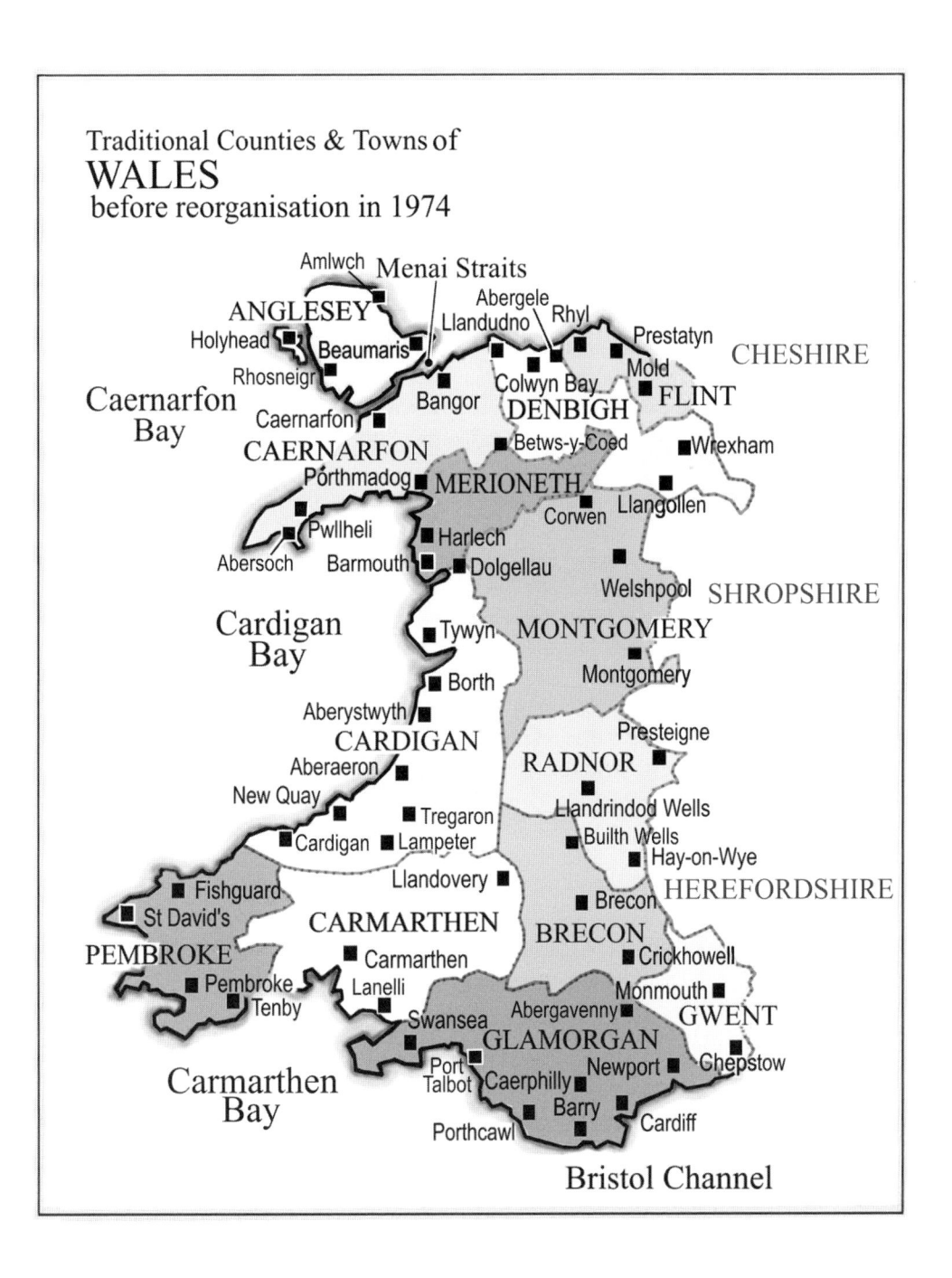

Traditional Counties & Towns of
WALES
before reorganisation in 1974

Blaenau Ffestiniog
Blaenau Ffestiniog in Gwynedd is a nineteenth century industrial settlement that gets its name from the older village of Ffestiniog (often referred to as 'Lan Ffestiniog'). The name was recorded in 1292 as 'Festinioc', and is thought to mean 'territory of Ffestin', the final suffix, 'iog' being a reference to a fortified position and a corruption of the Celtic word 'akon', meaning 'place (or territory)'. The 2011 National Census revealed that around eighty per cent of Blaenau Ffestiniog residents were Welsh speakers.

Borth-y-Gest
The Borth-y-Gest name comes from the Welsh word 'porth', meaning 'cove' or 'harbour'. It is overlooked by the hill called Gest (from 'cest', meaning 'paunch'), sometimes known by the alternative name, 'Moel-y-Gest', of which 'moel' means 'bare hill'. The place name may therefore be taken to mean 'harbour (near the) bare hill (shaped like a) paunch'. Locals often refer to the place simply as 'Y Borth' or 'Borth'.

Brecon
The market and minster town of Brecon in Powys has the Welsh name 'Aberhonddu', which means 'mouth of the Honddu', after the River Honddu, which meets the River Usk near the town. The Honddu river name comes from the Welsh 'hawdd', meaning 'pleasant'. During the Dark Ages the town was called 'Brycheiniog' and later known as 'Brecknock'. The name derives from Brychan Brycheiniog, the legendary fifth century Celtic king of Brycheiniog in South Wales. This became known as Brecknockshire (in Welsh, 'Sir Frycheiniog'), meaning 'the shire of Brycheiniog'. The nearby Brecon Beacons were the location of signal fires or beacons during medieval times.

Bryn-mawr
This township in Blaenau Gwent (sometimes spelled as one word, 'Brynmawr'), began life as Bryn-mawr farm, a name derived from the Welsh 'bryn', meaning 'hill' and 'mawr', meaning 'big'. Hence '(place on a) big hill'. The hill in question is the high upland plateau of Gwaun y Helygen, whose name means 'moorland of the willow tree'. Then in the nineteenth century the village underwent significant industrial development with the opening of the Nantyglo Ironworks and the name Bryn-mawr was commonly adopted for the settlement.

Builth Wells
The Welsh name for Builth Wells is 'Llanfair-ym-Muallt', which translates into English as 'church of Mair in Buallt (the cow pasture)'. In the mid-thirteenth century, the place name was simply recorded as 'Llanveyr', meaning 'St Mary's church', and by the end of that century as 'Lamueyr Buelth (or Buellt)'. In the nineteenth century, after a mineral spring was discovered in the town, the word

'Buelth' was changed to 'Buallt' to promote it as a spa town and the additional word 'Wells' was added to the place name.

Caergwrle
Caergwrle is a Flintshire village in North-East Wales. It was formerly known as Corley, to which the Welsh 'caer' (meaning 'fort'), was later added. This transpired in view of the myth of a giant called Corley (in Welsh, 'Gwrle'), who lived in the castle and reputedly is buried in a Neolithic mound nearby at Cefn-y-Bedd. In 1327 the name was recorded as 'Caer-Gorlei', meaning 'Gwrle's fort', and in 1601 it was known as 'Caergurley'.

Caerleon
Caerleon near Newport in Gwent (in Welsh, 'Caerllion'), was the site of a Roman military base for the Second Augusta Legion, who knew it by its Latin name, 'Isca Legionis', meaning 'Isca of the Legions'. Their fortified base was located on the site of an earlier Iron Age hillfort. 'Isca' is a Brittonic name meaning 'water', and was what the Romans called the River Usk, whose present-day name comes from a Celtic word meaning 'abounding in fish'.

Caernarfon
The region around Caernarfon in Gwynedd had been inhabited by the Celtic tribe of Ordocices, long before the Romans took occupation in the first century. In about 75 AD they established the military settlement of Segontium on the site of the present-day Norman castle. The place name breaks down into three separate elements: 'caer', a Welsh word denoting a fortress, and 'arfon', the name of the Welsh administrative district along the southern shore of the Menai Strait. The letter 'n' in the middle of the name is a shortened form of 'yn', meaning 'in'. Therefore, the name means 'fort in Arfon'.

Caerphilly
This historic South Wales town in Glamorgan (known in Welsh as 'Caerffili'), has a name that means 'fort of Ffili'. It is not known exactly who Ffili was, but he is thought by some to have been a Celtic man living before the Roman occupation of Britain. Others suggest St Ffili, who is said to have established the settlement that gave the town its name. It is known that the Romans built a fort here, which raises yet a third possibility, that Ffili might have been a Romano-British man. However, there is little tangible evidence for either hypothesis. The place name was recorded as 'Kaerfili' in 1271 and as 'Kaerphilly' in 1314.

Caersws
The village of Caersws on the River Severn in Powys has a place name made of two elements: 'caer' a Welsh word meaning 'fortress', and 'sws' which remains open to

interpretation, but the prevailing view is that it refers to the ancient Roman Queen Swys Wen, and that the fort was named 'Caer Swys Wen (or Gwen)' after her. 'Gwen' is an old word meaning 'fair'. The place name was recorded as 'Kairesosse' in 1470, as 'Kaersoys' in 1478 and 'Kaer Sws' in the mid-sixteenth century.

Caer-Went
Typically, Welsh places whose name begins with 'caer', indicate a fort of some kind, either an Iron Age or Celtic hillfort or a Roman military settlement. In this case, as the Roman town of 'Venta Silurum' it had been taken over from the Silures tribe, who had earlier known it as 'Venta', meaning 'market'. In time, the place name was corrupted to 'Gwent', a name that would be associated with the post-Roman Kingdom of Gwent and from which the modern county name is derived. In 1254 the place was recorded as 'Kaerwent'.

Caldy Island
In Welsh, this island off the coast of Pembrokeshire (sometimes spelled 'Caldey Island'), is 'Ynys Byr', but its name comes from the Scandinavian word 'cald' meaning 'cold', and 'ey', an island. Hence, 'cold island', which describes its location and the prevailing climate exposed as it is to seasonal gales from the south-west Irish Sea. The Welsh name means 'Pyr's island', after the sixth century Celtic saint, St Pyr (also known as St Piro) who was initially made abbot of the local monastery, before his tragic accidental death, and he was succeeded by Samson of Dol. The island's name appeared as 'Caldea' in the early twelfth century and as 'Kaldey' or 'Caldey' by 1291.

Capel Curig
This village in Conway has a name whose meaning is disputed. On the one hand it may be based on the dedication of the local chapel ('capel') to the seventh century Celtic bishop and saint, St Curig, who tradition has it established the church of St Julitta in Capel Curig. On the other, it has been suggested that the second word of the place name should more properly be taken from the Welsh word 'cerrig', meaning 'stones', in which case the place name might mean 'chapel of stones'. This last interpretation is supported by early versions of the place name, appearing as 'Capel Kiryg' in about 1536 and as 'Capel Kerrig' in 1578.

Cardiff
The Welsh name for the City of Cardiff is 'Caerdydd', which means 'fort on (the River) Taf (sometimes Taff)', based on 'caer', meaning 'fortress' and the name of the river. In Norman times the name was spelled in Middle Welsh as 'Caerdyf', which became the Anglicised spelling of Cardiff. The region of South Wales around Cardiff was the territorial land of the Silures, a Celtic tribe who were roundly defeated by Roman forces and their leader, Caractacus, exiled to Rome. There is an ongoing dispute concerning the name of the Roman fort at Cardiff.

Some have it as 'Tamium', loosely related to the River Taff, while others prefer 'Bovium' (sometimes 'Bomio'), not to be confused with the Roman town of that name in Tilston, Cheshire.

Cardigan
Cardigan in the County of Ceredigion has the Welsh name 'Aberteifi', which means 'mouth of the (River) Teifi'. It is not only the name of the town but that of the former historic County of Cardiganshire. The name Cardigan is actually an Anglicisation of the Welsh 'Ceredigion' (meaning 'Ceredig's land'). Ceredig is thought to have been one of the sons of the fourth century King Cunedda Wledig of North Wales, whose name meant 'The Imperator' ('the commander'). Welsh tradition has it that he invaded from the north to recover lands in Roman Britain that had been seized by Irish invaders.

Carmarthen
Carmarthen in South-West Wales was the main settlement of the Demetae tribe during the Roman occupation of Britain and claims to be the oldest town in Wales. At that time they knew it as 'Maridunum', but its original Celtic name meant 'sea fort'. The Romans are known to have established a fort there in 75 AD, and the modern place name means 'fort at Maridunum'.

Castle Cary
In some respects, this Somerset town has a duplicated place name. The word 'Cary' derives from the Celtic word 'caer', which could either mean a rock, a crag or a castle, suggesting that the place name could be interpreted as 'rock rock' or 'castle castle'. Of course, in reality, Castle Cary takes its name from River Cary.

Cemaes
The coastal fishing village of Cemaes is located on the north coast of Anglesey on Cemaes Bay, and its place name comes from the Welsh word 'cemais', which describes a bend or loop in a river or sea inlet, which are both distinctive characteristics of the local landscape.

Ceredigion
Once known as the historic County of Cardiganshire, as a result of the Local Government Act of 1972, it was succeeded by the Unitary Authority of Ceredigion in the larger County of Dyfed. The Welsh language is spoken by more than half the population of Ceredigion. (See: 'Cardigan'.)

Chepstow
The town of Chepstow in Monmouthshire (Gwent), is known in Welsh as 'Cas-gwent', and lies on the River Wye. Originally part of the Welsh Kingdom of Gwent, evidence has been found of human occupation, dating from the Mesolithic period

(around 5000 BC), and several Iron Age fortified camps are found in the area, that were thought to be established by the Celtic Silures tribe.

Childswickham
Located in Worcestershire near the Welsh border, the name of the village of Childswickham has decidedly Celtic roots. The name comes from a combination of Brittonic and Old English, typical of many place names in the Marches and border counties. The first element of the name comes from the Old English word 'cild', which could signify a child or a young man, usually of noble birth. The second element comes from 'wig', a Celtic word related to the modern Welsh 'gwig' meaning 'lodge' or 'wood', and 'waun', meaning 'marsh', 'moor' or 'upland pasture'. Alternatively, the final name element could equally be from the Saxon word 'ham', referring to a hamlet or settlement. Hence, the name translates as either 'young man's lodge on the moor (or in a meadow)' or 'young man's lodge in the hamlet'. In 706 AD the name was recorded as 'Childeswicwon' and the name was entered in the *Domesday Book* as 'Wicvene'.

Chirk
Chirk is a town in the borough of Wrexham, historically in the County of Denbighshire, and its name is thought to be an Anglicised form of the Welsh word 'Ceiriog', after the river on which it stands. The place is known in Welsh as 'Y Waun', which means 'the moorland'. It has been recorded by several variant names over the centuries, as 'Chirchland' in 1163, 'Circ' in 1164, as 'Circh' in 1166 and as 'Chyrke' in 1295. These variations have led to suggestions that the name may in fact be derived from the Old English word 'cirice', and simply means 'church'.

Clodock
This small Herefordshire hamlet has a name based on the dedication of its church to the Welsh Prince of Ewyas and sixth century saint, St Clydog. It was established as a settlement on the River Monnow in the foothills of the Black Mountains, close to the border with Wales. The name was recorded in Latin as 'Ecclesia Sancti Clitauci', which translates as 'church of St Clydog'.

Clun
Clun takes its name from the River Clun on which it stands. The name derives from the Brittonic word 'Colunwy', a root it shares with the Rivers Colne in Lancashire and Essex. The Clun family, after whom the place and river may have been named, trace their roots back to the Pictish tribes of Perthshire. Clun is a Shropshire border town that developed around the site of a Saxon church towards the end of the seventh century.

Colwyn Bay
'Colwyn', located at the mouth of the River Conwy, may be named after Gollwyn ap Tangno, Lord of Efionydd Arudwy in the eleventh century. The place name

means 'Bay of the River Colwyn'. An alternative explanation is that the Welsh word 'colywn' means 'puppy', referring to its small size. The place name was recorded as 'Coloyne' in 1334.

Conwy
The Celts named their original settlement which they knew as 'Caerhun' from the river on which it was established, probably a combination of the Brittonic word 'cawn' and the suffix 'wy', together meaning 'full of reeds'. The Romans built a fort at a place and called it 'Canovium', a Latinised version of the Celtic river name, which is now the River Conwy (or in Welsh, 'Aberconwy').

Corwen
The town of Corwen in Clwyd probably derives its name from a pre-Christian menhir, a standing stone known as 'Carreg-y-Big' (meaning 'pointed stone'), which is now incorporated into the porch of the village church. The name Corwen comes from the Welsh words 'cor', a sanctuary, and 'mean', a standing stone. Hence, 'sanctuary stone'. It was known as 'Corvaen' in 1254, as 'Korvaen' in the fourteenth century and recorded in its present-day name as early as 1443.

Cound
The Shropshire village of Cound (pronounced 'Coond'), is located on the River Severn and has been occupied since the Neolithic period with many Early Bronze Age artefacts unearthed in the vicinity and several early British hillforts in the surrounding area. The place is named after the River Cound, a Celtic river name whose meaning is unknown; the place was one of the most important shallow river crossings in the Welsh Marches. In the first century the Romans built a military fortress a mile and a half away at Uriconium, which emerged as one of the largest towns in Roman Britain.

Cricieth
The town of Cricieth lies on the Lyn Peninsula near Caernarfon in Gwynedd, and derives its name from the Welsh words 'crug', meaning 'hill', and 'caeth', meaning 'prisoners' or 'captives'. The reference almost certainly applies to the Norman castle which stands on the hill and would have been a place of incarceration. The name is often spelled 'Criccieth' (with a double 'c'). The castle was known as 'Crukeith' in 1273.

Crickhowell
The name of the town of Crickhowell in south-eastern Powys in Welsh is 'Crug Hywel', and is sometimes spelled 'Crughywel' or 'Crucywel'. The name comes from the nearby Iron Age hillfort called Crug Hywel, from the word 'crug', meaning 'mound' or 'hill'. It is thought to have been named after a man called Hywel, but

nothing is known of him, and this may be pure supposition. The present-day place name is an Anglicised version and translates as 'Hywel's mound'.

Cusop

The village of Cusop, which is located beneath Cusop Hill near Hay-on-Wye, was recorded in the *Domesday Book* as 'the Marcher Lordship of Cheweshope', which at that time formed part of the Ewyas Lacy Hundred in south-west Herefordshire. The area was named in part after the Norman knight, Walter de Lacy, who had been granted extensive land holdings in the Welsh Marches by William the Conqueror. The place name may mean 'Ceawa's enclosed valley'. The first element is thought to have been 'Cewe', similar to the word 'Cewydd', which was an Old Welsh name for St Swithin. In time the saint's name became Cewi, which along with the Old English word 'hop', referring to a small enclosed valley, completed the place name. Such mixtures of Welsh and English name elements are not uncommon in the Marches region.

Deganwy

The Clwyd township of Deganwy (sometimes spelled 'Degannwy'), is located on the Conwy Estuary, and was originally known in the Brittonic Celtic language as 'Decantouion'. It has been suggested that the name should be 'Din-Gonwy', meaning 'fort on the River Conwy', even though the entry in the *Domesday Book* describes it as 'the territory of the Decanae tribe', implying that they were the origin of the place name. However, there is indeed a castle overlooking the town that was at one time a residence of Maelgwn Gwynedd, a sixth century King of Wales, which tends to tip the balance in favour of the original premise.

Deiniolen

The village of Deiniolen in Gwynedd took its name after the Welsh prince and saint, St Deiniolen, who became the Bishop of Bangor, and to whom the local church is dedicated. The village was originally called 'Ebeneser', a biblical name taken by the Welsh Nonconformist chapel here, and its present-day name was only adopted in the twentieth century; this was based on 'Llanddeiniolen', the parish name, which means 'church of Deiniolen'. More than eighty per cent of the local residents speak Welsh.

Denbigh

In Welsh the name of the town of Denbigh is 'Dinbych', which comes from 'din', meaning 'fortress' and 'bych' or 'bach', meaning 'little' or 'small'. Therefore, the place name translates as 'little fort'. The fort in question was an earth mound hillfort built in 1282 by Gwenllian, daughter of Llywelyn ap Iorwerth (known as 'the Great'), King of Gwynedd. It was known for two centuries as 'Lesguenllean', meaning 'court of Gwenllian'. Under English rule the name was recorded as 'Dymbygh' in 1304 and as 'Dimbech' in about 1700.

Dinas Powis
Dinas Powis is a district of Penarth in the Vale of Glamorgan the first word of whose name is a Welsh word meaning 'fortified place'. The second word is related to Powys, the historic kingdom and current unitary authority in central Wales, which means 'province' or 'region'. The place name therefore translates a 'fortified place of Powis'. The Dinas Powis Iron Age hillfort dates from the third or second century BC, but was apparently abandoned by its Celtic creators during the Roman era. The place name was recorded as 'Dinaspowis' in 1187 and as 'Dinas Powis' in around 1262.

Dinedor
Dinedor is a Herefordshire village whose name is of Celtic origin and relates to the Welsh word 'dinas', meaning 'fort'. The entire place name translates as 'hill with a fort'. The aforesaid hill is the Iron Age hillfort known as Dinedor Camp, which later became the site of a Roman camp. (See also: 'Dinedor Camp Hillfort'.)

Doldarrog
The name of the village of Doldarrog comes from the Welsh words 'dol', meaning 'water-meadow' or 'flood plain', and 'carrog', a torrent or fast-flowing stream. This eminently describes the local topography, where several streams pour onto the flatter ground beside the River Conwy. In 1666 the village was known as 'Dole y Garrog'. There is also an alternative mythical version of the place name, based on a dragon called 'Y Garrog', who was said to prey on farm animals at pasture on the land (which became known as 'Garrog's meadow'), and was eventually lured to its death beside the river.

Dolgellau
Dolgellau in the Snowdonia National Park, derived its name from the Welsh 'dol', meaning 'water meadow', and 'cellau', meaning 'cells', a reference either to monastic cells, suggesting an early religious settlement, or possibly merchants' stalls or booths in a meadow beside a river, in this case the River Wnion. Over the years the name has been variously spelled as 'Dolgethley', 'Dolgelly', 'Dolgelley', 'Dolgelli', 'Dolgelleu' and 'Dolguelli', before arriving at its present-day form in the eighteenth century.

Dwygyfylchi
Dwygyfylchi is a district of Penmaenmawr in Conwy whose name derives from two Welsh words, 'dwy', meaning 'two', and 'cyfylchi', which signified a circular ring-fort or stronghold. Hence, the place name means '(place by) two circular forts'. In fact, several early British forts are found in the surrounding hills around here. In 1284 the place name was recorded as 'Dwykyuelchy', in 1413 as 'Dwygyvychi' and in the sixteenth century as 'Y ddwy gyfylchi'.

Dyfed
The historic County of Dyfed is thought by some to get its name from the Demetae, the original Celtic people who occupied the territory before the Romans came

to Britain. Others prefer the Deisi people as the source of the name; they were immigrants from Munster in Ireland who settled in Wales and western England. The name Deisi is derived from the word 'deis', which originally meant 'vassal'. The region was known as 'Dimet' in the tenth century, as 'Devet' in the late-thirteenth and as 'Dyuett' in the seventeenth. Dyfed was created in 1974 from the amalgamation of Cardiganshire, Pembrokeshire, and Carmarthenshire.

Dymock

Illustrating the extent of ancestral Welsh tribal lands across the present-day English border, the Gloucestershire village of Dymock shares a common Celtic heritage in its place name. It derives from the Welsh words 'din' meaning 'fort', and 'moch' or 'mocc' meaning 'pigs'. Hence, the entire name means 'fort of pigs'. As the village is located in the Forest of Dean it is assumed that pigs roamed and foraged throughout the woods here.

Ebbw Vale

The town of Ebbw Vale in Gwent derived its name from the River Ebwy on which it stands. Its Welsh name is 'Glynebwy', based on 'glyn', meaning 'valley'. Ebbw refers to 'eb', meaning 'horse', or the Welsh word 'ebol', meaning 'colt', along with 'gwydd', meaning 'wild'. This is generally seen as a reference to the wild and often tempestuous nature of the river here. However, others interpret the name as being more to do with horses, who may have drank or forded the river at this point, and that the 'wild' reference might be better translated as 'frisky', as is the nature of young colts, or to the Welsh ponies that still run free through the local hills. The town was earlier known as 'Pen-y-cae' and later as 'Glyn Ebwy', before finally becoming Ebbw Vale in around 1836.

Evercreech

The second element of this Somerset village name derives from a Celtic word similar to the Welsh word 'crug', meaning 'hillock'. The first element is less evident, but is thought to come either from the Old English word 'oefor', meaning 'wild boar', or derived from a Celtic word for a plant or a tree, possibly a yew. It is not unusual to find such Welsh-Celtic-English name combinations in border lands, which often poses problems in precise interpretation. Therefore, the place name could be taken to mean either '(place on a) hillock where boars are found', or '(place on a) hillock where (yew) trees grow'. In 1065 the name was recorded as 'Evorcric', and in *Domesday* as 'Evrecriz'.

Ewloe

The Flintshire village of Ewloe lies on the border with Cheshire and forms part of Deeside in the County of Clwyd. Little is known of the history of the Manor at Ewloe, although it had come under the jurisdiction of English Marcher Lords shortly after the Norman Conquest. Later, in 1257, it was recorded in the Chester

Plea Rolls that the Prince of Wales, Llywelyn ap Gruffydd, had regained Ewloe from the English and built a castle in the wood. Such fortified residences were not uncommon at that time as these contested territorial borderlands were frequently fought over by the English and Welsh. In fact, following the Battle of Ewloe in 1157, when the Welsh defeated Henry II's army, an earlier castle had been built as a stronghold for Welsh princes, who held it until the reign of Edward I. The place name comes from the Old English words 'oewell' (referring to the source of a river) and 'hlaw', a hill. Taken together they mean 'hill with a river source'. The name was recorded as 'Ewlawe' in 1281.

Flint
Flint gave its name to the County of Flintshire which was originally held by the Celtic tribe known as the Deceangli long before they were overrun by the Romans in the first century. The town of Flint has a name derived from the Middle English word 'flint', meaning 'hard rock'. This is seen as a reference to the hard stone strata on which Flint Castle was built by Edward I beside the River Dee in 1277. At that time it was known by its Norman French name, 'Le Chaylou'. In 1300 the name was recorded as 'Le Fflynt'.

Ganarew
There are two differing opinions as to the meaning of the name of this Herefordshire border town. Its Welsh name is 'Genau'r Rhiw', 'Gana-rhiw' or 'Gan-y-rew'. On the one hand it is suggested that the name refers specifically to Gwynwarwy, otherwise known as St Gunguarui. On the other, the Welsh words 'genau', meaning 'mouth' or 'opening of a pass', and 'rhiw', signifying a hill, have been offered as a different source for the place name. In this latter case the name might mean '(place by the) pass (or opening) on a hill'. The town is located in the south of Herefordshire, in the Welsh Marches and about two miles from Monmouth.

Glamorgan
In Welsh, Glamorgan is 'Morgannwg'. In its early history, it was probably named after a seventh century Welsh prince of Gwent named Morgan, which together with the Welsh word element 'glan', meaning 'shore', 'territory' or 'bank', produces a place name that means 'Morgan's territory (or shore)'. The prince in question was Morgan ap Athrwys, otherwise known as Morgan Mwynfawr, meaning 'great in riches'. This historic county of South Wales is sometimes referred to as Glamorganshire. The Vale of Glamorgan (in Welsh, 'Bro Morgannwg'), adds the Welsh word 'bro', meaning 'lowland' or 'vale', describing the valley in which the town and much of the county is located.

Glasbury
Sometimes known as Glasbury-on-Wye, this village is located near the English border, a fact which is reflected in the combination of Welsh and English elements

in the place name. 'Clas' is the Old Welsh word for a cloister or a monastic settlement or community, and the Old English word 'burh' signified a fortified place. Therefore, this Powys town's name translates as 'fortified town of the monastic community'. The Welsh name for the place is 'Clas-ar-Wy', meaning 'monastic community on the (River) Wye'. In 1056 the name was recorded as 'Clastbyrig', in 1191 as 'Glesburia' and in 1322 as 'Classbury'.

Glyn Ceiriog

This village near Wrexham in the Ceiriog Valley is sometimes known as 'Llansanffraid Glyn Ceiriog', a longer version of the place name that means 'church of St Ffraid in the Ceiriog Valley'. (St Ffraid is the Welsh name of St Bridget.) Over time the village has come to be known as Glyn Ceiriog, and locals often shorten the name even further to 'Glyn'. The River Ceiriog which flows through the valley has a Celtic name which means 'favoured one'. In 1291 the place name was recorded as 'Lansanfreit' and in 1590 as 'Llan san ffred glyn Kerioc'.

Gower

The Gower Peninsula near Swansea (in Welsh, 'Penrhyn Gwyr'), is a distinctive headland in South Wales that projects westwards into the Bristol Channel. The name comes from the Welsh word 'gwyr', which means 'curved', and describes the hook shape of the peninsular.

Gresford

The village of Gresford is a district in Wrexham whose Welsh name is spelled 'Gresffordd'. The ford to which the name refers is across the River Alun, and presumably its banks were green and verdant here judging by the place name, which translates as '(place by the) grassy ford'. It was entered in the *Domesday Book* as Gretford, and fell part in Wales and part in England, typical of many settlements in the Marches at that time.

Gwalchmai

The township of Gwalchmai on Anglesey was named in honour of the twelfth century court poet, Gwalchmai ap Meilyr of Trewalchmai, one of the earliest Welsh language poets who served in the court of King Owain Gwynedd. Many regard his best work and one of the most important medieval Welsh poems to be *Gorhoffedd Gwalchmai* (Gwalchmai's praise poem). The village was named 'Trefwalkemyth' in 1291 and as 'Trefwalghmey' in 1350, before the 'tref' element (meaning 'township') was dropped and the village name became 'Gwalghmey' in 1252.

Gwent

The historic and preserved County of Gwent in South-East Wales derived its name from the Celtic 'venta', signifying a market. The county roughly corresponds to what was called Monmouthshire before 1974. The Romans established a base at

'Venta Silurum', meaning 'Market (town) of the Silures', after the Celtic tribe whose territorial tribe lands it had been before the legions occupied it. After Roman withdrawal in the fifth century, the territory around Venta became the Kingdom of Guenta (later Gwent), which according to tradition was founded by Caradoc Freichfras (sometimes Vreichvras, also known as 'Caradoc ap Ynyr'). The chief town of the kingdom was the former Roman administrative centre, which became known as 'Caer-went', which translates as 'Fort Venta'.

Gwynedd

Gwynedd was originally the name of an ancient and powerful kingdom ruled by Cunedag (sometimes 'Cunedda') a Romano-British ruler in the eighth century, and has survived as an administrative county and unitary authority in North-West Wales. According to manuscripts by the monk and antiquary Nennius, Cunedda was instrumental in driving the Picts from Gwynedd. The county name was reinstated in 1974 to encompass most of the historic counties of Caernarvonshire and Merioneth with Caernarfon as its administrative centre. The name is thought to have come from Ireland and is derived from the Celtic Vendoti tribe, or in Brittonic, the 'Venii'. The county name properly translates as 'territory of the Venii'.

Harlech

The coastal town of Harlech gets its name from a combination of the Welsh words 'hardd', meaning 'fine' or 'fair', and 'llech', meaning 'rock' or 'slab'. Hence, the place name may be taken to mean '(place at the) fine rock', a reference to the location of Edward I's thirteenth century Harlech Castle, which stands on a prominent rock overlooking the sand dunes and the Irish sea below. It constitutes a perfect dominant and defensive position, exactly as was intended. Some sources have the name derived from 'Arddlech' (where 'ardd' means 'high'), in which case the name might mean '(place on a) high rock'. The name was recorded as 'Hardelech' in 1283, as 'Harddlech' in 1450 and as 'Hardelegh' in 1608.

Hawarden

This Flintshire town takes its common name from the Old English words 'heah', meaning 'high', and 'worthign' meaning 'enclosure'. Hence, '(place with a) high enclosure'. As the town does indeed stand on high ground overlooking the River Dee, the place name would appear eminently appropriate. In Welsh the place is known as 'Penarlag', derived from 'pennardd' which signifies high or rising ground, and 'alafog' probably meaning 'rich in cattle', but could alternatively have been the personal name of a man called Alaog. So, either '(place on) high ground rich in cattle', or '(place on) high ground (belonging to) Alaog'.

Hay-on-Wye

This is yet another border town that has been both a Welsh and an English possession during its time, a situation common in many settlements in the Welsh

Marches. The name comes from the Old English word 'haeg', meaning 'enclosure'. Hence, 'enclosure on the (River) Wye'. In Anglo-Saxon times, enclosures were a relatively new phenomenon; the countryside had been virtually wide open and unfenced, or 'common' beforehand, and separating a piece of land by enclosing it was both novel and noteworthy. This is evidenced by the number of British towns and villages which incorporate the element 'tun' (meaning 'enclosure' – or 'ton' in modern English) into their place names. Enclosures were similar to what we might now regard as fields, bounded by hedgerows or fences, but they might earlier have included small yards, paddocks, animal enclosures or arable plots. Various Enclosure Acts had been applied across Britain from the twelfth century but it would not be until the eighteenth century that widespread enclosure of land would take place. In its time, Hay-on-Wye would have stood out as a rare place of enclosure, sufficiently distinctive to use it as a place name. Due to boundary changes, the township lies on the border of Herefordshire and the Welsh County of Powys. The 'Wye' affix locates the town upon the river of that name. The township's name in Welsh is 'Y Gelli Gandryll', which means 'woodland of a hundred plots'.

Hodnet

This village on the Welsh-English border in rural Shropshire has a name which is from a Celtic derivation, similar to the Welsh words 'hawdd', meaning 'pleasant', and 'nant', a valley. Hence, the place name means '(place in a) pleasant valley'. The valley in question is that of the River Tern on which Hodnet is located. *Domesday* listed the place as 'Odenet' in 1086.

Holyhead

The town and port of Holyhead on the island of Anglesey has the Welsh name 'Caergybi', which translates as 'fort of Cybi', and sometimes as 'Ynys Gybi', meaning 'Cybi's island'. Holyhead means 'holy headland', based on the Old English 'halig', meaning 'holy', and 'heafod', indicating a headland or promontory. In 1315 the town name was recorded as 'Haliheved' and in 1395 as 'Holyhede'. St Cybi was a sixth century Cornish bishop who worked in North Wales and may have established a monastic settlement in Holyhead, which gave the town its religious connotation. The headland in question is Holyhead Mountain on the north-west of the island, and known in Welsh as 'Mynydd Twr', which means 'cairn mountain'. The word 'cairn' may be a misnomer, and could be a corruption of the word 'caestre', signifying a Roman fort or military garrison. This is supported by its various names over time: as 'Castro Kyby' in 1291 and 'Castelkyby' in 1310.

Kemble

This Gloucestershire village has a place name that translates as '(place at the) border'. The name comes from a Celtic word related to the Welsh 'cyfyl', technically meaning 'neighbourhood', but in this case specifically referring to a border, and most probably to the boundary of a tribal territory. The name was recorded in the late-seventh century as 'Kemele' and was listed in the *Domesday Book* as 'Chemele'.

Kenchester
This small Herefordshire hamlet was at one time a Roman fort located on the north bank of the River Wye and associated with a man called Cena. His name, together with the Old English word 'ceaster' which signified a Roman fort, produces a place name that means 'Roman fort associated with Cena'. The Roman name of the town was 'Magnis' or 'Magnae', possibly derived from an older Celtic name related to the modern Welsh word 'maen', representing a stone or stone pillar. *Domesday* recorded the name as 'Chenecestre'.

Kilpeck
Kilpeck has the Welsh name 'Llanddewi Cil Pedeg', and until the ninth century it was part of the Welsh Kingdom of Ergyng. Later it was taken over by the King of Mercia, and after the Norman Conquest came under the dominance and rule of the Marcher Lords, when William FitzNorman de la Mare was granted the manor by the Conqueror. The first element of the place name comes from the Welsh word 'cil', meaning 'corner' or 'nook' and the second from 'pedec', indicating a place where animal snares are set (most probably for rabbits or foxes). The place name therefore translates as 'corner or nook where animal snares are set'. The place was entered in the *Domesday Book* as 'Chipeete'. By around 1150 the name was written as 'Cilpedec'.

Knighton
Knighton's name in English has quite a different meaning to its Welsh name, which goes some way towards illustrating the confusion created in the Marches by successive English and Welsh border power struggles, and the frequently compromised solutions that resulted. In Welsh the place is called 'Trefyclo', a name based on the elements 'tref', a farm, 'y', meaning 'the', and 'clawdd', signifying a ditch. Hence, 'farm by the ditch', a reference to Offa's Dyke, the large linear earthwork that roughly follows the current border between England and Wales. It was an attempt by the eighth century Anglo-Saxon King Offa of Mercia to protect his territory from unruly Welsh border intrusions. Knighton claims that it is the only town in Britain that actually lies on the Dyke. The English place name, Knighton, derives from the Old English word 'cniht', and 'tun', an enclosure or estate. In this case, the place name might be taken to mean 'estate of the knights'. However, it is thought that the original Saxon word 'cniht' might have been more generalised in its usage, and could have included young men, servants or even followers. *Domesday* recorded the name as 'Chenistetune'. In 1193 the name was written as 'Cnicheton'. Nowadays, Knighton lies within the Ceremonial County of Powys.

Celtic Places and Placenames

Knockin
Knockin is a village in north-west Shropshire whose name means '(place by the) little hill'. It was formerly known as 'Cnukyn'. The name comes from the Celtic word 'cnoccin' and is similar to the Welsh word 'cnwc', meaning 'hillock' or 'little hill'. Its name in Welsh is 'Cnwcin'. The name was recorded as 'Cnochin' in 1165.

Kynaston
Kynaston is a small border hamlet in the Parish of Kinnerley of Shropshire. The place name is thought to be derived from the personal name of a man called Cyneweard (or Cynfyn) and the Anglo-Saxon word 'aston', meaning 'eastern farmstead'. Hence, 'Cyneweard's eastern farmstead'. It was recorded in the *Domesday Book* as 'Chimerstun'. Its Welsh name (which has exactly the same meaning as the English name), is 'Tregynferdd' and is derived from the word 'tre' or 'tref' meaning 'farm' and the aforementioned Cyneweard.

Lampeter
The township of Lampeter in Ceredigion has the Welsh name 'Llanbedr Pount Steffan', which translates as 'church of St Peter by Stephen's Bridge'. This derives from a contraction of the Welsh word elements 'llan', meaning 'church', 'Pedr', meaning 'Peter', 'pont', meaning 'bridge' and 'Steffan', meaning 'Stephen'. It is thought that at some time in its history, a man called Stephen was appointed as caretaker to the bridge over the River Teifi at this place. The name was recorded as 'Lanpedr' in 1284 and as 'Lampeter Pount Steune' in 1301.

Laugharne
The village of Laugharne on the south coast of the historic County of Carmarthenshire has the Welsh name 'Talacharn' (sometimes 'Treflan Lacharn'), based on the Welsh word 'tal', meaning 'tail' or 'end'. The place name is generally taken to mean '(place at the) end'. The second part of the name is obscure though some have it derived from the Coran Brook nearby. The English version of the name dropped the initial 'Ta'. It was already known as 'Talacharn' by the late twelfth century, and by the beginning of the thirteenth had the prefix 'aber' attached as 'Abercoran', meaning 'mouth of the Coran'. It was in 1868 that the name 'Laugharne' appeared, followed shortly after as 'Tal-Llacharn'.

Leominster
The Herefordshire border town of Leominster has a name whose origin dates from Celtic times, and meant '(land) at the streams'. This is thought to be a reference to the triangle of land on which the early settlement stood, formed by the confluence of the River Arrow (in Welsh, 'Afon Arwy', probably meaning 'stream'), and the River Lugg (in Welsh, 'Afon Llugwy', meaning 'bright one'). The town's modern name comes from 'leon' or 'lene', which the Celtic tribes called the region, and which is similar to the Old Welsh word 'lei', meaning 'to flow' or 'flowing'. Additionally,

the Old English word 'mynster' indicated a monastery, church or other religious settlement. There is an alternative view that it may refer to Earl Leofric of Mercia who once held land here. It is known that in 980 AD, Danes sacked Leominster and destroyed the nunnery, and it was Leofric who financed its rebuilding. On this basis the present-day place name means 'church (or religious settlement) in Leon'. In the tenth century the town was recorded as 'Leomynster' and *Domesday* listed it as 'Leofminstre'.

Llanberis
The name of the village of Llanberis in the Snowdonia National Park of Gwynedd comes from the dedication of its local church (in Welsh, 'llan') to St Peris, a little-known eleventh or twelfth century Welsh saint. The name actually began in a nearby hamlet called Nantperis (meaning 'valley of Peris'), while Llanberis as we know it today was called 'Coed y Ddol' (meaning 'wood in a meadow'). Over time the two settlements were conjoined to become present-day Llanberis. Nant Peris is still identified on some old maps as 'Old Llanberis'.

Llanbydder
The origin and meaning of the Llanbydder place name is contentious and the several supposed interpretations do little to clear up the confusion. The name was formerly spelled 'Llanybyther', which may be a corruption of 'Llanbedr' (meaning 'church of St Peter'), or of 'Llanybyddair', meaning 'church of the Ambuscade'. The place name was recorded as 'Thlanebetheir' in 1319, as 'Llanybyddeyr' in 1401, 'Llanybydder' in 1535 and 'Llan-y-byddar' in 1566. This raises the possibility that the last element of the name might derive from the Welsh word 'buddair', which is taken to mean 'buzzard' or possibly more generally as 'bird of prey'. However, what that might have to do with a church is unclear, so much so that it has been mooted that the 'llan' element of the name might itself be a corruption of 'nant', meaning 'valley'. In this case the place name would mean 'valley of the buzzards (or birds of prey)'. In the end, we may never know which.

Llandovery
In Welsh, the name of the Carmarthenshire town of Llandovery is known as 'Llanymddyfri', a name comprised of three elements: 'llan', a church, 'am', meaning 'near' and 'dyfri', meaning 'waters'. Hence, 'church near the waters'. The waters referred to are the River Bran, the River Gwydderig and the River Towy which all meet at this point. The place name was spelled as 'Llanamdeveri' in 1194 and as 'Lanymdevery' in 1383.

Llandrindod
Sometimes known as Llandrindod Wells, this township in the ancient County of Radnorshire, has a name based like many others around the local church, and was originally known as 'Llanddwy', which translates as 'church of God'

(based on the Welsh word 'Dwyw', meaning 'God'). However, when supposedly health-giving mineral springs were discovered in the town in the eighteenth century, it was quick to realise the potential for tourism that it offered and by the mid-nineteenth century it had become a popular spa town. For a time it was known simply as 'The Wells'. After undergoing several name changes in the early sixteenth century, including 'Llandynddod' in 1535 and 'Llan Yr dryndot' in 1543, it finally arrived at something approaching its present incarnation as 'Llandrindod' in 1549.

Llandudno

Llandudno is a seaside resort town on the Creuddyn Peninsula in the Borough of Conwy. The town takes its name from the sixth century missionary saint, St Tudno, who founded the original parish church on the Great Orme peninsula (in Welsh, 'Cyngreawdr'). Tudno is said to have been one of the seven sons of King Seithenyn, of the legendary Kingdom of Cantref y Gwaelod. He is the patron saint of Llandudno and the town and its parish church still bear his name.

Llanelli

Llanelli (formerly spelled 'Llanelly'), celebrates the fifth or sixth century Welsh saint, St Elli (or Ellyw) in its church and place name, which means 'church of Elli'. She (or He – nobody is quite certain), is said to have been a daughter, son or granddaughter of King Brychan of Brycheiniog (Brecknockshire), and was possibly a disciple of St Cadoc (known in Welsh as Cattwg Ddoeth, 'the Wise'), who is said to have established many churches in Cornwall, Brittany, Wales and Scotland.

Llanfair-pwll

Celebrated as the longest place name in the British Isles, this village in Anglesey has the full name 'Llanfairpwllgwyngyllgogerychwyrndrobwllllantysiliogogogoch'. The name is usually shortened to 'Llanfair-pwll', 'Llanfair PG' or 'Llanfairpwllgwyngyll', it is generally translated into English as 'The church of St Mary of the pool of the white hazels over against the fierce whirlpool and the church of St Tysilio of the red cave'. Occasionally however, the last element is interpreted as 'the cave of St Tysilio the Red'. In 1254 the name was recorded as 'Pwllgwyngyll'.

Llanfairfechan

The coastal resort town of Llanfairfechan in Conwy Borough has a name that translates as 'little church of Mary', based on 'llan', a church, 'Mair', the Virgin Mary, and 'bec han', meaning 'little'. The church is said to be little when compared to the much larger Church of St Mary a few miles away in Conwy town. In 1284 the place was recorded as 'Lanueyr' and in 1475 as 'Llanvair Vechan'. Almost half of its resident population are Welsh speakers.

Wales & the Marches

Llangefni
Llangefni is a small town on Anglesey whose name means 'church on the (River) Cefni'. The church is dedicated to St Cyngar (in Welsh, 'Cungar ab Geraint', also known as 'Docwin' and 'Dochau'), the fifth century saint and Patron Saint of Llangefni, who founded St Cybi's Monastery in Holyhead.

Llangollen
Llangollen is a town in Denbighshire that is named after an obscure sixth or seventh century saint, St Collen, and the church dedicated to him. Hence, 'church of St Collen'. Little is known of the saint, except that traditionally he is supposed to have arrived in a coracle and founded the first religious settlement here. He may also have been connected with Colan in Cornwall and with Langolen in Brittany. The place was recorded as 'Lancollien' in 1234.

Llanrwst
The patron saint of the church in this place is St Grwst (sometimes 'Gwrwst' or 'Gorwst') a sixth century saint also known in Latin as 'Sanctus Gwrwst' (known as the 'Confessor'). The place name reflects the church dedication to him. He was reputedly the son of Gwaith Hengaer ap Elffin, a Prince of Rheged of Cumbria and arrived in Wales around the year 540 AD and founded a monastic cell, the site of which is nowadays thought to be occupied by the Seion Methodist Chapel in Llanrwst.

Llantrisant
Llantrisant in Glamorgan derives its name from three Welsh word elements: 'llan' meaning 'church', 'tri' meaning 'three', and 'sant' meaning 'saint'. Hence, the name means 'church of three saints'. The saints in question are St Dyfodwg, St Gwynno and St Illtud. The Borough of Llantrisant was established by Royal Charter in 1346.

Ludlow
Lying close to the England-Wales border in Shropshire, with the Welsh name 'Llwydlo', the market town of Ludlow was the headquarters of the Council of Wales and the Marches from 1472 to 1689. It had been known as 'Lodelowe' in the twelfth century, based on the Old English word combination 'hlud-hlaew'. This was a reference to the River Teme on which it stands, and its many rapids, which explains the 'hlud' element of the name, meaning 'loud' ('loud waters'). The 'hlaew' element means 'hill', 'mound' or 'tumulus'. Hence, the name Ludlow means '(place on a) hill (mound) by the loud waters'. The mound in question, possibly an ancient British barrow or funeral mound, was removed in 1199 to build the parish church. In 1138 the place name was recorded as 'Ludelaue'.

Maentwrog
Maentwrog is a village in Merionethshire, located in the Vale of Ffestiniog and within the Snowdonia National Park. The place name means 'Twrog's stone'

or 'rock of Twrog'. According to legend, Twrog was a giant who is said to have thrown a boulder from the top of Moelwyn Mawr mountain into the settlement below, destroying a pagan altar. The stone is said to be the one in St Twrog's Church courtyard and is traditionally said to mark the saint's grave. The first element of the place name is 'maen', a Welsh word meaning 'stone'. In fact, the church is dedicated to the sixth century saint, St Twrog, probably a female, who was neither a giant nor responsible for hurling boulders from mountain tops. The place name was recorded as 'Mayntwroc' at the end of the thirteenth century.

Maesbrook

Maesbrook is a small Shropshire hamlet with a Welsh-sounding element in its place name; this is not surprising given its close proximity to the Wales-England border. It has been suggested that the first element of the name may be from the Welsh word, 'maes', which represents an open field, but on balance it seems more likely to be derived from the Old English word 'maere', meaning 'boundary'. The second element comes from 'broc', meaning 'brook'. Hence, the place name may be interpreted as either 'open field by a brook' or 'brook by the boundary'. *Domesday* listed the place as 'Meresbroc' in 1086 and in 1272 the name was recorded as 'Maysbroc'.

Menai Bridge

The town of Menai Bridge on Anglesey was known as 'Porthaethwy' before Thomas Telford built the suspension bridge which was completed in 1826 across the Menai Strait. 'Porth' is a Welsh word meaning 'ferry' which was formerly the primary source of crossing the strait to the mainland, and the old town name means 'ferry of the Daethwy'. The Daethwy were the original Celtic tribe whose territory the island was until Roman times. The Menai Strait, or in Welsh, 'Afon Menai', means 'River Menai'. The name 'Menai' is derived from the Welsh 'main-aw' or 'main-wy', meaning 'narrow water'.

Merthyr Tydfil

The Welsh word 'merthyr' means 'martyr', and the name of this town reflects the martyrdom of St Tudful (or 'Tydfil'), daughter of Brychan of Brycheiniog, a local chieftain, by Pictish tribesmen here in the fifth century. Reputedly, the town is her burial place. In 1254 the name was recorded as 'Merthir' and by the end of that century the name had emerged as 'Merthyr Tutuil'.

Moelfre

Many Welsh places share the word element 'moel' in their place name, and the coastal town of Moelfre on the east coast of Anglesey is just one of them. Others include Moel Tryfan in Gwynedd and Moel Sych in Powys. 'Moel' means 'bare' or 'bald' in Welsh. The final element of the name comes from 'bre', meaning 'hill'. Hence, '(place by the) bare hill'. The name was spelled 'Moylvry' in 1399 and 'Moelvre' in 1528.

Monmouth

In the Welsh language, Monmouth is called 'Trefynwy', which means 'town of Mynwy', and its English name, 'Monmouth', means 'mouth of the River Mynwy'. The river name was Anglicised to 'Monnowe' in the sixteenth century, having already undergone several variations, including 'Monemue' in around 1075, 'Mynu' around 1150, 'Monwy' in 1722, before finally arriving to its sometime English name of 'Monnow'. The town's original name was 'Abermynwy', which means 'mouth (or estuary) of the River Mynwy', but over time the 'aber' was replaced by 'tref', representing the town settlement rather than the river. It is thought that the river name comes from a Celtic word that might mean something like 'fast flowing'.

Neath

Neath is a town located just north of Port Talbot in West Glamorgan and took its name from the River Neath on which it stands, though the river is called the 'Nedd' in Welsh. It has been argued that the river name is of pre-Celtic origin and means 'shining' or 'brilliant', but an alternative suggestion for the source is 'nedi', which probably simply means 'river', and is of a similar root to the River Nidd in North Yorkshire. The Welsh name for the town itself is 'Castell-Nedd', meaning 'castle on the Nedd', a reference to the nearby Roman fort of 'Nidum'. The town's place name was spelled 'Neth' in 1191 and 'Neeth' in 1306.

Oswestry

The Shropshire town of Oswestry (in Welsh, 'Croesoswallt', meaning 'Oswald's cross'), has one of the best-preserved pre-Celtic Iron Age hillforts in Britain, having been constructed and occupied from 800 BC to the mid-first century AD. Located in the Wales-England borderlands, the place changed hands numerous times during the eleventh and twelfth centuries and still retains some Welsh street names. Two explanations exist for the origin of the place name. One has it named after a man called Oswald, which along with the affix 'treow', produces a meaning of 'tree belonging to Oswald'. Tradition has it that the man concerned was St Oswald, the seventh century King of Northumberland. In 1191 the place name was recorded as 'Oswaldestoe'. (See also: 'Old Oswestry Hillfort'.)

Pembroke

Located on the extreme south-west tip of Wales, Pembroke is called 'Penfro' in the Welsh language. The name means 'land at the end'. The name is derived from Celtic words related to the modern Welsh 'pen', meaning 'end' or 'head' (as in 'headland'), and 'brog' or 'bro', meaning 'land' or 'region'. The place was called 'Pennbro' around 1150 and 'Pembroch' in 1191.

Penarth

Penarth (sometimes hyphenated as 'Pen-arth'), is a port town in the Vale of Glamorgan which is located on a high promontory overlooking the Bristol Channel, and this is the source of its place name. It is derived from the Welsh words 'pen', meaning 'head' or 'end', and 'garth', a promontory or headland. Hence, the name translates as 'top of the headland'. The earliest record of the present-day name dates from 1254.

Penmaenmawr

Penmaenmawr in Conwy County Borough has a name that means 'great stone headland', based on the Welsh words 'penmaen', meaning 'stone headland', and 'mawr' meaning 'large' or 'great'. It was named after Penmaenmawr Mountain, the site of a former Iron Age hillfort, now effectively removed through quarrying. The stone reference in the name is apt considering the place's long history in the quarrying of granite, which was an important factor in the development of the village.

Penrhyn Bay

Penrhyn Bay (or in Welsh, 'Bae Penrhyn'), is a small town on the northern coast of Wales. Like Penmaenmawr, the village grew to increasingly depend upon limestone quarrying for its livelihood. The Welsh word 'Penryn' means 'headland' or 'promontory'.

Penrhyndeudraeth

Sometimes written in its hyphenated form as Penrhyn-deudraeth, the village was historically in the County of Merioneth. The place name comprises three elements: 'penryn', a promontory, 'dau', meaning 'two', and 'traeth', meaning 'beach', 'shore' or 'strand', which translates as 'peninsular (between) two beaches'. The two beaches referred to in the place name were known in the twelfth century as Traitmaur ('big beach') and Traitbochan ('little beach'). Upper Penrhyn was originally called 'Cefn Coch', meaning 'red ridge'.

Portarddulais

The name of the Glamorgan town of Portarddulais means 'bridge on the (River) Dulais'. Then name comes from the Welsh word 'pont', meaning 'bridge', 'ar' meaning 'on' or 'over', plus the name of the river on which the settlement was established. The river name comes from 'du' meaning 'dark' or 'black', and 'glais' meaning 'stream' or 'water'. Hence, the name translates as 'dark stream'. In the sixteenth century the place was referred to as 'Pen y bont aber Duleis' and in English as 'Dulais Bridge'. The bridge in question is thought to have been the former fourteenth century bridge which carried the road from Swansea to Carmarthen over the River Loughor (in Welsh, 'Afon Llwchwr'). The bridge was so named because of its position up from the mouth of the Dulais stream. It was also known as 'Y Bont Fawr' (meaning 'the big bridge').

Pontypool

The name of this town in Gwent, in the historic County of Monmouthshire, came about on account of the pool in the River Llwyd ('Afon Lwyd') which is crossed by a bridge, a fact that is reflected in the place name – a combination of the English word 'pool' and the Welsh word 'pont', meaning 'bridge', despite it having a perfectly good version of the name in Welsh, 'Pontypwl'.

Pontypridd
The name Pontypridd derives from the Welsh, 'Pont-y-ty-pridd', which translates as 'bridge by the earthen house'. This is a reference to the wooden bridges that formerly spanned the River Taff. Earthen houses were built with mud walls and occasionally wattle and daub, and a few were gathered around the successive bridges that were built here. A final new bridge (in Welsh, a 'pont y pridd') was built between 1746 and 1757 by William Edwards and by 1813 the name had been recorded as 'Pont yprydd'.

Porthcawl
Sometimes written as two hyphenated words ('Porth-cawl'), this coastal town in Glamorgan derives its name from 'porth', meaning 'harbour', and 'cawl', meaning 'sea-kale'. Hence, the place name means 'harbour where sea-kale grows'. Sea-kale (also called sea-colewort and scurvy grass), was frequently cultivated and its tender shoots pickled for long sea voyages, when it was used to prevent scurvy. The word 'cawl' is related to 'caul' (as in cauliflower). In 1632 the name was written as 'Portcall' and was recorded as 'Porth Cawl' in 1825.

Powys
Powys is a Unitary Authority in central Wales whose name comes from the Latin 'pagensis', meaning 'provincial', or 'pagus', meaning 'district' or 'province'. Hence, 'a provincial place'. The name implies that its resident population were 'country folk', that is, people who did not live in towns or major settlements, but were predominantly hill and valley people and farmers.

Prestatyn
As with many towns in Britain, places whose name includes the prefix 'prest' indicate some association with priests, monks or other religious personages (Preston and Prestwich for example), and the Flintshire town of Prestatyn falls into this category. The Old English word 'preosta', translates as 'of the priests'. The final name element comes from 'tun', signifying a farming community or farmstead and was typically expressed in Welsh as 'tyn'. Therefore the place name may be taken to mean 'farming community of the priests'.

Presteigne
Presteigne in Radnorshire, is known as 'Llanandras' in Welsh, and comprises 'llan' meaning 'church', along with the name of St Andrew, to whom the local church is dedicated. Hence, 'church of St Andrew'. The later name, Presteigne, is derived from the Old English words 'preost', a priest, and 'henn-maed' a border

meadow, reflecting its location on the Wales-England border. In this case the place name may be taken to mean 'priest's border meadow'. The name was recorded as 'Prestehemed' in 1137, as 'Prestene' in 1546 and in 1868 as 'Presteign, or Llan-Andras of the Welsh'.

Pwllheli
Pwllheli is a town on the Llyn Peninsula in Gwynedd whose name comes from the Welsh words 'pwll', meaning 'pool', and 'heli' meaning 'brine' or 'salt water'. The name may be taken to mean '(place by the) brine pool', though some prefer a meaning of 'salt water basin'. The basin in question was a tidal pool created in the thirteenth century when a sand bar was built to form the harbour.

Rhayader
The town of Rhayader is called 'Rhaeadr Gwy' in Welsh, which translates as 'waterfall on the (River) Wye'. It is sometimes referred to locally as 'Y Rhaeadr', simply meaning 'the waterfall'. Unfortunately, little still remains of the waterfall as it was destroyed in 1780 to make way for a bridge linking the town to Cwndauddwr and the Welsh Lakeland.

Rhondda
The river on which this town lies is the Rhondda, which also gave its name to the Rhondda Valley (in Welsh, 'Cwm Rhondda'). The name comes from the Welsh word 'rhoddni', meaning 'noisy' or 'babbling'. In fact there are two Rhondda rivers, the Rhondda Fawr, meaning 'Great Rhondda' and the Rhondda Fach, meaning 'Little Rhondda'. The place was known in the twelfth century as 'Rotheni'.

Rhosllanerchrugog
Rhosllanerchrugog is a village in Wrexham whose place name derives from the Welsh 'llannerch', meaning 'clearing' or 'glade', and 'grugog' meaning 'heathery', or 'crugog' meaning 'hilly'. The village is located on moorland (in Welsh, 'rhos'), and its name was traditionally written as 'Rhos Llanerchrugog', meaning 'the Llanerchrugog moor', which literally translates as 'moor of the heather glade'. In 1544 the place name was recorded as 'Rose lane aghregog' and in 1546 as 'Rhos Llannerch Riregog'.

Rhosneigr
Rhosneigr is a small village on the south-west coast of Anglesey, whose name is part-derived from the Welsh word 'rhos', a common prefix meaning 'moor' or 'moorland'. The second element of the name is thought to derive from the personal name 'Yneigr', the grandson of Cunedda Wledig, an important leader in the area during the fifth century. It is not known how the village came to be named in his honour. Hence, the place name means 'moorland of Yneigr'.

Wales & the Marches

Rhostryfan
This village in Gwynedd gets its name in part from a nearby hill called Moel Tryfan, itself named from the Welsh 'moel', meaning 'bare hill', and 'tryfan', meaning 'sharp peak'. The first element of the place name, 'rhos' means 'moor' or 'moorland', which translates the whole as 'moor by (Moel) Tryfan' or more specifically, 'moor by the bare hill with a sharp peak'.

Rhuddlan
Rhuddlan is a town in Denbighshire, and was historically in Flintshire. The town was the capital of Gwynedd for the Welsh King Gruffydd ap Llywelyn (1007–63); his family were the Welsh lords of Rhuddlan for generations. The name is derived from the Welsh words 'rhudd' and 'glan', respectively meaning 'red bank', a description of the distinctive red banks of the River Clwyd at this point. *Domesday* recorded the place name as 'Roelend' in 1086 and in 1191 it was written as 'Ruthelan'.

Rhyl
Rhyl's place name is a combination of the Welsh word 'yr', meaning 'the' and the Old English word 'hyll', a hill. In other words, the name simply means 'the hill'. Over the centuries the name has undergone many changes and variations, including 'Hulle' in 1292, 'Ryhull' in 1301, 'Hyll' in 1506, 'Yrhill' in 1578 and 'Rhil' in 1706, among many others. The paradox of Rhyl is that no such hill seems to exist near there; the surrounding landscape is a decidedly flat terrain, and if one had ever existed here such a mound has long since disappeared.

Rhymney
Rhymney is a town in the Borough of Caerphilly in Gwent, South Wales (historically in Monmouthshire), whose Welsh name is 'Rhymni'. It gets its name from the River Rhymney on which it stands. The river name comes from the Welsh 'rhwmp-ni', which means 'to auger' or 'to bore', a description of the boring or cutting action of the river at this place. The name apples to the town and the river, and was recorded as 'Remni' in 1101, as 'Rempny' in 1296 and as 'Rymney' in 1541.

Ross-on-Wye
Ross-on-Wye is a Herefordshire town in the Welsh Marches, located on the River Wye. The word 'ross' is derived from the Celtic 'ros', which could either refer to an outcrop or hill spur, or to moorland, as in the Welsh word 'rhos'. As the name suggests, the town is actually located on a hill overlooking the river. Therefore the place name translates as '(place on a) hill spur by the (River) Wye'. The river name is obscure, but is thought to mean 'mover' or 'conveyor' in reference to its fast-flowing current. The *Domesday Book* recorded the place as 'Rosse' in 1086.

Celtic Places and Placenames

Ruthin

The first element of Ruthin's place name means 'red'. However, the second element is more problematic. On the one hand it might come from the Welsh 'hin', meaning 'edge' or 'border', and on the other, it could be derived from 'din', meaning 'fort'. The first explanation might be a reference to its location on the edge of the River Clwyd. However, given that the remains of the thirteenth century red sandstone castle exist here, the second interpretation would appear to be the better one. The castle in question was referred to in 1545 as 'Y Castell Coch yng gwernfor', which translates as 'red castle in the great marsh'. Little is known about the town before the construction of Ruthin Castle in 1277, other than there is evidence of earlier Celtic and Roman settlements in the area. The Welsh spelling of the place name is 'Rhuthun'.

St Asaph

The original Welsh name for the City of St Asaph in Denbighshire is 'Llanelwy', which translates as 'church by the (River) Elwy'. The river name means 'driving (or forceful) one', a characteristic descriptive term which Celtic people often used of rivers. The city is believed to have been established around a sixth century monastery founded by the Celtic Saint, St Kentigern, which is now the site of the fourteenth century cathedral dedicated to St Asaph (in Welsh, 'Asaff'), the bishop of St Asaph. In 1291 the place name was recorded as 'Sanctus Asaphi'.

St David's

The City of St David's in Pembrokeshire, reputedly the smallest city in Britain, celebrates the sixth century bishop, David, the patron saint of Wales. In Welsh it is called 'Tyddewi', which is derived from 'ty', meaning 'house' (in this case, 'house of the Lord'), and 'Dewi' meaning 'David'. The present-day cathedral was built by the Normans and contains many relics, including the remains of St David, and has been a place of pilgrimage by nobility and royalty (including William the Conqueror, Henry II and Edward I), as well as commoners over the centuries.

Shrewsbury

In earlier times, Shrewsbury in the English County of Shropshire, was the capital of the Welsh Kingdom of Powys, and was known to the pre-Celtic Britons as 'Pengwern', meaning 'the alder hill', part of the territory of the Celtic Cornovii tribe. The town's name in the eleventh century was 'Scrobbesbyrig', based on the Old English 'scrobb', meaning 'scrubland', and 'burh', a stronghold or fortified place. Hence, the place name translates as 'fortified place in scrubland'. The Welsh name for the town is 'Amwythig', suggesting trees rather than scrubland. It has also been suggested that the first element of the place name might come from the personal name of a man called Scrobb, in which case the name might mean 'Scrobb's fort'. The town has been the subject of many territorial disputes between the English and Welsh over the centuries and in 778 AD, the Anglo-Saxons, under

King Offa of Mercia, took possession of it. The usual pronunciation of the place name is 'Shrows-bury'; however, while 'Shroos-bury' is perfectly acceptable, it tends to have fallen out of favour and is seen nowadays as rather antiquated. *Domesday* listed the town as 'Sciropesberie' in 1086.

Swansea
The original Welsh name for the South Wales City of Swansea is 'Abertawe', which translates into English as '(place at the) mouth of the (River) Tawe'. In the twelfth century the river name was 'Tauuy', probably a Celtic name meaning 'dark one', and the town name was recorded as 'Abertawi'. In 1150 the place name appeared as 'Aper Tyui'. At some point in the eighth or ninth century, the settlement came under Viking influence, in particular a Scandinavian called Sveinn (or Sweyn), whose base is thought to have been on an island in the Tawe estuary – hence the modern place name, 'Sveinn's island', derived from the Old Norse word 'ey' meaning 'island'. Some suggest that the Viking concerned might have been King Sweyn Forkbeard of Denmark (c.960–1014). In around 1165, the place name was spelled 'Sweynesse', in 1190 as 'Sueinsea' and in 1322 as 'Swanesey'.

Talgarth
Talgarth is a market town in southern Powys, whose place name comes from the Welsh words 'tal', in this context meaning 'brow' (as of a hill), and 'garth', a mountain ridge. Hence the name translates as '(place at the) brow of a ridge', which describes the town's location at the edge of a hill north-west of the Black Mountains. The name appeared as 'Talgart' in 1121, was recorded as 'Talgard' after 1130 and emerged in its present incarnation in about 1203.

Tenby
The Welsh name for the Pembrokeshire seaside town of Tenby is 'Dinbych-y-pysgod', which means '(small) fort of the fish', a reference to the town's long and ancient tradition as a fishing port. Located on Carmarthen Bay, the original settlement probably began life as a Celtic hillfort on Castle Hill, where the ruins of the thirteenth century Tenby Castle are now located. The English name is a corruption of the Welsh 'Dinbych', which derives from 'din', a fort, and 'bych' meaning 'little'. Hence, '(place by the) little fort'. The name was recorded as 'Dynbych' in 1275 and as 'Tynby' in 1369.

Tonypandy
Tonypandy lies in the Rhondda Valley of Glamorgan and its name means 'fulling mill on grassland (or pasture)'. It comes from the Welsh 'tonnau', meaning 'grassland' or 'unploughed land', 'pannu', which means 'fulling' (a process of deep cleaning animal furs, wools and hides), and 'ty', a house. The original fulling mill was driven by water from the River Rhondda. The area was occupied in prehistoric times as evidenced by several Bronze Age cairns as well as nearby earthwork

fortifications. The remains of an Iron Age settlement known as 'Hen Dre'r Gelli' have also been found on Mynydd Y Gelli Hill near Tonypandy.

Tredegar

Tradegar is a town near Newport in Blaenau Gwent, whose name means 'farmstead of Tegyr'. The Welsh word 'tre' represented a farmstead, and Tegyr seems to have been an early owner of it. However, an alternative suggestion is that it comes from the Old Welsh 'treff' meaning 'estate' or 'village', and 'deg ewr' meaning 'ten acres', in which case the place name could be interpreted as 'farm with ten acres'.

Tregaron

Tregaron in Ceredigion (sometimes 'Trev-Garon'), is said to derive its name from Caron, a second century Welsh king who is reputedly buried here, and who was canonised after his death. The village name means 'village (or settlement) of (St) Caron', after the dedication of the local church to the saint. The place name was recorded as 'Karoun' in 1281 and as 'Caron alias Tre Garon' in 1763.

Treorchi

The Glamorgan town of Treorchi (sometimes spelled 'Treorci' in Welsh and 'Treorchy' with a 'y' in English), stands on the River Gorci (or 'Orchy'), a tributary of the River Rhondda. This is the root of the place name, which translates as 'settlement on the (River) Orchy'. The origin of the river name is unknown. The 1875 Ordnance Survey map of the area referred to the stream as 'Nant Orky', which translates as 'Gorky Brook'.

Tywyn

Tywyn is a coastal resort on Cardigan Bay in Gwynedd, whose name is often spelled in English as 'Towyn'. The name derives from the Welsh word 'tywyn', meaning 'beach', or 'sand dune', which describes the extensive dunes found north and south of the town. The name means '(place by the) sand dunes'. It was recorded as 'Thewyn' in 1254 and as 'Tewyn' in 1291.

Upleadon

The Gloucestershire border village of Upleadon takes its name from the River Leadon on which it stands. The place name means '(place) higher up the (River) Leadon', identifying it as further upstream than the neighbouring village of Highleadon. The river runs through Herefordshire and Gloucestershire before it forms a tributary of the River Severn. The river name is of Celtic origin, and means 'broad stream'. Upleadon appears in the *Domesday Book* as 'Ledene' in 1086.

Welshpool

The town of Welshpool lies just three miles inside the Welsh border, historically in the county of Montgomeryshire, and now part of the Unitary Authority of Powys.

The name derives from the Old English words 'welisc' and 'pol', indicating a pool in Wales. The pool in question is at the place where the Lledin Brook joins the River Severn. The Welsh name for the town is 'Y Trallwng', which translates as 'the very wet swamp', based on 'y', meaning 'the', 'tra', meaning 'very', and 'llwng', a swamp. Originally known as 'Pola', the Welsh part of the present-day place name is thought to have been added in 1835 to distinguish it from the English town of Poole in Dorset. In 1477 the name was recorded as 'Walshe Pole'.

Wem

The Shropshire town of Wem was the territory of the Celtic tribe of Cornovii, the Iron Age people who occupied this area of borderland well before the Roman Conquest of Britain. They are thought to have been responsible for the nearby hillfort at Bury Walls. The name comes from the Old English word 'wemm', which signified filth, mud or dirt, producing a place name that means 'dirty (or muddy) place', a probable reference to the marshy terrain that surrounded the original settlement. *Domesday* recorded the name as 'Weme' in 1086.

Wormbridge

Wormbridge is a village in Herefordshire, whose name means what it says: 'bridge over the Worm (Brook)'. The river name is of Celtic origin, as with so many of these country villages near the Welsh border, and is thought to mean 'dark stream'. The name was recorded as 'Wermebrig' in 1207.

Wrekin, The

The Wrekin is a distinctive hill, topped by an Iron Age hillfort built by the Cornovii tribe, and rises out of an otherwise flat Shropshire Plain. The Celts called the hill 'Uriconio', meaning 'town of Virico', and the Wrekin name is thought to derive from the early Celtic word 'Wrikon'. In 47 AD the Romans burnt the fort to the ground, moving the defeated Cornovii to Wroxeter. However, the place name had emerged as 'Wreocensetun' by the eleventh century as part of the Kingdom known as 'Wreocensæte', a name which included a reference to the Roman fort, and was probably given to it by Mercian Anglo-Saxons. For centuries what we now call the Wrekin was known as Mount Gilbert, a name which the Normans gave it after a hermit who lived there. *Collins English Dictionary* records the Wrekin's significance as a common figure of speech in the West Midlands, where phrases like 'round the Wrekin' and 'all round the Wrekin' are used to describe a long-winded and tedious explanation that would have been better had it been more directly and clearly said.

Wrexham

Lying on an ancient territorial border between Wales and England and protected by a series of Celtic Iron Age hillforts, Wrexham was an early and important settlement in the domain of the Cornovii tribe. After Roman withdrawal from Britain, the settlement became part of the Kingdom of Powys. An early record of the name was in 1161 when it was written as 'Wristlesham', after a man called Wyrhtel, and a water-meadow which existed where the Rivers Gwenfro and Clywedog met. In Old English, such a meadow or flood plain was referred to as a 'hamm'. Hence, the name may be taken to mean 'Wyrhtel's water-meadow'. In 1291 the name was written as 'Gwregsam'. In present-day Welsh, the name is spelled 'Wrecsam', which is a phonetic version of its English name – both are pronounced exactly the same, with the initial 'w' as a silent letter. The accepted pronunciation is therefore 'reck-sam'.

Wroxeter
The fourteenth Roman legion (Legio XIV Gemina) called Wroxeter by the Latin name, 'Virconium Cornoviorum' when they established it as a legionary fortress and staging post for a planned invasion of Wales, beside the River Severn. It was a large settlement, with more than five thousand inhabitants at its height, and had seen human habitation for at least 1,500 years before the Romans arrived in Britain, with evidence of Bronze Age burial mounds in the region. It was hitherto the territorial capital of the Cornovii tribe, who called it 'Uiroconion' before their subjugation. The Roman name for the settlement, typical of their custom, adapted the original Celtic name and identified it as Virocnium, the territory of the Cornovii. The place name 'Wroxeter' translates as 'Roman fort near the Wrekin'.

Part Seven

Celtic River Names

Around two-thirds of the rivers of Great Britain and Ireland have names that originated in the Brittonic and Giodelic Celtic languages or have even earlier origins. They are among the oldest of all British names and it was on their banks that the earliest settlements would have been established. Some names may have been commonly used since Neolithic times and adopted by the Celtic settlers who migrated to Britain from the Continent in the fourth century BC.

Shrine to Coventina, goddess of springs, wells and rivers, Carrawburgh, Northumberland.

Celtic Places and Placenames

These ancient names tended to be descriptive of the unique nature of rivers, where concepts like 'flowing', 'gushing', 'turbulent', 'shining', 'dark' and 'deep' are common. Some have much simpler meanings, like 'water' or 'river'. Many were named after gods like Lugus and Coventina, as well as many other spirits and nymphs that were believed to occupy river waters. Some reflected the local topography, and were named after the deep gorges, territorial boundaries or wooded landscapes through which they flowed, while others described the flora and fauna of the riverside, naming places where otters or deer were seen or where oak trees grew. This was unlikely to have been on the basis of an inherent sense of conservation or an emotional attachment to nature (however endearing such an idea might be), but on a more pragmatic level, such names provided clues as to good places to hunt, where to find food, or to gather fuel and obtain other natural resources.

In the main, these ancient names tend to have survived better in the northern and western regions of Britain, where other invasive influences had less impact. Further south and east, later Romano-British culture tended to modify original river names, as did the Anglo-Saxons who ascribed Old English names to them, while Vikings tended to impose their own Scandinavian names.

The problem of interpreting Celtic river names is that their meanings were never written down. Thankfully, modern Welsh still retains much of their character and gives a clue as to their significance.

The Rivers

Aire
The Yorkshire River Aire may come from the Brittonic word 'isara' meaning 'the strong one', in which case Aire originally meant 'strong river'. Below Leeds the river is partially canalised, and is known as the Aire & Calder Navigation. It finally flows into the River Ouse at Airmyn, a name based on the Old English word 'myn', meaning 'river mouth' or 'estuary'.

Arun
In the second century, Ptolemy called the River Arun in West Sussex the 'Trisantonis', based on a Brittonic word meaning 'trespasser', a probable reference to its seasonal tendency to flood the surrounding countryside. The river was known as 'Arnus' in the upper reaches, from the Celtic word 'arno', meaning 'to run' or 'flow'. The town of Arundel may mean 'Arno-dell', or 'dell (valley) of the flowing river'.

Axe
The River Axe in South-West England has its source in the Mendip Hills and flows into Weston Bay on the Bristol Channel. The name derives from a Brittonic word

meaning 'abounding in fish'. This is also the same root as for the Rivers Exe, Esk and Usk, and is related to the Welsh word for 'fish'.

Avon
Avon is a common river name throughout mainland Britain, with around ten being called by it, based on the common Brittonic word 'abona', which is related to the Welsh word 'afon', simply meaning 'river'. Therefore, technically the name of any River Avon literally translates as 'river river'.

Bann
The River Bann is the longest river in Ulster. It has an Irish Gaelic name, 'An Bhanna' and its Ulster Scots name is 'Bann Watter'. The name is derived from the ancient Celtic and means 'river goddess'. There is also a River Bann in County Wexford, in the south-east of Ireland.

Boyne
The Irish name for the River Boyne, which rises in the Bog of Allen in County Kildare, is 'An Bhoinn' or 'Abhainn na Boinne'. This is an ancient river which Ptolemy referred to as 'Bouwinda' or 'Boubinda'. According to Irish mythology the river was created by the Celtic goddess Boann, and 'Boyne' is an Anglicised version of her name. As the river enters County Meath it becomes known as 'Smior Fionn Feidhlimthe', meaning 'the marrow of Fionn Feilim'.

Calder
The name of the West Yorkshire River Calder is thought to come from an ancient British expression, which means 'hard (or violent) water', and is closely related to the modern Welsh word 'caled', meaning 'hard'. There are also two River Calders in Lancashire, one of which is a major tributary of the River Ribble and the other of the River Wyre. There are others of this name in Renfrewshire and in the Scottish Highlands.

Cam
This East Anglian river's original name was the 'Granta', named after the town that grew up around it, which was known in Old English as 'Grantebrycge', which became the City of Cambridge. The river reflects the modern town name, but is still called the Granta in its upper reaches. Cambridge was an important Roman river crossing known to them as 'Great Bridge'. There are other River Cams in Gloucestershire and in Somerset.

Carron
Several hypotheses exist as to the meaning of the name of the River Carron, which rises in the Campsie Fells and flows into Scotland's Firth of Forth. Most accept

that it probably comes from a Brittonic expression which is similar to the modern Welsh 'caer avon', meaning 'river of the forts', a possible reference to Roman fortifications built on its banks as defence against Pictish incursions. Others have cited a different Gaelic origin meaning 'winding river'. Ptolemy called the river 'Itys'.

Chew
The River Chew rises in north Somerset before flowing seventeen miles through the Chew Valley to become a tributary of the River Avon at Keynsham. The name 'Chew' is of Celtic origin, and is thought to mean either 'gushing (or winding) water'.

Cocker
The River Cocker in the Lake District of Cumbria gets its name from the Brittonic Celtic word 'kukra', meaning 'crooked one'. It flows from a source in the Buttermere Valley, and joins the River Derwent at the town of Cockermouth.

Colne
The name of the River Colne (or Colne Water) in Lancashire, probably comes from the ancient Brittonic, but the meaning is uncertain. However, some have suggested it derives from the Celtic word 'cal', meaning 'stone', in which case the name could mean 'stony river'. There are other rivers of the same name in Essex, Hertfordshire and West Yorkshire.

Clyde
The River Clyde is known in Gaelic as 'Abhainn Chluaidh', and in Scots, 'Clyde Watter', or 'Watter o' Clyde'. It flows into the Firth of Clyde. Ptolemy recorded the name as 'Klota' and the Roman historian Tacitus similarly referred to it as 'Clota'. This was based on the earlier Cumbric name, 'Clud' or 'Clut', thought to mean 'pure' or 'cleansing'.

Dart
The River Dart in Devon has a name that is thought to be Brythonic Celtic, and means 'river of oak trees', a reference to the ancient native oak woods that line the banks of the Lower Dart. The name has occasionally been spelled as 'Darant'. The river has its source on Dartmoor and finally enters the English Channel at Dartmouth, the mouth of the River Dart.

Dee
The River Dee in Aberdeen bears the name of a Celtic river goddess, and means 'goddess' or 'holy one'. The name comes from the word 'deva'. The River Dee in Chester, which rises in Snowdonia in North Wales has the same root and meaning.

Derwent
Three English rivers share the name Derwent: in Cumbria, Derbyshire and Yorkshire. They are thought to derive their names from the Brittonic 'Deruentiu', meaning 'forest of oak trees'.

Don
The Yorkshire River Don (also known as the River Dun), derived its name from the Celtic word 'Dana', simply meaning 'water' or 'river' and is synonymous with Danu, a Celtic mother goddess and figure in ancient Irish mythology, who is also thought to be known as Anu, Ana, Anann or Anand. There are other rivers of the same name in Lancashire, Tyne & Wear and Northumberland as well as in Aberdeenshire, Scotland.

Doon
The River Doon has the Scottish Gaelic name, 'Abhainn Dhuin', and flows from Loch Doon in the Galloway Forest of Ayrshire, before entering the sea in the Firth of Clyde. The name is thought to come from the Gaelic, 'duin', which means either 'hill' or 'hillfort'.

Douglas
The River Douglas, which is also known as the River Asland (or Astland), flows through Lancashire and Greater Manchester in North-West England and is a tributary of the River Ribble. The name 'Douglas' is derived from the Brittonic elements 'dub', meaning 'black', or 'dark', and 'glass', related to the Welsh 'du-glais', signifying a stream or a brook. Hence, 'black (or dark) river'. The river has a section that has been partly canalised and is officially known as the Douglas Navigation.

Eden
The River Eden in Cumbria was known to the Romans as the 'Itouna', and was recorded as such by Ptolemy. This name derives as a Celtic name that simply means 'water' or 'rushing'. There is also a River Eden, a tributary of the River Medway in Kent, and another of the same name in Fife, Scotland.

Elwy
The River Elwy (called 'Afon Elwy' in Welsh), is a tributary to the River Clwyd. The name contains two elements: 'el', meaning 'swift' and 'wy', a common element in Welsh river names, which simply refers to 'water'. Hence, 'swift-flowing water'.

Erne
The River Erne (in Irish, 'Abhainn na hEirne' or 'An Eirne') is the second longest river in Ulster, and forms part of the border between Northern Ireland and the Republic, flowing some sixty-four miles before entering the ocean at Donegal Bay.

Along with Lough Erne, its name comes from a mythical princess named 'Eirne', or from 'Erainn', the name for an ancient ethnic group who dominated Ireland in the proto-historic period. Ptolemy named them 'Ivernioi', from which is derived the name of the island, 'Ivernia', and the Romans called 'Hibernia'.

Esk
Two rivers in England and four in Scotland go by the name of the River Esk. The river's name is derived from the Brittonic word 'iska', meaning 'abounding (or plentiful) in fish', and is related to the modern Welsh word 'pysg', meaning 'fishes'. This interpretation also applies to other British rivers of similar names, including the Axe, Exe and Usk.

Fal
The River Fal rises on Goss Moor and enters the English Channel at Falmouth. In the Cornish language, its name is 'Dowr Fala', though its exact meaning is unknown. The word 'fal' in Cornish is problematic, as it could mean either 'prince' or 'spade', neither of which are particularly helpful, nor seem connected to the river name, which continues to be a mystery.

Findhorn
The River Findhorn (in Scottish, 'Uisge Fionn Eireann' and in Gaelic 'Fionn Eire'), means 'white Ireland'. The 'white' element probably refers to the white sands of the estuary coast as the river enters the Moray Firth, though the Irish connection is obscure. An alternative suggestion is that it may possibly be a corruption of 'fionn-ear-an', meaning 'an east-flowing river'.

Fleet
The River Fleet in London has a name derived from the Old English word 'fleot', meaning 'tidal inlet', and gives its name to Fleet Street. It was also formerly known as the Holborn, deriving from the word 'bourne' or 'burn', meaning 'stream', which gave its name to the district of Holborn.

Fowey
The River Fowey has its source in Bodmin Moor. The name comes from the Cornish name, 'Fowydh', which means 'beech tree river', a reference to those that historically lined the banks of the river's lower reaches.

Forth
The Scottish tidal River Forth is thought to have derived its name from a pre-Celtic expression, 'vo-rit-ia', which means 'slow running'. This developed as 'Foirthe' in Old Scottish. Its Gaelic name is 'Uisge For' or 'Abhainn Dubh', meaning 'black river'. The Romans knew the waterway as 'Bodotria' and the Vikings called it 'Myrkvifiord'.

Foyle

The Irish name for the River Foyle in Northern Ireland is 'An Feabhal', a reference to Febail, father of the eighth century mythical Bran, whose story tells of an epic voyage which he undertook. Ptolemy described a river mouth which he called 'widhu', meaning 'tree' in his second century work, *Geographia*, which is thought to refer to the Foyle. It may come from the Gaelic word, 'poll' or 'phuill', generally indicating a pool, but in this case a stream. It has also been argued that the name is derived from the French word 'fouille' (meaning 'excavation'), possibly referring to early digging out to deepen or widen the river banks as it flows through Dublin city centre, though this is rather speculative. The name appears as 'Foyle' and 'Foyll' in Dublin city records of the thirteenth century.

Frome

The River Frome (historically known as the 'Froome'), is a small river in Gloucestershire whose name comes from the Brittonic word 'ffraw' meaning 'fair' or 'brisk', a reference to its fast-flowing current. There are other River Fromes –in Gloucestershire, in Bristol and in Herefordshire. The river was once also known as 'Stroudwater'.

Humber

According to Geoffrey of Monmouth's twelfth century chronicle, *Historia Regum Britanniae*, (History of the Kings of Britain), the Humber was named after Humber, the legendary king of the Huns, who invaded Britain in the twelfth century BC, and who drowned there during battle. In medieval literature, the Humber, along with the Thames and the River Severn, was counted as one of the three principal rivers of Britain. The ancient Kingdom of Northumbria and later the County of Northumberland took their names from the river, and translate as '(people who live in) land north of the Humber'

Irwell

The origin of the name of the River Irwell in Lancashire is obscure, but many believe that it comes from the Anglo-Saxon 'ere-well', meaning 'white spring'. The first element of the name may also derive from the ancient Brittonic river name element, 'ar', which means 'flowing', or 'rising', a possible reference to the river's propensity to flood, on account of its source in the Peak District from which it provides a major flow-off and drainage during heavy seasonal rainfall.

Lagan

The River Lagan in Ulster has the Irish name 'Abhainn an Lagain', which translates as 'river of the low-lying district'. In the second century, Ptolemy described the river which he called 'Logia'. In Old Irish, the original name for the River Lagan was 'Laogh', which means 'calf'. In 1605, the river was also known as 'Owenmore' (or in Irish 'Abhainn Mhor'), meaning 'big river'.

Leith
The River Leith (in Gaelic, 'Uisge Lite'), north of the City of Edinburgh, known in Scottish as the 'Water of Leith', flows through the city and enters the ocean via the Firth of Forth. The word 'leith' is from the Brittonic word 'lejth', and means either 'damp' or 'moist', or possibly 'grey' or 'flowing' – nobody seems quite certain. There is another River Leith in Cumbria.

Leven
The name 'Leven' is derived from the Gaelic 'uisge leamhna', meaning 'elm bank'. Several British rivers have this name, including one in Dunbartonshire and one in Fife, as well as others in North Yorkshire and in the Lake District of Cumbria.

Liffey
The River Liffey (in Irish, 'An Life'), flows through the centre of the City of Dublin. It had previously been known as 'An Ruirthech', meaning 'fast (or strong) flowing'. The plain through which it originally ran was called 'Liphe', which eventually became the river name. The word is derived from the identical source as the Welsh word 'llif', meaning 'stream'.

Lune
The River Lune rises in Cumbria and flows through Lancashire into the Irish Sea. Its name may come from the Brittonic words 'ion', meaning 'full' or 'abundant', and 'ea', a river. Hence, 'full (or abundant) river'. It has also been suggested that there is a possibility that the name could refer to Ialonus, a Romano-British god of forests and woodlands, who was known to have been venerated throughout Lancashire.

Medway
The Kentish River Medway (also historically known as the 'Medwege'), is thought by some to have derived its name from the ancient Celtic word, 'medu', meaning 'mead', a sweet alcoholic brew made from honey, inferring that it contained sweet water. Others take a different viewpoint and believe the ancient Britons called the Medway 'Vaga', meaning 'to travel', to which the Saxons added the prefix 'med', meaning 'middle', possibly reflecting the fact that the Medway effectively divides the county east and west. The Romans called the river 'Fluminus Meduwaeias' and the Saxons knew it as the 'Medwaeg'.

Mersey
The seventy-mile-long River Mersey rises in Stockport at the confluence of the Rivers Tame and Goyt, and flows into the Irish Sea at Liverpool. It historically marked the boundary between Lancashire and Cheshire. The name may come from a Celtic-derived Anglo-Saxon word meaning 'boundary river'; it also formed the border between the ancient kingdoms of Mercia and Northumbria.

Neath
The South Wales River Neath has the Welsh name 'Afon Nedd'. Its course runs south-west from the Brecon Beacons before entering the Irish Sea near Swansea Bay. The name derives from 'Nedd', which was the original name of the river. It is thought to be a Celtic or pre-Celtic name, but its precise meaning is obscure. Some suggest that it means 'shining' or 'brilliant' and others that it may simply mean 'river'.

Ness
The River Ness has the Scottish Gaelic name 'Abhainn Nis', and flows from the northern end of Loch Ness to Inverness, The word 'Ness' is a Pictish name derived from 'Nessa', the name of an ancient river goddess, who according to Scottish mythology was thrown into the water by the one-eyed giantess Beira and effectively became part of the loch and the river which bears her name.

Nidd
The River Nidd is a tributary of the River Ouse in North Yorkshire whose name has the pre-Celtic meaning 'brilliant' or 'shining'. The Nidderdale valley, in the river's upper reaches, was designated as an Area of Outstanding Natural Beauty in 1994.

Ouse
There are five rivers called Ouse in Britain, including in Orkney, in Yorkshire and Sussex, as well as the Great Ouse and the Little Ouse in East Anglia. The origin of the name is uncertain, but some suggest 'Usa', as recorded in 780 AD. Others prefer a Romano-British origin, possibly from the word 'udso', which probably translates as 'water'. Yet others cite the pre-Celtic word 'udsos', meaning either 'water' or 'slow flowing river'.

Penk
The Staffordshire River Penk gets its name from the township of Penkridge through which it runs. The name derives from the Celtic words 'pen crug', meaning 'ridge of a hill', a reference to an earthen mound or tumulus thought to be the location of a long-lost Roman fort known as 'Pennocrucium'. The town name means 'ridge by the (River) Penk'.

Ribble
Ptolemy's second century map of Britain marks the Ribble estuary as 'Belisama aest', named after the river goddess which the local Celtic tribes venerated. She was known as Rigabelisama, meaning 'Queen Belisama', referred to as the 'Most Shining One', and this is the meaning of the original river name. The first mention of anything approaching the name Ribble occurs in the *Vita Sancti Wilfrithi* (The Life of St Wilfrid) in the early eighth century. Wilfred is the patron saint of Preston

Celtic Places and Placenames

and in his biography are lands identified as 'iuxta Rippel', which translates as 'around the Ribble'. The Saxons called it the 'Ripel' which was taken to mean 'tearing', Hence, 'the tearing one', a reference to the river goddess's power, as evidenced in the raging tidal currents that often beset the Ribble estuary and cause river bank erosion.

Severn
The River Severn rises in the Cambrian Mountains of Wales and flows into Shropshire through Worcestershire and Gloucestershire before emerging at its estuary in the Bristol Channel. In Welsh, the river name is 'Hafren', meaning 'boundary', so called because for much of its course it marked the ancient boundary between England and Wales. The Romans called the river 'Sabrina', based on a mythical Celtic nymph who was thought to have drowned in the river. The word 'Severn' is a later derivation of the Roman name.

Shannon
The River Shannon in the Republic of Ireland has the Irish name 'Abha na Sionainne', meaning 'river of Sionann'. According to legend, Sionann was the wisest being on Earth, but she drowned in the river before being carried out to sea. She eventually emerged as the goddess of the river. According to Ptolemy's *Geographia* the river was called 'Senos', meaning 'to bind', similar to the modern English word 'sinew', a reference to its long meandering estuary as it approaches Limerick.

Soar
The River Soar is a tributary of the River Trent and is the main river of Leicestershire. Its ancient name comes from 'ser', meaning 'flowing'. It is thought that it may have been earlier known as the 'Leir', from Brittonic 'Ligera' or 'Ligora', a similar source to the Loire in France and many other similar names throughout Western Europe.

Stour
There are at least six rivers called Stour in the United Kingdom: in Dorset, Kent, Suffolk, Warwickshire and Worcestershire, as well as other smaller waterways of the same name. The precise meaning of the name remains open to argument. Some maintain that it comes from the Celtic word 'sturr' meaning 'strong'; others suggest a Germanic root which meant 'large' or 'powerful', while the Scandinavian word 'stor' suggests 'big' or 'great'. Finally, it has been mooted that 'Stour' simply derives from 'dwr', the Welsh word for water.

Taff
The River Taff (or 'Taf') has the Welsh name 'Afon Taf'. It rises as two rivers in the Brecon Beacons ('Taf Fechan', meaning 'Little Taff', and 'Taf Fawr', meaning

'Greater Taff), and runs on through Merthyr Tydfil before flowing into the Severn Estuary near Cardiff. The river name is thought to be similar in origin to the name 'tawe', as in the River Tawe, possibly signifying 'still and deep flowing'.

Tamar

The River Tamar (in Cornish, 'Dowr Tamar'), forms most of the border between the counties of Devon and Cornwall. The river was recorded in *The Anglo-Saxon Chronicles* in 997 AD, as the site of a Viking incursion into Cornwall. It is named after a beautiful mythical nymph called Tamara, who having refused to return home to the underworld with her father, was turned into a bubbling spring which became the source of the River Tamar.

Tame

There are three rivers called Tame in Britain: one in Stockport, Greater Manchester, one in Wolverhampton and another in the North Yorkshire. The name is synonymous with other river names, including the Thames, the Thame and the Tamar. The name is thought to be Celtic, but the meaning is unclear, although 'dark river' or 'dark one' has been suggested. Others think it may simply mean 'river'.

Tay

The River Tay, or in Scottish Gaelic, 'Tatha', is the longest river in Scotland and flows from the northern slopes of Ben Lui near Dundee for one hundred and seventeen miles before reaching the Firth of Tay. The meaning of the name is not clear, but some argue that it has the same root as 'tain', meaning 'flow' or 'flowing'.

Tees

The name of the northern English River Tees is thought to be Celtic or even pre-Celtic in origin, and may be related to the Brittonic Welsh word 'tes', meaning 'heat', and could also mean 'surging (or excited) river', a possible ancient reference to the High Force waterfall in upper Teesdale.

Teme

The River Teme is a Welsh river whose name is 'Afon Tefeidiad', which rises in mid-Wales to flow through the border Counties of Shropshire, Herefordshire and Worcestershire before joining the Severn a few miles below Worcester. This ancient river name is similar to many others in England, including the Team, Thames, Thame, Tame and the Tamar. These names derive from an older Celtic Brittonic word 'Tamesa' ('Temese' or 'Tamesis'), possibly meaning 'the dark one'.

Test

For many years the River Test in Hampshire was known as the River Anton. The present name comes from the Celtic Brittonic and probably relates to the Welsh word 'tres', meaning 'tumult' or 'uproar', or 'trais', meaning 'force'. It was recorded as 'Terstan' around 877, as 'Tarstan' in 1045 and as 'Terste' in 1234.

Thames
See: 'Tame'.

Trent
The name of Britain's second longest river, the River Trent is thought to come from two Romano-British words, 'tros', meaning 'over', and 'hynt', meaning 'way'. Taken together they could be either an indication of the frequency with which it overflowed its banks, or else a reference to a place where the river might be crossed over, or forded. It has also been suggested that the Romano-British expression 'tri-sent', meaning 'great through-path, or thoroughfare', might be appropriate, given its primary route for navigable transport inland in Roman times.

Tweed
The Scottish Borders River Tweed has the Gaelic name 'Abhainn Thuaidh', and in Scots is called 'Watter o Tweid'. The word 'Tweed' comes from a Celtic Brittonic word meaning 'border', a reference to its location as the historic border between Scotland and England.

Tyne
The word 'tin', is a potential source for the name of the River Tyne, as it was a Celtic word that meant 'river'. It may also be derived from 'tei', a word in a pre-Celtic language that might mean 'to flow' or 'flowing'. It has been suggested that it might be the river that Ptolemy referred to as 'Tina'. The Anglo-Saxons called it 'Tinanmude'.

Tywi
The River Tywi is known in English as the River Towy and in Welsh as 'Afon Tywi'. It is the longest river flowing entirely within Wales, beginning in the Cambrian Mountains before it emerges into Carmarthen Bay. The Welsh word 'tywyll' is thought to be the origin of the river name and means 'dark', reflecting the fact that parts of the river meander through dark, narrow valleys.

Usk
See: 'Axe' and 'Exe'.

Wear
It is thought that the river identified as 'Vedra' on the Roman map of Britain is the River Wear. It rises in the Pennine Hills of North-East England and enters the North Sea near Sunderland. Its name may be derived either from the Brittonic 'wejr', meaning 'bend', or 'wei', which probably meant 'to flow' or 'flowing'.

Wharfe

The original name of the River Wharfe in Yorkshire is thought to be from the Brittonic word 'werf', meaning 'liquid' (or possibly 'water'). This was replaced later by Viking settlers who used the Old Norse word 'hverfi', meaning 'to turn' to identify it, which would have been a reference to its meandering course. The river gave its name to Wharfedale, the valley through which it runs.

Wye

The River Wye forms part of the border between England and Wales and has the Welsh name 'Afon Gwy'. Its exact meaning is obscure, but some have suggested the Welsh word 'weag', meaning 'wave' might be relevant. For a time in its history it was known as the 'Vaga', and it was later recorded in a tithe map as 'Vagas'. Two other English rivers have the name Wye, one in Derbyshire and another in Buckinghamshire.

Wyre

The Lancashire River Wyre has a name of Celtic Brittonic origins, similar to the Old Welsh 'wei', meaning 'flowing'. It rises in the Forest of Bowland in Lancashire and flows into the Irish Sea at Fleetwood.

Yeo

The River Yeo runs through Somerset and Dorset before entering the English Channel on the south coast of England. It is also known as the River Ivel, a name derived from the Celtic river name 'gifl', meaning 'forked river'. It appeared in a Saxon charter of 880 AD as 'Gifle', and was recorded in the *Domesday Book* as 'Givele'. Later the name appears to have been influenced by the Old English word 'ea', meaning simply 'river'.

Part Eight

Celtic Mountain Names

Mountains and hills were often regarded by Celtic peoples as of mystical or religious significance, imbued with the spirits of ancient gods. This attitude of reverence was widespread across all parts of the archipelago with the same or similar names being common. As an example, the god Lugh (sometimes Lug or Lugus), whose place of worship was often on mountains, was revered throughout the Celtic world.

Despite the variety of Brittonic dialects that must have been present in Iron Age Britain, certain word elements seem to have been fairly constant. The Gaelic Irish word for 'mountain', or 'peak' ('bean' or 'beinn'), is a case in point, in that it is equivalent to the word 'ben' or 'bienn' in Scottish Gaelic, and very similar to 'bann' in Welsh.

Like rivers, many mountain names remain obscure, and are so ancient that many of their derivations have been passed down through the generations by word of mouth and through folklore, with all the vagaries implicit in that form of communication. What can be reasonably deduced of their meanings often relies on the modern forms of Gaelic that survive in Ireland, Scotland and Wales.

Eroded rock formations, Kinder Scout, Derbyshire Peak District.

Lugh (Lugus), Warrior Sun God, Musée de St-Remy, Reims.

Celtic Places and Placenames

The Mountains & Hills

Aonach Beag
Aonach Beag (also known as 'Ben Alder'), is a mountain in the Highlands of Scotland. The name means 'small ridge', although it is not actually smaller than Aonach Mor (whose name means 'big ridge'), it being much higher at more than 4,000 feet above sea level.

Ben Macdui
Ben Macdui, on the Cairngorms plateau, is the second highest mountain in Britain after Ben Nevis. Its name in Scottish Gaelic is 'Beinn Mac Duibh', meaning either 'MacDuff's Hill' or sometimes 'Hill of the Black Pig', a reference to its shape. Ben Macdui is said to be haunted by the legendary Am Fear Liath Mor, also known as the 'Greyman'.

Ben Nevis
Ben Nevis (in Scottish Gaelic, 'Beinn Nibheis'), is the highest mountain in the British Isles. There are several interpretations of the meaning of the mountain's name, but a widespread opinion is that it probably derives from 'beinn-bhathais', variously translated as 'heaven's clouds' and the last element, 'bathais', as meaning the 'top of a man's head'. On this basis a fair translation might be 'mountain with its head in the clouds'. However, the 'Nibheis' element of the Gaelic name is sometimes translated as 'malicious' or 'venomous'. Ironically, it has also been referred to as the 'mountain of Heaven'.

Blen Cathra
For many years Blen Cathra (sometimes one word, 'Blencathra'), in the Northern Fells of the Lake District, was known as 'Saddleback', on account of the shape of the mountain when viewed from the east. Even Ordnance Survey listed it as such on its maps. The name comes from the Cumbric words 'blain', meaning 'top' or 'summit', and 'cadeir', meaning 'seat' or 'chair'. Hence, the name means 'summit of a chair-like mountain'.

Buachaille Etive Mor
The name of the mountain of Buachaille Etive Mor at the head of Glen Etive in Argyll & Bute comes directly from Scottish Gaelic and translates as 'the herdsman of Etive'. It is frequently referred to simply as 'The Buachaille'. The name 'Etive' is thought to mean 'little fierce one', a reference to an ancient Celtic goddess who was associated with the River Etive and its related sea loch.

Cader Idris
Cader Idris is a Welsh mountain in the Snowdonia National Park. The Welsh word 'cadeir', means 'seat' or 'chair', and the 'Idris' element of the name refers to a

person called Idris. The name means 'Idris's chair', referring to the 'hollowed-out' chair-shape of the mountain. Idris ap Gwyddno was a seventh century prince of Meirionnydd who was sometimes referred to as Idris Gawr, or 'Idris the Giant'.

Cairngorms
The Cairngorms is a range of mountains and a Scottish National Park whose Gaelic name is 'Mhonaidh Ruaidh', which translates as 'red (or russet) coloured mountains'. The park has five of Britain's six highest mountains as well as having fifty-five 'Munros' (mountains over 3,000 feet above sea level).

Cambrian Mountains
The term Cambrian Mountains (in Welsh, 'Mynyddoedd Cambria'), has historically been applied to the whole of Wales's mountain ranges, but is nowadays chiefly used to describe those in mid-Wales, which are known in Welsh as the 'Elenydd'.

Carrauntoohil
At almost 3,500 feet above sea level, Carrauntoohil, on the Iveragh Peninsula in the Reeks District in County Kerry, is the highest mountain in Ireland. Its Irish Gaelic name is 'Corran Tuathail', which means 'Tuathal's sickle'. This may have been a reference to Tuathal, the son of Ughaire, the tenth century King of Leinster. The 'sickle' element is obscure, but it may refer to the hooked curvature of the mountain.

Cat Bells
Cat Bells (sometimes spelled as one word, 'Catbells'), is a fell overlooking Derwentwater in the Lake District of Cumbria, whose unusual name is thought to be a corruption of 'cat bields', meaning 'shelter (or lair) of the cat', an ancient reference to the wild cats that once roamed these hills.

Cheviot Hills
Straddling the Scottish Borders and County of Northumberland, the Cheviot Hills derive their name from a single mountain, the Cheviot. They are part of the Southern Uplands of Scotland and the northern Pennines. The name is thought to be of Celtic origin, from a word similar to the modern Welsh 'cefn', meaning 'ridge(s)'.

Chiltern Hills
The Chiltern Hills cover an area of some fifty miles stretching across the counties of Oxfordshire, Buckinghamshire, Hertfordshire and Bedfordshire. Their name is believed to be Brittonic in origin, possibly related to the word 'Celt' (or 'Keltoi') itself. Others suggest that there is evidence in Anglo-Saxon records to suggest that the local Cilternsaete (the 'Chiltern settlers') may have given their tribal name to the range.

Celtic Places and Placenames

Clee Hills

Actually, there is no Clee Hill as such, but it is a range which includes Brown Clee Hill and Titterstone Clee Hill. The small village of Cleehill is located on the southern slopes of Titterstone Clee Hill. It is thought that the hills are probably named from the Old English word 'cleo', meaning 'rounded hill'.

Cnoc na Peiste

Cnoc na Peiste (also known in English as 'Knocknapeasta'), is a mountain in County Kerry, part of the MacGillycuddy Reeks range, whose name means 'hill of the serpent'. The reference to serpents is not clear, but historically they have been creatures associated with rebirth or a creative life force, as well being harbingers of evil and chaos from the underworld.

Fan Fawr

Fan Fawr is a mountain in the Forest Fawr area of the Brecon Beacons in Powys, South Wales, whose name translates from the Welsh as 'big peak'. Fan Fawr is the highest peak of a ten-mile-wide plateau and upland area located between the central Brecon Beacons and the Black Mountains.

Galtymore

Galtymore (sometimes 'Galteemore'), is one of the Galty (or 'Galtee') Mountains which stretch across the counties of Limerick and Tipperary. It has the Irish Gaelic name 'Cnoc Mor na nGaibhlte', meaning 'big hill of the Galtees'. Several interpretations of the word 'galtee' have been suggested, but most agree that it probably means 'woods' or 'woodland'. The mountain has also been called 'Sleibhte na gCoillte', which literally translates as 'mountain of the forests'.

Glyder Fawr

Glyder Fawr is a mountain in Snowdonia, part of the Glyderau mountain range. It is the fifth highest mountain in Wales and the name comes from 'Glyder', a derivation of the Welsh word 'Gludair', meaning 'heap of stones'.

Grampians

The Grampian Mountains in the Highland region of Scotland derive their name from 'Mons Graupius', a name given by the Roman historian Tacitus, following a defeat of Pictish tribes by forces under Agricola in 84 AD. The range covers much of the central Highlands and its highest peak is Ben Nevis.

Helvellyn

Helvellyn is a mountain in the Cumbrian Lake District which is located between Ullswater, Thirlmere and Grasmere. It is the third highest peak in the district after Scafell Pike and Scafell. The name of the mountain comes from two Cumbric (or possibly Old Welsh) words, 'hal', meaning 'moorland' or 'upland',

and 'velin', meaning 'pale yellow', which taken together produce a name that means 'pale yellow moorland (or upland)'. This is thought to be an attribution related to the colour of vegetation on its slopes in summer and autumn.

Kinder Scout
Kinder Scout (formerly known as 'Kinder Scut') is a high moorland plateau in the Derbyshire Peak District and the highest point in the county. The plateau is famous for its distinctive eroded rock formations, known as 'Woolpacks', on account of their resemblance to the traditional method of wool-packing and baling. The mountain's name is thought to derive from ancient Celtic and means 'wide views', which perfectly describes the panoramic vistas it presents across the Cheshire Plain, Greater Manchester and southern Lancashire. Kinder was the setting for a 'mass trespass', when in 1932 around five hundred walkers from around Manchester walked from Hayfield to Kinder Scout where they staged a mass trespass in protest, and to secure right of access to open country over what had previously been closely guarded private land. As a consequence, Kinder is nowadays freely open to all walkers.

Lammermuir Hills
The Lammermuir Hills in the East Lothian region of southern Scotland have the Gaelic name 'An Lomair Mor'. Two explanations have been offered as to its meaning: one has it derived from the Gaelic 'lann barra mor', meaning 'flat (or level) place on the big height', while the other suggests the simpler and more literal translation 'lamb's moor'. Either is possible. Over time the name has been variously spelled as 'Lombormore', 'Lambremore', 'Lambermora' and 'Lambirmor'.

Lomond Hills
The Lomond Hills are located in west-central Fife and Perth & Kinross in Scotland and are also known as the Paps of Fife. The word 'paps' means 'breasts', a reference to the two prominent and similarly shaped tops of the East and West Lomond. The 'Lomond' name may have derived originally from a Pictish word similar to the Welsh word 'llumon', meaning 'beacon'. Hence, 'beacon mountain'. There is also a suggestion that it may be a derivation of the Gaelic 'lom monadh', meaning 'bare hill'. It was first recorded 'Lomondys' in 1315.

Mendip Hills
The Mendips are a range of limestone hills in northern Somerset. The origin of the name 'Mendip' is unclear, though it has been suggested that it might come from the Celtic word 'monith', meaning 'mountain' or 'hill', possibly with the added Old English suffix 'yppe' meaning 'plateau' or 'upland'. Another interpretation relies on the Brittonic term 'mened' (related to the Welsh word 'mynydd'), meaning 'moorland'. Finally, some cite the Old English words 'moen' and 'deop', together meaning 'mighty' and 'awesome'. The fact is that the passing centuries have shrouded the name in obscurity.

Mourne

The Mourne Mountains of County Down are the highest and possibly the most dramatic mountains in Northern Ireland. Often referred to as 'The Mournes', their Irish name is 'na Beanna Boirche', derived from the ancient Mughdhorna tribe (in modern Irish, 'Murna' or 'Mourna'). The Gaelic name 'na Beanna Boirche', is thought to mean 'the peaks of the peak district', but they are sometimes referred to as 'the peaks of Boirche', a reference to a third century king of Ulster.

Ochil Hills

The Ochil Hills, or in Scottish Gaelic, 'Monadh Ochail', is a range north of the Forth Valley in Scotland. They cover much of the historic County of Clackmannanshire, as well as Perth & Kinross and a part of Fife. The name Ochil was recorded as 'Okhel' in the thirteenth century, and may be of Pictish origin, possibly related to 'ogel' meaning 'ridge'. It has also been suggested that it may derive from the Welsh adjective 'uchel' meaning 'high' or 'tall'.

Peak District

The Peak District of Derbyshire lies at the southern end of the Pennine range, which has been inhabited since the Middle Stone Age as well as the Neolithic, Bronze and Iron Ages, with the remains of henges like Arbor Low near Youlgreave and the Nine Ladies stone circle at Stanton Moor. It was also the site of the Iron Age hillfort at Mam Tor. Ironically, the district is more commonly said to be of rounded hills, rather than peaks. The origin of the name is thought by some to be a corruption of 'Pict District', suggesting an early occupation by invading tribes from over the Scottish borders. However, a more likely explanation is that it is much later and comes from the Old English word 'Pecsaetan', which literally translates as 'peak dwellers', and referred to the Anglo-Saxon 'Peaklanders' or 'Peakrills', as they were known. Before the Anglo-Saxon invasions, the area had been the territory of the Celtic Brigantes tribe.

Pennines

The range of hills known as the Pennines, which run as a backbone down the length of northern England, is a relatively recent appellation, which though probably in common use, was not actually recorded as such until the eighteenth century. Two possible explanations exist for the origin of the name: one has it from the Celtic word 'penn', simply meaning 'hill', while another cites the Apennines, which similarly run down the length of Italy, as a likely influential source of the name.

Pen y Fan

Pen y Fan (pronounced 'Pen a Van'), derives its name from the Welsh words 'pen', meaning 'peak', 'beacon' or 'summit', along with 'y', meaning 'the', and 'fan' or 'ban', meaning 'hill' or 'mountain'. Hence, the name may be translated as something like 'the mountain's peak' or 'the beacon's summit'. It is the tallest peak in the Brecon Beacons of South Wales, and on its summit stands a well-preserved Bronze Age cairn.

Pen-y-Ghent

Pen-y-ghent (sometimes spelled as one word, 'Penyghent'), in the Yorkshire Dales is the smallest of the Yorkshire Three Peaks. In the Cumbric language the word 'pen' indicated the top or head, usually when applied to hills and mountains, while the obscure word element 'ghent' is thought to mean either 'edge' or 'border'. Therefore, the name when translated from the Celtic may mean 'hill (summit) on the border' or 'hill of the border land'.

Purbeck Hills

The Purbecks are a ridge of chalk downs in Dorset, part of the Southern England Chalk Formation. The hills take their name from the peninsula known locally as the 'Isle of Purbeck'. The name 'Purbeck' was recorded in 948 AD as 'Purbicing', meaning 'of the people of Purbic', of which 'Purbic' is thought by some to be a Celtic name, but could also derive from the Anglo-Saxon word 'pur', referring to a male lamb. Yet others prefer the Saxon word 'pur' as meaning 'bittern' or 'snipe', and 'beck' meaning 'beak', although this reference is difficult to explain.

Quantock Hills

The earliest record of the Quantock range of hills in Somerset appears as 'Cantuctun' around 880 AD in a Saxon charter. Later, in the *Domesday Book* it was entered as 'Cantoctona', 'Cantoche' and 'Cantetone'. However, the word 'cantuc' is a Celtic term meaning 'rim' or 'circle', and the Old English suffix 'tun', signified a village or early settlement. Therefore the name translates as 'settlement by a circle of hills'.

Scafell Pike & Scafell

Scafell Pike is the highest mountain in England and is located in the Lake District National Park of Cumbria. The name was traditionally spelled 'Scawfell' (and pronounced as such), until Ordnance Survey entered the name as 'Scafell' on their map of 1865. However, the shepherds who worked the slopes continued to use the old pronunciation well into the twentieth century, and frequently referred to the summits as 'the Pikes'. The word 'fell' comes from the Viking word 'fjell' meaning 'mountain'. The name 'Scafell' is thought to derive from the Old Norse words 'skalli fjall', meaning either 'the fell with the shieling' (that is, a night hill shelter for sheep or shepherds), or 'the fell with the bald summit', and is first recorded in 1578 as 'Skallfield'.

Sgurr na Stri

Sgurr na Stri is a mountain trail located on the Isle Of Skye in the Highland region of Scotland, which is familiarly known as 'The Peak of Strife', owing to its rank as a 'technically difficult' climb. A literal translation of the Gaelic name is 'the mountain of the old woman'. In explanation of this ancient chauvinistic interpretation, *The Skye Guide* comments that '…she is a tough old woman, with a steep and boulder-strewn face'.

Sidlaw Hills

The Sidlaws are a range of Scottish hills in Perthshire and Angus. Their Gaelic name is 'na Sidhbheanntan'. The element 'sid' probably comes from 'sidhe', meaning 'fairy' or 'sacred', no doubt a reference to the prehistoric cairns that are still dotted around the hills, along with 'bheanntan', meaning 'peaks'. The word element 'law', is a Lowland Scots word based on the Old English 'hlaw' referring to a mound or tumulus which stands out from the surrounding landscape. A reasonable translation of the whole name might be 'sacred mound or peak'.

Slieve Binnian

Slieve Binnian is one of the Mourne Mountains of County Down. The word 'slieve' is Gaelic for 'mountain'. In Irish Gaelic the name is 'Sliabh Binnean', which translates as 'mountain of the little peaks (or horns)'. In around 1568 the name was recorded as 'Great Bennyng'.

Slieve Lamagan

Slieve Lamagan (sometimes one word, 'Slievelamagan') is part of the Mountains of Mourne in County Down. Its Gaelic name is 'Sliabh Lamhagain', which translates as 'creeping (or crawling) mountain'. The name came about in view of the fact that it is one of the most difficult to climb in the whole range and its peak has to be ascended in a crawling position. It is sometimes also known as 'Slieve Snavan'.

Snowdon

Snowdon is the highest mountain in Wales, and is second only to Ben Nevis in Great Britain. The name 'Snowdon' comes from a combination of the Old Saxon words 'snaw' and 'dun', together meaning 'snow hill'. Its name in Welsh is 'Yr Wyddfa', which means 'the tumulus' or 'the barrow', thought to be a reference to the cairn at its summit which tradition has it was placed over the mythical giant Rhitta Gawr after his defeat by King Arthur.

Sperrins

The Sperrin Mountain range stretches across areas of County Derry and County Tyrone in Northern Ireland. Their Irish name, 'Sliabh Speirin', is derived from the Gaelic words 'sliabh', which can refer to a single mountain or a mountain range, and 'speirin', meaning '(mountain with a) little spur of rock' or '(mountain of the) little pinnacle'.

Trossachs

The Stirlingshire Trossach Hills (in Gaelic, 'Na Troiseachan'), have a name which may come from a Brittonic Celtic word 'tros', similar to the Welsh word 'traws', meaning 'across' and is generally taken to mean 'transverse (or across) hills', a reference to the way they traversally divide Loch Katrine from Loch Achray.

Tryfan

Tryfan is a mountain in the Ogwen Valley of Snowdonia in North Wales. The name 'Tryfan' is thought to derive from 'try' and 'ban', meaning 'top' or 'peak', which when taken together translate as 'very high peak'. By tradition it is the final resting place of the Arthurian knight, Sir Bedivere.

Part Nine

Bronze & Iron Age Hillforts

Recent research by Oxford University has found that there are 4,147 hillforts in Britain. These defensive Bronze and Iron Age hillforts give a clue to the kind of enmity that frequently existed between Celtic tribes and the fierce territorial disputes which must have been commonplace at that time. It has also been suggested that apart from intertribal warfare, the establishing of such sites could have been in response to periodic invasions from continental Europe.

Earlier hillforts tended to be slightly built 'univallate' types (that is with a single line of defensive earth ramparts). Around three or four hundred years later many had been expanded as 'bivallate' (two defensive lines), and 'multivallate' (several or many defensive lines). Construction would have been done entirely by hand using horn or rudimentary bronze or iron shovels, and earth carried up the ever-steeper growing slope in baskets – an enormous undertaking. It has been suggested that much of the work might have been carried out by enslaved prisoners taken in battle. However, many of these hill constructions were not exactly forts at all, but merely hilltop settlements, often only occupied during summer months, and the

Pen y Crug Hillfort, Brecon Beacons, Powys.

term 'fort' is little more than a generic name for hilltop settlements. Further, many were not actually established on hills.

Some of the oldest were constructed four and a half thousand years ago, but most were begun between about 700 and 500 BC in the later Bronze and Iron Ages, often over the site of these earlier prehistoric settlements. Not all, but most featured deep ditches and earthen or stone ramparts that were probably topped by wooden stockades or palisades. Many later hillforts evolved to include roundhouses, longhouses and granary huts, in preparation for extended sieges or for longer sustained habitation. Such 'forts' maintained more or less continuous habitation until the Roman invasion of the first century.

While some commentators see them as primarily military installations, and only used at times of war, the debate continues as to their precise purpose, and others think they operated as self-contained socio-economic entities. These were arguably the first civilised settlements, the earliest embryonic settled towns, at least when viewed in an historical context. It has been suggested that they might have only been occupied in summer time, as their exposure to the worst weather in winter probably meant that its resident population, along with their livestock, would have sought milder conditions in the valleys below.

Many forts remained in practical use until Roman times, when its people were often forcibly ejected and their hill settlements either destroyed, abandoned or sequestered as Roman military stations. A large number of these enforced abandonments took place soon after 43 AD, when the Roman commander Vespasian undertook a campaign to subdue southern Britain by attacking around twenty hillforts. Against his sustained military onslaught, native Britons could offer only paltry resistance, so that by the year 48 AD, the Romans had subdued all the Celtic territorial tribelands from south of the River Humber in the east and the Severn Estuary in the west.

Roman occupation effectively saw an end to the age of hillforts. The increasing pacification and 'civilisation' of resident tribes, saw many abandoning ancient sites to live in so-called 'vicus', civilian settlements which grew up alongside Roman camps. During the Late Iron Age enclosed and unenclosed settlements with the characteristics of early towns, which the Romans called 'oppida', became more common. They had reached a point in the first century AD where they became the rule, rather than the exception. These lowland settlements were based less on defence, as the hillforts had tended to be, but on trade, agriculture and industry. Oppida were most common across southern and eastern England and were often promoted and encouraged by an ever-expanding Roman Empire and the increased trading opportunities and wealth that brought with it.

Prolonged Roman occupation invariably saw many Britons becoming assimilated and intermarrying to become 'Romano-British' and evolving a culture that is often referred to as 'Roman Britain' so that long abandoned hillforts were soon overgown and lost in the landscape. However, thanks to aerial photoghraphy, many have re-emerged to bear witness to a heroic and an ancient warrior people and to an almost forgotten and seldom understood culture.

The Hillforts

Abbotsbury Castle
This Dorset earthwork sits high on a Wears Hill overlooking the English Channel. It was constructed by the Durotriges tribe, and is comprised of double ramparts which encircle an enclosure of about four acres, though the entire site measures around ten acres. It was occupied by the Celts until the Roman Second Augustinian Legion under Vespasian took possession, before moving on, after which it was effectively abandoned.

Ambresbury Banks
The Iron Age hillfort at Ambresbury Banks, generally described as a 'slight univallate hillfort', is located on a gravelly sand ridge overlooking the Lea Valley in Epping Forest. It is thought that the fort was once occupied by the Romano-British leader Ambrosius Aurelianus as part of his defence against the encroaching Saxons. The name 'Ambresbury' actually translates as 'Ambrosius's fort'. Various artefacts have been unearthed at the site, including fragments of red, grey and black pottery, flints and arrow heads. The hillfort was probably built to mark the boundary between the territory of the Catuvellauni and Trinovantes tribes.

Barbury Castle
Barbury Castle lies within the North Wessex Downs on the Old Ridgeway track in Wiltshire and encloses an area of more than twelve acres within a double rampart and with entrances on its eastern and western sides. Construction took place over a period of hundreds of years, perhaps beginning with a single soil rampart, and with a second added at a later date. It was first occupied about 2,500 years ago and continued in use until the Roman occupation, when they took it over and established a small military settlement within its perimeter.

Battlesbury Camp
This Wiltshire hillfort dates back to the first millennium BC when construction began on the plateau at the top of the Battlesbury Hill. Bronze Age people created the bivallate defensive perimeter here, comprising an earthwork with two banks, each separated by a ditch, and virtually inaccessible on all sides. Many graves have been found outside the north-west entrance, which suggests that the inhabitants met with a violent end, possibly at the hands of Roman legionaries or as a result of intertribal warfare. Several barrows were found to contain human cremated remains as well as carefully laid out and complete skeletons, while others contained primitive bead necklaces, jewellery and other artefacts.

Badbury Rings Hillfort
Badbury Rings is an Iron Age hillfort in Dorset and comprises three rings, of which the innermost dates from between 500 and 600 BC. It was occupied by the Durotriges

tribe at the time of the Roman conquest of Britain. Of its two surrounding ditches, the outermost encloses an area of some forty-one acres. Excavations of the site in 2004 found pottery dated to the Late Iron Age, though other material suggested a much earlier occupation. The fort was abandoned during the first century, possibly driven out by the Second Augustan Legion (Legio II Augusta) led by Vespasian. Its former inhabitants were moved to a nearby lowland settlement called Vindocladia (present-day Shapwick). The Badbury Rings site has been restored to grazing pasture land.

Bratton Camp

The earthwork defences of the Iron Age hillfort were built at Bratton Camp near Westbury on Bratton Down in the Salisbury Plain (sometimes called Bratton Castle), over 2,000 years ago. The protected settlement contained round houses, granaries, stores and workshops to sustain its inhabitants. The site has two ditches and banks which together enclose an area of about twenty-three acres, but it has sustained damage and substantial degradation as a result of quarrying. The hillfort is fourteen hundred feet long, over nine hundred feet wide at the east end, tapering to almost four hundred feet at the west end. Roman and Saxon coins found within the enclosure suggest later occupations long after its Celtic builders had abandoned it. Two nineteenth century investigations unearthed quantities of pottery, animal bones and three human skeletons, as well as a cremation platform for one or two adults.

Brecon Beacons

There are several hillforts in the Brecon Beacons of which those at Garn Goch form the largest in South Wales. The name Garn Goch means 'red hill' on account of the colour its bracken covering in the autumn. It comprises two Iron Age hillforts: 'Y Gaer Fawr', meaning 'the big fort', and 'Y Gaer Fach', meaning 'the little fort'. The two camps share a ridge location just above the village of Bethlehem, between Llandeilo and Llangadog, and were constructed in the Early Bronze Age. The site covers an area of twenty-eight acres, surrounded by thirty-feet-high stone ramparts and with a huge burial cairn. It is situated on the territorial boundary of rival the Silures and Demetae tribes. Of these, it is known that the Silures, led by Caradog (also known as Caractacus), resisted the Roman advance, while the Demetae may have collaborated with the Romans in the defeat and expulsion of the Silures from the site.

Bredon Hill

The hillfort at Bredon Hill in the Vale of Evesham is known as the Kemerton Camp. It was built by the Dobunni tribe and is located on a ridge with two sets of ramparts and ditches. A burial ground containing the decapitated remains of some fifty men, along with their weapons, has been found near the entrance to the inner rampart, which suggests a bloody battle took place here, either against the Romans or some other opposing tribe. Whatever the outcome, the fort was abandoned soon afterwards, and it appears to have been resettled later by the Romans, judging by the hoard of Roman coins found here during twentieth century excavations.

British Camp
British Camp is Bronze Age hillfort dating from about 3,500 years ago, and located at the top of Herefordshire Beacon in the Malvern Hills. The earth defences follow the contour of the hill and were enlarged over successive centuries. Archaeological excavations suggest that it was permanently occupied, and that the inner ward would have had dwellings for up to four thousand people. It is not known whether Roman forces ever occupied the fort, though legend has it that the Celtic chieftain Caractacus made his last stand here. There certainly was an armed conflict before the fort was abandoned in the middle of the first century. The top of the hill was later occupied by the Normans, who built their own motte and bailey fortification on the site.

Bury Castle
Bury Castle is located near Selworthy in Exmoor and is a relatively small fortified Iron Age settlement constructed on the spur of a hill, a so-called 'promontory fort'. Originally, its univallate earthwork was six-and-a-half feet high with an outer ditch of similar depth. More earthworks were added later and its ramparts reinforced with a timber palisade. On the north-east corner there are stone foundations, possibly part of a strengthened portal gateway. On the crest of the ridge some way above the enclosure is a cross-ridge earthwork, which was probably a lookout post.

Caesar's Camp
Caesar's Camp is a 2,400 year old univallate Iron Age hillfort located in Bracknell Forest in Berkshire. The origin of the name is not known, but its proximity to the so-named Devil's Highway, an old Roman road, may have led to the structure's incorrect attribution to the Romans. The fort encompasses an area of just over seventeen acres and is surrounded by a mile-long ditch. It was constructed around 500–300 BC by the Atrebatic tribe, and may have come under the control of Cunobelin, king of the Catuvellauni tribe sometime during the first century. The fort is unique in that it is the only one known in Berkshire.

Carnsew Hillfort
This late-prehistoric Celtic hillfort is situated on the slope of a prominent hill overlooking the Hayle Estuary at Carnsew in Cornwall. Its defences include two ramparts, the outer surmounting a fifty-feet-high escarpment. The site has never been excavated, but there is evidence for post-Roman activity as well as a late fifth or early sixth century burial. The site has suffered a great deal of damage as a result of nineteenth century landscaping to create 'The Plantation' park, as well as a deep railway cutting. During these works in 1843, the fifth century burial stone,

known as the Cunaide Stone, was unearthed by workmen and now forms part of an exhibition in the Hayle Heritage Centre.

Castlelaw
The remains of Castlelaw hillfort lie at the summit of Castle Law hill in the Pentland Hills of Midlothian. Originally it would have consisted of three earthwork ramparts laid out in concentric rings surrounding a low foothill, a so-called 'contour fort', with intermediate ditches and timber palisades. A sixty-five-feet-long earth house, possibly used as a storehouse, has been uncovered in the middle ditch, and was probably a later addition. This small fort probably housed a community of farming families, with huts grouped inside a simple timber palisade. Finds of Roman jewellery, pottery and glass bottle fragments suggest that its native inhabitants were actively dealing with Roman traders in the latter half of the first century.

Castle Pencaire
Castle Pencaire is an Iron Age hillfort on Tregonning Hill near Porthleven in Cornwall. It is roughly oval-shaped and constructed with a pair of ramparts and ditches with two entrances. The round enclosure measures a little short of three hundred by two hundred and sixty feet with a rampart up to eight feet high and a ditch five feet deep. The remains of hut circles have been found in the fort interior but they are badly deteriorated as a result of mining and quarrying. The hill also contains the remains of burial mounds and medieval field systems, but due to the heavy undergrowth covering the site and its generally poor condition, it has been placed on the Heritage at Risk Register by Historic England. The site also suffered serious deterioration in the twentieth century as a result of the industrial extraction of china clay.

Caterthun
The Caterthuns are a ridge of hills near Brechin in Angus. It contains two Iron Age hillforts, known as the White Caterthun and the Brown Caterthun. The first consists of an oval drystone wall structure, whose pale colour gives the fort its name. It was probably built by Pictish tribes. Inside the main ward are the footings of roundhouses and rectangular enclosures as well as a deep well or cistern cut directly into the rock. Brown Caterthun was constructed between 700 BC and 200 BC and consists solely of earth embankments and ditches – hence, its name.

Cadbury Castle
Cadbury Castle in Somerset was formerly known as 'Camalet', which tradition has it was the site of King Arthur's legendary court at Camelot. The fort's four raised earthwork terraces were surrounded by wooden fences for extra protection. During the Iron Age, Cadbury probably belonged to the Dumnonii tribe before they were driven out by the Durotriges. Even so, in 70 AD the Durotriges came up against a superior Roman force and fought what must have been a heated and bloody battle.

In the event, they were defeated and the Roman legionaries subsequently destroyed the fort and burned down the surrounding village.

Caer Caradoc

This multivallate South Shropshire hillfort camp, located on a high hogback ridge near Church Stretton, was built in the Iron or late Bronze Age, and has several raised earthwork terraces and ditches, many of which have been incorporated into the natural rocky outcrops of the hillside. It is named after the British chieftain and resistance leader, Caractacus, known in Welsh as Caradog (or Caradoc), and it translates into English as 'Caradog's fort'. According to legend it was here that the Battle of Caer Caradog took place, when Caractacus made his final stand against the Roman legions in the year 50 AD, leading an army thought to have been made up of Ordovices warriors, possibly supported by Silures tribesmen. What is known for certain is that the battle was fought by a combined Celtic force at a camp somewhere in the Malvern Hills – whether that was here or not is open to question, though as with all 'historic' legends, the story is compelling. Caractacus and his family were taken in chains as prisoners to Rome. The hillfort has been designated a Scheduled Ancient Monument.

Castle-an-Dinas

Occupying more than twenty acres of hilltop, Castle-an-Dinas is one of the largest and best preserved hillforts in Cornwall. It stands on Castle Downs near St Columb Major and was probably completed in the second century BC. The site was established at a strategic location guarding trade routes through Cornwall. It consists of three ditches and concentric earth ramparts, probably topped by wooden palisades, and there are two Bronze Age barrows at its centre, suggesting that the site had seen human habitation long before the hillfort was constructed. During the English Civil War the hill is where Royalist forces camped for two nights before surrendering to Parliamentarian troops under Lord Fairfax in March 1646.

Cissbury Ring

The West Sussex Iron Age hillfort known as Cissbury Ring was constructed sometime towards the end of the fourth century BC, though its earthworks were probably built as late as 250 BC. It is a univallate fort (a hilltop enclosure with a single earth rampart accompanied by a ditch). It is the largest hillfort in Sussex and its perimeter encompasses around sixty-four acres. The site also contains a Neolithic flint mine, one of the earliest known in Britain. It has been argued that the name is derived from 'Caesar's fort' after the Roman Emperor Julius Caesar, or 'Cissa's fort', after the South Saxon King Cissa. However, prevailing opinion is that it was more likely to derive from 'Sithesteburh', as the place was known during the reign of Ethelred, which translates as 'the last (or the latest) fort'. This is supported by the comparatively late date of its construction when compared to others which were built a thousand years earlier or more. The fort was abandoned sometime in the middle of the first century, and was later settled by farming communities during the Romano-British period as they moved to live within its ramparts and ploughed the hilltop into crop fields.

Cleeve Hill Camp
Located above the village of Southam in the Cotswolds, Cleeve Hill Camp is a multivallate hillfort that lies one of the highest points on the Cotswold Scarp of Cleeve Hill (also known as 'Cleeve Cloud') in Gloucestershire. The Iron Age site comprises an irregular crescent-shaped site which stretches for three hundred and fifty yards, and consists of two earth banks and two ditches. There are the remains of four circular buildings in the camp, all constructed in stone and without mortar, and there are traces of watch-towers on the summit. Unfortunately, subsequent quarrying and nineteenth century landscaping to construct a golf course has seriously degraded the site.

Countisbury Hill
This Iron Age univallate promontory fort on Exmoor is also known as Countisbury Castle, and commonly referred to as Wind Hill. It encloses an area of just over eighty-six acres. The remains of the east earth rampart are about fifty feet high, and the ditch is approximately twelve feet wide, and one hundred feet long. The remains of the defensive outwork have been significantly reduced by agriculture over the centuries. Countisbury Castle was recorded in the *Domesday Book* as 'Contesberie', and is thought to have been the fortified hill where the Viking Ubba, the brother of Ivar the Boneless, suffered a heavy defeat at the hands of the Anglo-Saxons at the Battle of Cynwit in 878 AD.

Danebury Ring
The hillfort at Danebury in Hampshire is one of the most heavily studied in Britain because it is what is known as a 'developed hill fort'. It was begun in the sixth century BC and constructed in three stages: first, a single ditch and an earth bank rampart reinforced with timber, in all enclosing an area of twelve acres. The following centuries saw the banks raised and strengthened and ditches deepened. Later still, the final stage involved the creation of a network of banks to slow down any attacking force. There is rudimentary evidence of granary stores and roundhouses within the inner ward, suggesting that the fort was intended for prolonged habitation, possibly sustaining around three hundred people, and was not merely a military installation. It is thought that the Danebury fort was probably constructed by the Attrebates tribe, whose capital was at Silchester. The site was abandoned at the beginning of the first century and the fact that more than a hundred buried bodies have been found in funerary pits, most bearing battle wounds, makes it reasonable to suppose that Danebury fell as a result of an armed assault. Its fate probably echoed that suffered by many other hillforts that were overcome by the Roman legions. By the end of the first century, apart from a single farmstead and grazing for cattle, the hillfort had outlived its usefulness.

Darren Camp

The Darren Camp in Ceredigion (known in Welsh as 'Banc y Darren'), is a strategically placed univallate hillfort located high on a rock outcrop of a natural sloping escarpment in between the valleys of Nant Silo and Peithyll. It was probably built around 800 BC as a single rampart encompassing an area of around one hundred and nine acres. There is a Bronze Age cairn within the interior, one of several burial markers on the hill that are thought to pre-date the fort. Much of the original structure has been obscured by subsequent open cast mining in what became known as the Darren Lode, a vein of ore bearing silver and lead which was exploited by the Romans.

Dinas Dinlle

Dinas Dinlle hillfort in Gwynedd is set on a sixty-five-feet-high hill of glacial drift sediments overlooking the sea and Caernarfonshire coastal plain. It was constructed as a polygonal fort with a double semi-circular rampart and ditch in the late Iron Age. It was occupied later by the Romans, who might have built a lighthouse on the site in the second or third century. The name Dinas Dinlle comes from the legendary Welsh figure, Lleu Llaw Gyffes, whose story is told in the *Mabinogian*. According to local folklore, Lleu is supposed to have built the original fort and gave his name to it. The word 'Dinlle' derives from the Old Welsh 'din', meaning 'fort' and 'Lle', which is short for Lleu. Its location on the coast has seen its size diminish considerably over the centuries due to sea erosion, with up to one hundred feet of the site being lost on the western side. Of note are the remains of a stone roundhouse with walls over seven feet thick, arguably the largest ever found in Wales.

Dinedor Camp Hillfort

Dinedor Camp is a promontory hillfort situated near to Dinedor Cross on a hill spur overlooking the Wye Valley in Herefordshire. It dates from the second century BC and is almost three hundred and seventy yards long and one hundred and seventy yards wide. The single ten-feet-high rampart on its steep southern slope would have been topped by a wooden palisade and may have been revetted with stone. The summit of the hill is the site of a Roman camp, possibly occupied at one time by the Second Governor of Britain, Marcus Ostorius Scapula, who was responsible for the defeat and capture of the British tribal leader Caractacus. Archaeological excavations in 1951 unearthed quantities of Iron Age and Roman pottery fragments, as well as coins, an iron axe head and Neolithic flints. The structure is now largely obscured by trees and vegetation.

Dun Aonghasa

Known in Irish Gaelic as 'Dun Aengus', this is one of several prehistoric hillforts on the Aran Islands of County Galway. The name translates as 'Fort of Aonghas', and may have been a reference to King Aonghus mac Umhor, a figure in ancient Irish mythology. The fort is thought to have been built in the second century BC by the southern Irish Celtic tribe known as the Builg, a name that may be related to the Belgae people of Gaul. The site appears to have been originally created by heaping piles of rubble against large upright stones, and by supplementing this primitive defence later with three more dry stone walls along the western side. The site encompasses an area of about fourteen acres. Many of the original walls have been have been restored to their original height of twenty feet, and are easily distinguished by the use of mortar, which was not originally employed in their construction.

Eddisbury Hillfort

Eddisbury hillfort, also known as Castle Ditch, is an Iron Age univallate hillfort near Delamere, one of seven such forts in Cheshire. Its construction was probably begun in the second century BC and expanded in the early first century AD, before it was virtually destroyed by the Romans. The site was reoccupied in the sixth to eighth centuries and in 914 the Anglo-Saxon township of Eddisbury was established. The fort began as a single rampart and ditch on the eastern part of the hill. Later, it was extended westwards, to occupy the whole hilltop, and additional ramparts and ditches were added to improve its defensibility. Over the centuries the original site has been degraded by agricultural ploughing within the fort's perimeter and by a stone quarry on its northern side.

Fin Cop Hillfort

Twenty-first century excavations of the Fin Cop promontory hillfort overlooking Monsal Dale in the Derbyshire Peak District revealed the often vicious intertribal warfare that occurred between Celtic settlements. Several hundred human remains were unearthed within the fort's thirteen-hundred-feet-long ditch; most were of women (of which one was pregnant), and the remainder were children, babies and infants, all bearing signs of a massacre, with stabbings, strangulation and dismemberment. The stone revetted wall had also been toppled into the ditch and rocks thrown in to cover the graves. The total absence of any male corpses suggests that they were probably killed elsewhere or taken off as slaves. No personal possessions were found amongst the skeletons, valuables were probably taken as trophies. The construction of the hillfort dates from between 440 BC and 390 BC, but it had not been completed at the time of the massacre. The outer perimeter enclosed an area of about ten acres. An Early Bronze Age bowl barrow, one of five others, was also discovered within the bounds of the fort which contained a dry-walled grave containing the remains of a cremation, as well as ceremonial food urns, an arrowhead and evidence of other burials. Animal bones in the ditch, suggest the fort's inhabitants kept cattle, sheep and pigs.

Hambledon Hill

The hillfort at Hambledon Hill in Dorset saw more or less continuous occupation from the fifth to the mid-third century BC, and was built by the Durotriges tribe, whose territory included all of present-day Dorset. The site features evidence of agricultural activity and is comprised of a number of enclosures linked by a causeway. It is a good example of a 'contour fort', that is one where the earth ramparts and terraces follow the contours of the hillside. Initially, it would have been a univallate construction, with a single ditch and rampart, and over time was developed into a better defended multivallate system. By the late first century, the site had been abandoned, having fallen prey to the advance of the Roman Second Augustan Legion (Legio II Augusta), a fate shared by the neighbouring fort on Hod Hill, as with many others in South-West England.

Kimsbury Camp
The Iron Age hillfort at Kimsbury, also known as Castle Godwyn, is located on Painswick Beacon in the Cotswolds of Gloucestershire. The fort is a large multivallate construction, located on the summit of Painswick Hill. Unfortunately, succeeding generations have almost devastated the original site, as apart from some of the ramparts which remain more or less intact, a golf course has overtaken much of the fort and part of its seven-acre interior has been extensively quarried for stone. The original construction entailed three earth ramparts with two intermediate ditches. The site was occupied from around 400 BC until 43 AD, coincidentally the year that the Romans landed on the shores of Britain.

Kinver Camp
This is a univallate promontory Iron Age hillfort located on a high sandstone cliff at the northern end of Kinver Edge in Staffordshire. It is comprised of a massive rampart and outer ditch along two of its four sides, the other two being protected by a steep escarpment. The earth rampart stands some twenty-six feet or more high and the ditch is about seventy-nine feet wide. A brick-built structure was constructed outside the rampart bank as a Home Guard post during the Second World War.

Liddington Castle
Liddington Castle fort, also known as Liddington Camp, is a late Bronze Age and early Iron Age univallate hillfort which occupies a flat plateau on the Marlborough Downs in Wiltshire. It is one of several located on or near the Ridgeway, and is reputedly the oldest in Great Britain, having been built in the seventh century BC, and was in use for the next two thousand years. The construction consists of a simple earth bank reinforced with balks of timber with a ditch in front. The eastern entrance appears to have been significantly reinforced with several sarsen stones surrounding it. Local tradition has it as the place where King Arthur won a victory over the Saxons at Mount Badon, but there is no evidence to support the claim.

Lodge Hill
Lodge Hill hillfort is located on a narrow ledge overlooking the River Usk north of Caerleon in Wales. It was probably begun in the seventh century BC. Its defences are

now densely overgrown with trees and bracken, but originally consisted of several banks and ditches, with ramparts almost thirty-three feet high in places, The massive stone and earthen bank defences were reinforced by vertical wooden posts. The main enclosure is over 437 feet long and just under 220 feet wide. Archaeological digs in the twentieth century unearthed the footings of a roundhouse, as well as a small post-built rectangular building. The Romans established their own legionary fortress nearby as a base for the Second Augustan Legion, dismantled most of the defences and connected it by a track and earth ramp into the original hillfort. The site was known to the Saxons as 'Belinstocke', meaning 'stronghold (or fort) of Belin', having been occupied by the Silures tribe who abandoned it shortly after the Roman occupation.

Loughton Camp

Loughton Camp is a small univallate hillfort in Epping Forest in North London which comprised a single bank and ditch earthwork rampart of which only a vestigial three feet high rise survives. It was probably constructed by the Trinovantes as a defence against the warring Catevellauni tribe around 500 BC. The now heavily forested site encompasses around ten acres and is also believed to have been a temporary camp used by the Romans on their way to the defeat of the Celtic tribes at Wheathampstead. Local tradition has it that Boudicca used the camp during her rebellion, before her defeat by Roman forces in 61 AD, although there is no actual evidence for this. It is generally thought that the fort may have been used as an animal enclosure and defensive rallying point during times of war.

Maiden Castle

Maiden Castle, one of some thirty hillforts in Dorset, is an Iron Age construction with a network of ramps and ditches, and is one of the largest and most complex hillforts in Europe. It was a relatively late construction, its multiple white chalk ramparts only built in the first century BC, though there is evidence that the hilltop has been occupied for around six thousand years. Over time the structure became ever more intricate as additional rings of defensive ramparts were constructed around the original single earthwork, and the entrances might have been timber-faced, making it what is known as a 'developed hillfort' of a multivallate form. The remains of more than fifty bodies were found in excavations on the site in the 1930s, many having died from horrific injuries, which reveals a tragic end to its Celtic builders and inhabitants. This was likely to have been at the hands of Roman legionaries led by Vespasian, who was hell-bent on subduing the Atrebates, Dumnonii, and Durotriges tribes in south-west Britain. By the year 47 AD, the hillfort began to be abandoned but retained some residence for a few decades, probably including a few Roman settlers, as Roman artefacts and coins have been found near the east gate. The Romans went on to establish the town of Durnovaria (modern Dorchester) nearby, which had been the ancient regional capital of the Durotriges tribe.

Celtic Places and Placenames

Mam Tor Hillfort

The Derbyshire Peak District hill of Mam Tor was built by the Celtic Brigantes tribe. It is sometimes known as the 'Shivering Mountain' because of the periodic landslides of the loose shale on its eastern side. The hillfort on the summit has been defined as a 'slight univallate hillfort', a description of its small enclosure of around sixteen acres surrounded by a single line of defence and one ditch. The name 'Mam Tor' translates as 'mother hill'. It dates from the late Bronze Age, and what remains of its ramparts can still be traced around the hilltop as well as vestiges of the two gateway entrances, despite erosion over time. Quantities of pottery as well as a polished stone axe, a bronze axe fragment, four whetstones and fragments of shale bracelets were found in excavations of the site by Manchester University in the 1960s. It had clearly known human habitation long before the fort was constructed with evidence of funeral barrows dating from the Late Neolithic to the Late Bronze Age (c.2400–1500 BC).

Mellor Hillfort

Mellor is the site of the only hillfort known to have existed in Greater Manchester. Situated on a hill near the village of Mellor at the edge of the Derbyshire Peak District, this Iron Age fort overlooks the Cheshire Plain, and lay forgotten until it was rediscovered during excavations at the end of the Old Vicarage garden and partially beneath St Thomas's Church by the University of Manchester in 1998. The settlement was established by the Brigantes tribe and saw continuous occupation for at least three thousand years, and like many others it was abandoned during the Roman period, probably in the fourth century. Roman glass shards and Iron Age pottery fragments, an amber necklace, arrowheads and a flint dagger were discovered in the inner ditch and a forty-two-feet-long roundhouse was unearthed on the site. The large number of flint fragments also suggest that, apart from being a place where funerary rituals were probably enacted, it may also have been a so-called 'knap site' for the production of flint tools.

Midsummer Hill Camp

This Scheduled Monument in the Malvern Hills of Herefordshire comprised a large multivallate hillfort containing four embanked ramparts, four hundred stone hut circles, a dyke and a pillow mound, and dates from about 800 BC. The camp is unusual in that its ramparts enclose two hills and the intervening valley known as Hollybush. Its Celtic inhabitants called it 'Dyn Mawr', meaning the 'Great City'. The structure measures approximately 1200 feet long by about 790 feet wide. The pillow mound had been thought to be Roman, but relics from both the Bronze and Iron Age have been found in excavations, suggesting Roman re-use of an existing older burial site. Neolithic, Bronze and Iron Age pottery and other artefacts including charcoal, flints and iron, have revealed that the hillfort was constructed during the fifth century BC and was occupied for the following five centuries. It was probably abandoned after being destroyed by fire during the Roman Conquest in 48 AD.

Mither Tap
Possibly occupied as early as 1000 BC, the hillfort of Mither Tap in Aberdeenshire stands at over sixteen hundred feet above sea level, and the most easterly of the several summits of the Bennachie range. Its defences would have developed by Pictish tribesmen over time, eventually to consist of thirty-three-feet-thick inner and outer stone ramparts. It has been argued that the Battle of Mons Graupius, where the Romans defeated the Caledonian tribes, was most probably fought on its slopes in 83 AD.

Mooghaun
Mooghaun (or in Irish, 'Muchan'), is a late Bronze Age hillfort in County Clare, built around 950 BC on a craggy hill, some two hundred and sixty feet above sea level, and is thought to be the largest in Ireland. Its construction involved building three concentric limestone ramparts, twenty feet thick in places, of which the outermost encloses an area of around twenty-seven acres. The site is now almost entirely overgrown with trees, bracken and other vegetation and the remnants of its stone walls are covered in moss. In 1854, construction of the Limerick & Ennis Railway about half a mile from the hillfort unearthed a box containing many gold ornaments and pieces of jewellery, which became known as the Mooghaun Hoard or the 'Great Clare Find', a treasure trove that now resides part in the National Museum of Ireland and part in the British Museum.

Old Bewick
Also known as Bewick Hill Moor Camp, this is one of three hillfort sites on Bewick Moor in Northumberland. It was a very small settlement, possibly housing two or three families at most and is comprised of two circular stone walls with banks and defensive ditches enclosing an area of hillside and set against the edge of a cliff. The site also has several cup-and-ring marked rocks, similar to those found on many hillsides in the region. These hand-carved examples of rock art were probably made in Neolithic or Bronze Age times, and their purpose or meaning remains a mystery, but they clearly had some symbolic relevance to the people who made them.

Old Oswestry
Old Oswestry in Shropshire (known in Welsh as 'Caer Ogyrfan'), is an example of a multivallate hillfort, one of many found in eastern Wales and the Marches. The two main ramparts encompassed the entire hilltop and were made of a clay base with support from timber and boulders, before the whole structure was covered with earth. It is disputed as to whether building began in the eighth or fifth centuries BC. It was probably occupied by the Cornovii or Ordovices tribes (nobody is quite sure which), and had continuous occupation until the Romans arrived in Britain in the first century. Though it seems to have avoided any direct conflict with Roman occupation forces, it was abandoned shortly after their arrival. The actual construction was a protracted affair, with many stages of development,

beginning as a few unfortified roundhouses; banks and ditches were added later until they finally enclosed an area of thirteen acres. Following its abandonment, the site was incorporated into an earthwork known as Wat's Dyke. The identity of Wat is unknown, but his dyke pre-dates that of the better known and longer one built by King Offa in the eighth century.

Old Sarum

The hillfort at Old Sarum is located about two miles north of Salisbury in Wiltshire at a place that controlled an important intersection of two ancient trade paths and the River Avon. There is evidence that the site has been occupied for at least five thousand years, but the hillfort as it exists today was probably established around 400 BC and occupied by the Atrebates tribe, whose territory it was right up to the Roman conquest of Britain in the mid-first century. At this time they are thought to have expelled its inhabitants, set up their own military fort within its earthworks and called it 'Sorviodunum'. It was used in turn later by the Anglo-Saxons and the Normans, who built a castle and the first Salisbury Cathedral in the inner bailey in the eleventh century. The fort was constructed by building a double earthen bank with an intermediate ditch and an entrance on the eastern side, so that it eventually enclosed an expansive oval-shaped area, to create what was reputedly the largest hillfort in Britain.

Pen y Crug

Pen y Crug Iron Age hillfort in the Brecon Beacons National Park (commonly referred to as 'The Crug'), was typically constructed around the summit of the hill, and originally comprised multiple lines of rounded earth ramparts, the innermost standing some thirteen feet tall. These were reinforced with stone and topped by a wooden defensive palisade. The hill summit overlooks the valley of the River Usk. The Romans were quick to realise the strategic advantage of building their own fort, and in about 75 AD they defeated and expelled the native Silures tribe and constructed 'Brecon Gaer', reinforced it with stone defences, and established a flourishing settlement of their own within the old hillfort.

Pilsdon Pen

Pilsdon Pen is a 900 feet-high hill in Dorset situated at the end of Marshwood Vale near Beaminster. At the summit stands an Iron Age multivallate hillfort of the Durotriges tribe, one of four hillforts overlooking the western end of Marshwood Vale, and reputedly the highest in Dorset. The fort's two earth banks are up to twenty-three feet wide and some four feet high, either side of an eight-and-a-half-feet-deep ditch producing an enclosure of almost eight acres. The remains of fourteen round-houses were uncovered within the enclosure during archaeological surveys undertaken by the University of Birmingham in the 1960s. The discovery of two Bronze Age burial mounds suggest that the site was in use long before the hillfort was constructed. There were also a number of post-medieval 'pillow mounds', thought to have been husbanded rabbit warrens, to supply its occupants with a readily available source of meat. Also found in the fort were hundreds of sling stones, fragments of domestic pottery, part of a crucible used in metal working, a Gallo-Belgic gold coin and other Roman objects including a ballista bolt.

Poundbury Camp

Also known as the Poundbury Hill hillfort, this fifteen-acre Dorset earthwork near Dorchester was begun during the Middle Bronze Age (c.2200–1570 BC). Its makers, the Durotriges tribe, chose to locate it on an escarpment of the Upper Chalk, and designed it to overlook and control the valley of the River Frome. The defences consisted of two banks and two v-shaped ditches. The fort contains at least one burial barrow dated from the late Iron Age, and later a section of a Roman aqueduct was incorporated in the western and northern parts of the site, as well as a nearby Roman cemetery. Soon after their invasion in the mid-first century, the Romans founded the town of Durnovaria alongside the hillfort and named it after the tribe whose territory it had been before their arrival.

Prideaux Castle

Prideaux Castle is a multivallate hillfort situated at the end of a prominent inland spur near Luxulyan in Cornwall. It has several alternative names: some refer to it as Prideaux Warren, others as Prideaux War-Ring, and more commonly it is known as Prideaux Hillfort. The name is of Cornish origin, and the earliest occupation near the site dates from the Bronze Age. It is almost circular in design and has three clearly defined earth and rubble banks and ditches with a fourth still partially visible in places. Excavations have uncovered numerous flints, sling stones, stone axes and shards of so-called South-West Decorated pottery. The site is heavily overgrown with trees and currently used for cattle pasture.

Rainsborough Camp

Rainsborough Camp is a fifth and sixth century BC bivallate Iron Age hillfort one mile from Charlton village in Northamptonshire. The fort is roughly oval in shape and encompasses an area of about six and a half acres. Due to successive ploughing and crop cultivation over the centuries, together with extensive landscaping in the nineteenth century, what remains of the outer ditch is almost featureless. Slight traces of a ditch outside the outer rampart on the west side are now all that can be seen above ground. However, archaeological excavations in the 1960s revealed that the inner rampart had been reinforced with three tiers of stone walling over six feet in height, with a clearly distinguishable ditch, and the west entrance had what is thought to have been flanked by stone guardrooms. It is thought that Rainsborough was one of the earliest hillforts to employ such stone-faced ramparts. The original fort suffered extensive fire in the early fourth century BC and in the late second century BC the site was refortified and the entrance was rebuilt. Roman artefacts have been found scattered across the area and nearby including bone and pottery fragments as well as flint spearheads. The site is nowadays covered with turf, trees and bushes, and the banks have suffered significant deterioration due to extensive root systems and infestation by rabbits, whose warrens further threaten to undermine its structure.

Rathgall
Rathgall in County Wicklow (or 'An Rath Geal' in Irish), could be interpreted to mean either 'the ring fort of the foreigner' or 'the white or bright fort', and is sometimes known locally as the 'the Ring of the Rath'. It is a large multivallate hillfort near the town of Shillelagh, built on the edge of a ridge and comprising four concentric earth and stone walls dating from the Bronze Age. It is one of the largest hillforts in Ireland and encompasses around eighteen acres. A house was unearthed within the inner stone circle during excavations carried out by University College, Dublin in the 1970s, where a number of hearths and post-holes were discovered, as well as more than fifty thousand fragments of pottery, a number of bronze objects and over eighty glass beads. The quality of these artefacts suggests that the house was occupied by a person or family of some high rank. As further evidence of its importance, during the excavation there was a discovery of a Bronze Age factory for metalworking, where the manufacture of swords, axes and spearheads would have taken place.

Ravensburgh Castle
Ravensburgh Castle hillfort is located on an outcrop of the Barton Hills, one mile south-west of Hexton in Hertfordshire. It is a large oval-shaped enclosure covering sixteen acres and its outer perimeter encompasses twenty-two acres. The site is strongly defended by a double rampart and ditch on the north, west and south sides, with a much stronger rampart on the vulnerable east side. It has been estimated that the hillfort's ramparts were some forty-six feet high, and that nineteen thousand balks of timber would have been employed in the construction of its thirteen hundred yard perimeter. Consequently, the fort is said to be the biggest hillfort in south-east England. Traditionally it has been thought to have been the headquarters of the Celtic chieftain, Cassivelaunus, who led a confederation of Celtic tribes against the army of Julius Caesar. In the event, according to the story, five tribes surrendered to Caesar and revealed the whereabouts of Cassivelaunus's stronghold, which was attacked and severely burned, before the chieftain surrendered in 54 BC. Nowadays, Ravensburgh Castle is heavily overgrown, densely wooded and is on private land, therefore access to the site is strictly limited.

Sutton Walls Hillfort
Sutton Walls is an Iron Age hillfort located on the River Lugg flood plain four miles north of Hereford. The fort is also thought to be where King Offa of Mercia had his palace, and according to *The Anglo-Saxon Chronicles* it was where Offa arranged

for the murder of Ethelbert II of East Anglia in 794 AD. The hillfort was first settled in the third century BC and saw continued occupation the next six hundred years. Excavations in 1948 unearthed twenty-four human skeletons, many of which bore evidence of decapitation. The site is now very badly degraded, with almost two-thirds of the central ward quarried for sand and gravel, while in more recent times it was used as a site for landfill, a practice that only ceased in 1985. Added to this, bad management has resulted in the site becoming densely overgrown with trees and scrub. Consequently, Historic England placed it on the Heritage at Risk register, and a detailed conservation management plan has been drawn up for the monument.

Tap O' Noth

Carbon dating places the construction of the Aberdeenshire hillfort at Tap O' Noth in the third century and excavations by the University of Aberdeen identify it as probably of Pictish origin. The hill on which the fort stands rises to more than eighteen hundred feet above sea level, making it the second highest in Scotland. There appear to have been up to eight hundred round houses within its bounds at one time, which would have housed up to four thousand people, possibly also qualifying it as one of the largest known post-Roman settlements in Europe. The enclosure covered of around fifty-two acres of the summit and was originally surrounded by a single stone rampart which may have been more than twenty feet thick in places. Later, a second wall consisting of a row of huge boulders was constructed lower down the hill on its northern and eastern sides, many of which were subsequently plundered for building materials. A shallow overgrown depression, thought to have once been about six feet deep, may have served as a rainwater well or cistern. Like many others throughout Britain, Tap O' Noth hillfort was abandoned by the end of the first century.

Traprain Law

Traprain Law is a hill four miles east of Haddington in East Lothian and the site of one of Scotland's largest Late Bronze Age hillforts. The fifth century hoard of two hundred and fifty Roman coins is probably the largest ever found throughout the Roman Empire. Traprain Law hill stands some seven hundred and twenty feet above sea level, and the fort encloses around forty acres. It had been occupied continuously for at least a thousand years, from the middle of the first millennium BC to the middle of the first century AD. In Roman times it was a major settlement of the Votadini tribe. Bronze Age artefacts have been found on the hill and there are numerous typical Neolithic cup-and-ring marks cut into its rocks. The exact purpose and meaning of these inscribed carvings is unknown, but Neolithic and Bronze Age activity of this kind on Traprain suggests that it had religious significance to the Votadini and was used as a ceremonial burial place. Nowadays it is probably best known for the discovery of the so-called 'Traprain Treasure' in 1919.

Celtic Places and Placenames

Tre'r Ceiri Hillfort

Tre'r Ceiri is an Iron Age hillfort which is almost fifteen hundred feet above sea level, located on Yr Eifl in the Llyn Peninsula of Gwynedd. Its name translates as 'town of the giants' and it is reckoned to be one of the best preserved hillforts in Britain. Probably built around 200 BC, its stone wall perimeter once measured a little over two thousand feet and encircled a six-acre enclosure; many are almost completely intact, standing up to thirteen feet high. The site appears to have been occupied throughout the Roman period, during which time its defences were strengthened. Fragments of Roman pottery and glassware as well as several copper torcs, beads, knives and rings were unearthed in recent digs; all are now on display in the National Museum of Wales. The hillfort was not finally abandoned until the fourth century.

Wandlebury Camp

The circular multivallate Iron Age hillfort of Wandlebury Camp is located on Wandlebury Hill in the Gog Magog Downs of Cambridgeshire, and was built with two concentric ditches separated by a bank which enclosed an area some one thousand and fifty feet in diameter. The fort is also known as the 'Wandlebury Ring' on account of its circular configuration. The substantial outer ditch and an inner rampart bank are constructed of chalk rubble and earth, and the inner ring would have had an additional wooden palisade. It was constructed in about 400 BC by the Iceni tribe, initially with a single bank, but with a second timber-revetted rampart and ditch being added in the first century BC. The Saxons called it 'Wendlesbiri' which translates as 'Waendal's fort'. It is thought that the fort was occupied until the late first century, and there is evidence of subsequent Roman occupation. A number of storage pits have been uncovered which contain a many artefacts and remains, including metal pins, brooches, ferrules and knives, as well as bone needles and combs, spinning and weaving implements, a quantity of pottery fragments and animal bones.

Warbstow Bury Hillfort

Warbstow Bury is Cornwall's second largest Iron Age hillfort; it is a multivallate construction with three ramparts, built around 2,500 years ago on a prominent ridge some 800 feet above sea level, overlooking the River Ottery near Launceston. Inside the fort is a seventy-two feet long pillow mound known as the Giant's Grave, which according to local folklore it is the final resting place of the Giant of Warbstow who was killed by the Giant of Beacon. The ramparts are up to nineteen feet high, with ditches almost nine feet deep. Of its three ramparts, the two outer walls are overgrown with bracken and the third is incomplete. The inner rampart stands about fourteen-and-a-half feet tall. The fort offers views over the north coast of Cornwall, and is reckoned to be one of the best preserved in the British Isles.

Warham Camp

Warham Camp is a circular multivallate Iron Age hillfort near Warham in Norfolk, and has been described by the University of East Anglia as 'the best preserved hillfort in the county'. It was constructed with double banks, almost ten feet in height and with ditches ten feet deep, enclosing an area of over four hundred feet in diameter. It has been dated to the last few centuries before the Roman invasion of Britain and was probably built by the Iceni tribe who occupied it until they were virtually exterminated by the Roman army in 61 AD following the revolt and uprising by the tribe led by Queen Boudicca. Currently, the site is in two areas separated by the channel of the River Stiffkey, and situated on a south-west facing slope above the river flood plain. It originally curved around the fort on the south-west side but was diverted in the early eighteenth century. The old river course has been filled in, but it can still be made out by aerial photography. Archaeological excavations reveal that the camp saw Roman occupation after the surviving Iceni were driven out, and that it may have been used even later by the Danes.

Wincobank

Wincobank is a univallate Iron Age hillfort in Sheffield, Yorkshire, and stands on the summit of an isolated sandstone hill overlooking the valley of the River Don. The hillfort is comprised of an elliptical enclosure of around two-and-a-half acres, surrounded by a single rampart which was originally built as a wall eighteen feet thick. The wall was made up of large stones set against an earthen and rubble core, reinforced with balks of timber, and with an external ditch. Excavation in 1899 showed that the ditch had an original depth of around six feet. Though it was earlier thought to have been a Roman construction, later evidence revealed it to have been built by the Brigantes tribe, as part of a defensive line against the northward advance of the Roman legions under Agricola. The Brigantes initially succumbed to Romans forces in around 72 AD but continued to rebel during the late second and early third centuries. Excavations have revealed burnt, charred and vitrified stone timbers, indicating that the rampart was destroyed by fire, probably as a result of intertribal warfare. One of the earliest records of the hill and the fort name was as 'Wincowe' in 1442, probably derived from the personal name of an Anglo-Saxon called Wineca, together the Old Scandinavian word 'haugr' meaning 'mound' or 'hill'. Hence, 'Wineca's hill'.

Woden Law

Woden Law Iron Age hillfort is located almost fourteen hundred feet high on Woden Law Hill, part of the Cheviot range, overlooking Kale Water in the Scottish Borders region. It is thought to have been built in several stages before its completion, at which time it consisted of four volcanic rock ramparts, some more than eighty feet deep, along with several lines of ditches and embankments. Five raised-earth banks are located some seventy feet from the fort itself and remain intact apart from two short breaks in their line. The inner rampart was faced with stone up to about nine feet thick and supported an inner dry-built rubble core taken from outcrops at the summit, and surrounds the remains of a number of timber roundhouses. Later, additional southern and eastern earthworks were constructed, thought by some to be the remains of Roman siege-works, as it is known that Roman forces occupied the site and used it for training exercises; even later, in the third century the site was re-used by local inhabitants. The fort was abandoned by the Celts shortly after the arrival of Roman forces.

Yeavering Bell Hillfort
Yeavering Bell is a hill in the Cheviot Hills of Northumberland and the location of the largest Iron Age hillfort in northern England. Its collapsed stone ramparts would originally have been over eight feet high, were almost ten feet thick, and enclosed an area of around thirteen acres. In the main enclosure there are the remains of about one hundred and thirty round houses and a ditch surrounding what would have been a burial cairn. It is thought that Yeavering Bell was regarded as a holy mountain by the Celtic people of the region and would have been a site of religious importance. It was probably occupied by the Votadini tribe well into the first century AD. The discovery of Roman pottery and coins on the site suggest that the fort was still being used long after the Roman invasion of Britain. The 'Bell' is actually the name of the entire hill, and its summit is 1,158 feet above sea level.

Part Ten

Cairns, Barrows, Henges, Monoliths & Stone Circles

More than a thousand Bronze and Iron Age stone monuments are known to exist in the British Isles and Ireland. Among them are stone circles, standing stones, henges, megaliths and funeral barrows. Many date back more than twenty thousand years, but it is estimated that most were typically constructed about three thousand years ago. Of these it is probably monuments like Stonehenge that immediately spring to mind as the most internationally celebrated and probably the best known. But there are many more.

Various theories exist as to their purpose. Some argue that they had a spiritual or religious significance as places of worship, others identify them with burial rituals while yet others prefer to think of them as astrological timepieces set to mark the arrival of the summer and winter solstices. Truth to tell, we may never completely

Castlerigg Stone Circle, near Keswick, Cumbria.

understand their meaning and significance, but what is certain is that they were evidently important to the people who built them. Why else would such arduous tasks be undertaken in their construction and installation? We cannot say with any certainty how some of the colossal lumps of stone were raised, or how millions of tons of earth were moved without the benefit of modern machinery. What prompted these people to engage in such massive enterprises is an enigma, but what is certain is that they were clearly compelled and highly motivated. There are more questions than answers.

Stone Circles
There are two categories of stone circles: 'recumbent' (or 'axial') circles, and 'concentric' circles. Briefly, recumbent stone circles contain a single large stone placed on its side, often flanked by smaller stones, reducing in size. On the other hand, concentric stone circles consist of a circular or oval arrangement of two or more stone circles set within one another.

Cairns
In its simplest form, a cairn is a pile of stones. Such structures have been used since prehistoric times and are commonly found throughout Europe. They were often erected as landmarks and to mark trails, boundaries and special places, used as burial monuments or for ceremonial or ritual purposes.

Cists
Cists (sometimes known as 'kists' or a 'kistvaens'), are burials in a chest or stone box – an early form of sarcophagus or coffin.

Chambered Tomb
Commonly found in burial mounds which are typically accessed through a stone-lined portal and divided into one or more side chambers. These were generally quite complex structures and usually inferred that the tomb had been the burial site of a high status chieftain, leader or priest.

Cromlech
A cromlech is a circle of vertical standing stones, often found around a burial tomb or place of worship. Many cromlechs date from the Neolithic and Bronze Ages in the second half of the fourth millennium BC, and most are commonly found in Wales, but some survive in Brittany, England and Ireland. They are most likely to have been places of worship and tribal gatherings.

Monoliths and Megaliths
A monolith is a single erect stone, known in the Cornish language as a 'menhir', similar to the modern Welsh words 'maen' and 'hir' which taken together mean

'long stone'. The word 'megalith' means 'many stones'. Such standing stones are located either singly or in groups; there are an estimated fifty thousand examples in Ireland, Great Britain and Brittany, of which Carnac is probably the best known.

Henges
The word 'henge' is a backformation from Stonehenge in Wiltshire, and consists of groups of standing stones or wooden posts, usually arranged in a circle with an internal ditch enclosing a flat area. Henges sometimes contained ritual stones or other ceremonial structures.

Dolmens
A dolmen, also known as a portal tomb, portal grave, or quoit, is a single-chamber tomb, usually consisting of three or more vertical standing stones supporting a large flat horizontal capstone or 'table', often weighing several tons. Dolmens generally have a 'portal' or doorway opening into the burial chamber. The word 'dolmen' is derived from the Celtic words 'daul', meaning 'table' and 'maen', a stone. Dolmens were typically covered with earth or smaller stones to form a barrow.

Barrow
A barrow, also known as a tumulus, burial mound or kurgan, is a mound of earth and stones raised over a grave or graves. Many dolmens are effectively barrows as they cover stone burial chambers, and some barrows are large enough to be classified as small hills. Their size and complexity generally indicates the status of the person who was buried inside.

The Stone Circles, Barrows & Monuments

Arbor Low Henge
Although somewhat smaller, this prehistoric henge monument in the Derbyshire Peak District has been called 'the Stonehenge of the North'. It consists of a stone circle of fifty limestone slabs surrounded by large earthworks and a ditch, enclosing an area measuring around three hundred by two hundred and seventy-five feet. Most of the stones have toppled over and lie flat on the ground, probably due to the shallow holes in which they were originally set, while a single stone still maintains an almost upright position. At the centre of the circle are six smaller blocks, thought to have once formed a small rectangular enclosure, known as the 'cove'. A round cairn or barrow was added later, and excavations in the early twentieth century revealed that cremations were carried out there, and the presence of human skeletal remains, flint scrapers and arrowheads were also discovered around the cove.

Celtic Places and Placenames

Avebury

Avebury Henge and Stone Circles in Wiltshire are unique in that the village of Avebury lies partly within the henge and outer circle of stones, and roads split the monument into four parts. The outer stone circle is roughly a quarter of a mile across, enclosing an area of about thirty acres, and contains two smaller circles within it. The circles were built during the Neolithic period, roughly between 2,850 and 2,200 BC and qualify as the largest stone circle in Britain, originally consisting of about one hundred standing stones. Many of the original stones were removed, toppled or destroyed in the Middle Ages, when the site was suspected of being used for pagan or devil worship.

Ballina Dolmen

This megalithic tomb is located on Primrose Hill in Ballina, County Mayo, and is often referred to as 'the Dolmen of the Four Maols'. It has also been called 'The Table of the Giants' and 'The Cloghgle Portal Tomb'. Its central feature is a Bronze Age burial cairn covered by a five-feet-long roof stone which rests on three supports. The four Maols were the brothers Mael Mac Deoraidh, Maelcroin, Maeldalua and Maelseanaigh. Legend tells how King Guaire Aidhne usurped the throne from Ceallach of Connacht, who had withdrawn to a monastery and had become Bishop of Kilmoremoy. While acting as students under Ceallach, the four brothers contrived to assassinate him to secure Guaire's claim to the throne. They were brought to trial, quartered and hanged at Ardnaree, known as 'The Hill of Execution', before being buried on Primrose Hill. The murderous brothers are known as the four Maols from the Irish word 'maol', which means 'bald', a reference to the shaved heads, or 'tonsures', common in religious houses at that time.

Barclodiad y Gawes

This so-called 'passage grave' in Llangwyfan, Anglesey, was originally a ninety-feet-long stone-covered cruciform cairn, but following the theft of much of its stone for building materials it was replaced by a concrete shell, and its interior secured behind locked iron gates. The whole grave has subsequently been covered with turf to better resemble what the site might have looked like when it was constructed during the Neolithic era. The name Barclodiad y Gawes means 'Giantess's apronful', which comes from an ancient legend which tells of a giant woman, who was carrying a number of large stones in her apron, before she dropped them in a pile on the ground here. The grave is made up of a long passageway leading to a central area with a terminal chamber with east and west side chambers. The interior is decorated with intricate zig-zag patterns, chevrons and spirals, typical of Celtic decoration. The cremated remains of two young males were found within one of the side chambers during excavations in 1952.

Cairns, Barrows, Henges, Monoliths & Stone Circles

Beacon Hill

Beacon Hill round barrow is a prehistoric burial mound located on a ridge in Old Clee beside Cleethorpes cemetery in Lincolnshire. The mound measures forty-five feet by twenty-five feet and is ten feet high. A large urn was found in the central chamber, containing cremated remains, some charcoal and four small funerary urns. Later, an Anglo-Saxon burial took place here, disturbing its fabric and changing its use into a beacon site.

Belas Knap

The Neolithic long barrow of Belas Knap on Cleeve Hill near Cheltenham, Gloucestershire, is distinctive for its false entrance and side chambers. The trapezoid-shaped barrow is also known as a 'Cotswold-Severn Cairn'. Its mound was probably constructed around five thousand years ago and used for successive burials until the four chambers, which contained the remains of thirty-one people, were deliberately blocked and the barrow was covered with earth to hide its entrances. Nineteenth century excavations unearthed the skeletal remains of five small children, the skull of an adult male dated around 4,000 BC, various horse and pig bones and fragments of pottery as well as a serrated flint blade; all these were found among the rubble blocking the false entrance.

Boskednan

The stone circle at Boskednan is located in an area of isolated moorland to the south-east of Carn Galve in Cornwall and is made up of nine standing stones (known as the 'Nine Maidens' or the 'Nine Stones of Boskednan'), as well as two others that have fallen over. It seems probable that there were up to twenty-three stones originally, most of which were removed and broken up over time to create farm walls and outbuildings. The complete arrangement would have encircled a two hundred feet perimeter. Its granite stones would have been erected in the late-Neolithic or early Bronze Age. Nineteenth century excavations uncovered a cist burial outside the circle which contained an urn and shards of pottery of a type known as 'Cornish Trevisker Ware' dating from the early Bronze Age. The remains of three more barrows lie to the north of the circle. In 2009 a team of archaeologists raised the two fallen stones, so that there are now eleven standing upright in the circle.

Bryn-Celli-Ddu

Bry-Celli-Ddu is a Neolithic passage tomb near Llanddaniel Fab on Anglesey. The outer barrow mound contains an inner stone circle, and is known as a 'circle henge'. The name 'Bryn-Celli-Ddu' translates as the 'Mound in the Dark Grove'. The mound is encircled by a one hundred and five feet diameter ditch in which stand fourteen stones. Inside, a narrow passage leads to an octagonal chamber. The tomb's capstone bears ornate incised carvings on both sides, a replica of which has been placed outside the rear of the chamber. Only a few surviving human bones and remains have been found in the tomb, but several other artefacts were discovered, including two flint arrowheads, quantities of mussel and limpet shells and a few stone beads.

Callanish Stones
The Callanish standing stones (in Scottish Gaelic, 'Clachan Chalanais'), are located near the village of Callanish on the west coast of the Isle of Lewis in the Outer Hebrides and date from the late Neolithic era. The arrangement is a cruciform pattern in a circle of thirteen stones with a diameter of just over thirty-seven feet, and with a thirteen-ton monolith stone at its centre. Two other parallel rows of stones form an avenue leading to the circle. East of the circle's central stone are the remains of a later chambered tomb. The site was originally encircled by a ditch, but agricultural ploughing has erased all trace of it above ground, and what remains is entirely grassed over. Local tradition has Callanish as an ancient site of druidical worship and ritual. After its abandonment sometime before 1,000 BC the whole site was covered with turf and it was not until the mid-nineteenth century that it was fully uncovered.

Castlerigg
The stone circle at Castlerigg near Keswick in Cumbria is one of the earliest megalithic sites in Britain. It dates from around 3,000 BC and comprises thirty-eight free-standing stones, some up to ten feet tall. Castlerigg is unusual in that there is a rectangle of standing stones in the middle of the circle – what lies beneath is unknown, as is their purpose. The absence of any archaeological investigation leaves it as a wide open mystery.

Chettle Long Barrow
Chettle Long Barrow lies at the north-east corner of Eastbury Park on the boundary with Tarrant Gunville in Dorset. The mound is one hundred and ninety feet long and seventy-two feet wide, with a maximum height of just under ten feet. The Neolithic site is now very overgrown with bushes, weeds and dense undergrowth and is surrounded on both sides by ploughed fields. Sometime before 1767 a quantity of human bones were removed from the mound and re-interred elsewhere, in order to create a hollow and to construct a grotto within it, a whim of Bubb Doddington, the First Lord Melcombe.

Chun Quoit
The chambered tomb of Chun Quoit near Morvah, Cornwall, stands as an isolated monument on bleak exposed moorland, and is one of the best preserved of all Neolithic quoits in Cornwall, dating from around 2,400 BC. The dolmen consists of four upright stones about five feet high, three of which support a fairly circular mushroom-shaped capstone. It is thought that the monument would have originally been covered by a thirty-five feet diameter round earth barrow.

Chun Quoit Dolmen, Cornwall.

Coldrum Long Barrow

Also known as the Coldrum Stones, this chambered long barrow is located near the village of Trottiscliffe in Kent and dates from around 4,000 BC. It was constructed around fifty stone megaliths and contained twenty human remains, thought to have been part of an ancestor worship cult. The site is badly dilapidated, the inner chamber having collapsed, and much of the stone masonry subsequently taken for building materials. The monument is reckoned to be one of the best surviving of the so-called 'Medway Megaliths'.

Culliford Tree Group

This Culliford Tree barrow group is, unsurprisingly, covered with trees – hence its name. It dates from the early Bronze Age and is part of the Dorset Ridgeway. The actual long barrow is the most prominent of the small group of mounds located in a field at the eastern edge of Came Wood on the lane to Whitcombe. It is one hundred and eighteen feet in diameter, almost sixteen feet high and encircled by a ring of trees which were planted in 1740. An excavation in 1858 revealed four separate skeletons buried at a shallow depth near the top of the mound. Several jewelled ornaments were found with one of the female remains, including amber beads from a necklace, two with gold plates on their bases. Several feet lower down in the mound was an Early Bronze Age funerary urn containing cremated ashes and bones, as well as a small pottery accessory vessel. The barrow later became the meeting place of the courts of Culliford Tree Hundred.

Doll Tor

Doll Tor is a small circle of six standing stones, which along with a low cairn, are situated in a small wood in Derbyshire. The stones are on average about three feet in height and the circle is around twenty feet in diameter. The ring of stones was once connected by a dry stone wall. A rectangular grave pit below the cairn was excavated in 1931–34 and found to contain evidence of a female cremation. Four other cremated remains were subsequently uncovered round the inner edge of the stone bank, before it was all eventually filled in to form the cairn. Crude attempts were made by unknown persons to re-erect some of the fallen stones in the 1930s, but the site was later restored to its earlier condition by the Peak National Park Authority and Historic England.

Drombeg

Drombeg Stone Circle in Glandore, County Cork is also known as 'The Druid's Altar'. The name 'Drombeg' translates as 'the small ridge'. It was built sometime between 1,100 and 800 BC, and originally comprised seventeen standing sandstone menhirs and a recumbent (or 'axial') stone bearing two inscribed cup marks. The circle contains two taller portal stones placed opposite the recumbent stone, and the site is orientated south-west towards the setting sun at the time of the Winter Solstice, suggesting an astronomical or astrological significance. Only thirteen of the original stones still remain. In 1957, excavations were carried out on the gravel floor inside the circle where a central pit was discovered containing a broken pot holding the cremated remains of an adolescent male.

Dunkery Beacon

Dunkery Beacon is located at the summit of Dunkery Hill in Somerset, and is the highest point on Exmoor at just over seventeen hundred feet. Debates continue concerning the origin of the name with several other earlier spellings including 'Duncrey' and 'Dunnecray' suggesting that it comes from the Welsh word 'din' meaning 'fort' and 'creag' meaning 'rock'. The site has known human habitation since around 2,000 BC. Several cairns and burial mounds have been unearthed, as well as the remains of two Iron Age hillforts on the lower slopes. The main cairn is at the top of the site and comprises an oval stony mound measuring up to one hundred and twelve feet long and eighty-eight feet wide. The 'Beacon' element of the place-name records its location as a warning beacon or signal fire, which was employed to warn at the approach of the Spanish Armada in 1588 and of impending attack during the Monmouth Rebellion in 1685.

Easter Aquhorthies

The Easter Aquhorthies stone circle is located near Inverurie in Aberdeenshire and is thought to be the best preserved example of a recumbent stone circle in Scotland. The stones seem to have been intentionally selected by its builders for their colour; of the ring of nine stones, eight are of grey granite and one of red jasper, while there are two other grey granite stones alongside a recumbent red granite stone, which have distinctive crystal and quartz striations and flecks. The circle measures some sixty-four feet in diameter, and is almost circular in plan. The recumbent stone measures about thirteen feet in length and is thought to weigh around nine tons. The name 'Aquhorthies' derives from a Scottish Gaelic word meaning 'field of prayer' or possibly 'field of the pillar stone'. The 'Easter' element of the name is a misnomer, almost certainly a corruption of the name of East Aquhorthies farm nearby.

Five Wells
Five Wells is a chambered stone tomb on Taddington Moor in the Derbyshire Peak District, dating from between 4,500 and 2,000 BC. There were originally two back-to-back limestone chambers, and the entire site may have once been overlaid by a fifty-six feet diameter mound. The western chamber is in a very dilapidated state with collapsed portals and missing stones, many thought to have been taken to build dry stone walls in the eighteenth century. The eastern chamber is better preserved, and still retains a pair of upright portal stones about five feet tall, another pair of large slabs, and a smaller stone at the back. The original capstone slab has disappeared. The remains of an estimated twelve human figures were recovered from the two chambers in an 1846 excavation, and three more were found in an 1862 dig. A number of Neolithic and Bronze Age artefacts were also unearthed here, including an arrowhead, a knife, several shards of pottery of the types known as 'Neolithic Plain Ware' and 'Peterborough Ware'.

Goatstones
Located near to Ravenshaugh Crags in Northumberland, Goatstones is a so-called 'four poster' stone circle. Although it comprises four standing stones, arranged at each corner of a square formation, the term 'circle' is only notional. It is of a fairly rare type, typically found in the Scottish region of Perthshire. The stones are set low in the ground, and stand a little over two feet high. The southern stone fell over at some time in its history and now leans at a shallow angle. The eastern stone is covered with badly weathered cup marks. The name 'Goatstones' is thought to come from 'Gyet-Stones', which translates as 'wayside stones', a possible reference to an old droveway nearby.

Goward Dolmen
The Goward Dolmen is a megalithic cromlech located in a farmer's field in the townland of Gowar between Hilltown and Castlewellan in County Down. Locally, the monument is known as 'Pat Kearney's Big Stone'. Pat Kearney lived in a thatched cottage nearby and for many years acted as the caretaker and guide to the monument; all that remains of the cottage nowadays are a few moss-covered stones. The dolmen's capstone is estimated to weigh around fifty tons. However, due to a collapsed supporting stone at the rear, the capstone has shifted

sideways and now lies tilted at an acute angle. The portal tomb dates from around 2,500–2,000 BC. Excavations of the site in 1834 unearthed a cremation urn and a flint arrowhead.

Greycroft Stone Circle
Greycroft Stone Circle is located in a field at Seascale How Farm in Cumbria, located only a few hundred yards from the sea. The ring of ten standing stones (all that remain of the original twelve), encompasses a diameter of just over ninety-eight feet, and a single detached outlying stone stands a hundred or so feet away. In 1820, the local farmer, James Fox, buried all but one of the stones to improve his ploughing, and they were not recovered and restored to their upright positions until 1949, when an excavation was undertaken by staff and pupils from Pelham House School in Calderbridge. As well as human remains, several Bronze Age artefacts, including flints, a jet ring and a Neolithic stone axe were found in a low mound burial cairn that was unearthed within the circle.

Grey Wethers Circles
The two prehistoric Grey Wethers Circles are located at the foot of Sittaford Tor on a plateau north of Postbridge in Dartmoor. The northern circle is made up of twenty upright granite slabs forming a circle of about one hundred and five feet in diameter, while the southern circle is slightly larger with twenty-nine stones. The name is thought to derive from the fact that from a distance, the stones were thought to resemble a flock of sheep – (a 'wether' is a castrated male sheep). Local legend has it that at midnight every Midsummer Eve, the stones take their former shapes as sheep, and graze on the slopes of Sittaford Tor until morning. Most of the stones had fallen over so that less than twenty remained standing in the combined circles before they were restored to their upright positions by Robert Burnard in 1909. Burnard's dig also found that the inner ward of the circles contained large quantities of charcoal, suggesting sustained use of fire, probably cremations, over many years.

Heston Brake Long Barrow
Heston Brake Long Barrow is a somewhat neglected chambered tomb (or dolmen), located in a field on a hill overlooking the Severn Estuary in Portskewett, Monmouthshire. It has stood here for more than 4,000 years. Nine of the original thirteen megaliths are still standing; the missing four stones were victims of both vandalism and theft for local farm building materials. A two-feet-high stone known as the 'chopping block' suggests the possibility of the site being used for ritualistic or sacrificial purposes during Neolithic times. The stones are of a conglomerate glacial erratic type and known as 'puddingstones' or 'plum-puddingstones'. The original barrow would have been covered with earth, but by the nineteenth century most of it had been removed or disappeared through weather erosion and what remains is now partially obscured by undergrowth.

Hoe Hill Long Barrow

Also known as 'Cromwell's Grave', How Hill is a well-preserved Neolithic long barrow located a few hundred yards west of Hoe Hill Farm in Lincolnshire. The rectangular-shape barrow is badly overgrown with grass, hawthorns, beech trees and other bushes and now forms a collapsed depression, probably the result of a failed internal wooden structure at some point in its history. The earthwork and its buried remains are from the early Neolithic period, and the site is surrounded by an almost disappeared 'marker' ditch, which probably delineated the bounds of its ritual significance. Excavations have unearthed samples of worked flint, Beaker pottery and a barbed arrowhead, as well as animal bone dated to the Neolithic period, sometime between 3,905 and 3,640 BC. The barrow is known as Cromwell's Grave because according to local tradition it is the burial place of a Roundhead soldier who was captured by Royalist sympathisers and executed here.

Kilclooney Dolmens

The larger of the two dolmens at Kilclooney near Ardara in County Donegal dates from around 3,500 BC, and is thought to be one of the best in Ireland. The arrangement is made up of an exceptionally large capstone supported by two upright portal stones. Finally, there is a back stone of red Ardara granite, in this case known as a 'chocking stone', whose function was an aid to manoeuvring the capstone into place, to adjust its angle and thereby maintain an otherwise ungainly and awkward equilibrium. The whole structure was built to enclose a tomb chamber, and would have originally been covered by a mound of stones and earth. A smaller dolmen, located some thirty feet behind the other, and separated from it by a field wall, probably formed a secondary chamber within the cairn of stones. Fragments of early Neolithic pottery have been found in the chamber of the larger dolmen.

Lanyon Quoit

Lanyon Quoit is a prehistoric chambered tomb located north-west of Madron in Cornwall. It would have originally been covered with an earth and stone mound, all of which have now gone, revealing the remains of an impressive stone chamber. During a severe storm in the early nineteenth century the monument collapsed and was largely restored to its upright position in 1824, but only three of the uprights could be re-erected, as a fourth had been broken during the collapse. According to local folklore, the monument was the last resting place of the bones of a giant – hence the alternative names for the dolmen – 'Giant's Quoit' or 'Giant's Table'.

Loanhead of Daviot Stone Circle

The Loanhead Stone Circle is located on a ridge overlooking the village of Daviot in Aberdeenshire, and is a fine example of a so-called 'recumbent' stone circle. It incorporates a sixty-nine-feet diameter ring of eight upright standing stones and a massive stone slab lying on its side (the recumbent stone). The granite stone monument was constructed in the early Bronze Age, and encompasses a slightly raised cairn of small rocks and stones, known as a 'kerbed ring cairn'. A stone coffin box, or 'cist', which was unearthed on the eastern edge of the ring in 1934, contained an incense cup and cremated human remains. Further work following the discovery revealed a sunken stone wall next to the main circle, which turned out to be an ancient cemetery dating from the second century BC, complete with thirteen burial pits and urns containing the remains of at least thirty bodies.

Marown
In a field near Marown on the Isle of Man known as 'Magher y Chairn' (the Field of the Lord), stands a collection of stones called St Patrick's Chair. This is one of the so-called 'chair' monuments on the island, from which, according to tradition, St Patrick was said to preach. The arrangement consists of three standing granite stone pillars, of which two are inscribed with a cross. Surrounding the site are a pile of other stones, which may have originally formed some sort of structure, but subsequent deterioration and damage has left their purpose a puzzle which archaeologists are still unable to decipher. The arrangement is most probably of Bronze Age origin and may be the remains of a burial chamber, and would have been covered with an earth mound. The inscribed crosses were a later mediaeval addition, as the site was acquired by early Christian missionaries to the island.

Matfen Stone
The Matfen Stone (also called 'Stob Stone') is a single standing Bronze Age menhir, located opposite Standing Stone Farmhouse south of Matfen a few miles north of Hadrian's Wall in Northumberland. The weathered stone demonstrates how water erosion over time has carved deep grooves down all four sides. There is evidence of incised cup marks on three of the faces. Cup-and-ring marks are typical of much prehistoric rock monuments, and often include swirls and concentric ring markings whose exact significance is not exactly understood, but are thought to have some ritualistic or religious significance.

Men-an-Tol
The standing stone arrangement at Men-an-Tol, near Madron in Cornwall is thought to have been installed around 3,500 years ago. Of its four standing granite stones, it includes one of only two upright hole-pierced stones known in Cornwall, with a nineteen inch diameter hole at its centre. The two side stones and six other stones lie recumbent and partially buried nearby. The purpose and meaning of the installation is hotly disputed. In 1993 the Historic Environment Service of Cornwall concluded that it had originally been part of a larger stone circle of around twenty stones, but that they had been partially realigned following an excavation in 1815; others believe it may have been a burial dolmen, of which the holed stone formed the capstone. Local folklore attributes the stone as having a guardian fairy, known as a 'piskie', who can perform miraculous cures, especially to children with rickets,

and that women passing through the hole at full moon are guaranteed to become pregnant. In Cornish, 'Men an Toll' means 'stone of the hole'.

Merrivale Rows
The Merrivale Rows are pair of long stone rows (numbering more than one hundred and fifty standing stones in all), that cross east–west over Longash Common in Dartmoor. Close by are the remains of a Bronze Age settlement of roundhouses, a stone circle, standing stones and a number of earth burial mounds, probably built between about 2,500 and 1,000 BC. The northern double row stretches for almost 600 feet, while the second row, which almost runs parallel, is longer, measuring some 865 feet in length. A stone ring in the middle of the rows is thought to be the burial place of some important person. Another burial place is marked nearby with a stone-lined burial chamber, or 'cist'.

Nine Stones Close
Nine Stones Close (sometimes known as 'Grey Ladies'), is a small stone circle located on the edge of Harthill Moor near Winster in Derbyshire. Flints and shards of pottery found at the site date from the Bronze Age. Of the original nine megaliths, seven were known to be still standing in 1847, but only four still remain today, as several were removed after that date for farming use, at least one being employed as a gate-post in a nearby drystone wall. As two of the stones had either fallen over or leaned badly, they were re-erected in 1936 and embedded in concrete. Local folklore has fairies sometimes gathering there to dance. This is thought to be the origin of its Grey Ladies name, as the so-called 'ladies' represent the fairies who are supposed to dance there at midnight. Another tradition says that it was the stones themselves that were magically transformed into dancing women at midnight.

Normanton Down Barrows
Normanton Down is a Neolithic and Bronze Age barrow cemetery located on Salisbury Plain near Stonehenge. The site consists of three long barrows, and around forty round barrows comprised of a variety of different types. A distinctive feature of the site is the so-called 'Bush Barrow', which is located on the ridge. Substantial quantities of burial artefacts and grave goods have been unearthed from the site, including a selection of amber beads and pendants, gold beads, cups, bronze daggers, bronze pins and a carved bone flute.

Pentre Ifan Burial Chamber
The name Pentre Ifan actually means 'Ivan's village'. The capstone of this burial chamber measures sixteen and a half feet in length and weighs some sixteen tons. The complete complement amounts to seven stones in all. The chamber was set within a shallow pit, and would have originally been covered by a mound of stone

and turf. The principal stones are of the same Pembrokeshire dolerite blue stones that are found at Stonehenge, quarried in the nearby Preseli Hills and were put in place about 5,500 years ago. Reputedly, Pentre Ifan in Pembrokeshire is the largest and best preserved Neolithic dolmen in Wales.

Plas Newydd

The Plas Newydd prehistoric dolmen (a 'cromlech') is located a few hundred yards from the shore line of the Menai Straits in Anglesey. In fact, there are two adjacent burial chambers here: the larger of the two has an enormous weighty oblong-shaped capstone, supported by five large upright stones. The smaller chamber has proportionally smaller supporting stone pillars. It is thought that this may have acted as an entrance chamber for the larger one. Other stones nearby suggest that the original site was much larger, and that earth mounds would once have covered the entire monument.

Rollright Stones

These megalithic monuments are located near the village of Long Compton, between the Oxfordshire and Warwickshire boundary, on the edge of the Cotswold Hills, and their construction covered a period of around two thousand years, spanning the Neolithic and Middle Bronze Age eras. Parts of the monument are obscured by trees, but the site includes a stone circle, a portal dolmen, a menhir, a round cairn and a round barrow surrounded by a ditch. The first of the monuments to be constructed was the 'Whispering Knights', a portal dolmen which dates to the early or middle Neolithic period. It consists of four large standing stones and a fallen capstone which remains leaning against them at an angle. The stones enclose a six and a half feet square chamber. The 'King's Men' stone circle was a later construction of the late Neolithic or early Bronze Age, and may once have consisted of over one hundred stones of a local Oolite limestone, of which seventy still remain standing. A solitary standing stone, known as 'The King Stone', was probably erected around 1,500 BC as a permanent memorial to the burial ground. Local mythology has it as a monument to an ancient deceased king. It has suffered significant degradation through unscrupulous souvenir hunters and is consequently now guarded by a tall iron railing fence. Excavations have revealed a number of flint blades. As to the place name – some believe it to be derived from the Old English 'Hrolla' and 'landriht', which could be interpreted as the 'property of (a man called) Hrolla'. Others prefer an older Celtic source combining 'rodland' and 'ricc', signifying a wheel-shaped area or a stone circle.

Rudston Monolith

The Rudston Monolith, located in Rudston churchyard in the East Riding of Yorkshire, is reputedly the tallest prehistoric monolith in the United Kingdom at over twenty-five feet tall. The single stone slab monolith dates to the late Neolithic or early Bronze Age period and was cut from agglomerate Moorstone grit and weighs about forty-four tons. An excavation in the late eighteenth century speculated that its depth below ground may be as great as its height above it. At some time in its history the top of the stone appears to have been broken off; it may originally have been pointed and stood twenty-eight feet high. It is thought that during Anglo-Saxon times, zealous priests may have rededicated the otherwise pagan monument to the Christian faith and have affixed a cross on top of it, fuelling a compelling hypothesis as to why the original point is missing. In fact it supports a possible explanation of the place name, as 'rood' is an Old English word for a cross. On this basis, 'Rudston' could be interpreted as 'rood-stone' (stone with a cross). The top of the monolith is now protected by a lead hood.

Silbury Hill

The large Neolithic chalk and clay mound at Silbury Hill in Wiltshire was begun in about 2,500 BC and is the largest man-made structure in Europe, rivalling even the Egyptian pyramids in its height of ninety-eight feet and a volume calculated to be more than five hundred and fifty thousand tons. The site covers an area of about five acres and despite numerous excavations, no burials or graves have been found, and the purpose of the structure remains a mystery. Silbury is a designated UNESCO World Heritage Site.

Silbury Hill, Avebury, Wiltshire.

Spinster's Rock

Spinster's Rock is reputedly the best surviving example in Devon of a Neolithic burial chamber. It is located in a field on Shilstone Farm, west of the village of Drewsteignton. The dolmen comprises a large granite capstone supported by three upright stones in a tripod arrangement. Originally the stones would have been covered with earth or smaller stones. The monument was erected sometime between 3,500 BC and 2,500 BC and may have contained many burials. The collapse of the stone chamber has prompted a local legend which asserts that the monument lay in a fallen state before it was re-erected by three passing female wool spinners one morning before breakfast. Consequently, it became known as 'spinner's rock', a title which eventually morphed into 'spinster's rock'. The legend is fanciful, of course, but the dolmen did actually collapse and was fully restored in 1862.

St Lythans Burial Chamber

St Lythans in South Glamorgan is a Neolithic dolmen that stands in a field in the small village of St Lythans near Cardiff. The monument was originally covered by an earth mound and measured about ninety feet in length with a capstone weighing about thirty-five tons. The single stone chamber is only a vestige of what would have been a once much larger burial site. The place has never actually been excavated but human remains and fragments of pottery were found when the chamber was cleared in 1875. Other later finds included a fragment of polished stone axe, flint flakes and a leaf-shaped flint arrowhead. The monument is known locally as 'gwal-y-filiast', and translates as 'kennel of the greyhound bitch'; its exact significance is unknown, though some think it to be a reference to its one-time use as a kennel for greyhounds.

Stannon Circle

Stannon stone circle is located in a remote spot near St Breward, two and a half miles south-east of Camelford on Bodmin Moor, Cornwall. It comprises forty-seven standing stones and thirty-two recumbent stones laid in a one-hundred-and-forty-feet diameter ritual circle. Originally, there may have been as many as eighty-two stones on the site, as well as a hut circle settlement, several cists, and what is believed to have been a much later Romano-British building. Excavations carried out in the late 1960s suggest that the Middle Bronze Age settlement may have had a population of around one hundred people. The site is laid out in such a way as to mark the point at which the sun rises at certain times of the year. Along with the circle, it is thought to have been of ceremonial significance, as the tallest of the remaining standing stones aligns almost exactly with the twin peaks of Rough Tor.

Stanton Drew

The arrangement of standing stones at Stanton Drew in Somerset consists of three late Neolithic stone circles, dating from around 2,500 BC, and an associated group of stones (known as the 'Cove'), as well as a nearby fallen sarsen stone (now recumbent), known as 'Hautville's Quoit' which lies across the river to the north on an alignment. This large stone may have been significantly bigger than it exists today as it has been ravaged by pieces having been broken off at some time to repair roads. The 370 feet diameter circle, known as the 'Great Circle', is the second largest in England after Avebury. Originally, the circle consisted of around thirty menhirs of which only twenty-seven remain, most no longer standing upright. The deep circular ditch that surrounded the circle would probably have had one or two banks, making it a true henge.

Stenness Standing Stones

The Standing Stones of Stenness are located a few miles from Stromness in Orkney, and date from around 3,100 BC. The remaining four of the original twelve stone megaliths stand some nineteen feet tall – a fifth stone lies prone on the ground, reputedly toppled by a local farmer intent on clearing the land for ploughing. It is thought that there would have originally been a surrounding ditch and a peripheral earth bank. A six feet square hearth revealed at the centre of the stone circle contained ash, burnt bone, charcoal and broken pottery, suggesting ritual cremation; an older house that pre-dated the erection of the stones, may have once stood on the site. The name 'Stenness' derives from the Old Norse expression 'steinn-nes', which translates as 'stone headland'.

Stonehenge

Stonehenge is the original henge, after which all other 'henges' derive their name. This ancient Wiltshire monument has generated a great deal of attention over the years, both nationally and internationally. The oldest elements of this complex monument were probably the Heel Stone and the North Barrow, followed in around 3,000 BC by the digging of the circular ditch with an inner and outer bank, enclosing an area of over three hundred and twenty-eight feet in diameter. The installation of the circle of thirteen stones, each weighing around twenty-five tons, came later in around 2,500 BC. They include large sarsens and smaller bluestones, as well as the four Station Stones just outside the circle. The whole site seems to have been associated with ritual burials since its inception, as an archaeological excavation in 2013 unearthed some fifty thousand cremated fragments of human bones, estimated to be the remains of about sixty people. Speculation abounds as to the function or purpose of its construction. It has been thought to be a site of astronomical observation, as a religious druidical site, as an association with the wizard Merlin of Arthurian legend and as a mystical place of healing.

Stoney Littleton

Stoney Littleton Long Barrow (also known as the Bath Tumulus and the Wellow Tumulus), located near the village of Wellow in Somerset, is a Neolithic chambered tomb, dating from about 3,500 BC. The barrow features three sets of paired side chambers off an entrance gallery and central passage, with a seventh single chamber at the far end. The site remained relatively intact until around 1760 when a local farmer broke in looking for building stone and emptied the chambers of their contents. Later nineteenth century excavations revealed evidence of cremations having been performed in the barrow when the bone remains of three individuals were unearthed.

The Nine Stones
The Nine Stones Bronze Age stone circle near to the village of Winterbourne Abbas in Dorset is a relatively small monument at just twenty-six feet in diameter. Seven of its conglomerate stone megaliths are partially buried and only around three feet still stands above ground. Two remaining stones appear larger, and as they are spaced much more widely apart than the other seven it is thought that this may have formed an entrance to the circle. Local folklore associates the site with the Devil, who is said to have turned nine children to stone here. Consequently, the monument is also known as 'the Devil's Nine Stones' and 'the Nine Ladies'. It is also a ritual site for modern druids who periodically hold ceremonies here.

Tomnaverie
Tomnaverie is a Bronze Age recumbent stone circle of a type only found in north-east Scotland, and is located near Tarland in Aberdeenshire. It is comprised of a large stone lying on its side, flanked by two upright stones which once surrounded a burial cairn dating from around 4,500 years ago. Excavations have revealed that the site was used for cremations, as evidenced by the charred human bone fragments and the quantity of charcoal found in a pit where the original recumbent stone would have stood. It has also been suggested that the site may have been used for astronomical observations as in midsummer the moon would have been framed by the recumbent stone in the south-west. The circle measures fifty-six feet in diameter with a smaller circle of kerb stones around a no longer existent cairn.

Wayland's Smithy
The Neolithic chambered long barrow of Wayland's Smithy is located near the village of Ashbury, a mile or so from the world famous Uffington White Horse in Oxfordshire. It comprises an original oval-shaped timber chamber, which dates from around 3,590 BC, where the remains of fourteen people were discovered. Later, a second, larger stone chambered barrow was overlaid on the first, doubling its height. Legend has it as the home of Wayland, the Saxon god of metalworking – hence the name by which it has been known since the tenth century. The entire structure would have been covered with earth dug from two six feet deep ditches which now form the perimeter of the site.

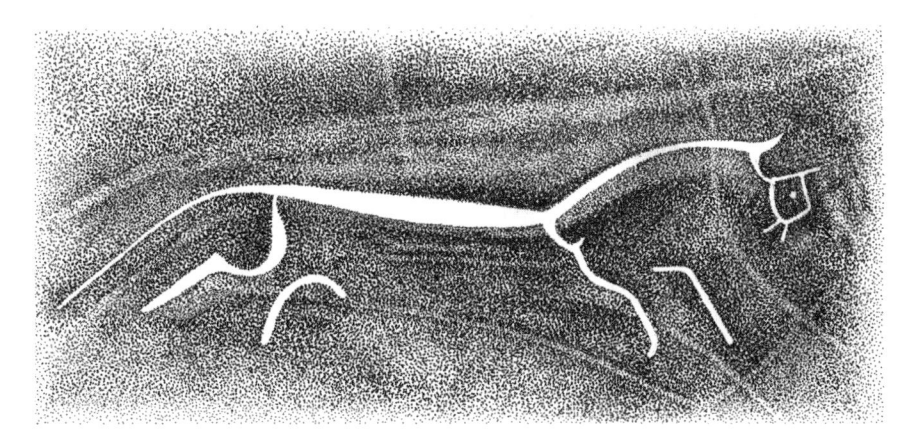

Uffington White Horse, Oxfordshire.

West Kennet Long Barrow
West Kennet Long Barrow near Silbury Hill in Wiltshire is of a type known as the Cotswold-Severn Group, and dates from around 3,650 BC. The mound contained the cremated remains of around forty-six bodies, men, women and children, before its chambers were sealed with earth and rubble in about 2,000 BC. Massive limestone sarsen stones were also installed to block the entrance and a false entrance was created to waylay grave robbers. It is thought that the monument was more than a burial place as its sheer size and dominant location suggest that it may have been used for other ceremonial or religious purposes. Excavations in the barrow have unearthed a variety of grave goods and burial artefacts including pottery and beads, as well as flint and stone tools and implements.

Yeavering Battle Stone
Yeavering Battle Stone is a Neolithic or Bronze Age standing monolith in the shadow of the Yeavering Bell hillfort in Northumberland. It now marks the place where the Battle of Yeavering took place between English and Scottish forces later in 1415. The stone stands just over seven feet tall above ground level, but having fallen over in 1890 and been re-erected in 1924, its exact purpose as well as its position and orientation remain uncertain.

Yellowmead
The Bronze Age stone circles at Yellowmead near Sheepstor were only discovered in 1921, having lain beneath a thick covering of Devonshire heather for many centuries and only coming to light when the extensive burning off of the heathland on Yellowmead Down took place. What lay beneath the scorched earth was an almost concentric stone circle of four rings around a thirteen feet diameter burial

cairn. The central circle comprises twenty-two stones, and the outer rings have thirty-two, twenty-seven and thirty stones respectively.

Yockenthwaite

The stone circle on Yockenthwaite Moor in Langstrothdale, North Yorkshire, consists of twenty-four three feet tall megaliths arranged almost edge to edge in a circle some twenty-five feet in diameter. They have been identified as 'kerbstones', once part of a burial or ring cairn, where the remains of a tribal chieftain are thought to have been buried. The original earth mound covering has disappeared through natural weathering erosion over time. Just north of the circle are the remains of another possible burial cairn. The name 'Yockenthwaite' is probably of Scandinavian origin, where the 'thwaite' element is an Old Norse word meaning 'clearing', and Yocken is thought to be a corruption of 'Eogan', the personal name of the man who created the clearing in what would have been a densely forested area in prehistoric times. Hence, the place name translates as 'Eogan's clearing'.

Part Eleven

Celtic Crosses

It has been suggested that Celtic high crosses may have been introduced originally by St Patrick as an aid to his conversion of the pagan tribes of Ireland and Britain. However, despite its popularity in Irish folklore there is no evidence for this, and the distinctive form of the crosses pre-dates the birth of the saint. What is certain is that early Christian missionary monks did introduce them into Britain.

Celtic High Cross, Llanddwyn Island, Anglesey.

As to their origin, it is commonly held that the ring on the cross relates to a Celtic Moon goddess, symbolised by a 'nimbus' (or ring), and that its location beneath the superimposed cross symbolised Christ as the god above all others. This would have been a concept that early Celts and Pictish tribes would have understood and with which they could easily identify. Thus the traditional Christian cross combined with the pagan sun symbol saw the birth of the Celtic cross.

The crosses fall into two main categories: first, the so-called Celtic 'High Cross', which is a tall standing stone pillar, topped by a decorative wheel cross. The second is the 'Cross Slab' type, an earlier form which would have had religious or Biblical scenes as well as a cross inscribed upon it. This latter type was generally no more than six feet tall and was more akin to a conventional gravestone.

Celtic crosses were particularly prevalent in Ireland, where hundreds of them began to appear in cemeteries from the seventh century onwards, to a point where they are often referred to 'Irish high crosses', and form part of what is sometimes called 'monastic Irish art'. About sixty crosses are known to exist in Ireland alone, and the style continued well into the twelfth century.

Celtic-style ringed crosses reappeared in the mid-nineteenth century in Irish graveyards, and their revival developed into more than a religious icon, but became a potent symbol of Celtic, and especially of Irish cultural identity. However, as their popularity increased they became widespread across all areas of the British Isles – throughout Cornwall, Wales, England and Scotland. The appearance of these often-called 'sun crosses' or 'wheel crosses' are also found in Europe.

This Celtic revival saw wheels and ornamental crosses becoming very popular in decorative items such as brooches, Scottish kilt pins and other jewellery ornaments with the middle classes. The style had a significant influence on Continental Art Nouveau style and in the English Arts & Crafts movement. However, the actual term 'Celtic Crosses' was probably a nineteenth century invention, coined in reaction to the burgeoning stylistic revival.

The Crosses

Ahenny Crosses
The small village of Ahenny in County Tipperary, in the ancient Kingdom of Ossory, is noted for its eighth century group of Celtic high crosses, which includes the nearby Killamery and the Kilree High Crosses. They are thought to have been based on earlier wooden forms, whose Celtic knot work, interlaced swirls, spiral patterns and bosses were reproduced later in sandstone and granite. The Ahenny north cross is generally thought to be the finest example of the group. It stands just over ten feet tall with a conical shaped capstone, which may represent a bishop's mitre. The bases of all the crosses are carved with scenes from the Bible, but they have not weathered well and as a result they are now difficult to interpret.

Celtic Crosses

Aberlemno Pictish Cross
The so-called Aberlemno Cross in Angus is actually a cross inscribed upon a flat stone, known as a 'Pictish cross slab', and stands some seven feet tall in the Aberlemno churchyard. The front face of the stone bears an inscribed Celtic cross set against a background of entwined beasts, while the reverse side pictures a battle scene between Pictish and Northumbrian warriors, and is thought to portray the Battle of Dunnichen which took place nearby in around 685 AD. Three other stones also stand here beside the Brechin to Forfar Road. All four stones are counted among the finest examples of sculpted Pictish stones in Scotland.

Camus Cross
Sometimes spelled as one word, and also known as 'Camuston' (in Scottish Gaelic, 'Camus Croise'), the small township of Camuscross is located on the Panmure Estate near Carnoustie on the Isle of Skye, and is the location of an early medieval standing stone. This Pictish red sandstone cross dates from the tenth century and stands about six and a half feet tall. It depicts the Crucifixion on one face along with decorative scroll patterns and foliage, and Christ in Glory, thought to be holding the Book of Remembrance, on the other. The cross once stood on a small mound, which was first opened in about 1620 and found to contain a skeleton, a food bowl and a gold oval ring which is thought to have been a pommel mount for a bronze weapon, possibly a dagger.

Carew Cross
The eleventh century Celtic cross in Carew, Pembrokeshire, is believed to commemorate Maredudd ab Edwin, who ruled the region of Deheubarth in South Wales with his brother Hywel, in the eleventh century. The Latin inscription on the base translates as 'The Cross of Margiteut son of Etguin'. It is possible that the dedication to Maredudd was added later to an already existent cross. It has been described as 'one of the finest early Christian monuments in Wales'. Actually an assembly of two different stones, the wheel head and shaft come from quite different sources and its two separate parts are joined by a stone-cut tenon joint. The cross is decorated with elaborate knot motifs and intricate cord-plaiting with circular, plain and looped oval rings and Greek-style key-patterning. Its original location is not known but it was moved into its present position at the entrance to Carew Castle in the twentieth century.

Drumcliffe High Cross
This Irish high cross stands in a location that was once the site of a sixth century monastery founded by St Colmcille in the village of Drumcliffe (sometimes spelled 'Drumcliff', and known in Irish Gaelic as 'Droim Chliabh'), in County Sligo. It is one of three that remain in the former graveyard of the old abbey. The main high cross stands over twelve feet high, and is decorated with carvings of Adam and Eve,

Cain slaying his brother Abel, Daniel in the lion's den and other Biblical scenes, as well as decorative Celtic knot motifs representing the Tree of Life.

Duleek High Cross

The small sandstone High Cross in the County Meath village of Duleek is located near to the derelict Church of Ireland which is thought to have been founded by St Cianan. In Irish, Duleek is 'Daimhliag Chianain', which translates as 'the church stone of St Cianan'. The ninth century cross is small by high cross standards, and being a little under six feet tall, it is one of the smallest in Ireland. It features carved figures, a depiction of the Crucifixion, scenes from the life of the Virgin Mary, and what is thought to portray the presentation of Jesus at the temple. Other sides contain various Celtic decorative elements and at the centre of the cross are seven raised spirals which are thought to represent the dance of the planets around the sun.

Edderton Cross Slab

This Pictish red sandstone cross-slab monument dates from the eighth or ninth centuries and stands in the old Edderton graveyard on Easter Ross in the Highland region of Scotland. Its minimal decoration includes a Celtic cross carved in low relief above a carving of a mounted horseman in a semi-circular arched base. Buried lower down and partially obscured below ground level are incised depictions of two more horsemen.

Iona Abbey High Crosses

The crosses at Iona Abbey on the Isle of Mull are claimed by some to be the most beautiful and intricately carved Celtic crosses in Scotland. There are four surviving high crosses here, the remnant of over a thousand that are thought to have once stood here in the Middle Ages. The four remaining are St Matthew's Cross, St John's Cross, St Oran's Cross and St Martin's Cross. A reconstructed replica of the eighth century St John's Cross stands outside the entrance to St Columba's Shrine. It apparently fell over soon after its erection due to a flaw in the stone, and is now housed in the abbey's Infirmary Museum, held up by wooden supports. It was originally a ringless cross, but four segments were added with concrete in the 1920s, but blew down on a number of occasions. St Martin's Cross, stands on its original site outside the abbey. It was carved from a single slab of grey stone more than twelve hundred years ago and decorated with bosses and interlaced serpents. It also depicts scenes from the Bible including the Virgin and Child, Daniel in the lions' den, David and Goliath, as well as King David and King Saul. The reconstructed crosses of St Oran and St Matthew are on display in the Abbey Museum. The crosses are thought to mark the location of St Colmcille's grave.

Kells High Crosses

The town of Kells in County Meath is famous for two things: *The Book of Kells* and its Celtic high crosses. Three of the five crosses, as well as the base of a fourth, are in the grounds of the Abbey of St Colmcille, which was founded in 807 AD by monks fleeing Viking attacks. The fifth, and probably best known, is the Market Cross. It lay broken and toppled for many years after being used as a gallows by Parliamentarian soldiers during the Civil War. This late-ninth or early-tenth century sandstone cross is sometimes called the 'Gate Cross', as it once stood outside the monastery's eastern gate. It is decorated with scenes that include Christ in the tomb, Daniel in the lions' den, the sacrifice of Isaac, Adam and Eve and the temptation of St Anthony. On the base are hunting scenes, as well as images of birds, animals, centaurs and a battle scene. The other crosses at Kells include the tenth century West Cross (sometimes called the 'Ruined or Broken Cross'), the Cross of St Patrick & St Columba, which is the earliest of the Kells crosses, the remains of the base of the North Cross, and the East Cross (sometimes known as the 'Unfinished Cross') which depicts the crucified Christ at its centre.

Kildalton Great Cross

The High Cross of Kildalton on the Scottish Isle of Islay, sometimes known as the Kildalton Great Cross, is generally associated with St John's, St Martin's and St Oran's crosses in Iona. Dating from the late-eighth century, the ringed cross was probably carved by the same stonemason as the Iona crosses. It was cut from a single slab of local grey-green epidiorite stone. Carvings on the monument depict Daniel slaying a lion, Cain murdering his brother Abel, the sacrifice of Isaac, and the Virgin Mary flanked by angels. Other parts of the cross are decorated with intricate carved reliefs of interlacing spiral-work and fantastic animal forms including serpents, lions and birds. The cross is located in the graveyard of the ruined and roofless thirteenth century Kildalton Chapel, and a concrete copy was made for display in the National Museum of Antiquities of Scotland in the late nineteenth century.

Kilree High Cross

The ninth century Kilree High Cross in County Kilkenny stands in a field west of the ruined church and Round Tower. Its sandstone column and cross are very badly weathered, but scenes including the Adoration of the Magi and Daniel in the lions' den have been identified, as well as a hunting scene, several bosses, spirals and other geometric designs symbolising growth, death and decay. The centre of the cross is thought to represent God and the lower circle may represent the winter sun, demonstrating the continuing prevalence of pagan beliefs even among early Christian converts. The cross was probably originally fitted with a long- disappeared capstone. Kilree gets its name from the Gaelic 'cill ri', meaning 'church of the king'. Legend has it that King Niall Caille, who drowned in the King's River at Kells, is buried beneath the cross.

Killamery High Cross

The ninth century Killamery High Cross stands in Killamery cemetery in County Kilkenny on the site of an early medieval monastery which was founded by

St Gobhan in 632 AD. It is part of the western Ossory group of Celtic crosses, which was named after the Osraige tribe whose territory this was from the first to the twelfth centuries. The badly weathered cross is around twelve feet tall and its shaft is decorated with marigolds. It is sometimes referred to as the 'Snake-Dragon Cross' on account of its distinctive wheel head, whose central boss is surrounded by interlaced snakes and a dragon with its mouth wide open. Faces of the monument are carved with a hunting scene, fret and key patterns, depictions of Adam and Eve, Noah and John the Baptist, as well as a sun-swastika symbol. A worn inscription is carved on the base of one side of the cross which reads 'OR DO MAELSECHNAILL', said to be a prayer for Maelsechnaill, a ninth century High King of Ireland.

Kirriemuir Sculptured Stones

This series of carved Pictish stones were found in the grounds of Kirriemuir Church in Angus. Among the stones are two known as Kirriemuir One and Kirriemuir Two, which depict a variety of well-defined figures, among them are mounted huntsmen and animals including a dog and deer. Kirriemuir One is carved on both sides and is decorated with Pictish symbols. It also bears a mirror and comb symbol as well as figures identified as Saints Anthony and Paul; it has been dated to the late-ninth or early-tenth centuries. Kirriemuir Two is a cross-slab carved and decorated in relief on both faces. Its central cross is decorated with interlacing knot work and with four figures surrounding it at each corner of the stone. The upper two figures are either cloaked or winged and the two lower figures are clerics holding books. The stones now reside in the Meffan Institute in Forfar.

Llangadwaladr Cross

Standing over a grave in St Cadwaladr's Church in Llangadwaladr, Anglesey, there is a small Celtic cross, known as the 'Cadfan Stone', which commemorates Cadfan of Gwynedd, King Cadwaladr's grandfather, who died in 625 AD. The graveyard was once part of a royal monastery and Cadfan is said to have spent his last years in contemplation there. The inscription on the seventh century tombstone in the church wall reads in Latin, 'Catamanus Rex Sapientisi Mus Opinatisim Us Omnium Reg Um', which translates as 'King Catamanus (Cadfan) wisest (and) most renowned of all kings (lies here).'

Margam Stones

Possibly one of the most important collections of Celtic stone crosses in Britain is housed in the Margam Stone Museum in an old schoolhouse near Port Talbot in South Wales. The collection includes seventeen sixth and tenth century stone monuments, of which six are Celtic crosses, including the Great Cross of Cobelin, which originally stood outside Margam churchyard. It is described as a 'disc-headed cross-slab', and is decorated with Celtic knotwork, flanked by effigies of the Virgin Mary and St John, and standing in a square base that is engraved with a hunting scene. Most of the stones had been set as milestones on Roman roads before being collected together in the nineteenth century and displayed in the museum.

Monasterboice High Crosses

The ruined Monasterboice monastery in County Louth was founded by St Buite in the sixth century and is famous for its ninth and tenth century high crosses, of which the best known is Muiredach's High Cross. It is also known as the South Cross and is one of three Celtic sandstone crosses that survive in the old monastery grounds. An inscription at the base of the west face reads in Gaelic 'Or Do Muiredach Las Ndernad In Chros', which translates as 'a prayer for Muiredach who had this cross made'. This is a reference to Muiredach mac Domhnall, one of the monastery's most celebrated abbots, who died in 923 AD. The sandstone cross is decorated on one side with scenes from the Old Testament, and from the New Testament on the other. In the centre of the wheel-circle is a depiction of the Crucifixion and on the reverse side is a carving representing the Christ in Judgement. The North Cross is the plainest of the three and appears to have been left unfinished, though it does contain a simple depiction of the crucified Christ. The West Cross (sometimes called the Tall Cross) has an elaborately carved head and a long shaft which contains panels depicting biblical scenes, and its east side shows a carving of Christ in Glory. The site also contains a round tower, a sundial and several stone cross slabs.

Moone High Cross

The Moone High Cross stands in the ruins of the monastery in Moone, County Kildare, which was founded by St Palladius in the fifth century and dedicated to St Columcille. The cross dates from the ninth or tenth century and is claimed to be the second tallest Celtic cross in Ireland, standing around seventeen feet tall. It was discovered in three pieces – a base, shaft and head – in the abbey graveyard in 1835 when it was re-erected as a complete cross. Among the fifty-one sculpted biblical scenes depicted on its shaft are Daniel in the lions' den, the sacrifice of Isaac, the three children in the fiery furnace and Christ's miracle of the five loaves and two fishes. Other carvings on the shaft depict characters from the Bible, as well as Celtic symbols, including mythical and other fantastic creatures and a great deal of ornate decorative work. The granite cross is also known as 'St Columba's Cross', and currently stands inside the ruined abbey church beneath a protective glass canopy. The wheel-head represents the crucified Christ and may be of a later date, having suffered some damage.

Ruthwell Cross

This eighth century stone cross, found today in the village of Ruthwell in Dumfriesshire, originally stood at Priestside on the Solway Firth. It is elaborately carved with Latin and Runic inscriptions as well as scenes from the life of Christ, and thought to be one of the most important surviving sculptures of Anglo-Saxon

Britain. The cross was virtually destroyed as an 'idolatrous monument' by the Presbyterians on the orders of the General Assembly of the Church of Scotland in the seventeenth century. Carvings on the shaft of the monument include scenes of the Crucifixion, the Annunciation, Mary Magdalene and John the Baptist. There are also depictions of Mary and Joseph's flight from Egypt, as well as St Paul and St Anthony breaking bread. The cross was carefully restored by the Reverend Henry Duncan in the early nineteenth century before being moved into a purpose-built apse in the secure environment of Ruthwell Church.

St Dogfan
The so-called 'Cwgan Stone' is a cross-slab stone which was found in St Dogfan's Church in Powys during restoration in the 1850s. It is thought to date from the ninth century and was later decorated with an incised Celtic cross as a tombstone for Cwgan, son of Prince Ethelstan of Powys who died in the eleventh century. The inscription on the stone reads 'Cogom Filiu(s) Edelstan', which roughly translates as 'Cwgan, son of Edelstan'. The monument is now preserved in the south aisle of the church.

Truro High Cross
Standing in a cobbled square near Truro Cathedral, the nine hundred year old high cross is one of Cornwall's oldest. It was unearthed during excavations in St Nicholas Street in 1958 and was erected outside the Marks & Spencer store in the city centre. Unfortunately, the cross was the subject of an accident in February 2019, when an elderly driver crashed his car into it, breaking the cross into four pieces. It has only recently been restored and erected near the cathedral, which is thought to have been its original location.

Part Twelve

Brittany

Celtic Migrations
Even a cursory encounter with the subject of the Celts, demonstrates that historically and culturally, Brittany has long been aligned to South-west England and to Cornwall in particular. This is largely due to the migrations that took place in the face of increasing incursions on their ancient tribal lands in Britain, first by the Romans, and later by Anglo-Saxons in the third and fifth centuries. Forced to leave their tribal homes and territories, they crossed the ocean to establish settlements in the peninsula of north-west Brittany.

These Celtic migrants were predominantly of the powerful Venetii tribe, but there were others, including the Ambiliati, Boiocasses, Diablintes, Lexovii, Menapii, Morini, Namniti, Nannetes, Osismii and Redones.

Despite their new adopted homeland being foreign to them, evidently they still regarded themselves as Britons. The colony's high kings and tribal rulers continued to call themselves 'Bretenanwealde', which translates as 'ruler of the Britons', and Brittany as 'the land of the Britons'. Ironically, as a further continuing

Standing stone alignments, Carnac.

reference to their former homeland, they called the extreme western tip of Brittany 'Cornouailles', which remains the French name for Cornwall.

The Romans had known Brittany as 'Armorica', meaning, 'land by the sea' or 'coastal region' (in Latin 'Gallia Lugdunensis'), and its Celtic peoples as 'Gauls', so that their tribal lands gradually became widely known as 'Gallia'. Their early Celtic language, 'Gaulish', was spoken by the Celtic inhabitants of a much wider region which was not only restricted to Brittany, but included Luxembourg, Belgium and a significant part of Switzerland. Over time, Celtic tribes were forced further westward by advancing Germanic tribes like the Franks; it was they who eventually gave the name to the country we now call France, 'the land of the Franks'.

The Breton Language

Breton is a dialectic form of the Brittonic group of Celtic languages, closely related to Cornish and Welsh. In recent years it has undergone an important revival, promoted by an emergent Breton organisation called 'Diwan', which is a federation of schools that actively lobby for Breton to be officially recognised as a legitimate language of France. More than a quarter of a million Bretons now speak it, mainly in the western half of Brittany.

More than any other factor, it is perhaps its geographical remoteness, like that of Cornwall, which has protected the Celtic culture and language of the Breton peninsula. This insularity has enabled its people to develop a strong sense of independence and cohesiveness, and to maintain the local customs and traditions that ultimately identify them as a unique people, the characteristics of which are typified in Breton art, music and culture. The region is now internationally recognised as one of the so-called Six Celtic Nations and is a member of The Celtic League and Celtic Congress.

Celtic Places in Brittany

Amiens

Although Amiens is located in the Somme Département of Hauts-de-France, its Celtic roots are well documented. It was originally in the tribal territory of the Ambiani, a confederation of tribes living in northern Gaul. Their name stems from Gaulish word 'ambi', meaning 'both sides' (as in 'ambidextrous'), plus the suffix 'ani', which taken together mean '(the people who live) on both sides', a reference to the two banks of the River Somme. The Ambiani capital was Samarobriua (meaning 'bridge on the River Somme'), from the Gaulish 'Samara', their name for the Somme, and 'briua', meaning 'bridge'. This was the site of the present-day City of Amiens.

Brest

Brest is a major port city in the Finistère Département in Brittany. The name was first recorded as 'Bresta', probably derived from the Celtic word 'brigs', meaning 'hill'. The original settlement dates back to the Gallo-Roman times but it was not until the seventeenth century that it was established as a military base, after which it emerged as an important trading port on the Atlantic coast.

Carnac

Carnac is located on Bay of Quibéron, in the Département of Morbihan, and is known as 'Karnag' in Breton. In French its inhabitants are called 'Carnacois'. The site was erected between the fifth and third millennia BC by the pre-Celtic people of Brittany. Its 7,000 year old avenue of eleven rows of standing stones is not unique, many other similar arrangements exist elsewhere, but the sheer number of standing stones and the scale of the alignments at Carnac place it in a class of its own. Its age pre-dates Knossos in Crete, Stonehenge in Wiltshire and the Pyramids in Egypt. The exact significance of the stones has been debated for many years. Some argue that they represent a druidical religious site, others see them as ancient territorial markers, or symbolic structures designed to reinforce group identity. According to many legends, the stones may represent a guardian army, or perhaps they were an important place of worship – others believe they had some astronomical or astrological purpose.

Finistère

Finistère is an excellent example of the common heritage shared by Bretons and Cornishmen. In Breton, the place is called 'Penn ar Bed', which translates as 'head (or end) of the world', and the Cornish name for Land's End is 'Pedn-an-Wlas', which has an almost identical meaning – 'head (or end) of the country'. Like its Cornish counterpart in England, Finistère is the most western department in France. The present-day name comes from the Latin words 'finis terrae', ascribed to the region by the Romans, and meaning 'end of the earth'.

Nantes

Although Nantes is now located in the Loire-Atlantique Département, it has decidedly Gallic origins. Originally, it was one of the major cities of the historic Province of Brittany and the ancient Duchy of Brittany, before being officially separated following the French Revolution in 1789. During the Gaulish period it was the capital of the Namnetes, a Celtic people who were allied with the Venetii, and whose territory extended south as far as to the River Loire. In Breton, the city is called 'Naoned'. The Romans knew the place as 'Condivicnum', and it later became known as 'Namnetes' or 'Nannetes', after the Gaulish tribe, which over time emerged as Nantes.

Quimper

Quimper is the capital of the Finistère Département as well as having been the ancient capital of Cornouaille, Brittany's most traditional region, whose name translates as 'Cornwall'. Its Breton name is 'Kemper' (which is similar to the Welsh word 'cymer'), meaning 'confluence'. This reflects its location at the confluence of the rivers Le Steir, L'Odet and Jet.

Rennes
It is believed that the Celtic tribe known as the Redones (sometimes 'Reidones') occupied the territory in eastern Brittany sometime in the second century BC and established a settlement, which they called 'Condate', at the confluence or the Ille and Vilane rivers; this would eventually become the City of Rennes and Brittany's administrative capital. The name Redones comes from the Gaulish word 'redo', meaning 'driving a chariot'. Along with the Venetii tribe, the Redones and other southern British Celtic tribes were recorded as having submitted to Julius Caesar after being defeated in battle at Sambre in 57 BC, which may have hastened their eventual migration to Brittany.

St Malo
In the Breton language, this historic Breton port in Ille-et-Vilaine is known as 'Sant-Malou'. It was founded in the first century BC by the Gauls, and later became known by its Roman name 'Reginca'. In its present-day incarnation, St Malo was founded by the Welsh Christian monk St Maclou (or 'Maclovius', c.520–621), after whom the place was named; he was one of the seven founder saints of Brittany, who built the church on the site of the Roman city

Vannes
Vannes in the Département of Morbihan is known in Breton as 'Gwened'. Its name comes from the Venetii, a seafaring Celtic tribe who lived in the south-western region of Armorica (present-day Brittany) before the Roman invasions. The Venetii (sometimes 'Vannetais'), were eventually defeated by Julius Caesar's fleet in 56 BC. Following the defeat, the Romans renamed the Venetii's chief settlement 'Darioritum' and systematically punished its former Gaulish owners. Following Roman withdrawal, from the fifth to the seventh centuries, the remaining Gauls assimilated the successive immigrant Britons who had fled the Anglo-Saxon invasions of Britain. Thereafter the settlement reverted to its Breton name, as 'Gwened' and in time reflected the early Celtic tribal name, 'Vannetais', as Vannes.

Bibliography

BARTLETT, PROF. THOMAS, *Ireland, a History* (Cambridge University Press, 2010).
BEACHAM, P. & PEVSNER, N., *The Buildings of England – Cornwall* (Yale University Press, 2014).
BRADLEY, RICHARD, *The Prehistory of Britain and Ireland* (Cambridge University Press, 2007).
BRODRIBB, WILLIAM JACKSON & CHURCH, ALFRED JOHN (Translators), *Tacitus: Life and Death of Julius Agricola* (CreateSpace Digital Services, 2018).
BURY, JAMES BAGNELL, *The Life of St Patrick and his Place in History* (Dover Publications, 2008).
CLARE, SISTER FRANCIS MARY (Margaret Anne Cusack), *An Illustrated History of Ireland* (Irish National Publications, 1868).
COLLIS, JOHN, *The Celts: Origins, Myths & Inventions* (The History Press, 2003).
CORPUS OF ELECTRONIC TEXTS (CELT), *Documents of Ireland* (University College, Cork, 2016).
CUNLIFFE, BARRY, *The Ancient Celts* (Second Edition, Oxford University Press, 2018).
DAFYDD, MYRDDIN ap (Ed), *Welsh Place names Explained* (Carreg Gwalch, Lanrwst, 2016).
DAVIES, ELWYN (Ed), *A Gazetteer of Welsh Place names* (University of Wales Press, 1967).
DRISCOLL, STEPHEN T., GEDDES, JANE, & HALL, MARK A (Eds), *Pictish Progress (Studies of Northern Britain in the Early Middle Ages)* (Brill NV, Leiden, 2011).
DYER, J., *Hillforts of England and Wales* (Shire Publications, 2003).
EKWALL, (Prof) EILERT, *English River Names* (Clarendon Press, 1928).
FLANAGAN, DEIRDRE & LAURENCE, *Irish Place names* (Gill Books, Dublin, 1994).
FORDE-JOHNSTON, J., *Hillforts of the Iron Age in England and Wales: a Survey of Surface Evidence* (Liverpool University Press, 1976).
GOG, GWILI, *Understanding Welsh Place names* (Northern Eye Books, 2015).
GWYNN, STEPHEN, *The Famous Cities of Ireland* (Maunsel & Co. Ltd., Dublin, 1915).
HANNAN, R. J., *A Dictionary of Ulster Place names* (Queens University, Belfast, 1992).

HARBINSON, P., *Pre-Christian Ireland, from the First Settlers to the Early Celts* (Thames & Hudson, 1994).
HARDING, DENNIS, *Iron Age Hillforts in Britain and Beyond* (Oxford University Press, 2012).
HOGG, A. H. A., *Hillforts of Britain* (Hart-Davis MacGibbon London, 1975).
JACK, THOMAS C., *Ordnance Gazetteer of Scotland* (Grange Publishing, Edinburgh, 1885).
JAMES, S., *Exploring the World of the Celts* (Thames & Hudson, 1993).
LEWIS, SAMUEL, *The Topographical Dictionary of England* (Archive Books, London, 1831).
LEWIS, SAMUEL, *A Topographical Dictionary of Ireland*, 1837 (Genealogical Publishing Company, Baltimore, 1995).
MACKILLOP, JAMES, *A Dictionary of Celtic Mythology* (Oxford University Press, 2004).
MCKAY, PATRICK, *Place names of Northern Ireland* (Publisher: Clo Ollscoil na Banriona, 2007).
MARTIN, PROF. G. H., and WILLIAMS, Dr A., *Domesday Book – a Complete Translation* (Penguin Books, 2003).
McKAY, PATRICK, *A Dictionary of Ulster Place names* (Queens University, Belfast, 1999).
MILLS, A. D., *A Dictionary of British Place names* (Oxford University Press, 1991).
MOORE, PROF. A.W., *The Surnames & Place names of the Isle of Man* (Elliot, Stock, London, 1890).
NICOLAISEN, W. F. H., *Scottish Place names* (Publisher: John Donald, Edinburgh, 1976).
OPPENHEIMER, STEPHEN, *The Origins of the British* (Published by Robinson, New Edition, 2007).
ORDNANCE SURVEY, *Guide to Gaelic Origins of Place names in Britain* (2005).
ORR, PHILIP, *New Perspectives: Politics, Religion & Conflict in Mid-Antrim, 1911–14* (Ballymena, 2011).
OWEN, HYWEL WYN, *The Place names of Wales* (University of Wales Press, 2015).
PEVSNER, SIR NIKOLAUS, *Pevsner Architectural Guides – The Buildings of England* (Penguin Books, 1951).
ROOM, ADRIAN, *A Dictionary of Irish Place names* (Appletree Press, 1994).
SAVAGE, ANNE, *The Anglo-Saxon Chronicles* (Book Club Associates, London, 1982).
SHARKEY, JOHN, *Celtic High Crosses of Wales* (Published by Llygad Gwalch Cyf, 1998).
STEVENS, HENRY, N., *Ptolemy's Geography* (Forgotten Books, 2018).
TROUNSON, J., *Mining in Cornwall, Volume One* (Moorland Publishing Company, 1981).
WATSON, W. J., *The Celtic Place names of Scotland* (Berlin Limited, Edinburgh, 2004).

Useful Online Resources

BEFORE THERE WERE COUNTIES, An Irish Territorial History (sites.rootsweb.com/~irlkik/ihm/irehstry.htm).
CLANS OF IRELAND (clansofireland.ie).
CORNISH PLACE NAMES (cornwalls.co.uk/culture).
CULTURE NORTHERN IRELAND (culturenorthernireland.org).
GAZETTEER OF SCOTLAND (scottish-places.info).
HISTORIC CORNWALL (historic-cornwall.org.uk).
IRISH WALLED TOWNS NETWORK (irishwalledtownsnetwork.ie).
LENDINNING, D., Ptolemy's Celtic Tribes in Britain (romanplaces.eu/ptolemy-s-celtic-tribes-in-britain/ptolemy-s-celtic-tribes-in-britain).
LIBRARY IRELAND (libraryireland.com/HistoryIreland).
MEGALITHIC IRELAND (megalithicireland.com).
NATIONAL ARCHIVES (IRELAND) (nationalarchives.ie).
PLACE NAMES WALES (wales.com).
SCOTCLANS (scotclans.co.uk).
SCOTLAND, Fox, Bethany, (University of Helsinki, 2007).
SCOTTISH ORIGINS (scottishorigenes.com).
SCOTWEB (scotweb.co.uk).
STONE CIRCLES (stone-circles.org.uk/stone/index.htm).
ULSTER HISTORICAL FOUNDATION (ancestryireland.com/history-of-the-irish-parliament/constituencies).
WELSH PLACE NAME SOCIETY (historypoints.org/index.php?page=the-welsh-place name-society).

Index

Aber- (prefix) 86, 159, 161
Aberaeron (Ceredigion) 157
Aberavon (Port Talbot) 157
Abercorn (West Lothian) 86
Abercraf (Brecknockshire) 159
Abercrombie (Fife) 86
Aberdare (Glamorgan) 159
Aberdeen (City of) 88
Aberfeldy (Perth & Kinross) 88
Aberfoyle (Stirling) 88
Abergavenny (Monmouthshire) 159
Abergele (Conway) 159
Aberlady (East Lothian) 88
Aberlemno Pictish Cross (Angus) 259
Aberlour (Moray) 88
Abermaw (see: 'Barmouth') 161
Abernethy (Perth & Kinross) 90
Aber-soch (Gwynedd) 159
Abertillery (Gwent) 160
Abbotsbury Castle Hillfort (Dorset) 218
Aboyne (Highland) 90
Acharacle (Argyl & Bute) 90
Achnashellach (Highland) 90
Achonry (Sligo) 36
Acts of Union:
    (Ireland) 33
    (Scotland) 84
    (Wales) 156
Adare (Limerick) 36
Advent (Cornwall) 8
Agha- (prefix) 36
Aghadoe (Kerry) 36
Aghadowey (Derry) 36

Aghagallon (Amtrim) 36
Aghagower (Mayo) 36
Aghalane (Cavan) 36
Aghinver (Fermanagh) 36
Agricola, General Julius *ix*, 32, 83, 106, 210, 235
Ahenny Celtic Crosses (Angus) 258
Ailsa Craig (South Ayrshire) 90
Airdrie (North Lanarkshire) 90
Aire, River 194
Alness (Ross & Cromarty) 91
Alt-/Allt- (prefix) 36
Altachullion (Cavan) 36
Altamooskan (Tyrone) 36
Altnahinch (Antrim) 37
Altarnun (Cornwall) 9
Ambleston (Pembrokeshire) 160
Ambresbury Banks Hillfort (London) 218
Ambrosius Aurelianus 218
Amesbury (Wiltshire) 160
Amiens (Somme) 266
Amlwch (Anglesey) 160
Andreas (Isle of Man) 76
Anglesey (Island of) 160
Anglo-Saxon Chronicles 132, 232
Angus (Unitary Authority) 91
Annaclone (Down) 37
Annacotty (Limerick) 37
Annadorn (Down) 37
Annaghdown (Galway) 37
Annals of Ulster, The 104
Annan (Dumfries & Galloway) 91
Annet (Cornwall) 9

Index

Anstruther (Fife) 91
Antonine Wall 91
Antrim (County) 37
Aonach Beag/Aonach Mor (Highland) 208
Applecross (Highland) 92
Arbor Low Henge (Derbyshire) 212
Arbory (Isle of Man) 76, 77
Arbroath (Angus) 92
Ard- (prefix) 38
Ardara (Donegal) 38
Ardee (Louth) 38
Ardnamurchan (Highland) 90, 92
Ardfinnan (Tipperary) 38
Ardnaree (Mayo) 39
Ardrishaig (Argyl & Bute) 92
Ardrossan (North Ayrshire) 92
Ards Peninsula (Down) 39
Artraighe (Celtic tribe) 71
Arun, River 194
Arvagh (Cavan) 39
Argyll (& Bute) 91, 92, 96, 108, 114, 124, 129, 136, 148, 208
Armagh (City of) 39
   County Armagh 56, 57, 65, 72
Arran, (Isle of) 118
Athleague (Roscommon) 39
Athlone (Westmeath) 40
Attrebates (Celtic tribe) 223
Auchinleck (East Ayrshire) 93
Auchterarder (Perth & Kinross) 93
Auchtermuchty (Fife) 93
Aughrim (Wicklow) 40
Aultbea (Highland) 93
Auterii (Celtic tribe) 65
Aviemore (Highland) 94
Avoka (Wicklow) 40
Avon, River 160, 195, 196, 229
Axe, River 194
Ayr 94
   East Ayrshire 93, 104, 114, 123, 136

North Ayrshire 92, 96, 97, 100, 104, 105, 120, 123, 127, 142
South Ayrshire 90, 94, 114, 131, 146, 149

Badenoch (Highland) 94
Bala (Gwynedd) 161
Ballabeg (Isle of Man) 76
Ballachulish (Highland) 94
Ballantrae (South Ayrshire) 94
Ballasalla (Isle of Man) 76
Ballater (Aberdeenshire) 94
Ballina Dolmen (Mayo) 240
Ballinalack (Westmeath) 40
Ballinasloe (Galway) 41
Ballaugh (Isle of Man) 76
Bally-/Balli-/Baill- (prefix) 41
Ballybetagh (Dublin) 41
Ballyclare (Antrim) 41
Ballyconnell (Cavan) 41
Ballymena (Antrim) 42
Ballynahinch (Connemara) 41
Balamoral (Aberdeenshire) 95
Banchory (Aberdeenshire) 94
Banff (Aberdeenshire) 94
Bangor (Down)
Bangor (Gwynedd)
Bangor-on-Dee (Clwyd)
Bann, River 195
Bannockburn (Stirling) 94
Bantry (Cork) 43
Barbury Castle Hillfort (Wiltshire) 218
Bargoed (Gwent) 161
Barmouth (Gwynedd) 161
Barra (Western Isles) 95, 116
Barregarrow (Isle of Man) 76
Barrhead (East Renfrewshire) 95
Barry (Glamorgan) 162
Bathgate (West Lothian) 95
Battlesbury Camp (Wiltshire) 218
Bearsden (East Dunbartonshire) 96
Beaumaris (Anglesey) 156
Beddgelert (Gwynedd) 161

Celtic Places and Placenames

Bede ('the Venerable') 132, 145
Bedruthan Steps (Cornwall) 9
Beith (North Ayrshire) 96
Belcoo (Fermanagh) 43
Belfast (City of) 43
Belgae (Gaulish tribe) *viii*, 225
Bellananagh (Cavan) 43
Bellanamallard (Fermanagh) 43
Bellanamullia (Roscommon) 43
Benbecula (Western Isles) 96
Benbo (Leitrim) 44
Ben Macdui (Cairngorms) 207
Ben Nevis (Highland) 207
Ben Vorlich (Dunbartonshire) 97
Bettws-y-Crwyn (Shropshire) 162
Betws-y-Coed (Conway) 162
Biggar (South Lanarkshire) 97
Bishop Rock (Isles of Scilly) 9
Blackwater, River 67
Blackwaterfoot (North Ayrshire) 97
Blaenavon (Gwent) 162
Blaenau Ffestiniog (Gwynedd) 164
Blaenau Gwent 164, 190
Blair Atholl (Perth & Kinross) 97
Blairgowrie (Perth & Kinross) 97
Blanii/Eblani (Celtic tribe) 51
Blantyre (South Lanarkshire) 97
Blencathra (Cumbria) 208
Boat of Garten (Highland) 97
Bodmin (Cornwall) 9, 25, 27
    Bodmin Moor 8, 9, 11, 21, 198, 252
Boho (Fermanagh) 44
Bonhill (West Dunbartonshire) 98
Bonnybridge (Falkirk) 98
Bonnyrigg (Midlothian) 98
Borth-y-Gest (Gwynedd) 164
Boskednan Stone Circle (Cornwall) 241
Bothwell (North Lanarkshire) 99
Boyne, River 51, 67, 195
Braaid (Isle of Man) 76
Badbury Rings Hillfort (Dorset) 218
Braddan (Isle of Man) 77

Braemar (Aberdeenshire) 98
Bratton Camp (Wiltshire) 219
Bray (Wicklow) 44
Breage (Cornwall) 10
Brechin (Angus) 99, 22, 259
Brecon (Powys) 164
    Brecon Beacons 201, 202, 210, 213, 219, 230
Bredon Hill (Worcestershire) 219
Bressay (Shetland) 99
    Bressay Sound 128
Brest (Brittany) 31, 266
Breton (Language) 33, 154, 266, 267, 268
Bridge of Allan (Stirling) 99
Brigantes (Celtic tribe) 212, 228, 235
Brigid (Celtic deity) 58, 59
British Camp Hillfort (Herefordshire) 220
Brodick (North Ayrshire) 100
Brora (Highland) 100
Broxburn (West Lothian) 100
Bruree (Limerick) 44
Bryher (Isles of Scilly) 10
Bryn-Celli-Ddu (Anglesey) 241
    Bryn-Celli-Ddu Tomb Mound 154
Bryn-mawr (Gwent) 164
Buachaille Etive Mor (Argyll & Bute) 208
Buckie (Moray) 100
Bude (Cornwall) 10
Budock Water (Cornwall) 10
Builth Wells (Powys) 164
Burntisland (Fife) 100
Bury Castle Fort (Somerset) 220
Bute (see: Argyl & Bute)
Butler, James 59
Buttermere, Lake (Cumbria) 196

Cadbury Castle (Somerset) 221
Cader Idris (Snowdonia) 208
Caer Caradoc Hillfort (Shropshire) 222
Caergwrle (Clwyd) 265

Index

Caerleon (Gwent) 16, 165, 226
Caernarfon (Gwynedd) 156, 165, 169
    Caernarfonshire 174, 224
Caerphilly (Gwent) 156, 165, 187
Caersws (Powys) 165
Caer-Went (Gwent) 166
Caesar, Julius 222, 232, 268
Caesar's Camp Hillfort (Berkshire) 220
Cairngorms (Moray) 208, 209
Caithness (Highland) 100, 117, 122, 137, 150, 152
Calder, River 195
Caldy Island (Dyfed) 166
Caledonii (Pictish tribe) 83, 108
Callander (Perth & Kinross) 101
Callanish Stones (Isle of Lewis) 82, 242
Calstock (Cornwall) 11
Camborne (Cornwall) 11
Cambrian Mountains 202, 209
Cambuslang (South Lanarkshire) 101
Camel, River 19, 22
Campsie Fells (Stirling) 101, 195
Camus Cross (Isle of Skye) 259
Cannalidgey (Cornwall) 11
Capel Curig (Clwyd) 166
Cape Wrath (Highland) 101
Caractacus/Caradog 166, 219, 220, 222, 224
Caradon Hill (Cornwall) 11
Cardigan (Ceredigion) 167
    Cardiganshire 157, 172
    Cardigan Bay 190
Cardinham (Cornwall) 11
Carew Cross (Pembrokeshire) 259
Carharrack (Cornwall) 12
Carlisle (City of) *ix*
Carlow (County) 44
Carluke (South Lanarkshire) 101
Carmarthen (Dyfed) 167, 184, 239
    Black Book of Carmarthen 154
    Carmarthen Bay 189, 204
    Carmarthenshire 171, 178, 179

Carnac (Brittany) 239, 267
    Carnac megalithic alignments 265
Carnfree (Roscommon) 45
Carnoustie (Angus) 102, 259
Carnsew Hillfort (Cornwall) 220
Carrauntoohil (Kerry) 209
Carrick- (prefix) 44
Carrickbeg (Galway) 44
Carrickboy (Longford) 44
Carrickcarnan (Louth) 44
Carrickfergus (Antrim) 44
Carrickmore (Tyrone) 44
Carron, River 98
Carryduff (Down) 46
Carstairs (South Lanarkshire) 102
Carthew (Cornwall) 11
Cassivelaunus (Celtic chieftain) 232
Castle-an-Dinas (Cornwall) 12
    Castel-an-Dinas Hillfort 222
Castle Cary (Somerset) 167
Castle Pencaire Hillfort (Cornwall) 19, 221
Castlerigg Stone Circle (Cumbria) 237, 242
Castletown (Isle of Man) 76, 77, 78
Cat Bells (Cumbria) 209
Caterthun Hillforts (Angus) 221
Cauci / Caucoi (Celtic tribe) 45
Cavan (County) 36, 37, 39, 41, 43, 45, 46, 49, 58, 59, 60, 62, 63, 66
Celtic/Irish High Crosses 50, 257, 258, 259, 260, 261, 263, 264
Cemaes (Anglesey) 167
Ceredigion (Unitary Authority) 167, 178, 190, 224
Chapel Amble (Cornwall) 12
Chacewater (Cornwall) 12
Chepstow (Gwent) 167
Chettle Long Barrow (Dorset) 242
Cheviot Hills (Scottish Borders/ Northumberland) 209, 235, 236
Chew, River 195
Childswickham (Worcestershire) 168

Chiltern Hills 209
Chirk (Clwyd) 168
Chun Quoit (Cornwall) 242, 243
Chysauster (Cornwall) 13
Cilternsaete (Celtic tribe) 209
Cissbury Ring (West Sussex) 222
Clandyboy/Clandeboy (Down) 46
Clare (County) 46, 48, 53, 59, 60,
    71, 229,
    Richard FitzGilbert de Clare 59
Claudius (Emperor) *vi, viii*
Cleave Hill Camp (Gloucestershire) 222
Clee Hills (Shropshire) 210
Clifden (Galway) 46
Clodock (Herefordshire) 168
Cloghfin (Tyrone) 47
Clota (Celtic river goddess) 196
Clovelly (Devon/Cornwall) 13
Clun (Shropshire) 168
Clyde, River 101, 110, 153, 196
    Firth of Clyde 100, 104, 115, 120
Clyst Honiton (Devon) 13
Cnoc na Peiste (Kerry) 210
Coatbridge (North Lanarkshire) 102
Cocker, River 196
Colby (Isle of Man) 77
Coldrum Long Barrow (Kent) 243
Coldstream (Scottish Borders) 102
Coleraine (Derry) 47
Colne, River 196
Colonsay (Argyl & Bute) 103, 136
Colwyn Bay (Clwyd) 168
Colyton (Devon) 13
Comber (Down) 47
Connacht, (Province of) 47, 48, 55,
    69, 70
Connemara (Galway) 42, 48
Corcomroe (Clare) 48
Cork (City of) 41, 48
    County Cork 43, 56, 60, 69, 244
Cornovii (Celtic tribe) 13, 15, 188,
    191, 192, 229
Cornwall, (Duchy of) 7

Cound (Shropshire) 169
Countisbury (Devon) 13
    Countisbury Castle Hillfort 13, 223
Coupar Angus (Perth & Kinross) 103
Cowdenbeath (Fife) 103
Craigavad (Down) 48
Crail (Fife) 103
Crantock (Cornwall) 14
Crawford (South Lanarkshire) 103
Crediton (Devon) 14
Creech St Michael (Somerset) 14
Cregneash (Isle of Man) 77
Crickhowell (Powys) 169
Cromarty (Ross & Cromarty) 103
    Cromarty Firth 91, 118, 147
Cromwell's Grave (Burial barrow) 247
Crotraighe (Celtic tribe) 71
Crumlin (Antrim) 48
Cubert (Cornwall) 14
Culliford Tree Group Barrow
    (Dorset) 243
Cullompton (Devon) 14
Culmore (Derry) 49
Culross (Fife) 104
Cults (Aberdeen) 104
Cumbernauld (Ross & Cromarty) 104
Cumbrae (North Ayrshire) 104
Cumnock (East Ayrshire) 104
Cusop (Herefordshire) 170
Cuthbert, Saint 14, 34, 124, 132,
Cymric (Celtic tribe) 105

Daingean (Offaly) 48
Dalbeattie (Dumfries & Galloway) 105
Dalby (Isle of Man) 77
Dalkeith (Midlothian) 105
Dallas (Moray) 105
Dal Riata, (Kingdom of) 45, 61, 93,
    114, 120
Dalry (North Ayrshire) 105, 129
Dalwhinnie (Highland) 105
Dalziel (North Lanarkshire) 106
Danu (Celtic deity) 197

Index

Darren Camp Hillfort (Ceredigion) 224
Dart, River 196
D'Avranches, Hugh 157
De Bonville, Simon
De Brus, Robert ('the Bruce') 116
De Burgo/De Burgh, Richard 55
De Clare, Richard FitzGilbert 59
De Lacy, Walter 170
De Courci/De Courcy, John 51, 60, 67
De Montgomerie, Roger 157
Dee, River (Aberdeen) 88, 90, 95, 99, 124, 148
Dee, River (Flintshire/Cheshire) 161, 173, 196
Deganwy (Clwyd) 170
Denbigh/Denbighshire (Clwyd) 168, 170, 181, 187, 188
Deiniolen (Gwynedd) 170
Deise (Celtic tribe) 71
Dematae (Celtic tribe) 167, 171, 219
Derry/Londonderry (City of) 33, 36, 47, 49
   County Derry 49, 51, 52, 58, 62, 64, 72, 214
Derry- (prefix) 49
Derrynacreeve (Cavan) 49
Derwent, River 196
Devil's Dyke (Dumfries & Galloway) 91
Devon (County of) 15
Dinas Dinlle Hillfort (Gwynedd) 224
Dinas Powis (Glamorgan) 171
Dinedor (Herefordshire) 171
   Dinedor Camp Hillfort 224
Dingle, (Kerry) 49
   Dingle Bay 58
Dingwall (Highland) 106, 147
Dobunni (Celtic tribe) 219
Doldarrog (Clwyd) 171
Dolgellau (Gwynedd) 171
Doll Tor Stone Circle (Derbyshire) 244
Dolmen of the Four Maols 39, 240

Domesday Book 9, 10, 11, 12, 13, 14, 15, 16, 18, 23, 24, 26, 27, 28, 29, 30, 156, 160, 168, 170, 172, 174, 176, 177, 178, 179, 182, 187, 189, 190, 191, 205, 213, 223
Don, River 196
Donagh- (prefix) 50
Donaghcloney (Down) 50
Donaghcumper (Kildare) 50
Donaghmore (Down & Tyrone) 50
Donaghmoyne (Monaghan) 50
Donegal (County) 50
Doon, River, 197
Dornoch (Highland) 106
   Dornoch Firth 106
Douglas (Isle of Man) 78, 80
Douglas River (Lancashire) 197
Down (County) 50
Downpatrick (Down) 51
Drogheda (Louth) 51
Drombeg Stone Circle (Cork) 243
Dromineer (Tipperary) 51
Druids *vii*, *viii*, 254
Drum-/Drom- (prefix) 51
Drum (Monaghan) 51
Drumahoe (Derry) 51
Drumbeg (Down) 51
Drumcannon (Donegal) 51
Drumcliffe High Cross (Sligo) 259
Drumcree (Westmeath) 51
Drumcroon (Derry) 51
Drumnadrochit (Highland) 106
Dryburgh (Scottish Borders) 106
Dublin (City & County) 33, 36, 41, 52, 55, 60, 64, 68, 69, 70, 72, 199, 200, 231,
Duleek (Meath) 51
   Duleek High Cross 260
Dumbarton (Strathclyde) 97, 107, 142
Dumfries & Galloway 91, 105, 109, 115, 116, 124, 126, 129, 130, 131, 133, 135, 140, 142, 145, 146, 148, 152

Celtic Places and Placenames

Dumnonii (Celtic tribe) 13, 14, 15, 221, 227
Dun- (prefix) 52
Dunaff (Donegal) 52
Dunbar (East Lothian) 106
Dunblane (Perth & Kinross) 107
Dundalk (Louth) 52
Dundee (City of) 107, 203
Dundrum (Down) 52
Dunfermline (Fife) 108
Dungannon (Tyrone) 53, 68
Dungiven (Derry) 52
Dunkeld (Perth & Kinross) 108
Dunkery Beacon (Somerset) 244
Dunluce (Antrim) 52
Dunmoyle (Tyrone) 52
Dunoon (Argyl & Bute) 108
Duns (Scottish Borders) 108
Dunterton (Devon) 15
Durness (Highland) 108
Durotriges (Celtic tribe) 218, 221, 225, 227, 230, 231
Dwygyfylchi (Conwy) 167, 171, 172
Dyfed (Historic County) 177
Dymock (Gloucestershire) 171

Easter Aquhorthies (Aberdeenshire) 244
Easter Ardross (Highland) 108
Easter Ross (Highland) 109, 260
East Linton (East Lothian) 109
East Wemyss (Fife) 109
Ebbw Vale (Gwent) 172
Ecclefechan (Dumfries & Galloway) 109
Edderton Cross Slab (Highland) 259
Eden, River 41, 146, 197
Edenderry (Offaly) 53
Edinburgh (City of) 109, 118, 128, 137, 145, 200
Eddisbury Hillfort (Cheshire) 225
Egloskerry (Cornwall) 15
Eilean Donnan (Highland) 109
Eire (Republic of Ireland) 32, 33, 35, 52

Elgin (Moray) 110, 130
Elwy, River 197
Emly (Tipperary) 53
Ennis (Clare) 53
Enniscrone (Sligo) 53
Enniskillen (Fermanagh) 33, 43, 54
Eoghanacht (Celtic tribe) 71
Erdini (Celtic tribe) 46, 61
Eriu (Celtic deity) 63
Eriskay (Outer Hebrides) 110
Erne, River 46, 197
Erne, Lough (Fermanagh) 46, 54, 57, 64, 198
Erskine (Renfrewshire) 110
Esk, River 126, 133, 198
Evercreech (Somerset) 172
Ewloe (Clwyd) 172, 173
Exeter (City of) 15, 24, 27, 30

Fahan (Fermanagh) 54
Fair Isle (Shetland) 110
Fal, River 198
Falkland (Fife) 111
Fan Fawr (Powys) 210
Fannich (Highland) 111
Fauldhouse (West Lothian) 111
Fenagh (Leitrim) 54
Feniton (Devon) 15
Feock (Cornwall) 16
Fergus the Great (Dal Riata) 45, 47, 57, 108
Fermanagh (County) 36, 43, 56, 58, 60, 64
Fettercairn (Aberdeenshire) 111
Fife (Unitary Authority) 111
Fin Cop Hillfort (Derbyshire) 225
Findhorn, River 198
Fingal (Dublin) 64, 69
Fingal's Cave (Inner Hebrides) 112
Finglas (Dublin) 55
Finistère (Brittany) 19, 266, 267
Finn, River (Donegal/Tyrone) 55
Fir Bolg (Celtic tribe) 53, 54, 71

278

Firth of Clyde 90, 94, 100, 104, 108, 115, 120, 127, 142, 196
Firth of Forth 91, 104, 111, 112, 117, 124, 135, 144, 195, 199
Firth of Tay 107, 203
FitzOsbern, William 156
Five Wells Stone Tomb (Derbyshire) 245
Fleet, River 198
Flint (Township) 171
Flintshire (Clwyd) 160, 164, 172, 175, 185, 187
Flotta (Orkney) 112
Fochabers (Moray) 112
Forres (Moray) 112
Forteviot (Perth & Kinross) 113
Fortrose (Highland) 113
Forth, River 99, 111, 198
Foula (Shetland) 113
Fowey, River 198
Foyle, River 199
Frome, River 199

Gairloch (Highland) 113
Galachiels (Scottish Borders) 113
Gallen (Offaly) 55
Galloway (Dumfies & Galloway) 113
Galston (East Ayrshire) 114
Galtymore (Limerick/Tipperary) 210
Galway (County) 37, 38, 41, 45, 46, 55, 56, 57, 60, 224
Ganarew (Herefordshire) 173
Gangani (Celtic tribe) 45
Garn Goch (Brecon Beacons) 219
Garras (Cornwall) 16
Gaul/Gaulish/Gallic *viii*, 73, 82, 225, 266, 267, 268
Gerrans (Cornwall) 16, 25
Giant's Causeway (Antrim) 56
Giant's Ring (Antrim) 43
Gigha (Argyl & Bute) 114
Girvan (South Ayrshire) 114
Glamis (Angus) 114

Glamorgan (Gwent) 159, 161, 162, 165, 171, 173, 181, 182, 183, 184, 185, 189, 190, 252
Glasbury (Powys) 173
Glasgow (City of) 94, 96, 101, 114, 132, 139, 142, 152
Glastonbury (Somerset) 16, 17, 20
Glen Affric (Highland) 114
Glenavy (Antrim) 56
Glencoe (Highland) 115
Gleneagles (Perth & Kinross) 115
Gleneig (Highland) 115
Glen Maye (Isle of Man) 78
Gloucestershire (County) 157, 172, 176, 190, 195, 199, 202, 223, 226, 241
Glyder Fawr (Snowdonia) 210
Glyn Ceiriog (Clwyd) 174
Goatstones Stone Circle (Northumberland) 245
Gog Magog (Cambridgeshire) 234
Gordon, Earl Charles 90
Gorticashel (Tyrone) 56
Gougane Barra (Cork) 56
Gourock (Inverclyde) 115
Goward Dolmen (Down) 245
Gower Peninsula (Swansea) 174
Grampians (Highland) 83, 111, 133, 210
Grampound (Cornwall) 17
Greenock (Renfrewshire/Inverclyde) 115
Gresford (Wrexham) 174
Gretna (Dumfries & Galloway) 115
Greycroft Stone Circle (Cumbria) 245
Grey Wethers Circles (Devon) 246
Grey Ladies Stone Circle (Derbyshire) 249
Gugh (Isles of Scilly) 17
Gulval (Cornwall) 17
Gunwalloe (Cornwall) 17
Gwalchmai (Anglesey) 174
Gwent (Historic County) 174

Gwinear (Cornwall) 18
Gwynedd (Unitary Authority) 175

Hadrian/Hadrian's Wall
    (Northumberland) *ix*, 84, 91,
    116, 248
Hambledon Hill (Dorset) 225
Hamilton (South Lanarkshire) 116
Hamilton, Sir Alexander 60
Harlech (Gwynedd) 156, 175
Harris: see 'Isle of Harris'
Harrowbarrow (Cornwall) 17
Hawarden (Flintshire) 175
Hayle (Cornwall) 18
    Hayle, River 24, 30
Heanish (Outer Hebrides) 116
Hebrides (Island Group) 85
Hebrides Overture (Fingal's Cave) 112
Heddon-on-the-Wall
    (Northumberland) 116
Helland (Cornwall) 18
Helvellyn (Cumbria) 210
Hendraburnick (Cornwall) 18
Henge 237, 239
Hereford (City of) 157
Heston Brake Long Barrow
    (Monmouthshire) 246
Highland (Region) 117
    Highland Clearances 83
Hodnet (Shropshire) 176
Hoe Hill Long Barrow
    (Lincolnshire) 247
Holyhead (Anglesey) 161, 176
Holywood (Dumfries & Galloway) 117
Hoy (Orkney) 117, 147
Hugh Town (Isles of Scilly) 18, 24
Humber, River 217
Huna (Highland) 117

Iberni/Uterini (Celtic tribe) 48
Iceni (Celtic tribe) *ix*, 234, 235
Illogan (Cornwall) 19
Inchcolm (Fife) 117

Inchkeith (Fife) 117
Inish-/Inis- (prefix) 56
Inishannon (Cork) 56
Inishbeg (several) 56
Inishbofin (Donegal) 57
Inisheer (Galway) 56
Inishfree (Donegal) 56
Inishmore (Galway & Fermanagh) 57
Innerleithen (Scottish Borders) 118
Innishmaan (Galway) 38
Innishowen (Donegal) 57
Inver- (prefix) 118
Inveraray (Argyl) 118
Inverclyde (Unitary Authority) 118
Invergordon (Highland) 118
Inverkeithing (Fife) 118
Inverness (Highland) 93, 118, 151, 201
Inverleith (Edinburgh) 118
Inverurie (Aberdeenshire) 118, 244
Iona (see: 'Isle of Iona')
Ireland, Republic of (see 'Eire')
Irvine (North Ayrshire) 120
Irwell, River 199
Islay (Inner Hebrides) 116, 120,
    140, 261
Isle of Man *x*, 74, 75, 77
Isles of Scilly 7, 8, 19
Iona, Isle of (Inner Hebrides) 78, 120
    Iona Abbey High Crosses 260
Iverni (Celtic tribe) 66, 198

Jedburgh (Scottish Borders) 121, 137
John o'Groats (Highland) 121
Jura (Argyl & Bute) 122
Jurby (Isle of Man) 78

Keady (Armagh) 57
Keith (Moray) 122
Kells (Meath) 57, 260, 261
    Book of Kells 57
    Kells High Crosses 260
Kelso (Scottish Borders) 122
Kemble (Gloucestershire) 176

Index

Kenchester (Herefordshire) 177
Kennoway (Fife) 122
Kerrier (Cornwall) 19
Kerry (County) 36, 58
Kil-/Kill- (prefix) 57
Kilbride (various) 58
Kilcar (Donegal) 58
Kilcronaghan (Derry) 58
Kilclooney Dolmens (Donegal) 247
Kilcock (Kildare) 58
Kildalton Great Cross (Islay) 261
Kildare (County) 58
Kilfenora (Clare) 59
Kilfullert (Down) 59
Kilkenny (Leinster) 59
Kill (Cavan) 59
Killadeas (Fermanagh) 58
Killamery High Cross (Kilkenny)
Killashandra (Cavan) 59
Killarney (Kerry) 60
Killcullan (Kildare) 58
Killevy (Armagh) 58
Kilmacolm (Inverclyde) 122
Kilmarnock (East Ayrshire) 123
Kilpeck (Herefordshire) 177
Kilsyth (Lanarkshire) 123
Kilwinning (North Ayrshire) 123
Kimsbury Camp (Gloucestershire) 226
Kincardine (Fife) 123
Kings:
    Aonghus mac Umhor 224
    Arthur 16, 29, 160, 214, 215, 221, 226, 253
    Athelstan 7, 24, 27
    Brian Boruma/Boru 67
    Brychan Brycheiniog 8, 15, 164, 180, 182
    Caron 190
    Charles I 42
    Cissa 222
    Cnut ('Canute') 125
    Cunedda Wledig 167, 175, 186
    Cunobelin 220
    David I 126, 129, 131
    Edward I 60, 75, 99, 156, 173, 175, 188
    Edward II 59
    Edward the Confessor 28
    Edwin of Northumbria 109
    Ethelred 25, 222
    Guaire of Connacht 240
    Gruffydd ap Llywelyn 173, 187
    Haakon IV 86, 104, 126, 148
    Harold I 156
    Henry II 173, 188
    Henry VIII 156
    Hywel ap Cadell 156, 259
    James I 49, 67
    James V 59, 139
    John 40
    Kenneth I (Cinaed macAlpin) 113
    Llywelyn ap Iorwerth 170
    Maelgwn Gwynedd 170
    Malcolm II 146
    Niall Caille 261
    Offa of Mercia 157, 177, 189, 230, 232
    Owain Gwynedd 174
    Penda of Mercia 31, 146, 157
    Sweyn Forkbeard 189
    Tuathal of Leinster 209
    William I ('the Conqueror') 157, 170, 177, 188
    William III ('of Orange') 40
    William ('the Lion') 91, 99, 108, 135
Kinder Scout (Derbyshire) 206, 211
Kinghorn (Fife) 124
Kinross (Perth & Kinross) 124
Kinsale (Cork) 60
Kinver Camp Hillfort (Staffordshire) 226
Kintyre (Argyl & Bute) 124
Kirkcaldy (Fife) 122, 124, 128
Kirkcudbright (Dumfries & Galloway) 124, 148
Kirkintillock (East Dunbartonsthire) 125
Kirkwall (Orkney) 125, 135, 142

Kirriemuir (Angus) 125
    Kirriemuir Sculptured Stones 262
Knighton (Powys) 177
Knock- (prefix) 60
Knock (Down) 60
Knockaderry (Limerick) 60
Knockainy (Limerick) 60
Knockalough (Clare) 60
Knockcroghery (Roscommon) 61
Knockduff (Cavan) 60
Knockglass (Waterford) 60
Knockin (Shropshire) 177
Knockmaroon (Dublin) 60
Knockmoy (Galway) 60
Knocknapeasta (see: 'Cnoc na Peiste')
Knockninny (Fermanagh) 60
Knoydart (Highland) 125
Kyleakin (Highland)
Kyle of Lochalsh (Highland) 126
Kynaston (Shropshire) 178

Ladock (Cornwall) 19
Lady Isabella Wheel (Isle of Man) 78
Lagan, (Town & River) 37, 61, 199
Lagin (Celtic tribe) 62
Lairg (Highland) 126
Lammermuir (Scottish Borders) 126
    Lammermuir Hills 211
Lamorna (Cornwall) 19
Lampeter (Ceredigion) 178
Lanark (South Lanarkshire) 126
Land's End (Cornwall) 20
Langholm (Dumfries & Galloway) 126
Lanyon Quoit (Cornwall) 247
Laoighis/Liogis (Celtic tribe) 61
Laois (County) 61
Larbert (Falkirk) 127
Largs (North Ayrshire) 127
Larne (Antrim) 61
Lasswade (Midlothian) 127
Lauder (Scottish Borders) 127
Laugharne (Dyfed/
    Carmarthenshire) 178

Laurencekirk (Aberdeenshire) 127
Laxford (Highland) 127
Leith (Edinburgh) 200
    Water of Leith/Leithen Water 118
Leinster, (Province of) 39, 61, 62
Leitrim (County) 61
Lellizzick (Cornwall) 20
Leofric, Earl of Mercia 179
Leominster (Herefordshire) 156,
    178, 179
Lerwick (Shetland) 128
Leslie (Fife) 128
Lesmahagow (South Lanarkshire) 128
Letterkenny (Donegal) 62
Leuchars (Fife) 128
Leven (Fife) 128
Leven, River 98, 128
Lewis, Isle of (Outer Hebrides) 82,
    116, 120
Lezant (Cornwall) 20
Lezayre (Isle of Man) 79
Liddesdale (Scottish Borders) 128
Liddington Castle (Wiltshire) 226
Liffey, River 51, 68, 200
Limavardy (Derry) 62
Limerick (County) 62
Linlithgow (West Lothian) 129
Lis- (prefix) 63
Liscloon (Tyrone) 63
Liscolman (Antrim) 63
Liscolman (Wicklow)
Lisduff (Laois) 63
Lisfinny (Waterford) 63
Lislea (Antrim) 63
Lismore (Waterford) 63
Lisnacree (Down) 63
Lispole (Kerry) 63
Lisrodden (Antrim) 63
Little Minch (see: 'Minch')
Lizard Peninsula (Cornwall) 7, 17,
    22, 23
Llanberis (Snowdonia) 179
Llanbydder (Carmarthenshire) 179

Index

Llandovery (Dyfed) 179
Llandrindod (Powys) 179
Llandudno (Clwyd) 180
Llanelli (Dyfed) 180
Llanfairfechan (Clwyd) 180
Llanfair-pwll (Anglesey) 180
Llangadwaladr Cross (Anglesey) 262
Llangefni (Anglesey) 181
Llangollen (Denbighshire) 181
Llanrwust (Denbighshire) 181
Llantrisant (Glamorgan) 181
Loanhead of Daviot Stone Circle (Aberdeenshire) 247
Lochaber (Highland) 129
Lochgelly (Fife) 129
Lochgilphead (Argyl & Bute) 129
Lochinvar (Dumfries & Galloway) 129
Lochinver (Highland) 130
Loch Lomond (Argyl & Bute) 130
Loch Ness (Highland) 130
Lochmaben Stone 145
Lockerbie (Dumfries & Galloway) 129
Lodge Hill Hillfort (Gwent) 226
Lomond Hills (Fife) 211
Lonan (Isle of Man) 79
Londonderry (see: 'Derry')
Looe (Cornwall) 20
    Looe, River 20
Lossiemouth (Moray) 130
Lough- (prefix) 63
Lough Beg (Antrim) 63
Lough Derg (Donegal) 63
Lough Erne (Fermanagh) 64
Lough Mourne (Monaghan) 63
Lough Ramor (Cavan) 63
Loughros (Donegal) 64
Loughton Camp Hillfort (Epping/London) 227
Louth (County) 64
Luceni (Celtic tribe) 58
Ludgvan (Cornwall) 20
Ludlow (Shropshire) 157, 181
Lugadii (Celtic tribe) 58

Lugh/Lugg/Lugus (Celtic deity) 64, 102, 205, 207
Lune, River 200
Lusk (Dublin) 64
Luss (Argyl) 130
Lywelyn ap Gruffydd 187

Machars (Dumfries & Galloway) 130
Maentwrog (Merionethshire/Gwynedd) 181
Maesbrook (Shropshire) 182
Maetae (Celtic tribe) 99
Maghera- (prefix) 64
Maghera (Derry) 64
Magheracloone (Monaghan) 64
Magheralin (Down) 65
Magheramena (Down) 65
Magheramore (Wicklow) 65
Maiden Castle (Dorset) 227
Malew (Isle of Man) 79
Malin/Malin Head (Donegal) 65
Mallaig (Highland) 131
Mam Tor (Derbyshire) 212, 228
    Mam Tor Hillfort 228
Manannan (Celtic deity) 78
Manx Language *ix*, 4, 33, 74
Marazion (Cornwall) 20, 28
Marches (See: 'Welsh Marches')
Marhamchurch (Cornwall) 21
Markinch (Fife) 131
Marown (Isle of Man) 76, 248
    St Patrick's Chair, Marown 74, 248
Matfen Stone (Northumberland) 248
Maughold (Isle of Man) 79, 81
Mawgan (Cornwall) 21
Maybole (South Ayrshire) 130
Mayo (County) 36, 39, 40, 65, 240
Mearns (Renfrewshire) 130
Meath (County) 65
Medway, River *viii*, 197, 200
Megdale (Dumfries & Galloway) 131
Mellor Hillfort (Greater Manchester) 228

Celtic Places and Placenames

Melrose (Scottish Borders) 131
Menai Straits (Anglesey) 165, 182, 249
    Menai Bridge 182
Men-an-Tol (Cornwall) 7, 248
Menapii (Celtic tribe) 54, 66, 72, 73, 265
Merrivale Rows (Devon) 249
Mersey, River 200
Merthyr Tydfil (Mid-Glamorgan) 182, 203
Midlothian (Unitary Authority) 132
Midsummer Hill Camp (Herefordshire) 228
Milngavie (East Dunbartonshire) 132
Minch, The (Outer Hebrides) 116, 132, 144
Minginish (Highland) 132
Minions (Cornwall) 21
Minto (Scottish Borders) 132
Moate (Westmeath) 65
Moelfre (Anglesey) 182
Moffat (Dumfries & Galloway) 133
Monaghan (County) 65
Monasterboice High Crosses (Louth) 263
Monmouth (Gwent) 183
    Monmouth Rebellion 244
Montgomeryshire (Powys) 190
Montrose (Angus) 133
Monzievaird (Highland) 133
Moone High Cross (Kildare) 263
Morar (Highland) 133
Moray (Unitary Authority) 133
    Moray Firth 99, 113, 134, 141
Morwenstow (Cornwall) 21
    Morwenna, Saint 21, 22
Mountrath (Laois) 66
Mourne Mountains (Down) 212
Mousa (Shetland) 134
Muck (Inner Hebrides) 134
Muckle Flugga (Shetland) 134
Mughdhorna (Celtic tribe) 211
Muir of Ord (Highland) 134

Mull, Isle of (Argyl & Bute) 120
Mulla- (prefix) 66
Mullagh (Cavan) 66
Mullaghanee (Monaghan) 66
Mullaghcarn (Tyrone) 66
Mullaghglass (Armagh) 66
Mullaghroe (Sligo) 66
Mullion (Cornwall) 22
Mungo, Saint 114, 115, 117
Munster, (Province of) 46, 57, 66, 72
Mylor Bridge (Cornwall) 22

Naas (Kildare) 66
Nagnatae (Celtic tribe) 65, 70
Nairbyl (Isle of Man) 80
Nairn (Highland) 134
Nannetes (Celtic tribe) 265, 267
Nanstallon (Cornwall) 22
Nantes (Loire-Atlantique) 267
Navan (Meath) 67
Neath (West Glamorgan) 182
    Neath, River 201
Nectonos (Celtic river deity) 89
Nennius 37, 175
Ness, Loch (see: 'Loch Ness')
    Ness, River 129, 200
Newport (Gwent) 165, 190
Newry (Down) 67
Newstead (Scottish Borders) 135
Newtownards (Down) 39, 67
Nidd, River 183, 201
Nigg (Highland) 135
Nine Stones (Dorset) 254
Nine Stones Close (Derbyshire) 241, 249
Nithsdale (Dumfries & Galloway) 135, 146
Normanton Down Barrows (Wiltshire) 249
North Berwick (East Lothian) 135
North Ronaldsay (Orkney) 135

Oban (Argyl & Bute) 136
Ochil Hills (Perth & Kinross) 92, 212

Index

Ochiltree (East Ayrshire) 135
Offaly (County) 44, 48, 67
Offa's Dyke 157, 177
Old Bewick Hillfort
    (Northumberland) 229
Old Oswestry Hillfort (Shropshire) 229
Old Sarum Hillfort (Wiltshire) 230
Omagh (Tyrone) 33, 67
Onchan (Isle of Man) 80
O'Brien, Donal Mor 62
Oppida 217
Orighella (Celtic tribe) 70
Oronsay (Inner Hebrides) 103, 136
Orkney (Unitary Authority) *x*, 136
Orphir (Orkney) 136
Ossory (Kingdom of) 59
Oswestry (Shropshire) 157, 183
    Old Oswestry 229
Oxmantown (Dublin) 68
Oxnam (Scottish Borders) 137
Oykel, River (Highland) 137

Padstow (Cornwall) 22
Paisley (Renfrewshire) 137
Partition of Ireland 33, 35, 40
Patrick, Saint 43, 47, 51, 52, 53, 56,
    58, 67, 69, 72, 73, 74, 79, 81, 248,
    257, 261
Peak District (Derbyshire) 199, 206,
    211, 212, 225, 228, 239
Peebles/Peebleshire (Scottish Borders)
    109, 118, 137
Peel (Isle of Man) 80
Pelynt (Cornwall) 22
Pembroke/Pembrokeshire (Dyfed) 157,
    172, 183
    Earl of Pembroke 59
Penarth (Glamorgan) 183
Penicuik (Midlothian) 137
Penk, River 201
Penmaenmawr (Clwyd) 184
Pennines, The 212
Penrhyn Bay (Conwy) 184

Penrhyndeudraeth (Gwynedd) 184
Pentland Firth (Highland) 138
Pentland Hills 90, 221
Pentreath (Cornwall) 23
Pentre Ifan Burial Chamber
    (Pembrokeshire) 249
Pen y Crug Hillfort (Powys) 216, 230
Pen y Fan (Powys) 212
Pen-y-Ghent (Yorkshire) 213
Perranarworthal (Cornwall) 23
Perranporth (Cornwall) 23
Perranzabuloe (Cornwall) 23
Perth (City of) 138
    Treaty of Perth 75
Petroc, Saint 9, 10, 15, 22, 25, 28
Phillack (Cornwall) 24
Picts/Picti/Pictish (Celtic tribes) 27,
    32, 51, 55, 61, 71, 82, 83, 88, 90,
    91, 92, 94, 109, 111, 113, 117, 118,
    123, 124, 125, 128, 130, 134, 136,
    137, 138, 139, 140, 141, 143, 168,
    175, 182, 195, 201, 210, 212, 221,
    229, 233, 258, 259, 260, 262
Piran, Saint 7, 9, 23, 27
Pilsdon Pen Hillfort (Dorset) 230
Pitcaple (Aberdeenshire) 138
Pit- (prefix) 138
Pitcorthie (Fife) 138
Pitglassie (Highland) 138
Pitlochry (Perth & Kinross) 138
Pittenweem (Fife) 139
Plaid Cymru 156
Plantation of Ulster 33, 47, 49, 54,
    60, 61
Plas Newydd Dolmen (Anglesey) 250
Pliny the Elder 81, 116
Polmadie (Glasgow) 139
Pontypool (Gwent) 184
Pontypridd (Monmouthshire) 185
Portarddulais (Glamorgan) 184
Port Erin (Isle of Man) 80
Port Soderick (Isle of Man) 80
Port St Mary (Isle of Man) 80

Port Talbot (West Glamorgan) 183, 262
Porthcawl (Mid Glamorgan) 185
Porthleven (Cornwall) 24
Porthloo (Cornwall) 24
Portmahomack (Highland) 139
Portree (Skye) 139
Poundbury Camp Hillfort (Dorset) 231
Powys (Kingdom of/Unitary Authority) 177, 185, 188, 190, 192
Praze-an-Beeble (Cornwall) 24
Prestatyn (Flintshire) 185
Presteigne (Powys) 185
Prestwick (South Ayrshire) 146
Prideaux Castle Hillfort (Cornwall) 231
Probus (Cornwall) 24
Ptolemy, Claudius 37, 39, 40, 46, 48, 50, 52, 54, 58, 62, 65, 66, 72, 73, 112, 120, 194, 195, 196, 197, 198, 199, 201, 202, 204
Purbeck Hills (Dorset) 213
Pwllheli (Gwynedd) 186

Quaich, River (Perth & Kinross) 139
Quantock Hills (Somerset) 213
Quethiock (Cornwall) 25
Queens:
    Boudicca 227, 235
    Elizabeth I 42, 45
    Elizabeth Bowes-Lyon 114
    Maeve/Medb/Meabh of Connacht 38, 42, 44, 48, 59
    Mary Tudor 61
    Victoria 95
Quies (Cornwall) 25
Quimper (Brittany) 267

Ra-/Rath- (prefix) 68
Raasay (Hebrides/Highland) 116, 140
Rahugh (Westmeath) 68
Rainsborough Camp (Northamptonshire) 231
Rame (Cornwall) 25
Ramsey (Isle of Man) 79, 80

Rannoch Moor (Highland) 140
Raphoe (Donegal) 68
Ratallan (Roscommon) 68
Ratass (Kerry) 68
Rathconrath (Westmeath) 69
Rathgall Hillfort (Wicklow) 232
Rathgar (Dublin) 68
Rathmoyle (Kilkenny) 68
Rathnure (Wexford) 68
Rattray (Perth & Kinross) 140
Ravensburgh Castle (Hertfordshire) 232
Redgorton (Perth & Kinross) 140
Redones/Reidones (Celtic tribe) 265, 268
Renfrew (Renfrewshire) 140
Rennes (Brittany) 268
Rhayader (Powys) 186
Rhins of Galloway (Dumfries & Galloway) 140
Rhobogdii (Celtic tribe) 50
Rhondda/Rhondda Valley 186, 189
    River Rhondda 189, 190
Rhosllanerchrugog (Clwyd) 186
Rhosneigr (Anglesey) 186
Rhostryfan (Gwynedd) 187
Rhuddlan (Flintshire) 187
Rhyl (Flintshire) 187
Rhymney (Gwent) 187
Ribble, River 195, 197, 201
Rinns of Islay (Argyl) 141
Rollright Stones (Oxfordshire) 250
Rona (Western Isles) 141
Ronaldsay: see 'North Ronaldsay'
Ros-/Ross- (prefix) 69
Roscommon (Town & County) 69
Roscor (Fermanagh) 69
Roscrea (Tipperary) 69
Roseland (Cornwall) 16, 25, 28
Rosemarkie (Highland) 141
Ross (Ross & Cromarty) 141
Ross-on-Wye (Herefordshire) 187
Rossbeigh (Kerry) 69
Ross Carbery (Cork) 69

Index

Rossglass (Down) 69
Rosyth (Fife) 141
Rousay (Orkney) 141
Rudston Monolith (Yorkshire) 250
Rum (Hebrides/Highland) 142
Rutherglan (South Lanarkshire) 142
Ruthin (Clwyd) 188
Ruthwell Cross 263

Sabrina (Celtic river deity) 202
Saltcoats (North Ayrshire) 93, 142
Samson (Isles of Scilly) 25
Sancreed (Cornwall) 25
Sanquhar (Dumfries & Galloway) 142
Santon (Isle of Man) 81
Saul (Down) 69
Scafell/Scafell Pike (Cumbria) 210, 213
Scilly Isles (Isles of Scilly) 9, 29
Scapa Flow (Orkney) 112, 143
Scone (Perth & Kinross) 143
    Stone of Scone 45
Scoti/Scotii (Celtic tribe) 65, 72, 82, 83
Seaton (Cornwall) 26
Selgovae (Celtic tribe) 135, 143
Selkirk (Scottish Borders) 143
Sennen (Cornwall) 26
Severn, River 165, 169, 190, 191, 192, 199, 202, 203, 217, 246
Sgurr na Stri (Highland) 213
Shannon, River 40, 61, 62, 202
Shetland (Unitary Authority) *x*, 85, 99, 105, 110, 113, 128, 134, 143, 147, 148, 150, 151
Shiant Islands (Outer Hebrides) 144
Shrewsbury (Shropshire) 157, 188
Sidlaw Hills (Perthshire/Angus) 114, 214
Silbury Hill (Wiltshire) 251, 255
Silures (Celtic tribe) 165, 166, 168, 175, 219, 222, 227, 230
Skara Brae (Orkney) 144
Skeabost (Skye/Highland) 144

Skerray (Highland) 144
Skerries (Dublin) 69
Skye, Isle of (Inner Hebrides/Highland) 116, 121, 126, 132, 139, 140, 144, 145, 150, 151, 213, 259
Slamannan (Falkirk) 144
Sleat (Skye) 144
Slemish (Antrim) 69
Slieve- (prefix) 70
Slieve Ban (Down) 70
Slieve Binnian (Down) 214
Slieve Donard (Down) 70
Slieve Gallion (Derry) 70
Slieve Lamagan (Down) 214
Slievemore (Tyrone) 70
Sligo (Town & County) 36, 46, 53, 66, 70, 71, 109, 259
Snaefell (Isle of Man) 81
Snowdon/Snowdonia (Gwynedd) 171, 179, 181, 196, 208, 210, 214, 215
Soar, River 202
Soay (Inner Hebrides) 145
Solway Firth 145, 263
South Ronaldsay (see: 'North Ronaldsay')
Spanish Armada 244
Spanish Head (Isle of Man) 77
Spanish Legion, Ninth (Legio VIII Hispana) 83
Sperrins (Derry/Tyrone) 214
Spinster's Rock (Devon) 252
Stannon Stone Circle (Cornwall) 252
St Asaph (Clwyd) 16, 188
St Blazey (Cornwall) 26
St Breward (Cornwall) 27, 252
St Buryan (Cornwall) 27
St David's (Pembrokeshire) 188
St Dogfan/Cwgan Stone (Powys) 264
St Germans (Cornwall) 25, 27
St Helen's (Cornwall) 27
St Helena (Cornwall) 18
St Ives (Cornwall) 18, 27, 31
St John's Cross (Iona) 260

St Keverne (Cornwall) 28
St Lythans Burial Chamber (South Glamorgan) 252
St Malo (Brittany) 268
St Martin's (Isles of Scilly) 28, 29
St Martin's Cross (Iona) 260
St Matthew's Cross (Iona) 260
St Mawes (Cornwall) 25, 28
St Michael's Mount (Cornwall) 21, 28
St Morwenna (Cornwall) 21
St Oran's Cross (Iona) 260, 261
St Patrick's Chair, (Isle of Man) 74, 248
   St Patrick (see: 'Patrick, Saint')
St Pyr/Piro (Pembrokeshire) 166
St Quivox (South Ayrshire) 146
Stanton Drew (Somerset) 252
Stenhousemuir (Falkirk) 145
Stenness (Orkney) 145
   Stenness Standing Stones 253
Stevenson, Robert 147
Stirling (Aberdeenshire) 95, 99, 106, 146
Stob Stone (Northumberland) 248
Stonehenge (Wiltshire) 237, 239, 249, 250, 253, 267
Stoney Littleton Barrow (Somerset) 253
Stornaway (Western Isles) 156
Stour, River 202
Strabane (Tyrone) 70
Stranraer (Dumfries & Galloway) 146
Strath- (prefix) 147
Strathclyde (Region) 104, 107, 147
Strathearn (Perth & Kinross) 113, 147
Strathmiglo (Fife) 147
Strathpeffer (Highland) 147
Strathspey (Moray) 94
Stromness (Orkney) 147, 253
Strongbow (Richard de Clare) 59
Sulby (Isle of Man) 81
   River Sulby 81
Sullom Voe (Shetland) 147
Sumburgh Head (Shetland) 147
Sutherland (Historic County) 148

Sutton Walls Hillfort (Herefordshire) 232
Swansea (City of) 159, 174, 184, 189, 201

Tacitus, Publius Cornelius 31, 83, 108, 196, 210
Taff, River 202
Talgarth (Powys) 189
Tallaght (Dublin) 70
Talland (Cornwall) 29
Tamar, River *ix*, 7, 11, 202, 203
Tame/Thames/Thame, Rivers 199, 203
Tamesis 203
Taranis (Celtic deity) Frontispiece illustration
Tarbert (Argyl & Bute) 148
Tarbet (Highland) 148
Tay River 88, 111, 138, 203
   Firth of Tay 107
Tean/Teän (Isles of Scilly) 29
Tees, River 203
Teme, River 181, 203
Tenby (Pembrokeshire) 189
Test, River 203
The Nine Stones (Dorset) 254
Threave (Dumfries & Galloway) 148
Threepwood (Ayrshire) 148
Thurso (Highland) 138
Tintagel (Cornwall) 22, 29
Tipperary (Town & County) 51, 70, 210, 258
Tiree, Isle of (Inner Hebrides) 116, 149
Tobereendoney (Clare) 71
Tobermory (Inner Hebrides) 149
Tomintoul (Moray) 149
Tomnaverie Stone Circle (Aberdeenshire) 254
Tonypandy (Glamorgan) 189, 190
Towednack (Cornwall) 29
Tranent (East Lothian) 149
Tredegar (Gwent) 190
Tregaron (Cardiganshire) 190

Index

Trent, River 202, 203
Treorchi (Glamorgan) 190
Tre'r Ceiri Hillfort (Gwynedd) 234
Tresco (Isles of Scilly) 29
Trevone (Cornwall) 30
Troon (South Ayrshire) 149
Trossachs (Stirlingshire) 215
Truro (Cornwall) 12, 19, 24, 30
    Truro High Cross 264
Tryfan (Snowdonia) 215
Tuathal of Leinster 209
Tull-/Tully- (prefix) 71
Tullaherin (Kilkenny) 71
Tullamore (Offaly) 71
Tullintrain (Derry) 71
Tulloha (Kerry) 71
Tullycarnet (Down) 71
Tullyhogue (Tyrone) 71
Tummel, River (Perth & Kinross) 138, 149
Turriff (Aberdeenshire) 150
Tweed, River 102, 118, 122, 131, 204
Tyne, River 109, 204
    Tyne & Wear (County) 197
Tyrone (Town & County) 55, 68, 70, 71, 214
    Hugh of Tyrone ('Clanaboy') 46
    Tyrone's Rebellion 33
Tywi (Towy), River 204
Tywyn (Gwynedd) 190

Uamh Bheag (Perth & Kinross) 149
Uffington White Horse (Oxfordshire) 254, 255
Uig (Skye, Highland) 150
Uist (Outer Hebrides) 96, 110, 116, 134, 150
Ulbster (Highland) 150
Ullapool (Highland) 150
Ulster (Province of) 72
Unst (Shetland) 150
Uny Lelant (Cornwall) 30
Upleadon (Gloucestershire) 190

Urquhart (Highland) 151
Ushnagh (Westmeath) 72
Usk (Monmouthshire) 164, 194, 197, 226, 240

Vannes (Brittany) 268
Vartry, River (Wicklow) 72
Vaternish (Skye) 151
Velabri/Vellibori (Celtic tribe) 58
Vendoti (Celtic tribe) 175
Veneti/Vannetais (Celtic tribe) 265, 268
Vennicnii (Celtic tribe) 50
Veryan (Cornwall) 25, 30
Vespasian, Emperor 160, 219, 227
Vinderii (Celtic tribe) 39
Voluntii (Celtic tribe) 39
Votadini (Pictish tribe) 109, 132, 233, 236

Wandlebury Camp (Cambridgeshire) 234
Warbstow (Cornwall) 30
    Warbstow Bury Hillfort 234
Wardlaw (Highland) 151
Waterford (County) 58, 63, 72
Wat's Dyke (Shropshire) 230
Wayland's Smithy (Oxfordshire) 254
Wear, River 204
Welsh Marches, The 134, 157, 168, 169, 170, 173, 174, 176, 177, 181, 187, 229
Welshpool (Powys) 190
Wem (Shropshire) 191
Western Isles (Outer Hebrides) 40, 95, 116, 120, 141, 146, 151
West Kennet Long Barrow (Wiltshire) 255
Westmeath (County) 73
Westray (Orkney) 151
Wexford (Town & County) 72, 73
Whalsey (Shetland) 151
Whithorn (Dumfries & Galloway) 152
Wick (Highland) 152
Wicklow (Town & County) 73

Celtic Places and Placenames

Wigtownshire (Dumfries & Galloway) 130, 140
Wishaw (North Lanarkshire) 152
Wormbridge (Herefordshire) 191
Wrekin, The (Shropshire) 191, 192
Wrexham (Clwyd) 156, 191
Wye, River 167, 205
Wyre, River 205

Yarrow (Scottish Borders) 152
Yeavering Battle Stone (Northumberland) 255
Yeavering Bell Hillfort 236
Yell (Shetland) 152
Yellowmead Stone Circles (Devon) 255
Yeo, River 205
Yockenthwaite Stone Circle (North Yorkshire) 256
Yoker (Glasgow) 152

Zennor (Cornwall) 31
Zetland (see: 'Shetland')